British Railways
STATION TOTEMS
The Complete Guide

Dave Brennand & Richard Furness

crecy.co.uk

British Railways Station Totems

The Complete Guide

Dave Brennand & Richard Furness

crecy.co.uk

ISBN 9781800351417
First published in 2002
This edition published 2022

A CIP record for this book is available from the
British Library

Printed in Turkey by Pelikan

Crécy Publishing Limited
1a Ringway Trading Estate
Shadowmoss Road
Manchester M22 5LH
www.crecy.co.uk

Contents

The remains a WR Darby End Halt totem after the station closed in 1964.

Acknowledgements

This book is truly the product of a team effort. Although we may have written, researched and laid out the book, the contents and gathering of much information gleaned over the last twenty years has come from many sources. During the drafting phase, Alan Young and Tim Clarke were absolute towers of strength. Not only did they use their considerable knowledge of railway history and the BR network to improve the text, they contributed many photos from their extensive libraries. In addition, Alan Young drew many of the regional maps and both gentlemen contributed scholarly texts to various chapters. The entire volume is all the richer for their eagle-eyed proof-reading. We sincerely thank you for your support and friendship over many years in helping us produce this 'Totem Encyclopaedia'. Special mention goes to Alf Miles, Pete Sargieson and John Wells for their unstinting advice, contributions and further checking of our text. Also, looking over our shoulders throughout was Ian Faulkner, whose exploits in our hobby we feature in Chapter 3.

Many totem photos came from Simon Turner at GWRA Auctions, Pershore and David Jones of GCRA auctions at Woodford Halse, in addition to those from our joint Totem

Blake Street, Staffordshire *circa* 1970.
Totem Study Group (TSG) library

Study Groupg (TSG) library. Other totem pictures came from Roger and Sandra Phipps at Talisman Auctions and from Tony Hoskins, formerly of GWRA. New data came from Graham Carr, Nick Catford, Jim Connor, Barry Gayton, Mike and Paul Matthews, Andy Meeks, Joss Mullinger and Trevor Smith and others mentioned in the text: thank you all.

The Frontispiece image, our original choice for the front cover, is a recent painting of *King Edward* I about to leave **Birmingham Snow Hill** on the *Inter City*. The artist and long-time friend Barry Price is watching the now Didcot-preserved *King 6023*, with a collectable Snow Hill totem immediately over his head. This image and Phillip Hawkins's glorious study of the *Cornishman* on page 274 is a time I (RF) vividly remember. Thank you both for enhancing our work so artistically.

Last, but certainly not least, our greatest gratitude goes to our wives Belinda Brennand and Judi Furness for their tolerance of the literally thousands of hours we have spent in front of our computer screens to develop this book.

AUTHORS' NOTE: Throughout this book we have highlighted those stations fitted with totems in **bold print,** such as the two stations mentioned in the Foreword that follows; **Seer Green & Jordans** and **Stratford.**

Foreword by Geoff Courtney
(*Heritage Railway* magazine)

There's something about totem station signs that no other item of railway memorabilia possesses. Nostalgia plays its part, but the emotion a totem sign can elicit is far deeper than just that. A station name can cut through to one's soul, to the very fabric of one's childhood or adolescence, to the gut feeling of days that were both happy and occasionally sad, to hopes fulfilled and unfulfilled.

Among the nameplates, cabside numberplates and other railwayana I have been fortunate to acquire over the past twenty-five years or so, are only two totems, but each draws me into a world that is private and mine alone. The first is **Seer Green & Jordans**, which recalls the village to which my family was relocated from the East End of London early in World War Two. The second is **Stratford**, the vast station, locomotive depot and works complex 4 miles from Liverpool Street that were at the core of my trainspotting, and thus my life other than school and Essex County Cricket Club, in the 1950s.

Dave Brennand and Richard Furness first collaborated on *The Book of British Railways Station Totems* that was published in 2002: it was an instant success and is now regarded as a collectors' item. The book I am privileged to write this Foreword for is a quantum leap from that, and serves as a reminder that we collectors, indeed those who have simply a peripheral interest in the subject, are fortunate to have two such dedicated researchers in our midst.

And my goodness, is this publication researched. Within its 352 pages are over 89,000 words, 2,647 images, including 2,000+ totems, 43 maps, and statistics galore. It is well-written and a geographic and visual

An ER survivor at Brampton, Suffolk, in 1982. *Alan Young*

cornucopia of unalloyed delight, taking readers from Scotland to England's West Country, from Wales to East Anglia. The fact that 'my' Essex is the hardest county to collect totems from, despite it having 94 stations fitted with the signs, is one of the pieces of apparent minutiae that populate the book, and there's something for everyone, whatever county they consider home.

The New Book of Station Totems will enchant, fascinate and educate. It is to be read at leisure with a glass in hand or a mindset of studied resolve. It recalls a railway system that, for better or worse, was far removed from that of today, when life was simpler and less formulaic, when stations were welcoming locations rather than barrier-laden fortresses, and signage was straightforward but still informative.

Totems fitted perfectly into that template. They told you what you needed to know and no more, they were standardised throughout the railway system, and have rightly earned their place in the railwayana hierarchy, with five-figure realisations at auctions no longer being a rarely encountered exception.

Richard and Dave have done this subject justice due to many, many hours of diligent and painstaking work, gritty determination, deep knowledge, and a belief that out there is a collectors' movement that has a thirst for what they have written about. Enjoy the result of their endeavours.

Geoff Courtney
Bedfordshire, December 2021

Abbreviations

AC	Alternating Current		LMS	London Midland Scottish (Rly)
BR	British Railways		LNER	London & North Eastern Railway
BTC	British Transport Commission		LNR	Leeds Northern Railway
BTF	British Transport Films		LNWR	London & North Western Railway
CC	Collectors Corner (Euston)		LP	Lower Panel (Totem)
CK&PR	Cockermouth Keswick & Penrith Railway		LSWR	London & South Western Railway
CLC	Cheshire Lines Committee		LT	London Transport (Underground)
CR	Caledonian Railway		LTSR	London Tilbury & Southend Railway
DC	Direct Current		LYR	Lancashire & Yorkshire Railway
DEMU	Diesel Electric Multiple Unit		MR	Midland Railway
DMU	Diesel Multiple Unit		NBR	North British Railway
ECML	East Coast Main Line		NER	North Eastern Railway/Region
ECR	Eastern Counties Railway		MSLR	Manchester, Sheffield & Lincolnshire Railway
ER	Eastern Region (BR)		NLR	North London Railway
EMU	Electric Multiple Unit		NR	Network Rail
FD	Face Drilled (Totem)		RCH	Railway Clearing House (relevant to some maps used)
FF	Full Flange (Totem)		REC	Railway Executive Committee
FGW	First Great Western		RIB	Running-in-Board (Station Signage)
FR	Furness Railway		ScR	Scottish Region (BR)
GCR	Great Central Railway		SDJR	Somerset & Dorset Joint Railway
GER	Great Eastern Railway		SECR	South Eastern & Chatham Railway
GNR	Great Northern Railway		SER	South Eastern Railway
GNSR	Great North of Scotland Railway		SR	Southern Railway/Southern Region (BR)
GSWR	Glasgow & South Western Railway		T&HJR	Tottenham & Hampstead Junction Railway
GWR	Great Western Railway		TOC	Train Operating Company
H&BR	Hull & Barnsley Railway		TSG	Totem Study Group
HF	Half Flange (Totem)		WF	Wide Flange (Totem)
HR	Highland Railway		WHL	West Highland Line
IOW	Isle of Wight		WR	Western Region (BR)
LBSCR	London Brighton & South Coast Railway		Y&NMR	York & North Midland Railway
LCDR	London Chatham & Dover Railway		YN&BR	York, Newcastle & Berwick Railway
LMR	London Midland Region (BR)			

Totems abound! The TSG-organised display at Yeovil's 150th anniversary, 29 July 2006. *TSG library*

Introduction and Background

Background

This greatly expanded book about railway station totems comes almost 20 years since our first edition was published in 2002. Even before 2002, the interest in collecting railwayana had been in full flow for nearly 40 years, starting when the railways began to modernise in the 1960s. Official sales of railway-related artefacts began at **Stoke on Trent** in 1964 and are still going strong approaching 60 years later. Even before 1964, private sales had taken place. Our 2002 book produced the first comprehensive listing both of totems in auction and those that had survived the decades of change. Its appearance provoked renewed interest and the gathering of much new information. In the past 20 years, we have made over 1,200 changes to the databases, quite a few deletions, others were discoveries, all based on traceable photographic evidence. The majority are first-time appearances in auctions, but previously unknown installations have added 43 new entries. Even today, as house and shed clearances occur, treasures long thought to have been lost or destroyed, are continually re-appearing. During this book's drafting, information was still emerging.

The BR network in 1952.

The iconic totem design appeared shortly after British Railways came into being on 1 January 1948. The Transport Act of 1947 laid the foundations for the re-organisation of the national railway network, due in part to the ravages of war and partly because of the financial problems its aftermath caused. Britain has a long, proud history of railway development, which began with early coal waggonways in the 17th century, but it was the railway-building mania of the Victorian era that laid the cornerstones for the 20th century sequence of events. The 19th century had seen hundreds of railway companies grow, merge and sometimes fold, as monetary constraints took hold. The Great War of 1914–18 sowed the seeds of a major re-organisation in 1923 when four main players, the Great Western (GWR), the London, Midland & Scottish (LMS), the London & North Eastern (LNER) and the Southern Railway (SR) came into existence. The economic damage of WWI had prompted a serious look at total nationalisation, but after much discussion (and some disagreement) that was rejected in favour of forming the 'Big Four'.

History repeated itself twenty years later, when the financial and physical damage from WWII forced yet more changes. War damage, as at North Woolwich on 4 April 1941 below, was extensive, thereby imposing nationalisation on the 'Big Four'. Many other main stations, **Coventry**, **Manchester Exchange, Middlesbrough** and **York**, for example, saw similar damage. Under Clement Atlee's Labour Government, the 1947 Transport Act made provision for the takeover of the 'Big Four', and British Railways (BR) appeared as the business name of the Railway Executive of the British Transport Commission (BTC). It required major investment to rectify huge war damage (which the 'Big Four' could ill afford) and the creation of a new corporate identity to rebuild the railways' image for the future. The 'Big Four' identities had served them well between 1923 and 1947, but BR wanted a different, more unified approach. The task of creating a new image and logo was given to the Public Relations and Publicity Department, based at BR headquarters in Marylebone, North London. The new logo had to be simple, but instantly recognisable, and history shows it quickly evolved to become one of the most famous of all the 20th century branding exercises.

The First 'Totems'

Even before BR launched their totem in February 1948, stations had been fitted with signage telling travellers where they were. At many stations these were wooden signs with metal letters, positioned at each end of the platforms. Today we would call them 'running-in boards' (RIBs) but, in reality, they were a form of early totem. In the 1930s, the LMS used a standard 'totem' at various positions along their station platforms. These we now call 'hawkseyes' and they come up for auction at regular intervals. They were not always the usual LMS crimson lake, as the Llandovery picture illustrates. Alongside we show the final colouring using Midland maroon and cream; below a late-1930s photo of Salford Priors (Warwickshire) depicts their platform use (see Stop Press page 350).

Running-in boards were white on black until 1934, when black lettering on a yellow background was introduced: then in BR times, maroon and cream was used (as Wadborough shows). Along the platforms and under lamps, rectangular metal plates were installed carrying the station's name (these are termed lamp tablets) and also carried regional colours, but not the colours that BR adopted in 1948 for their six regions.

The LNER used tablets with brown lettering on cream (Whitley Bay, the discoloured Frinton on Sea), while the LMS used yellow with black lettering (Daisyfield). GWR signage from **Starcross** is always sought after, so the B&W enamel tablet mentioning the ex-SR station at **Exmouth** is quite a rarity. The Southern Railway produced their glass in wooden frame tablets in traditional green (Queens Road, above), while a few Scottish stations also carried dark blue tablets but with lettering in a quite different but unknown font (such as at **Dunbar**). Indeed, this small collage shows no uniformity of signage font, but when shown together they emphasise post-WWI 'regionality' existence. Though not as colourful as the later BR totems, they are attractive and many lasted well into the BR era. Today, tablets such as those illustrated above appear regularly in auctions, but collectors seem to be more interested in the iconic totems from the BR era. Several national transport and heritage railway museums feature tablet collections as depicted in this sextet.

The Southern Railway, which covered an area that carried millions of commuters year-round, together with thousands of holidaymakers in the summer months, followed a totally different approach. Their corporate colour was green, so all their stations were adorned in green enamels with the station name itself in the form of a roundel, undoubtedly inspired by London Transport's famous underground signs. The LT signs first appeared in 1908 and the red-and-white circle and blue bar is one of the world's most instantly recognisable signs, adopted in various styles and colours worldwide. When an SR target is shown alongside an LT sign, the similarity is unmistakable.

The SR targets had one curious characteristic: they were not a standard width, even though the circle diameter was. The overall width changed according to the station's name, so some of them were a most curious shape, as Chard Junction shows.

When BR took over in 1948, thousands of SR targets were in place, particularly in Kent, Surrey and Sussex. Some of these were not taken down until decades later, as discussed in detail later in the book, while others were removed and replaced by totems in a seemingly random policy; sometimes they co-existed for many years, as at **Bingham Road** and **Clock House** for example.

A *Totem Exchange* study suggests more than 590 stations were fitted with targets, but a large percentage have not appeared in auction. Targets stretched from London down to the Kent coast, across Hampshire and Dorset, then into Devon and Cornwall. Examples from the two most-westerly counties rarely appear in auction and items from Dorset or the Isle of Wight are also especially desirable today. Notice in the Chard Junction target photograph how appendages were treated. These appeared as curved lettering in the lower half of the sign, as in these two pictures.

In our 2002 totem book, we explained that the possibility existed that a totem-shaped logo was first used by the Bassett-Lowke Company of Northampton. They were one of the world's finest model makers and Mike Green, the Bassett-Lowke Society Chairman, has sent us the following image from *The Bassett-Lowke Story* by Roland Fuller, published by New Cavendish Books. The B-L Society has confirmed that the earliest photographic evidence of the use of the totem emblem is in the 1954 catalogue, (picture below). None of the early post-war catalogues, adverts or company letterheads included it. The totem design therefore was indeed a BR design but the records we have seen show this must have been produced very rapidly, prior to the launch of the nationalised railway.

Reproduced with kind permission from Allen Levy and New Cavendish Books

BRs Station Totems Evolve

In October 1947, pre-BR executive meetings finally agreed to six regions within the new British Railways from January 1948. These were the Eastern Region (ER) based on the southern section of the old LNER; the London Midland (LMR), essentially the old LMS in England and parts of Wales; the North Eastern Region (NER), based on the northern English section of the old LNER; the Scottish Region (ScR), a merger of LMS and LNER routes and assets in Scotland; the Southern Region (SR) based on the routes of the former Southern Railway Company; and the Western Region (WR) based on the former Great Western Railway area. Each was run by a Chief Regional Officer, reporting to the BTC Board. Two of these (K.W.C. Grand of the WR and John Elliott of the SR) had strong advertising backgrounds, but others were less experienced in marketing and image building. Additionally, each of the regions had its own Public Relations/Publicity Officer and it was this group of six that was responsible for implementing signage and other BR publicity materials in their areas. In all six areas, the change of brand and image took a great deal of work. Sometimes the old signs were not taken down and were used until finally being replaced during the 1960s, '70s and '80s by 'modern' aluminium screen-printed examples.

Both the areas and assets of these six regions were very unbalanced, and this is evidenced by the sizes of the regional totem databases in each of the relevant chapters. The smallest was the NER (9% of all route miles operated), with the LMR by far the largest (29%). There were heavy concentrations of stations in Lancashire, Yorkshire, Kent, Lanarkshire and Surrey, with very few in most of the Scottish counties, Anglesey, Brecknock, Cardigan, Huntingdon and Radnor. When British Railways was launched, it had no corporate identity of its own. Today, if a major new organisation is launched, its brand is plastered everywhere well ahead of the appearance date. The BTC had not even considered its identity during the formative months, much to the annoyance of the Railway Executive, which oversaw BR. Relations were almost hostile and to avoid the imposition of the BTC logo, the RE created the closest thing British Railways had as a logo, a sort of elongated roundel, reminiscent of a simple model railway loop with passing places top and bottom.

Occasionally also known as the 'hot dog sausage' totem, it was designed by the RE's advertising officer A.J. White. The Railway Executive had sought London Transport's advice on a logo, but the latter wanted to keep well out of the conflict between the BTC and the Railway Executive. The standard logo, first presented in February 1948 during an RE press conference, was used as the corporate emblem and template for station platform nameplate signage, using the Gill Sans typeface, inherited from the LNER, and designed by Eric Gill (see below). This became the railway's corporate typeface from inception through to 1965, when Rail Alphabet lettering was introduced.

The high-level conflicts that arose early on grew steadily worse and they moved down the chain from the executive into senior management levels. The WR's K.W.C. Grand appeared especially uncooperative, as the GWR had always followed its own path, and he thought he could continue unchecked. Changes in June 1948 saw the former LMS lines in Essex moved to the ER, some LMR lines in Central and South Wales were transferred to the WR and the Silloth branch was transferred from the NER to the LMR. The SR's Southampton Docks was transferred in September 1950 to the Docks & Inland Waterways Executive.

Enamel station totems first began to appear in late 1949 or early 1950. The April 1948 BR manual Sign Standards detailed all station signage that had to be made. There were thousands of stations, but only a minority ever received totems. In addition, other station enamels had to be manufactured, some of which are shown in the following image extracted from the 1948 manual (courtesy of Mike Ashworth).

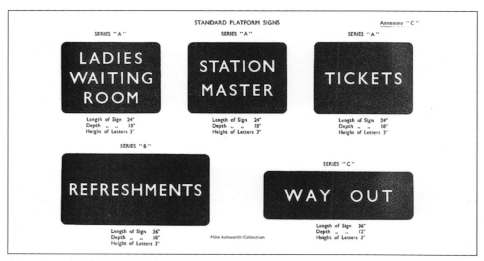

STANDARD PLATFORM SIGNS

SERIES "A"

LADIES
WAITING
ROOM

Length of Sign 24"
Depth .. .. 18"
Height of Letters 3"

SERIES "A"

STATION
MASTER

Length of Sign 24"
Depth .. .. 18"
Height of Letters 3"

Annexure "C"

SERIES "A"

TICKETS

Length of Sign 24"
Depth .. .. 18"
Height of Letters 3"

SERIES "B"

REFRESHMENTS

Length of Sign 36"
Depth .. .. 18"
Height of Letters 3"

Mike Ashworth Collection

SERIES "C"

WAY OUT

Length of Sign 36"
Depth .. .. 12"
Height of Letters 3"

Courtesy of Mike Ashworth Collection

Several UK firms had made and supplied enamel signs for a variety of industries plus road and transport usage; they were approached by the Railway Executive to become part of the supply chain for the refurbishment of stations across Great Britain. Three of these (with more listed in Chapter 2) were Garniers and Gowshalls, both in the London area, and Birmingham's Patent Enamel Company. Over the next fifteen years they made hundreds of thousands of signs, all notionally to the standard specification for size and colour, but of course minor process variations meant small differences arose.

The totem logo did not just appear on enamel signs. It was used on all paper publicity ephemera, on BR's road vehicles and on buildings in very large format (Chapter 7). Every timetable, handbill, information sheet and poster was reissued in the first months BR existed, so people were bombarded by the image after a positively slow start. The photograph that follows was a familiar sight in the 1950s and 1960s.

The colours adopted for the six regions reflected their heritage and soon the British Railways image was everywhere. Throughout each city, town or village, direction signs were erected, even if the station itself was not fitted with totems, showing travellers the location of the nearest station. It was therefore very difficult in the early 1950s to travel far without seeing a totem image; the two images below show examples from 'footballing' North London (ER) and coastal Lancashire (LMR). Even the shipping and harbour facilities inherited by BR were fitted with their standard enamels and totems, reinforcing the corporate identity.

BRITISH RAILWAYS

WHITE HART LANE
STATION

BRITISH RAILWAYS

HEYSHAM HARBOUR
AND STATION

The Regional Colours

The six new regions of British Railways were each given their own identities in the form of enamel station signs of different colours. These colours were historically based, in part, on former railway companies that were absorbed in the 'pre-grouping' of 1923 and partially on the heritage liveries of the 'Big Four' from 1923 to 1947. One of the sheer delights of collecting totems is to see all six regional colours together, as in the set alongside. Visiting auctions, swapmeets or some of the displays of public collections allows an appreciation of the intrinsic beauty of these artefacts.

Beginning at the bottom, the Southern Region used Southern Railway green. However, totems were not made using a consistent colour and three distinct variants can be found (light, mid- and dark green). The first SR totems were a darker green, as depicted by **Winchester City**. These half-flanged (HF) designs were replaced later by fully flanged (FF) variants, with all three shades appearing, albeit randomly, as discussed later.

A study of the SR database shows no clear pattern as to which colour appeared at each station, suggesting each of the suppliers may have worked to the whims of whoever was making the signs. There may have also been other historical factors in the minds of managers, especially as the Southern Railway had used green for their station targets. The **Charing Cross** shown on page 18 is, like the Winchester City alongside, the darkest colour BR (SR) used, and many examples are found in the SR database. Later, a much lighter shade of green as illustrated by the **Harrietsham** totem at the top of page 18 was introduced, but tonal variations were also made and fitted. The mid-green that BR also used, represented on page 18 by **Hersham,** is a clear variation, and placing three SR totems together accentuates the distinct tonal differences. A further example is given by the six SR totems shown together on page 256. Here, the light green **Marston Magna** contrasts markedly with the much darker **Lee for Burnt Ash**. Part of the reason may be the choice of manufacturer and the colour mix they used, but also as time progressed, the SR executives may have realised subtle changes of colour could also make the signs easier to read. **Hersham's** mid-green colour is the epitome of the SR.

TSG library

Courtesy South Devon Railway

The photograph of a preserved coach on the South Devon Railway at Buckfastleigh, Devon, shows how smart this livery is. Being wholly GWR based, the RE managers thought this was totally appropriate for the Western Region's new signage identity.

The **Lincoln Central** opposite carries the rich livery of the Eastern Region. This was a pure ultramarine blue livery, first used by the Great Eastern Railway from 1882 and well illustrated in this photo of the preserved Y14 class 0-6-0 loco built in 1912.

The Western Region comes next, represented in our 'big six' by **Birmingham Snow Hill**: this station closed in 1972, only to be rebuilt and re-opened fifteen years later. The GWR livery is one of the oldest, first seen in 1864. The public perception is that the GWR was a 'brown and cream' railway, and while this was true for rolling stock, it was not true for buildings and signage. Wooden nameboards had raised white letters and framing on a black background. A few nameboards in later years had maroon-brown backgrounds. Station notices, 'Waiting Room', 'Ladies', etc., had raised white letters and framing on a black background and not the perceived totem colours, later termed 'Chocolate & Cream'.

Sheringham (North Norfolk Railway). *Dave Hepper*

The LNER carried this tradition forward; the post-1923 enamels also proudly carried dark blue, but more akin to a royal blue. Therefore, the ER's choice of colour harks back over many decades of history – it is arguably the most striking of all.

A **Manchester Exchange** totem carries the regional livery of the largest region, the LMR. Burgundy and cream were the company colours initially of the Midland Railway and then its 1923 descendant the LMS. More correctly known as crimson lake, it dates back to 1883, but prior to that, Midland engines were painted green. The livery is shown to perfection on an OO-gauge model of an 1880s 0-4-4 tank locomotive, designed by Samuel Johnson at Derby Works.

When the Midland was absorbed into the LMS in 1923, this livery was retained, much to the annoyance of LNWR workers, who also became LMS employees. They wanted their heritage colours as the LMS livery, but black was not a good choice. Much later, however, BR took black and white as the 'modern' livery. Some of railways' finest sights were of Stanier's magnificent 4-6-2 maroon-liveried Pacifics storming up **Shap** and **Beattock** banks on the West Coast Main Line; these powerful machines suited the LMS choice of colour extremely well.

The NER's totems were tangerine, a curious choice, but again one where there was historical precedent. Some of the north-east's stations were fitted with dark orange enamels by the LNER and after red, dark blue and green were taken out, there was little choice. Yellow would have been unreadable at high speed.

Courtesy of Rails of Sheffield

The **Wakefield Kirkgate** totem shows this livery well, but early on the plain white lettering proved a little difficult to read in the gloomy north-east evenings, and almost impossible on days of bright sunshine. Later-produced totems had the white lettering attractively edged with black, and many examples can be found throughout this book.

The NER's orange pedigree is illustrated right by an LNER Durham lamp tablet, a totem forerunner, but Durham station itself never carried BR totems. This lamp tablet is about 18 inches in length, and because of the colour, it survived for many years into BR ownership. Several of the later BR-made totems matched this colour.

The final BR regional colour, for the ScR, featured at the top of page 17 is represented by a totem from world-renowned **Gleneagles**. This colour is loosely based on the later Caledonian Railway (CR) livery. Before 1910, CR locomotives were painted in Prussian blue, a colour not too dissimilar from the Great Eastern's livery. But this was expensive paint, and after 1910 it was mixed with white to give the more familiar lighter shade at a lower cost. The early livery is shown at the top of the following page. BR (ScR) therefore chose a vibrant colour from between these tonal extremes, and somewhat similar to the blue on the Saltire flag of Scotland.

Below, the post-1910 livery is carried by a Class 49 4-6-0 loco built in 1906 at St. Rollox.

Totems were quickly installed, but even as some stations were receiving their new signage, totems were being removed (on the ER in particular) in favour of fluorescent lighting in the late 1950s, with the station name carried on the lamp surface. In other places, totems lasted into the late '70s and early '80s, and throughout this book, Alan Young's photos show these collectable gems still hanging and proudly displaying their regional colours. Totems could be seen anywhere on the station, with their design being influenced by where they were mounted. Some in the LMR and NER were flat, so they could be screwed directly to walls and other prominent surfaces. The favoured place was underneath station lamps with the two photos below as typical examples.

The colour of the Gleneagles totem is about midway between these two historic liveries and in looking at many other ScR totems (Chapter 7), there are various shades of blue that existed, just as there was on Caledonian locomotives. But what is evident from all six of the regions is the homage BR paid to the considerable history they had inherited. It was almost as if they were obliged to make changes, but not very significant changes.

The Rapid Rise and Demise of Totems

In the 1950s and 1960s, the railways touched most people's lives. It was the time when both the authors became hooked on trainspotting and holidays, which were always taken by train, until the rise of the car and the building of roads in the late 1950s and early 1960s took place at a pace similar to the railway mania of the Victorian era.

Train journeys in the 1950s were one of our greatest joys and many stations, large or small, used to have activity, engine sheds, goods yards and signal boxes, where sometimes the friendly signalman used to let us in, to watch the engines. Today most of this has gone and trains are managed from control centres possibly 100 miles away.

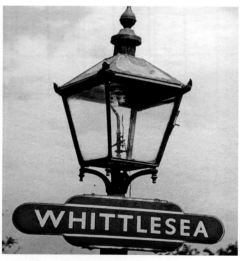

Left: November 1974. Above: July 1974. *Both photos by Alan Young*

Notice the stylish SR and GER platform lamps, today equally as collectable as the totems they once carried. Many UK gardens are now adorned with such artefacts.

How many of us can remember sitting or standing at the end of platforms at dusk, with notebooks and pencils at the ready as the old gas lamps flickered into life and then gloriously illuminated the enamels? The wonderful **Stratford** painting below by Peter Insole shows this memory to perfection, although with electric lighting in this instance.

Spandrels and Capitals, by Peter Insole, GRA. *Courtesy of the artist*

The rapid demise of station totems first occurred in and around London, especially to the east. Reference to the ER totem database (pages 84-96) shows that stations such as **Bethnal Green**, **Clapton**, **Stepney East** and **Stoke Newington** in London, or **Barking**, **Billericay** and **Rayleigh** in Essex, have no known survivors (so far!). Even as far north as **Cambridge** or into Norfolk and Suffolk, the totems came down hurriedly. Essex was particularly plundered, with no survivors recorded from 25 stations out of the 94 that were fitted; the two routes to **Southend-on-Sea** were badly affected.

Technology was advancing quickly during the 1950s, as working capital became available after the years of wartime austerity. The development of the fluorescent tube had a big impact on public lighting and was destined to be a major factor in the demise of totems. : From the late 1950s these lights were installed at many stations around the capital city and explains the absence of totem survivors from much of this area. The station name was embossed on the light cover so it could be read far more easily. Essex lost many of its totems as other parts of Great Britain gained theirs!

The East Coast Main Line also lost some of its totems early on and most of these are not known to have survived. ER aficionados would love **Potters Bar**, **Hatfield**, **Hitchin**, **Essendine**, **Grantham**, **Newark**, **Retford** or **Northallerton** (NER) in their collections. As can be seen from the picture below of **Sandy**, Bedfordshire, the fluorescent light being installed was much larger than the old lamp and its totem.

Changes afoot at Sandy station, Bedfordshire, in October 1977. *Alan Young*

The 'Beeching' Effect

The one single factor that hastened the demise of totems was the appointment in 1961 of Dr. Richard Beeching as Chairman of the British Railways Board, to look at ways of stemming the losses the railways were experiencing. The rise of the motor car and the building of roads meant people and goods could be moved more conveniently where they wanted, and more importantly, when they wanted. Beeching, ICI's Technical Director, was an eminent physicist and engineer before his Government appointment. His first report *The Reshaping of British Railways* was published in 1963, calling for the closure of one third of the nation's 7,000 stations. In addition, 5,000 route miles would be axed and 70,000 jobs would be lost, all for a net saving of around £130 million. The unions and most of the travelling public were very unhappy!

His second report (1965) included a total rebranding and change of corporate image, losing the regional colours and using black-and-white instead. After Beeching left BR, later in 1965, the changes really began, with the totems being removed at a faster rate. Look in the databases to see how many stations closed in the 1960s: Scotland was very badly affected. In came lower-cost signage using a new logo, the 'double arrow' symbol and stations soon started to carry this new brand. Such signs do not possess the intrinsic beauty of the regional totems and although some appear in auctions today, their current desirability appears to be far lower than early BR signage.

The Richard Beeching reports remain controversial to this day. His reorganisation and subsequent development proposals were based purely on economic grounds and totally ignored the sociological effects of closure. Many lines and stations were closed, for instance in the Scottish Lowlands and in mid- and south Wales. Hundreds of communities were left isolated, in much the same way that the high street bank closures are affecting communities today. The failure to consider important social aspects has resulted in many stations re-opening 20, 30 or 40 years after they closed, especially in Scotland. The expanded databases include more stations that have either been reopened or totally rebuilt since closure in each of the six regional chapters than in the 2002 book.

Totem Statistics

As a background to the project, the comprehensive databases that we have kept and updated for over 20 years were analysed to give an overall feel to the scale of the work. The top-level analysis for all this work is given on the following page. We have found that 2,720 different stations were adorned with totems, the LMR having the greatest number with 825 stations and the NER, with only 116, possessing the fewest. Survival rates are different for each region (overall is 92.2%) with the most survivors being in the SR; the ER had the lowest percentage of survivors. This region was the first to start installing totems and also the first to begin their removal.

The date of station closure is a significant factor in totem survival. In general, when stations closed, the signage was disposed of either by skip, sales or indeed other means! Scotland was especially savaged with just over half the stations being closed. Happily, ScotRail has reopened a high percentage of these, more than in any other part of Britain, but the largest number of our information 'gaps' remains in Scotland at 73, followed by the ER at 65. The 1960s saw swingeing economic cuts across all six regions, but the data also shows many stations were being closed even before the Beeching era. A total of 51 stations fitted with totems were closed in the 1950s, so these signs were in use for only a very short period. We also found that after some stations were closed, the signage was subsequently left in place for several years.

Totem Statistical Data

Region	Stations Fitted	Totems Survived	No data	Not in auction	1950s Closures	1960s Closures	Post 1970 Closures	Re-openings *
Eastern	383	317 (82.8%)	65 (17.2%)	45 (14.1%)	24 (6.3%)	83 (21.6%)	19 (4.9%)	6 (1.6%)
London Midland	825	779 (94.4%)	44 (5.6%)	60 (7.2%)	16 (1.9%)	271 (32.7%)	41 (4.9%)	54 (6.5%)
North Eastern	116	113 (97.4%)	3 (2.6%)	9 (7.7%)	2 (1.7%)	30 (25.6%)	10 (8.5%)	9 (7.7%)
Scottish	492	419 (85.2%)	73 (14.8%)	40 (8.1%)	7 (1.4%)	251 (50.7%)	7 (1.4%)	32 (6.4%)
Southern	498	491 (98.6%)	7 (1.4%)	30 (6.1%)	2 (0.4%)	72 (14.5%)	23 (4.6%)	15 (3.0%)
Western	406	390 (96.1%)	16 (3.9%)	31 (7.6%)	3 (0.73%)	106 (25.9%)	19 (4.6%)	19 (4.6%)

Totals	2720	2509 (92.2%)	* re-openings include heritage stations on preserved lines

EASTERN REGION

Station	County	Layout	Flange	Closed	Auction	Survived
DRAYTON	Norfolk		HF	1959		
GRIMSTON ROAD	Norfolk		HF	1959		
GRIMSBY TOWN	Lincolnshire		HF		✓	✓
KIVETON PARK	Yorkshire		HF		✓	✓
NEW BARNET	Hertfordshire		HF			
ST. OLAVES	Suffolk		HF	1959		
STAVELEY WORKS	Derbyshire		HF	1963		
STEPNEY EAST	London					
TILBURY RIVERSIDE	Essex	LP	HF	1992		
WATERBEACH	Cambridgeshire		FF		✓	✓

LONDON MIDLAND REGION

Station	County	Layout	Flange	Closed	Auction	Survived
BROADHEATH	Lancashire		FF	1962		
DOE HILL	Derbyshire		FF	1960		
HADFIELD	Derbyshire		HF		✓	✓
LEVENSHULME NORTH	Lancashire	2L	HF			
MANCHESTER LONDON ROAD (named Piccadilly in 1960)	Lancashire	2L	HF			
NEWTON FOR HYDE	Lancashire	2L	HF			✓
PADIHAM	Lancashire			1957		✓
SEACOMBE	Cheshire		HF?	1960		
ST. PANCRAS poster heading type 52in long	London				✓	✓
TRENT rectangular poster header type	Derbyshire		Flat	1968	✓	✓
WARBRECK	Lancashire			1960		
WIDNES	Lancashire		FF			✓
WITHINGTON & WEST DIDSBURY	Lancashire	2L	FF			

NORTH EASTERN REGION

NONE TO DATE						

SCOTTISH REGION

Station	County	Layout	Flange	Closed	Auction	Survived
AYTON	Berwickshire		FF	1962		
CLYDEBANK EAST	Lanarkshire	LP		1959		
DUNBAR	East Lothian		FF			
GAILES	Ayrshire		FF	1967		
GREENOCK LYNEDOCH	Renfrewshire	1L		1959		
KILBARCHAN	Renfrewshire		FF	1966		✓
MILLIKEN PARK (re-opened May 1989)	Renfrewshire		HF	1966	✓	✓
POMATHORN	Midlothian		FF			
ROSSLYNLEE	Midlothian		FF			
RENFREW SOUTH (replaced SOUTH RENFREW)	Renfrewshire	1L	FF	1967	✓	✓
RUTHERFORD	Roxburghshire		FF	1964		·
STEWARTON (re-opened June 1967)	Ayrshire		HF	1966		
STRATHBUNGO	Lanarkshire			1962		
WATERSIDE	Ayrshire		HF	1964	✓	✓

SOUTHERN REGION

Station	County	Layout	Flange	Closed	Auction	Survived
EARLSFIELD	London		FF			
GREENHITHE	Kent		BF		✓	✓
HORSLEY	Surrey		?			✓
YETMINSTER	Dorset		FF?			

WESTERN REGION

Station	County	Layout	Flange	Closed	Auction	Survived
PETERSTON	Glamorgan		HF	1964		✓
SALTNEY	Cheshire		FF	1960		

Discoveries since publication of the 2002 Totem book.

The Layout of This Book

This greatly expanded book compared to the 2002 *The Book of British Railways Totems* has been nearly twenty years in the making. During that time the interest in totem collecting has grown and so has the amount of information on station history and the provision of totems. The six regional databases contain far more entries, as more and more of them have appeared in auction, coupled with discoveries made in attics, garden sheds and other places of concealment. It seems that even more totems than was first realised were squirreled away in the 1960s and 1970s. The tables on the previous page cover all these information changes in a succinct manner.

This Introduction sets the scene for the book and is followed by a new Chapter 2. This contains extensive sections discussing various totem fonts and how they developed during the 20th century. The vitreous enamelling process, the cornerstone to successful totem manufacture, is covered in more detail and station signage policy is also discussed. Chapter 3 covers the rare and unusual, collecting themes and examples of some wonderful totem collections that exist within our hobby.

Chapters 4 to 9 are devoted to each of the six regions, which were formed in 1948. Each of the chapters follows roughly the same structure: the history of each region, then its totem geography, which is a more detailed study of the spread of totems in each region. We are indebted to Alan Young who is the major contributor to most of these sections. The geographical studies are based on Alan's writings for the Totem Study Group between 2003 and 2009 and have been expanded to encompass our most-recent research. Each of the chapters then contains two, three or four feature articles, sometimes with an area focus or sometimes a more regional focus; some are written by learned contributors. Each chapter then concludes with a review of every county within the relevant BR region, and discusses availability, rarity, or where there is little or no knowledge on totem

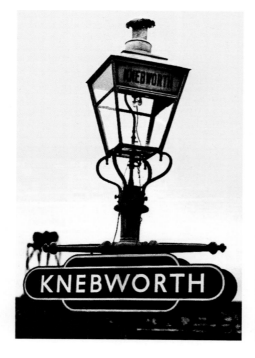

survival. Chapter 4 covers the Eastern Region, Chapter 5 the London Midland Region, Chapter 6 the North Eastern Region, Chapter 7 the Scottish Region, Chapter 8 the Southern Region and Chapter 9 the Western Region; many maps, *in situ*, totem photos and other relevant photos are contained therein.

Chapter 10 is a completely new section. During the past twenty years we have been amassing photographs of totems *in situ* during the years they were in use. These have confirmed that stations whose totems do not appear to have survived, were actually fitted, including locations such as **Albion** (LMR), **Bury-St-Edmunds** (ER), **Hamble Halt** (SR), **Newhaven** (ScR), **Northallerton** (NER) or **Yate** (WR), for example. The majority of these photos have not been published before and give our studies full traceability. Many have been sent to us by like-minded collectors and we give them appropriate credit.

Chapter 11 is the closure and subject wrap-up, including a learned dissertation by Tim Clarke on general BR signage policy. There is extra focus on the Southern Region to help explain why so many different variants exist and why some types from a few SR stations are much less common than others. It was due to passenger growth numbers and the ability of the network to cope during the totem years. The two pictures alongside show our deep affection for this era of Britain's railways. Finally, Stop Press includes the very latest information, surfacing after our manuscript was finished in early July 2021.

Photos by Alan Young

Totem Design Instructions

On 27 September 1948, British Railways published a document entitled *Code of Instructions for Station Name and Direction Signs*. This contained very detailed instructions for the production of station enamel signage, and it was sent out to prospective manufacturers for comment. The layout, font and manufacturing process to be followed were all included but, as subsequent history showed, not all the instructions were followed and, over the years, variations in lettering and layout took place. The key figures from this document are shown below.

BRITISH RAILWAYS TOTEM

The standard lettering was to be 3 inches high, and the name located within the centre section of the 36-inch-long totem. For those cases where a long station name appears, a scale was laid down for the letter height as a function of the number of station letters. Where appropriate, double- or even triple-lined layouts could be used within the central and lower panels to accommodate the full name of the station; different sized lettering was permitted, with examples shown below.

The table below details the letter size relative to the number of letters on the totem. The smallest allowed is 2 inches, but if the rules below do not permit the name to fit correctly, then Gill Sans Condensed font lettering may be used.

	Heights of letters (inches)	Maximum number of letters
	3.0	10
Standard	2.75	12
	2.5	14
	2.25	16
Minimum	2.0	18

Gill Sans Condensed does not appear that often on totems but where it does, the letters seem squashed together, contrasting markedly with standard Gill Sans, as the four pictures below clearly show.

'Words such as 'Central', 'Halt' or 'Junction' may be placed in the lower panel in 1 inch letters if there is insufficient space in the central panel'. The guide also permits letters larger than 3 inch, but the only region where this option was taken up was the ER and examples appear in Chapter 4 and in the Eastern Region database pages. With 36 inch long totems, these larger letters seem somewhat ungainly. Some totem examples were only made in very small numbers, as laid down in one of the design clauses, such as **Combpyne** with one totem and **Trench Crossing** with two.

The 1948 Code of Instructions did not just cover totems, it related to all station enamel signage from very large running-in boards (erected at the ends of platforms), large platform or directional signs, down to individual office signs for ticketing, refreshments, parcel rooms and similar functions. The *Code of Instructions* examined every part of the signs, especially the Gill Sans lettering. A small part of this is shown below left and discussed later in the chapter where station sign fonts are covered in more detail. Alongside is the Gill Sans alphabet and marked in the grey circles are the changes BR made to Gill's original designs. The length of the arms on letters 'E' and 'F', the descended 'J', plus the calligraphic tails on letters 'Q' and 'R' are the departures from 1928 Gill work.

Courtesy of Mike Ashworth collection

Wikipedia Commons image

Those station staff who were assigned offices were given their own signs (station master, porter, ticket inspector etc.,) so considering all the stations and all the signs required, the BR order ran into hundreds of thousands of items. Some carried the BR logo, but many did not. Outside the station there were direction signs to be supplied.

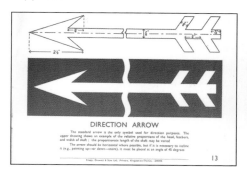

All the signs were made from a common material, VE CR4 grade steel, which was chosen because its mechanical properties deteriorate very slowly with respect to time. This makes the sign durable but considering many were only in use for a few years, the choice was somewhat wasteful. Because of the huge requirement, the specifications and design briefs were sent out to several companies who had experience with the supply of vitreous enamel sign manufacture. These included Mead McLean, Brutons, Gowshalls, Garniers, all from London, and Birmingham's Patent Enamel Company.

All these firms supplied various government and public bodies but Mead McLean had very relevant experience, having supplied the Southern Railway with its enamel targets. The general quality of the Mead McLean's signage was high, and the targets coped with the inclement weather with little deterioration. The target below was probably made around 1936/37 and the 'PUBLICITY DEPT' sign in the early BR years.

The manufacturing cost was on the expensive side because the process was labour-intensive, as the next section describes, so it was interesting that the first totem sales allowed today's treasures to be picked up for just a few shillings each. Even a decade later, the value had not increased that much; at Scunthorpe in January 1971, some Lincolnshire gems were available for only a few pounds.

Scunthorpe Auction at the BR Goods Shed, High Street East, Scunthorpe.

TOTEMS	Saturday 16th January 1971	TOTEMS
Sutton-on-Sea £3		1 Sutton-on-Sea & 1 Alford Town £5.50p
Sutton-on Sea with brackets £3.50p		1 Sutton-on-Sea & 1 Alford Town £7
1 Mablethorpe & 1 Sutton-on-Sea £5		1 Sutton-on-Sea & 1 Alford Town £5
1 Alford Town & 1 Sutton-on-Sea £4.50p		1 Mablethorpe & 1 Sutton-on-Sea £7.50p
2 Sutton-on-Sea £5		1 Skegness (price unrecorded)
Alford Town £4.50p		
Mablethorpe £5.50p		Many cast iron seatbacks were on offer
1 Sutton-on-Sea & 1 Mablethorpe £5.50p		still in their seats eg Willoughby Jnc.
1 Sutton-on-Sea & 1 Alford Town £5		
Sutton-on-Sea £5.50p		
1 Mablethorpe & 1 Alford Town		Many enamel boxboards also on offer.
& 1 Sutton-on-Sea £9		
2 Sutton-on-Sea & 1 Alford Town £9		Doorplates 3 to 4 in each lot 15/- to 30/-

Often they were sold in pairs (**Mablethorpe** and **Sutton-on-Sea** for example) to allow BR to divest themselves of them quickly. Clearly such a sale allowed local assets to be purchased so the population there could buy a piece of Lincolnshire history to cherish. Around the country, similar sales took place, offering different regional items of railwayana. What is fascinating about this Scunthorpe sales advert is how many **Sutton-on-Sea** totems were for sale, probably all those on the station being disposed of together as fifteen were on offer. Small lots of doorplate signs were for sale from 15s (0.75p) to 30s (£1.50) each, along with many cast iron and enamel boxboards.

The Vitreous Enamel Manufacturing Process

The process used to manufacture station totems is termed vitreous enamelling. It is a very old process, first documented in ancient Egyptian manuscripts. The basic process is the fusing of powdered glass at high temperatures onto any surface that can withstand the 750°C to 850°C hardening requirements. Documented evidence of its extensive use, especially on metallic surfaces, can also be found in manuscripts from ancient Greece and Rome, as well as the Celtic and Chinese civilizations. In the Middle Ages, it was extensively used to produce jewellery, pottery and durable domestic artefacts. The technique of porcelain enamelling on cast iron was developed in Central Europe in the early 1800s and once the steelmaking process had been perfected by Bessemer in the late 19th century, enamelled steel objects began to appear.

Research shows it was widely used in the UK, between the years 1880 and 1950, both for product advertising and street signage. The first purpose-built factory for making such signs was created by Benjamin Baugh in 1889 at Selly Oak, Birmingham, the Patent Enamel Company. This company was one of the manufacturers that British Railways approached to bid on their supply contract, once the totem design had been fixed. Another supplier was Garnier of London, who had established their factory in Strode Road, Willesden Green, in 1898. Each of the suppliers had a slightly different process, which may account for some of the variations in quality and colour.

The process requires very careful temperature control because any sudden or unwanted variations may cause spurious chemical reactions during firing. Once the manufacturing procedure has been perfected, the product is durable, weather-, chemical- and UV resistant, scratchproof and with long-lasting colour stability, all ideal properties for being outside in a British climate for many years. The disadvantage of enamel is the tendency to crack or shatter when the substrate layers are bent or stressed; this is reduced by careful thickness control when the layers are applied.

Further reduction of stressing can be made by careful matching of the glass thermal expansion coefficients to that of the steel body. However, the manufacture did not anticipate vandals bending the ends backwards on some half-flanged variants and, as a result of such cases, the fully flanged types were subsequently introduced. Below is an example of a totem badly treated in the West Midlands. It was once a pristine WR **Cradley & Cradley Heath** totem, but has suffered much trauma!

A rather sorry and damaged Cradley (Heath & Cradley) totem *in situ. Alan Young*

The most important first stage of the manufacture was the stamping out of the steel blank, followed by rigorous degreasing so the layers adhered evenly all over the steel surface. Tanks of acid were used to remove any surface grease. The blank then underwent numerous screening processes to build up the enamel slowly and evenly. A black or dark grey layer was first applied to bond directly to the steel and this was cured in an oven until strong fusion of the two layers occurred.

It was allowed to dry in a controlled atmosphere so that no impurities could harm the under-coating. The next layer would be a white or light-coloured substrate layer to form the basis for the subsequent applications of the required regional colours. The glass powder used was a mildly alkaline borosilicate glass, produced at around 1,200°C to make molten glass, which was then thermally shocked to produce the fine powder granules required for vitreous enamelling. These two base layers are critical to the long life of each totem. The white layer was usually a little thicker than the first dark layer to give a solid intermolecular bond. (These layers can be seen in cases where chips have appeared on the enamel's surface due to sudden damage or face drilling).

Once the substrate layers had been checked for quality, the actual process of screen printing could begin. It is a slow and painstaking process, as successive layers are applied, then fired between each application, so building up a thick layer of enamel on the steel base. The screens are made from fabric, usually silk, but sometimes nylon, stretched tightly onto wooden frames. They are held rigidly in place during the regional colour application before firing at between 800–850°C. At each subsequent firing, the temperature is lowered so the previously applied layer is not affected and does not melt. The whole process could take anything from a few days to three weeks, depending on the size and complexity of the enamel sign being made; totems took around two weeks. Large enamel advertising signs using multiple colours would take longer, using a different screen for each colour being applied. The same process is used for product advertising signs as well as station and public notices.

Eric Gill and His GILL SANS Typeface
Richard Furness & Alan Young

Throughout this book, there are thousands of examples of station signage, the vast majority using the familiar Gill Sans typeface: this section describes others that BR used. Its inventor was Arthur Eric Rowton Gill (1882-1940) a famous sculptor, typeface designer and printmaker who worked on the typeface for around two-and-a-half years, slowly refining and adjusting it. Before it appeared, he had been working for Stanley Morison on **Perpetua**, a serif typeface for the British offshoot of the USA-based Monotype Corporation. This is a worldwide company, which has been active in typesetting since its foundation in 1887. This typeface eventually appeared in 1926, around the time he was developing Gill Sans, so in the late 1920s, Gill became the most active and influential of the British font designers. His lifelong work was eventually recognised and he was named Royal Designer for Industry, the highest British design award, by the Royal Society of Arts, when it formed in 1936. The clarity of the lettering is shown to good effect in the main station sign for Lowestoft Central.

A typeface is a particular set of glyphs (an alphabet and its corresponding accessories such as numerals and punctuation) that share a common design. For example, Arial is a well-known typeface. A font is a particular set of glyphs within a typeface. Generally speaking, typefaces are not copyrighted but many fonts are. Regarding Gill Sans, Eric Gill had collaborated with Edward Johnston in the early days of a transport lettering project. In 1913, Frank Pick had commissioned Johnston to design a typeface for London Underground: the simple and clear Sans serif Johnston typeface was the result. In typography and lettering, a **Sans serif** (or more simply a Sans) letterform is one that does not have extending features (called 'serifs') at the end of strokes. Sans-serif typefaces tend to have less stroke width variation than serif types. They are often used to convey simplicity, modernity or minimalism, which attracted Eric Gill.

AaBbCc AaBbCc AaBbCc

The left-hand figure above is a Serif type, the centre figure is a Sans serif type and the right-hand figure illustrates the strokes present on each letter in the left-hand diagram, which have been removed in the centre figure. It was this simplicity of letters that Gill saw as the opportunity to build on Edward Johnston's work and create a clear railway font.

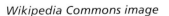

TSG Library

The left-hand figure above shows the differences between the Johnston Sans (shown in red) and the Gill Sans (shown in dark blue). Gill's work seems more simplistic and pleasing to the eye with respect to all five letters and even a simple dot is cleaner.

This led the LNER to adopt his typeface (but with modifications to upper case letters 'J' and 'R' as mentioned) for all their publicity, signs and even nameplates. Arguably the most famous of these is shown in the right-hand photo above, borne by steam's world speed record holder, Gresley's A4 **MALLARD**.

Gill never strayed far from his religious roots. Among his many and varied well known achievements were *The Canterbury Tales* (for Golden Cockerel Press) and the *Four Gospels.* For both these publications he designed new typefaces and produced wonderful illustrations. Readers may appreciate this true artisan's remarkable skill as an illustrator and typeface designer from the two examples below.

Courtesy Golden Cockerel Press

Courtesy of The Folio Society

The Second World War broke out in 1939 and just one year later, Eric Gill died. Ironically, his typeface was used extensively by the LNER throughout the war and its boldness symbolised the 'British Bulldog Spirit', which inspired the nation to get through this most difficult period of history. Eight years after his death, his Sans-serif typeface was to gain even greater visibility when British Railways selected it for signage and publicity throughout the country. In the early 1960s, after flirting with other fonts (*see* the section that follows), BR abandoned the restrained and elegant Gill Sans in favour of the punchier Helvetica Medium and its derivatives. The new fashion at that time was the use of largely lower case lettering for signage, but as the sentence below shows, it was not as clear as Gill Sans.

> This sentence is typed in 10pt Helvetica Medium merely to illustrate the typeface

Gill Sans came out of copyright in 2010, seventy years after Gill's death. As a consequence, it has received much attention in the past decade and derivatives have appeared regularly. Because Gill Sans is now widely available in PC software packages, it turns up in all sorts of publications, adding to the long list of its diverse users. Apart from the LNER, early users were Penguin paperbacks for their book covers and Betty's Tea Rooms of Harrogate in their advertisements. Later users were the *New Musical Express* for the Top 30 chart, (Sir) Paul McCartney for solo album lyrics, the BBC (adopted in 1997 as its corporate font though they are now moving away again), The Royal Society of Arts, Network Rail, Channel 4, and the Church of England.

> **This sentence is typed in 9.5pt Gill Sans merely to illustrate the typeface**

Possibly the largest examples in use today are on the Cunard liners, as these ships have their names painted in Gill Sans. British Rail gave up on Gill Sans but it has quietly returned to the railways courtesy of EWS freight vehicles. The recent installation of appropriately coloured green totems on the Lymington branch is an interesting development. These apparently use a 'light' version of Gill Sans reminiscent of the form used on LNER blue enamel running-in boards. We are probably not alone in hoping that this innovation is adopted elsewhere for information signage.

Gill Sans is one of 14 similar fonts making up the whole Humanist family. Gill worked on these for many years up to 1930, slowly refining and adapting. The upper and lower typefaces are shown together in the preceding left-hand figure for the first three letters of the alphabet. The upper case letters are modelled on Roman capitals with letters such as 'M' (as in the locomotive nameplate MALLARD) being in the proportions of a square with the middle strokes meeting in the centre of that square. The lower case letters 'a' and 'g' are slightly weird, being unbalanced compared to the other letters and, as the font weight increases, they become rather ugly. These are based on Carolingian script (an ancient Roman script used extensively by Emperor Charlemagne). The use of some of these letters is shown in the two pictures below, including the only totem to carry exclusively lower case lettering, **Besses o' th' Barn**.

Akzidenz Grotesk	a	g	t
Futura	a	g	t
Johnston	a	g	t
Gill Sans	a	g	t
Caslon	a	g	t

Notice the proportions of the letter 't' compared to the 'h' alongside it: they somehow look at odds with each other. In the computer font, this disparity in size is not present. The letter 'e' appears curiously shaped, reflecting the calligraphic basis of the font. It seems to overwhelm the letter 's' alongside. However, the clarity of the upper-case lettering on the rare Essex **WOOD STREET** totem is undeniable.

BESSES O' TH' BARN would have looked much better in capitals (as presented here) so it is curious as to why lower case letters were adopted at this location only. It is not commonly appreciated that not all BR signs were in Gill Sans. As time went by, BR began to take note of what other countries were doing in respect of public signs and towards the end of totem installation began to increasingly experiment with other fonts. This was a little curious, as they might have been developing their corporate identity quietly and in parallel. In 1964, BR had approached the Design Research Unit (DRU) to begin work on a new image. This organisation, founded in 1951, was one of the first generation of British Design Consultancies that combined expertise in architecture, graphic and industrial design, to promote image and brand awareness.

Totem Typefaces:
Not Always GILL SANS

Alan Young & Richard Furness

The familiar BR font used for totems, posters and timetables until the mid-1960s was inherited from the London & North Eastern Railway. Each of the 'Big Four' pre-nationalisation companies used sans serif capitals on station signs, but the LNER's **Gill Sans** was considered most suitable for the national network. The preceding article shows this closely resembled Edward Johnston's font for the London Underground Group. The vision of Frank Pick was most influential here, just as it was for his posters and other image enhancing signage, when he promoted and marketed rail travel.

BR set out to create standardised 'lamp tablets' in the six regional colours with the Gill Sans font size governed by the length of the station name. The guidelines permitted the use of Gill Sans Condensed for longer names, and this produced a distinctly different appearance from the standard version (e.g., at **Small Heath & Sparkbrook**). It seems that only the LMR, WR and SR used the condensed form. Early poster signs such as **Pendleton** (above) appear to have used a heavy Gill Sans Condensed font.

We get into interesting territory when BR departed from standard Gill Sans on totems. The conspicuously misshapen WR totems at **Radstock West** were an early, possibly unique, aberration (*see* the form of the 'O' and 'W'). **Moreton-in-Marsh** had similarly misshapen totems and curious looking print which, on close inspection, appears to be Gill Sans Condensed but with widely spaced characters. The severely distorted totem signs used at **Bath Spa, Kings Nympton** and **Helston** used an unidentified narrow Sans-serif font, and the letters 'B', 'E', 'M' and 'O' are distinctly non-Gill Sans.

Towards the end of the totem era the Southern and Western Regions staged a rebellion against Gill Sans. The SR had already played 'fast and loose' with the totem, trying out different shades of green, all-green signs, totems with both black and white flanges, 4-foot totems and wooden signs with what appears to be hand-lettered approximations to Gill Sans. Then in the early 1960s a substantial number of their stations received totems lettered in *Transport Medium* font. This Kinnear-and-Calvert-designed typeface, the property of the Government, was turned into a computer font by Nathanial Porter in 2011. It was adapted from **Akzidenz Grotesk**, a typeface dating from 1896 and now out of copyright. The much newer digital versions of both fonts however are still in copyright. Transport Medium, now termed New Transport or Transport New, is the familiar one in today's British road traffic signage.

> **This sentence is typed in 9pt Transport Medium merely to illustrate the typeface**
>
> **This sentence is typed in 9pt Akzidenz-Grotesk merely to illustrate the typeface**

Why, and exactly when, the Southern Region adopted this font is unclear, but research by John Wells suggests that it had to be post-1958, as the font did not previously exist, and was probably after 1961, because stations renamed in that year had Gill Sans signs. John suspects that these errant SR signs were installed no earlier than 1963. Indeed, in February–March 1963 the *New Design for British Railways* exhibition was held at London's Design Centre, and among the exhibits was a new 'house-style' livery for Rail Freight using the *Transport Medium* font (*Railway Magazine,* April 1963). It seems likely that in this time of reviewing BR's corporate image, the SR began to use Transport Medium. The confusion within BR regarding what fonts to use, and whether to continue using the totem, is demonstrated by the variety of typefaces in the 1963/4 passenger timetables. Significantly the name SOUTHERN REGION appears on the covers of both the winter 1963/4 and summer 1964 timetables in Transport Medium Capitals, accompanied by a muddle of other fonts on the cover and within the book.

Totem aficionado John Wells does not rule out the involvement of a road sign manufacturer in the production of the non-standard SR totems: perhaps the firm simply used Transport Medium because they had it 'in stock', and to the untutored eye it could pass for Gill Sans. However, a careful comparison of Gills Sans to Transport Medium shows it is distinctly different. The pair of totems below appeared with Transport Medium letters and notice they are produced in two different shades of SR green.

SR TOTEMS WITH TRANSPORT MEDIUM TYPEFACE

Balcombe, Banstead, Barnehurst*, Belmont, Chislehurst, Christchurch, Clapham, Cobham & Stoke d' Abernon (2L version), **Durrington-on-Sea, Earley, Eltham Park*, Esher, Fratton, Hackbridge, Hampton, Leatherhead, Lewisham*, London Road (Guildford), Maze Hill, Mortlake, New Milton, Oxshott, Oxted*, Petts Wood, Queenborough, Seaford, Shoreham, St. Denys, Staplehurst*, Streatham, Tadworth, Upper Warlingham** (2L version), **Warnham, Winnersh Halt, Woldingham** and **Woodside*.**

* these stations also had standard Gill Sans lettered totems (*see* database for flange information).

Simon Davies has studied the geographical distribution of non-Gill Sans SR totems and found them to be almost equally distributed between the Western, Central, and Eastern divisions. He has seen only fully flanged specimens and they are mostly mid-green in colour. John Wells reports lighter green shades but also a mid-blue/green one from **Durrington-on-Sea**. Some of these signs must have been displayed for a very short time. **Christchurch** and **New Milton** totems were possibly *in situ* from only 1963 until 1967, when the London **Waterloo** to Bournemouth stations (**Queen's Road Battersea** excepted) were given the Corporate Identity make-over.

At **Beddington Lane Halt** Transport Medium was used on the running-in and signal-box boards, but not on the totems. **London Road (Guildford)** totems were unique in using a lower case font for 'Guildford' in the lower panel. John Wells has noted that Transport Medium was also used on some early enamel black-and-white signs. The SR and LMR used it on some signal-box nameboards; at **Blackpool South** (and possibly elsewhere) the latter region even adopted lower case in the manner of road signs and of later BR practice.

The Western Region also went its own way with signage in the early 1960s. It had already shown individuality in using cream (rather than white) lettering on all brown totems such as **Hanwell**, honouring GWR livery, but in the early 1960s it seems to have abandoned brown in favour of black, with plastic black-and-white totems appearing at **Torquay**. The **Paddington–Princes Risborough** line saw some totems skilfully over-painted in black (including **Paddington, Denham Golf Club** and **Seer Green & Jordans**), but preserving the Gill Sans lettering: **Liskeard** and **Newquay** were similarly treated.

However, several stations were fitted with new signs using white letters on a black background, using a heavy grotesque font with a closer affinity to 19th Century styles than to the 1960s. The letters 'A', 'G', 'E' and 'L' are quite different from Gill Sans.

These rather strange-looking totems were installed only at **Bourne End, Devonport, Hayes & Harlington,** and **Langley (Bucks)**: the font type is unknown. The preceding two pictures show a **BOURNE END** *in situ* compared to an overpainted **Newquay**.

What looked like bold moves by the Western and Southern regions seem modest when compared with a Scottish Region experiment of 1959. The Glasgow 'North Side' Electrification scheme was inaugurated on 5 November 1960, but an article in *Railway Magazine* in February 1960 notes that 'at certain stations prototype signs of a new design have already been erected'; a photograph of **Westerton** includes a rectangular lamp-mounted sign looking disconcertingly like a later BR corporate identity design. These signs used dark lower case sans serif type on a yellow background. Presumably the choice of colour was derived from the electrification scheme logo, with its intersecting blue and yellow V shapes (right-hand photo).

This Scottish experiment is probably anathema to 'totemologists' but is interesting because it apparently pre-dated the Southern and Western totems with typeface variations, and it gave a foretaste of the corporate identity era. In 1965, British Railways changed its image, re-branded itself 'British Rail', abandoned regional colours, discarded totems and banished Gill Sans. Bland black-and-white signs, using *Rail Alphabet* (based on Helvetica Medium), eventually covered the railway network.

Station Signs with Transport and Rail Alphabet Fonts

In 1948, British Railways' decision to use Gill Sans lettering on regional background colours, was a style that persisted for fifteen years. However, the management was keen on rebranding and giving the railways a fresh image in the face of declining freight tonnage and passenger numbers. Around 1960, several important stations were earmarked for upgrades, one of these being **Coventry.** This was transformed using a modernistic approach, with the final result being rather faceless and bland, as captured in Ben Brooksbank's excellent photograph. Notice the fluorescent lighting installed at right angles to the platforms and the Brutalist style of the architecture.

Above: The newly rebuilt Coventry station in 1962. *Ben Brooksbank*

Right: Coventry station in 1961 during rebuilding. *WarwickshireRailways.com*

The preceding photo shows the former station during its rebuilding around 1961. It was here that BR decided to trial a new signage font designed by Jock Kinneir and Margaret Calvert called *Transport*. Its development started in 1957 and continued for a few years, building on the characteristics of both Helvetica and Akzidenz Grotesk.

This had begun to be used on Britain's road signs, apparently being more readable at high speeds and in inclement weather. It is shown below left alongside the later Kinneir and Calvert design for Rail Alphabet. There can be no doubt that both are influenced by Gills Sans, though lower case letters such as 'g' are an improvement.

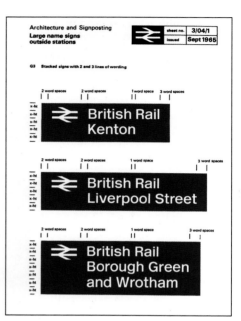

Helvetica (Left) and Rail Alphabet (Right) fonts compared. *Wikipedia commons*

Akzidenz Grotesk originated in Germany and developed to achieve iconic status in the post-war period as the preferred typeface of many Swiss graphic designers in what became called the 'International' or 'Swiss' design style. This became popular across the Western world in the 1950s and 1960s. Its simple and neutral design has also influenced many later typefaces, including those that became popular in the UK. It was from this that Helvetica was developed in Switzerland in 1957 and proved to be an excellent typeface for public signs, though this is not as clear as Gill Sans or indeed Frutiger that is used throughout this book. Helvetica could be seen at every in Swiss railway station and on rolling stock (as seen below) and has since formed the base font for many European public notices.

Kinneir and Calvert took this basic font and introduced their own bespoke letter-spacing system (as shown in the right-hand figure above) and in two slightly different weights to provide optimum visibility on both light and dark backgrounds. Their subsequent creation of Rail Alphabet was based on the need to improve readability indoors at stations and this was accepted and adopted by the new British Rail in 1965. It was first seen publicly at Liverpool Street station in London that year.

The 1965 total rebranding of British Railways included a new logo (the double arrow, as shown on page 34), a shortened corporate name 'British Rail', and sadly the total adoption of Rail Alphabet for all lettering other than printed matter including station signage, trackside signs, fixed notices, train interior information signs and train liveries. Key rebranding elements were still in use in the 1980s and Rail Alphabet was also used as part of the livery of Sealink ships until that company's privatisation (preceding photo of the *MV Caesarea*). By the end of the 1980s, British Rail's various business units were developing their own individual brands and identities and some decided to adopt other fonts; as a consequence, the use of Rail Alphabet declined.

Totem Usage and Signing Policy

The 1948 BR signage standard document discussed at the start of this chapter states that the totems were to be rigidly suspended from platform roofs, near to station lamps, so they could be more easily read at night and during inclement weather. Many of the *in situ* pictures throughout this book show such examples from all six regions, but often they were affixed to walls and other parts of the station. Some of the fixings were rather ungainly as at **Worcester Foregate Street** or **Windsor & Eton Central**.

Both photographs Tim Clarke

The majority however did conform to the guidelines and, in the golden light of dusk, as the gas lamps began to glow, some quite wonderful images were available, if you happened to be there and had a photographic eye. The **Hanwell** picture alongside is a perfect example, with a totem in good condition nearing the end of its working life.

Hanwell totem *in situ*, 7 June 1975. *Alan Young*

Similar sights were found in every region, such as this wonderful shot below of **New Southgate** in 1973. Totems were not always found below lamps or affixed to lamp standards. Many other places proved to be convenient, such as building walls or fences as in this image of **Boldon Colliery** (this station was renamed Brockley Whins in 1991, thereby reverting back to its original pre-1925 name).

Not all totems were mounted parallel to the platform and tracks. The preceding picture shows **Sunnymeads** in Buckinghamshire mounted at right-angles and there were other examples of installation not exactly in accordance with the guide. At some stations the totems were even displayed away from the platforms. Reference to *Jowett's Atlas* or the *RCH Station Handbook* lists all the stations that existed in 1948 and the small selection below is typical of the sights seen at stations up and down Britain in the 1960s, such as **Swindon**, **Hellifield** (courtesy Tim Clarke) and **West Bromwich.** The first picture shows totems were affixed to almost anything solid such to a wooden fence at the Wiltshire station on the main **Paddington** to **Bristol** line. Notice the modern lighting at **Swindon** that is not above the totem, most strange!

New Southgate *in situ,* in 1973. *Alan Young*

Boldon Colliery. *N. Skinner*

Sunnymeads station, June 1977. *Alan Young*

Below: West Bromwich station, 15 July 1967. *G.C. Lewthwaite*

Not all the stations inherited by British Railways in 1948 were fitted with totems; in fact the minority were so-adorned. As the installation progressed, spasmodically at first and then much faster, totems were being removed in the east as modern lighting was fitted, while simultaneously they were being installed in the west. As described in the regional chapters under 'totem geography', the process was somewhat random. Some small halts received them (but not always), while some mainline stations were fitted but others that were more far obvious candidates were not.

At its zenith, the British network possessed 6,747 stations, but totems were only installed at 2,720 of these, meaning that just over 40% were chosen to carry the new post-war British Railways image. These decisions were taken by the Regional Public Relations and Publicity Departments, so it not unexpected there were inconsistencies in signage policy. Many important stations were not fitted, as listed below. This was surprising as these stations would have been the perfect places to display BR's new Image. Three of Manchester's stations (**Central**, **Exchange** and **Victoria**) were fitted, as were **Birmingham's Snow Hill** and **New Street, Bristol Temple Meads** and **York**: an amazing 36 totems were provided for **Bournemouth West** and larger numbers were made for **Clapham Junction**. It is possible that cost may have been a factor in the decision not to fit totems in the list below, as most are large or very large stations.

Aberdeen	Ashford (Kent)	Banbury	Blackfriars
Bournemouth Central	Bridlington	Chichester	Crewe
Doncaster	Dover Marine	Durham	Edinburgh Princes Street
Edinburgh Waverley	Euston (London)	Fenchurch Street	Glasgow Central
Glasgow Queen Street	Glasgow St Enoch	Hull Paragon	Inverness
Liverpool Central	Liverpool Exchange	Liverpool Lime Street	Liverpool Street
Manchester Piccadilly	Marylebone	Middlesbrough	Newcastle Central
Norwich Thorpe	Nottingham Victoria	Plymouth	St Pancras
Sheffield Midland	Sheffield Victoria	Southampton Central	Victoria (London)
Yarmouth Vauxhall			

What is most intriguing is none of Liverpool's main stations were totem-provided, but many in the suburbs were; half of London's termini were fitted and half were not. Computer technology allows us to see what some of the totems from this list may have looked like. What price might these two be today if they had existed?

These reconstructions show the computer Gill Sans font developed after 2010 does not exactly match that adopted by BR. This clearly was of a slightly heavier weight than standard Gill Sans: these two reconstructed totems are lettered with 'computer Gill Sans'. It is interesting that new totems installed at Lymington and Barnstaple use this same lightweight Gill Sans letters; this is why they also do not look quite right. However, there is nothing like the real thing as shown in the collection below. When all six regional colours are displayed together, the effect is simply stunning! One-line, two-line and lower-panel designs are all present in this mainly city-based array.

TSG library files and the cover of the 2002 totem book.

Opening Comments

Station totems have been the subject of collecting ever since the first signs started to be withdrawn. Initially, many were sent to landfill sites and to scrap metal merchants and most of these were lost forever, as our databases indicate. Others were quickly snapped up by BR employees, eager to own a piece of history and by fledgling collectors, who immediately recognised their intrinsic value. This is quite different to their monetary value and as the decades have passed, some totems have increased in both fields, while for others the intrinsic value has been enhanced as their monetary value has slightly decreased. It is not our remit to discuss totem monetary values, but this volume offers our decades of experience to allow collectors to make more informed judgments. Throughout the book we often comment on rarity, but what is a rare item? It is defined as 'something that is unusual or uncommon', but for any totem, several factors are involved that make it uncommon. These include, but are not limited to, the number made, the station name, its location, the totem's condition and the number of survivors.

It is often said that 'beauty is in the eye of the beholder' and this is the intrinsic value mentioned above. This beauty seems enhanced when it comes to rare totems. Some stations, such as the oddly named **Combpyne** on the Lyme Regis branch, only had one totem. There were very few stations with just one totem, but when we study those with two or three, such as **Locheilside**, the number increases markedly; in contrast, at **Clapham Junction** or **Elmstead Woods**, the platforms were peppered with them. Totems from **Clapham Junction** are sought by many collectors, even though they are readily available. Usually the name, the location and the totem's condition are the key factors (some collectors like mint totems and others ex-station totems).

The number of auction appearances can be considered only a rough guide to rarity. However, we add a cautionary note, as the number of survivors or same-item re-sales may add bias to these figures. It is a fair assumption to make that a totem appearing for the very first time at auction today is generally considered as rare, especially in the 21st century, since auctions have been happening for more than sixty years. However, the enamel collecting scene is not just about auctions; many uncommon or unusual totems are firmly entrenched in collections and are unlikely to appear on the open market. Our databases show many hundreds of true rarities and we can only highlight a limited number here due to space constraints. We have chosen just one inspirational and rare totem from each region on this page.

It is perhaps true to say that the greatest rarities are those that we've never actually seen. Amongst these would be totems from stations closed in the early 1950s, followed by those from stations that were re-signed in the mid- to late 1950s. These include **Potters Bar** (re-signed by 1955), **Grantham**, **Newark Northgate**, **Cambridge** (re-signed by 1956), **Colchester**, **Bury-St-Edmunds** and **Newmarket** in the ER alone. Despite the vast numbers of stations fitted with totems in the LMR, we are still wondering if we will ever see the likes of **Aylesbury High Street**, **Denbigh**, **Macclesfield Central**, **Manchester London Road**, **Mold**, **Rickmansworth Church Street**, **Runcorn**, **Saltney Ferry (Mold Junction)**, **Stanmore Village** or **Towcester**? These are all exceedingly rare, if they have survived at all.

The NER has yielded only a handful of iconic rarities such as **Northallerton** and **Whitby West Cliff** (*see* Chapter 10, *In Situ* Files, for **Seaburn** and **Dinsdale**; both unknown survivors). Several tangerine totems have only been auctioned once. The Scottish Region probably has the greatest percentage of rarities relative to the number of stations fitted, simply because many small stations had very few totems installed. For desirables here we might choose **Ballachulish**, **Bridge of Orchy**, **Glenfinnan**, **Houston & Crosslee**, **Kyle of Lochalsh**, **Loch Awe**, **Morar**, **Rannoch** or **Strathcarron** as some of the nicest and rarest from a plethora of classic names.

Much of the alluring scenery is off the beaten track and a good proportion of the UK's population view Scotland as the ideal restful holiday destination for this reason. Unfortunately, there are many more who seek the sun, sea and sand overseas, as Scotland's climate can sometimes be inclement, even during the summer months.

Strathcarron, Ross & Cromarty in 1974. *Alan Young*

A common collecting theme will always be seaside resorts and many of these are highlighted in the six regional chapters that follow. Britain has over 7,000 miles of largely unspoilt and often remote coast, with hundreds of resorts and scenic destinations from which to collect totems. Devon, Cornwall, Pembrokeshire, Somerset, South Wales, Sussex and the Cambrian Coast all bring back happy memories. In LMR territory, the Lake District and the North Wales coast have some rare and evocative names to pick from (*see* pages 100 and 105).

The Northumberland coast offers almost 40 miles of beautiful panoramas, but few tangerine totems. We must head south to Yorkshire for good seaside names to collect (such as **Saltburn** or **Scarborough**). Lincolnshire can only muster three, **Mablethorpe**, **Skegness** and **Sutton-on-Sea**, while Norfolk, Suffolk and Essex contain many delightful totem resort names, albeit sometimes difficult to find.

The Southern Region spoils us with hundreds of miles of coastline and memories of great family holidays. From Kent in the east, to Cornwall in the west, in between lie dozens of desirable totem names; just a small sample might be **Hastings**, **Eastbourne**, **Seaford**, **Brighton**, **Weymouth**, **Seaton**, **Budleigh Salterton** and **Bude**. We were told during our research that **Budleigh Salterton** totems were sold by the station master on the last day of passenger service in 1967 for 15 shillings (0.75p) each!

Generally, the further west one travels, SR totems become more elusive, so the four Cornish 'greens', all closed in the 1960s are both rare and desirable. Many Devonshire SR stations fall into the same category. The wonderfully named **Ottery St Mary** has all the rarity attributes listed earlier and additionally, this totem has no public appearances. The Isle of Wight offers some beautiful beaches, quaint villages and a timeless world, but no resort totems; just three inland stations were fitted, with **Merstone** and **Mill Hill** being uncommon and rarely seen. Today, SR targets and other station signage from the Isle of Wight are all equally collectable.

The Welsh Valleys were a concentrated totem-rich area, but many have yet to be seen. We would choose **Aberbeeg**, **Dinas (Rhondda)**, **Llanharan**, **Pencoed**, **Ponthir**, **Tir Phil**, **Upper Pontnewydd** and **Ynyshir** as being very rare. The HF one-line **Barmouth Junction** is not known to survive, and neither is **Teignmouth** on Devon's south coast. Only a few survive from **Moat Lane Junction** or **Ross-on-Wye**, which are truly wonderful collectables. Just three flat irregular shaped totems were found in the WR; **Little Kimble**, **Moreton-in-Marsh** and **Radstock West**, all of which are rarities.

If we had to choose one WR rarity above all others it might be **Carbis Bay**. This gem appeared at a Sheffield auction in 1999; before then we were unaware that this station on Cornwall's **St. Ives** branch even had totems, or as it turned out, one totem! The image below shows the station in the 1960s. The back of the totem can be seen faintly at the bottom of the path down to the platform: **Looe** is another rare gem.

Private Collections

A new feature in this book is some of the best collections that have been assembled, often over many decades, some of which were put together in the early days of collecting, during the 1960s, '70s and '80s. Obviously, we do not divulge owner's names or locations, but they have allowed pictures of their treasures to be included to show what dedication and persistence can achieve. We start in South Wales with part of a stunning collection. The owner has a clear fascination with this mainly coal-mining industrial area that disappeared as the demand for coal fell. Rarities include **Cefn On**, **Llanbradach** and **Pontlottyn**. Some names also represent engine sheds, a theme that often inspires the collecting of railwayana artefacts.

Whilst featuring Wales, we have the chance to include a unique and rare totem; **Penychain** lies just 4 miles from **Pwllheli** on the Llyn Peninsula. Billy Butlin opened a holiday camp there in 1947 on land he had purchased for military use in WW2. The business grew in the '50s and '60s and other camps popped up all over the UK. An agreement was reached between Butlin's and BR that the station signs at Penychain would all be in the Butlin's colour scheme of yellow and blue, including the RIBs. We are aware of just two survivors and none yet appearing in a public auction.

The **Pontypool (Crane Street)** is the only survivor we are aware of. The station was on the former GW branch line from **Newport** to Blaenavon (closed 1962) and was one of only two stations on the line with totems (the other being **Upper Pontnewydd**, which is not thought to have survived). Another predominantly Welsh-themed collection, below, covers much of Wales, from **Amlwch** on Anglesey in the north down to **Pembroke Dock** in the south. **Craven Arms & Stokesay** is the interloper. There are some great rarities here, including WR **Llanidloes, Rhayader, Lampeter, Llandrindod Wells, Llangollen** and LMR **Amlwch, Cefn-Y-Bedd, Dolgarrog** and **Llangefni**. Most of this collection has been sold since this image was taken in the 1980s.

The ER is popular with collectors, but it is also very challenging, due to early re-signing and scarcity of survivors from some of London's suburban lines, as detailed in Chapter 4. The collection below follows the Lea Valley line in North London as it heads towards **Bishops Stortford** and **Cambridge**. Note the very rare **St. Margarets** (junction for **Buntingford**) on the **Hertford East** branch. Alongside is a selection from the former Tottenham & Hampstead Joint line from **Barking** to **Gospel Oak**.

Note that both **Burnt Mill** (renamed Harlow Town) and **Harlow** (renamed Harlow Mill) totems are missing from the Lea Valley line collection. It is worth noting that the **Harlow** has a sticker mark in the lower panel where the word 'Mill' used to be. Neither of this pair has been in auction thus far. Heading east from Liverpool Street, the next stop after **Stratford** is **Maryland** (formerly known as Maryland Point); we have evidence that just four HF totems were fitted here on the outer ends of the island platform. Travelling towards Essex, just **Forest Gate, Manor Park** and **Chadwell Heath** had totems until reaching **Ingatestone** on the main line towards **Ipswich**, and then they appeared at virtually every stop until Norwich Thorpe, which was sadly omitted.

Four different collections are featured here and if combined, they would complement each other well, with just a small gap between **Marks Tey** and **Ipswich**. The lower Norfolk display is wonderfully representative of the Broads and its surrounding area.

The former Stour Valley and Colne Valley lines once formed a lifeline for rural communities between **Cambridge** and **Colchester**. The 1960s pruning of these lines has today caused more road traffic and pollution than was foreseen in those blinkered years. On the plus side, most of the totems have survived including the unique Colne Valley set (below, right), all saved by one man who simply asked BR for a sign off each station in 1962. Sadly, that gentleman is no longer with us, but the whole collection is. Most of these are in near mint condition, as they only hung for two or three years. Although the ER has the highest casualty rate in terms of survivors, those displayed here are simply superb names from stations serving some of England's picturesque villages.

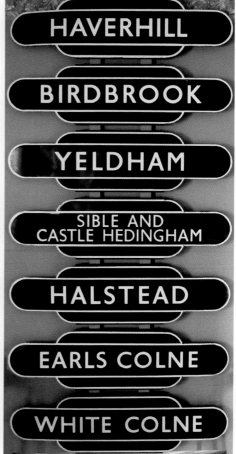

One of the most popular themes is the challenge to obtain the set of six regional colours; easier said than done when it comes to the NER example. Every LMR variant of the appendage 'Junction' is shown in the middle view. The right-hand image shows some rare Bedfordshire and Northamptonshire closed stations, all found at Collectors Corner, Euston, in the mid-1980s on the same day!

Whilst the collection above may appear to be random at first glance, it is in fact the product of many years hunting down 'bird names' on totems; the owner is obviously an ornithologist in addition to a totem collector. The Turkey Street (formerly Forty Hill) is the 'odd man out', as this station on the Churchbury Loop in Middlesex did not have totems, so a 'repro' had to be fabricated to fill an omission. The two collections featured below are full of surprises and gems. A mainly Yorkshire theme is present in the left-hand image below, with classic NER totems and the ER represented by rare **Darfield** and **Wath Central**. The right-hand collection is random with several desirable names. We would pick **Primrose Hill**, **Long Melford**, **Pelaw** and **White Notley** as gems.

The left-hand image above and the image below were photographed at an organised display in Derby, in the 1990s. The most striking aspect is the wonderful combination of the six colours together (*see also page 37*). We are so fortunate that these colours were chosen in 1948 and the country was divided into the six regions. Would totems be so collectible today had one colour, or even just plain black-and-white, been chosen instead?

When looking back at totem collecting, a few names stand out from the crowd when the subject of massive collections arises. Both the late Paul Carter and the late Richard Rutherford had collections of over 1,000 items each! Richard lived in north-west London and would visit Collectors Corner at Euston several times a week. The greatest collection that we are aware of is that assembled by legendary Ian Faulkner in the 1970s and '80s. Ian has given us permission to publish some views of his astonishing collection at its peak. The number of rarities would fill several pages if listed. Ian knew full well what the most desirable totems were and made a concerted effort to obtain them in sometimes convoluted deals. At one stage, he owned more than 1,600 different names and many duplicates, taking the total to just over 2,000. How on earth the roof beams in his house took all the weight of the totems in his loft, we will never know. We doubt if another collection will ever rival this beautiful array of BR enamels. Both authors were privileged to have visited Ian and spent many hours in his company. Much of the knowledge we have accumulated for our databases came from Ian and he is an inspiration to us all. Even during the development of this enlarged volume, he has continued to support and advise us.

Ian owned so many astonishing rarities and a few highlights include SR **Blandford Forum** and **Alresford**, WR **Swansea Victoria**, **Shipton for Burford** and **St. Budeaux Ferry Road**, MR **Dent** painted over a **Burnley Central** and **Ashby-de-la-Zouch**, ER **Six Mile Bottom**, NER **Blaydon**, double-sided **South Shields** and ScR **Langholm**.

The collection in the two images above could have been inspired by Ian Faulkner, as the same theme is present. Assembling just this collection was quite a tall order, with even more out of view. There are some rare signs from all over BRs network. We might choose **Dawlish Warren, Exeter (St. Thomas), Exton, Highbridge for Burnham-on-Sea, Ham Mill Halt** or **Thornaby** as six of the most highly prized.

Due to their scarcity, most collectors own just a few NE totems, but the Yorkshire collection below is pure tangerine! Decades have been spent in pursuit of the rarer examples: all three flange styles from **Scarborough Central** are included.

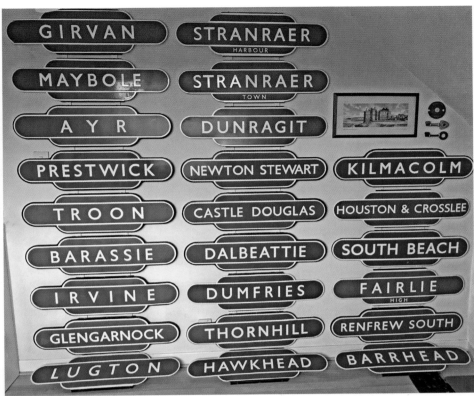

We now head north to Scotland to see two unrivalled county-themed collections, the Kingdom of Fife (alongside) and Ayrshire (above). Both are challenging counties to complete and, despite having nearly all of them, the Fife collection was thwarted by elusive **Lundin Links** and **Oakley (Fife)** totems. There were others in this collection out of view. The picture was taken in the 1980s and the collection has since been largely disbanded.

This astonishing sight of totems from the G&SWR lines in Ayrshire is most impressive, assembled patiently over thirty years! The owner is still in pursuit of **Dalmellington**, **Dunlop**, **Drybridge**, **Kirkcudbright** and others. Neither **Castle Douglas** or **South Beach** have been seen in public and **Houston & Crosslee** has been in auction just once.

There is nothing quite like the thrill of a train journey on the West Highland line (*see* page 189). Collecting a totem from every station, from **Helensburgh Upper** via the junction at **Crianlarich Upper** to **Fort William,** is one of *the* greatest collecting challenges in our hobby. We are privileged to show this WHL collection, which has taken more than twenty years to assemble. However, due to the scarcity of the more remote halts and the handful of totems installed, there are inevitably some gaps. The West Highland Extension line from **Fort William** to Mallaig is also challenging line to complete. Just **Banavie** and **Morar** are missing from the quartet below.

There is the added thrill of riding behind the steam hauled *Jacobite* service in the summer months. After **Glenfinnan**, as the line heads west, totems become much scarcer and none were fitted at Lochailort, Beasdale or Arisaig. Just **Morar** (*in situ* below) had a few before reaching the terminus at Mallaig, which was sadly not deemed worthy of having totems installed; what a highly collectable sign that would have been. Only the running-in boards carried the ScR blue colour, but we have photographic evidence that these were overpainted light green in the 1970s!

Alongside is the only complete collection of **Kyle of Lochalsh** line totems we have seen. The intermediate stations of Achterneed, Achanalt, Glencarron, Attadale, Stromeferry, Duncraig, Plockton and Duirinish were not furnished with totems. This septet took more than twenty-five years to assemble from one of the most scenic railway lines in the world. The line was threatened with closure, first in the early 1960s, then again in the early 1970s. Fortunately, common sense prevailed due to intense local and national lobbying, together with the need to service an expanding oil industry for the construction of offshore platforms at Drumbuie, near **Kyle of Lochalsh**. A Far North line collection would be extremely difficult to complete. After **Dingwall**, just **Tain, Bonar Bridge, Lairg, The Mound, Golspie, Wick** and **Thurso** had totems in this most remote part of Scotland. Both **Wick** and **Thurso** only had two or three totems each.

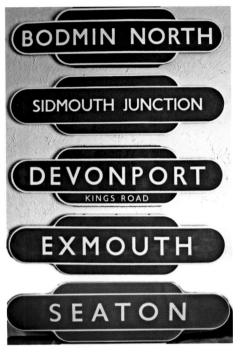

The two photos above show a quite superb Somerset & Dorset set and an equally impressive SR West Country collection, belonging to two different collectors. The 150th Anniversary Celebration of the opening of **Yeovil Pen Mill** station was held on 29 July 2006. One of the authors (RF) was asked to design a totem display, so seven TSG members combined to put 111 totems and 13 targets on view. Two of the many pictures taken are shown below, including an out of view WR **Evercreech Junction**. Records show, however, that **Yeovil Pen Mill** actually opened on 29 February 1854, so maybe the event was a bit like some railway services – running somewhat late!

Lower Panel Totems

One of the greatest attractions in totem collecting is the sheer variety on offer. Many questions have been raised over the years regarding the arrangement of lettering on totems and records are incomplete, as Chapter 11 briefly describes. We have been handed down a rich tapestry of wording layouts that often stray from those published in the *Code of Instructions for Station Name and Direction Signs* issued in 1948. Why were **Wath Central** signs made with Central in the lower panel and **Thorne South** made in one line? Why does lower panel **Kinross Junction** differ drastically from one-line **Thornton Junction**? Look at how **Bilston Central** is arranged in a totally different style to **Bicester North**. The variants are, thankfully, plentiful as it would be tedious if every totem conformed exactly to one standard layout.

The WR has just over 60 lower panel totems; here we find **Abergavenny Monmouth Road, Birmingham Snow Hill** and **Moor Street, Bristol Temple Meads, Cheltenham Spa Malvern Road, Crumlin High Level, Danzey for Tanworth, Exeter St. David's, Kensington Olympia, Severn Tunnel Junction, Uxbridge Vine Street** and **Worcester Shrub Hill** to name but a few. The WR also favoured adding the county names in the lower panel, so we find **Pengam (Glam), Westbury (Wilts)** and **Wellington (Salop)**. Countrywide, some stations possessed two different styles of totem alongside each other, but strangely this practice did not happen in the Scottish region. Prime examples are **Stourbridge Junction, Neath General, Clacton on Sea, Swanscombe Halt, Loughborough Junction** and **Lichfield Trent Valley.** There are of course many others. Some lengthy word layouts appear to be squashed (condensed Gill Sans lettering) when compared to the far more spacious lower panel arrangement.

A variety of words can be found in the lower panel, ranging from the more common examples such as 'Junction', 'North', 'High Level', 'Low Level', 'Lower, 'High', 'Central' and 'Halt', to the far more exotic names. A complete list of these would become onerous, but the following can be found: 'Beach', 'On Sea', 'Riverside', 'Sunnyside', 'West Cliff' and 'Wellington Road'. Another use of the lower panel was advertising nearby villages or branch lines; hence on the WR there is **Ashchurch for Tewkesbury**, **Llandaff (for Whitchurch)**, **Shipton for Burford,** with **Sandling for Hythe** on the SR.

We believe that **Wrexham Exchange** is unique by using 'Exchange' in the lower panel. The only other totems carrying this appendage are **Manchester Exchange**, **Bradford Exchange** and the rare **Barnsley Exchange**, all of which are two-line examples. (We have seen a poor photograph of a Barnsley Exchange *in situ*). Considering the high number of LMR totems, lower panel appendages were used only seven times to incorporate suffixes. Superb **Chapel-en-le-Frith Central** is a unique LMR lower panel design with well-balanced hyphens. Only a few one-line 'Halts' appear on the LMR and even these are scarce, as the following section describes.

A unique occurrence of a town name in the lower panel appears on **London Road (Guildford)** and, to add further interest, the sign maker used lower case lettering for the appendage. We rather like **Leyton Midland Rd.,** and **Chesterfield Midland** totems, as the word Midland on the ER sign looks rather incongruous! North of the border, there were a few unusual lower panel layouts, starting with **Stranraer Harbour**; the only LP 'Harbour' in any of the six regions. Exceptionally rare **Oakley (Fife)** was the only Scottish county name on a totem. **Maryhill Central** is more balanced than a one-line layout; oddly, **Maryhill Park** was also LP when one line would have easily fitted.

Three of **Pontefract**'s stations had the appendages **Baghill**, **Monkhill** and **Tanshelf**.

A Study of 'Halt' Totems
Alan Young & Dave Brennand

Station halts were introduced early in the 20th century with the commencement of steam motor rail services. The provision of waiting rooms, platform staff and even a roof to shelter from the elements were not common features of the most basic halt. The most remote villagers were often glad of the opening of a new station, however austere**.** The pre-grouping railway companies introduced many halts, or 'platforms' as they were sometimes referred to in public timetables from 1903, and tickets would be issued by the guard or even from a crossing keeper's hut. As platform lighting was rarely provided, these stations were often only served during daylight hours. The platforms, sometimes made from wood or reused sleepers, were often just enough to accommodate one or two coaches. The SR seemed to favour the word 'Halt', even using it on 12-coach platforms, such as those in Kent that were extended in the 1960s. There are no less than twenty-seven lower panel 'Halts' to be found in SR counties and several more using the conventional one-line layout. Looking at halts during the BR era highlights some interesting questions with regard to the provision of totems at some of the most remote halts and the lack of them at many more. Some regions seemed to have no interest in installing totems at their halts, with the ER, NER and ScR being the worst 'offenders'. The word 'Halt' does not appear on a single NER example and we only find it twice in the vast ER; at **Brundall Gardens Halt** in Norfolk and **Emerson Park Halt** between Romford and **Upminster**.

Just enamelled **Balgreen Halt** appears in Scotland, whilst wooden **Balmossie Halt** and **Golf Street Halt** can also be found north of the border. Both these painted single-line examples were originally in ScR light blue livery before they were 'improved' with the blandness of black letters on white.

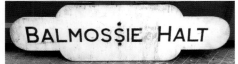

The LMR did not install any 'Halt' totems anywhere in Wales with the WR fitting just one flangeless totem at **Heath Halt Low Level**. The station at **Cefn On** with very few totems is a classic case of a station which appears to be a halt, but was not classified as such. The SR are to be congratulated for installing no less than thirty-five totems at their halts; the largest choice for the collector, and these come as one-line, two-line, lower panel and one of only two three-line variants at **Three Oaks & Guestling Halt**. The Sussex Coast was home to many halts with evocative names such as **Pevensey Bay Halt** and **Normans Bay Halt**. As we head further west, there were a cluster of halts between Chichester and **Havant**. Here we find **Fishbourne Halt**, **Nutborne Halt**, **Southbourne Halt** and **Warblington Halt**, a superb quartet. The most westerly of SR halts with totems was Devonshire's rare **St. James Park Halt** and the tiny station at **Combpyne** on the Lyme Regis branch was a classic halt-type station and photographic evidence shows just one totem situated several yards from the platform on a post.

On the BR system there were many stations, which were little more than halts, but they did not appear in timetables as such, so their totems did not carry the word.

The word 'Halt' was finally dropped from public timetables between 1969 and 1971. We have seen many ScR *in situ* photos of minor stations with the appearance of being just a halt where just two or three totems were installed; **Rutherford**, on the St. Boswells to **Roxburgh** line is a good example. The acquisition of these rarities is challenging and some may only appear once in a lifetime: **Idmiston Halt** is an example, appearing just once at auction in 2006. Considering the size of the LMR, they used 'Halt' totems at just four of their 825 fitted stations; **Canley Halt**, **Daimler Halt**, **Leire Halt** and **Rushcliffe Halt**, a somewhat suprisingly low number.

The WR faired better with eleven 'Halts' and the unique use of the word 'Platform' on **Wootton Wawen Platform**. The longest run of totemed halts on the WR was the 'Bumble Hole' branch in the West Midlands: **Baptist End Halt**, **Windmill End Halt**, **Darby End Halt** and **Old Hill (High Street) Halt**. These were simple wooden platforms upon opening, but were then replaced with concrete platforms and small waiting shelters with a few totems on each. Some of the totems on this branch remained *in situ* for several years after closure in 1964 and although some were badly vandalised, others survived without much damage. The example alongside

from **Windmill End Halt**, was found in a nearby canal; the flange has been completely eaten away by corrosion and there are a couple of holes, but the lettering and colour are relatively untouched.

Totem Restoration

The condition of a totem is always important, and some collectors will not purchase a badly creased or chipped totem. There are many rare totems where survivors have been found in the most appalling condition imaginable, with examples of **Ibrox** and **Balloch Pier** being shown below. The **Ibrox** totem from the west of Glasgow's city centre had some really deep damage, almost certainly due to local vandals. **Fort William** and **Aylesham Halt** had both been buried, but hours of careful restoration returned them to a semblance of their former glory.

Some **Balloch Pier** totems were allegedly thrown rather unceremoniously into Loch Lomond. However, the question arises as to how the sign acquired no less than five creases in the first place? The answer could possibly be that contractors folded the sign up before dumping them, but the truth may be even stranger; we don't really know. Restoration is sometimes a lengthy process, involving some heart-breaking decisions. If a totem is still creased when acquired, the hammering process to straighten it out will undoubtedly lead to the loss of even more enamel from the sign. After such a beating, the totem can take several days to 'settle down' to its new shape. During this settling time, some small enamel shards may 'ping' off, which is to be expected, as any induced stresses relax.

Some creases may leave a raised section after the straightening process, and this can sometimes be carefully removed using an angle grinder! Neither of these processes are for the unskilled and the image below taken by a professional restorer may seem incredible to most collectors, but if you want a straightened totem, there are not many choices available. Restoring totems is driven by personal taste and most look better after restoration, but we have seen some that are poorly repaired, with incorrect colours, which can make them look worse than before.

For the restoration to look really professional, the damaged areas should be filled with some kind of epoxy filler. Those in the trade will often use P38 Car Body Filler; the noxious fumes produced by this substance should not be inhaled for any length of time. The filler should always be left to dry rock hard for at least 24-hours before sanding down. The rough surface can be smoothed by using a sharp, long-bladed craft knife, held at an angle, and final levelling can be completed using various grades of 'wet & dry' abrasives and wire wool. Rubbing down should be confined to the filled area only, as enamel will scratch very easily if you go over the edge.

Once it is perfectly smooth restoration can progress to the painting stage, a truly dark art and sometimes the most frustrating part of the process. A sympathetically coloured primer or undercoat should be applied first. It is unlikely that you will find matching colours straight from a paint tin, but Phoenix Precision produce the six regional colours in small tinlets, so we suggest trying these first. Looking through the array of pictures in this book it becomes apparent that totems come in distinctly different shades, so trial and error sometimes plays a major part in obtaining the best colour match. Colours can appear different under fluorescent lighting and paint sometimes dries to a different shade than when it was applied. The inky dark violet colour of ER totems is very difficult to perfect, and the whole process requires a high degree of patience.

Repainting letters that may have been obliterated by damage or corrosion is quite challenging. This needs careful measurement and a very steady hand. We have seen many totems that have been varnished over perfectly good enamel, to cover up the lack of any shine. This tends to make the white areas go yellow after several years, so should therefore be avoided. Varnishing can also devalue a totem. The picture of the hugely rare **Dukinfield Central** proves what can be achieved with hard work. Whilst restoration does not always stand up to close scrutiny by the perfectionist, they are certainly a vast improvement on the damaged and creased item. Should you not like the restored totem, it will be a long wait for a good condition **Dukinfield Central**!

To the many seasoned collectors in our hobby, any mention of Quorn brings back memories of the railwayana collectors' boot sales in the preserved station car park. These were organised by Bob Withers for thirty years until he handed over the reins to the Great Central Railway in 2016. We have fond recollections of arriving there at 7.30am or before, unloading our wares and frantically peering into other car boots for great treasures. Some astonishingly rare totems have appeared at Quorn over the years, including a probably unique ER **Shoeburyness** totem found in *three pieces* by one of the authors in the late 1980s. Other collectors burst out laughing when they saw it, but another example has not been seen since. It has since been restored, but still shows many scars of its neglected and buried past.

Another great rarity was literally unearthed during platform rebuilding work in North London at Harringay Green Lanes in 2003 when a **Harringay Park** was found with no less than eight creases. These totems were replaced in 1958 when the station was renamed Harringay Stadium and fluorescent lighting was installed. The 'before' and 'after' pictures of this unique survivor are shown in Chapter 4 (*see* page 79). Some LMR, ER and a handful of SR totems are described as 'lightweight' in their construction. These were manufactured by J. Bruton & Son of Palmers Green, North London, and sometimes suffered from corrosion problems affecting the white areas before the main colour. This **Fazakerley** (since restored) is one example and others were **Alderley Edge**, **Greenfield**, **Huncoat** and **Preston**. Strangely, not all examples from these stations met the same fate and some survivors are in much better condition.

Collectors' Corner at London Euston

Collectors' Corner (CC) was *the* Mecca during its heyday in the 1970s and 1980s, for those of us passionate about collecting railway-related artifacts. The selling of railwayana to the public and the name Collectors' Corner was the brainchild of Chris Osman, who worked in the BR Stores Controller Department at Alperton, close to his home in Neasden. His boss was Major Kirby, who gave Chris the task of setting up sales of redundant handlamps, cast iron signs and totems in 1968. The Alperton stores were soon overwhelmed by the arrival of so much railwayana that alternative premises were required. The former horse stables in Cardington Street, just outside London's Euston station, proved to be the perfect home for the burgeoning enterprise. There was even a working water-powered lift. The official opening was in December 1969 and during the following three decades CC always made a profit for BR.

Due to the lack of co-ordination, BR wanted to centralise these sales and make the accountability easier, so CC took over all the regional sales (except the ER and NER, which were concentrated at York). Initially, most of the totems for sale were from the vast LMR, and these were then joined by those from the SR, particularly from stations undergoing their late 1960s corporate image 'upgrades'.

The remarkable and rare picture below from the early 1970s shows almost fifty totems, a fraction of the numbers coming onto the market at that time. Note the lack of any Scottish signs, which began to increasingly appear, mainly from the Glasgow area, towards the end of that decade. For the cost of one quality totem today, you could have bought all of these! Back then, few WR, ER and NER signs were for sale. Note that some names are repeated two or three times, with **Blackburn** (both conventional and poster header type), **Peckham Rye**, **Chorley** and **Albany Park** being examples. Some of these might be considered to be rare today, but they were certainly plentiful then and they have all survived, somewhere.

Collectors' Corner in 1982. *Mike Matthews*

BR poster for Collectors' Corner.

Before Cardington Street opened, sales were handled regionally at various locations: **East Croydon** and **Waterloo** (SR), **Stratford** and Norwich (ER), **Stoke on Trent** and **Derby** (LMR), **Reading** and **Swindon** (WR), Glasgow (ScR) and **York** (NER). In addition, a huge number of signs were also sold by individual managers at local stations.

Note: We are most grateful to Geoff Courtney and Heritage Railway magazine for permission to use extracts from their March 2021 article regarding Chris Osman and the background story of the formative days at Collectors' Corner.

Former TSG member Steve Page recalls his visits in the 1970s: 'Venturing up the staircase and opening the heavy door at the top, the smell from the gas heaters hanging down from the roof supports was immediately apparent. Stepping into the gloomy interior, I was confronted with rows and rows of shelves containing everything imaginable; but we are more interested in the totems and they were displayed on the wall, about halfway along on the right-hand side. I cannot remember any names from that first visit, only that most were priced at £3 each. None of the names could have meant anything to me, or I might well have bought one, even at that price, which represented quite a chunk of my pocket money! (My first totem purchase was still a year away). I left empty-handed, and set off towards **Clapham Junction**, for an afternoon of trainspotting, refreshed by lemonade and Lyons individual fruit pies.

made my way to the exit. As I reached the office I paused, and just on the off-chance asked if they had any Swale Halt totems left, "Sorry, they've all been sold", came the reply. A second person sitting in the office looked up and said: "There is one left, but it's damaged. I'll show you." Sure enough, in a closed-off area containing sold and reserved items, was a **Swale Halt** totem, complete with its fixing bracket. It had in the past received the attention of stone-throwers and had several large chips, but it was not creased. A modest amount of cash was parted with, and it became mine. It is now restored and one of my favourite items, bringing back memories of Sunday trips along the branch to **Sheerness-on-Sea** (where the sun never seemed to shine and where we would spend the afternoon shivering on the pebble beach).'

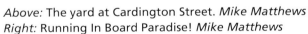

Above: The yard at Cardington Street. *Mike Matthews*
Right: Running In Board Paradise! *Mike Matthews*

Mike Matthews

'Over the next few years, I made occasional visits to CC, but did not start recording which totems were on sale until 1978. After then, visits became more frequent, particularly between 1982 and 1984, when I worked in London, and a lunchtime visit made an interesting diversion from the daily routine. Whenever I arrived, I would look to see what was in the outside yard, as the running-in boards there would often give an indication of which totems would be on sale inside. One day I arrived in the yard and leaning against the wall was a light green enamel RIB for **Swale Halt**, with the suffix 'Alight Here for Ridham Dock'. I hurried up the steps and headed to the totem wall, but there were no **Swale Halt** totems there. Disappointed, I finished looking round and

Bob Ballard was the manager at CC for many years and we fondly remember his happy band of busy assistants. Many collectors will have their personal memories of dealings at CC, which were always friendly and straightforward. It was sometimes possible to swap your spare items for items they had for sale. All this was happening several years before the mainstream railwayana auctions became established.

The 1980s totem prices would make many of today's collectors weep, often averaging £50 to £100 each. The dilapidated state of the building gave the place real character; the odd fern and damp walls were to be expected, but these were interior walls. There were water leaks after downpours and even pigeons flying around! One aspect of the totems on offer was their ex-station condition; none of the restoration and super shine we often see today. This worked to the buyers' advantage, of course. Nobody ever rushed you or tried to pressurise you to buy, it was pure joy.

Mike Matthews

For those collectors who did not get the chance to visit, we are fortunate to have been provided with some wonderful photos and memories from Mike Matthews and his son Paul, who visited frequently in the early 1980s. It must be remembered that not all the items for sale at this time were out on display, as there were storage areas unseen by the public, unless you knew the right staff member! Mike continues the CC story with some recollections of the remarkable sights at Cardington Street; 'My earliest memories were from 1974, when I drove into the cobbled yard through large double gates. The yard and buildings were originally horse stables dating back to LNWR times, serving Euston station way beyond the demise of horse-drawn vans in the 1940s, when mechanical horses took over – I even found an old derelict Scammel Scarab in one of the outbuildings, proving that it continued in use until the 1960s.

'The yard was adorned with various large items including many RIBs in a variety of colours. Access to CC was via a wrought iron staircase, and upon opening the door I was confronted by a veritable treasure chest of what we now call railwayana. There were walls full of totems, rows of lamps and signalling equipment unceremoniously dumped on the floors and stacked up by the walls. The staff had a small office in the corner (with a **Cardington** totem displayed on the wall) and a stable door, where I would ask to view items locked in some of the cabinets.

'It was a quaint, homely place where you could spend hours, unhurried by the hustle and bustle of London life. As the years passed by, the old first-floor building became more perilous, and this area was closed; whereby they moved everything into another ground floor building within the same site. As land prices increased, the whole site was sold off *circa* 1985 and demolished: a great shame as these were historically important buildings. They could have been converted for some other use, providing some old-world charm in an often-harsh concrete and glass city. A nearby building in Coburg Street was found, but it lacked the character of the old place. Over the years I purchased many items from CC, but unfortunately very few totems – big mistake!'

Our contributor John Wells remembers how the totems were assembled from all over the country: 'Regarding Scottish signs, these were gathered at Glasgow Central and loaded into a GUV or BG parcels coach, which would often be attached to an overnight express specifically for the purpose of getting the huge volume of signs to CC. There were RIBs, ancillary signs, doorplates and of course many hundreds of totems. The RIBs were far too cumbersome to be taken into the main sales area and these languished in the yard, sometimes for years before some crazed collectors (including me) would come along. During my time as a Secondman on the footplate at Euston it was a common sight to see Brute parcels trolleys full of ScR enamels sitting in the parcels area waiting for Bob Ballard and his assistants to take them over to CC.

'I well remember going to Euston station one day to watch a coach full of signs being unloaded; the porters had been amusing themselves by hanging several ScR **Singer** totems on the walls of Platform 20, the parcels unloading bay. **Waterloo** was another station where a huge amount of enamel signage would be collected from all over the SR before being shipped over to CC.'

Whilst researching our original paperback *Totem Book* in the late 1980s, I (DB) was fortunate enough to access the CC records with Bob Ballard's permission and compile a list of the totems sold during the 1970s and 1980s. These records did not show the earliest sales from 1969 or any of the items transferred from the old Clapham Museum, but they gave a fascinating insight into the thousands of totems that were sold. There was no indication of how many of each totem passed through CC, but it was common for some names to crop up twenty times or more: an example was **Clapham Junction**. Conversely, there were other rarer names on the list: **Ashburys for Belle Vue, Canley Halt, Carlisle, Hayfield, Irchester, Kilsby & Crick, Merthyr, Mount Florida, Radcliffe Black Lane, Silvertown, Town Green & Aughton** and **Wick,** where perhaps just one or two appeared. Unsurprisingly, the rarest examples always sold quickly. The rare **Hayfield** totem on the previous page has been to the USA and back!

In addition to the list above, Steve Page also noted the following totems for sale in the late 1970s and early 1980s: ER **Acle, Hornchurch, Mistley, Wrabness, Wroxham** and **Wymondham**, ScR **Brucklay, Camelon, Culter, Ellon, Fraserburgh, Glenfinnan, Kingussie** and **Udny**, SR **Rochester**, WR **Dovey Junction, Exeter (St. Thomas), Small Heath & Sparkbrook** and a very rare **Llantarnam,** which was probably on commission. From the official CC records, we know that at least 293 different LMR names were sold, 63 ScR, 138 SR, 53 WR and surprisingly just 14 ER and 3 NER names. There may well have been others unrecorded or sold on commission. (As an aside, many LMR totems were sold at **Carnforth** steam museum in the 1970s and early 1980s).

Collectors Corner, Euston, was a fantastic place, often used as a convenient meeting point to arrange deals and socialise with other enthusiasts in the yard. The inevitable relocation of the CC business to Coburg Street (a former NCP car park) happened in 1985 and then, in January 1998, it all sadly disappeared up to York, but commercially it did not seem as successful. This too succumbed to closure in 2001, thus ending an era, the like of which we will never see again.

Irregular and Unusual Totems

When it comes to displaying totems, the oversized 4-foot items are problematic. (We have avoided using metric units as totems were made using imperial dimensions). These were found at a few LMR locations; **Broad Street, Brondesbury, Harrow & Wealdstone, Liverpool Central Low Level, Manchester Central, Queens Park, Sandhills, South Kenton, Watford High Street** and **Willesden Junction**. In addition, all these stations had the standard 3-foot totems, except for **Liverpool Central Low Level** and **Queens Park**. A pair of 4-foot examples is shown below.

The largest LMR totems were those displayed at **Liverpool James Street**. These were incorporated into enamel panels, measuring 6–8 feet wide: an *in situ* picture is found on page 101. The SR was the only other region to sparingly use 4-foot totems, with **Clapham Junction, Exeter Central** and **Weymouth** being installed at strategic locations alongside the standard signs. **Exeter Central** kept its Southern Railway targets right up to the Corporate Identity era, so the installation of only 4-foot totems was unusual. **Waterloo** had several very large 6-foot painted wooden totems: an image of one of these is shown on page 244. Just a handful of LMR painted wooden totems existed at **Earby** (wood only), **Finmere, Mauldeth Road** and **Pleasington**. **Horton-in-Ribblesdale** had some odd-looking hand-painted steel totems, but the lettering was distinctly different from the regulation Gill Sans (page 140).

Awsworth, (closed in 1964) had some odd 'official' fibreglass totems. Just four stations carried these unusual enamelled flat steel totems (below) incorporated into poster board headings in addition to standard totems. They could be found at **Blackburn, Leicester London Road, Longton** and **Preston.** Both **Blackburn** and **Longton** examples have been auctioned. Further examples may still come to light.

Shotton (High Level) 1976. *John Mann*

Handsworth (& Smethwick) 1970. *John Mann*

Some regions embraced the idea of overpainting totems, either as an early form of what we now term recycling, or to save the cost of having replacement signs made after a station's renaming. Even the simple renewal or addition of lampposts, would necessitate some 'new' totems. The LMR used the practice sparingly at just seven stations: **Bletchley** (below o/p on **Berkhampsted**), **Chorley** (o/p on **Burscough Bridge** – below), **Cricklewood, Dent, Radlett, St. Albans City** and **Wembley Stadium.** We highlight these variants in Chapter 5, but we are limited in the space available to give the full information, as some of these might be 'one-offs'. The exception is **Wembley Stadium,** where the whole station was signed using former **Watford Junction** totems. This was just a single platform serving the stadium on a loop diverging from the GC Marylebone to **Wembley Hill** line. The loop and station were last used for the 1968 FA Cup Final and official closure was on 1 September 1969.

Some intriguing overpaints have been seen over the years, and they may not have always been officially sanctioned, but the trio we have included were. These show MR **Shotton High Level** with the 'High Level' appendage crudely painted over after the closure of **Shotton Low Level** in 1966, (subsequently re-opened in 1972). WR **Handsworth & Smethwick** was transferred in 1965 to the LMR, who promptly dropped the **'& Smethwick'** to avoid confusion with nearby **Smethwick Rolfe Street.**

The closure of the **Birmingham Snow Hill** to **Wolverhampton Low Level** line in 1972 took with it eight totemed stations, including the attractive names of **Priestfield** and **Swan Village.** Amongst them was another unsightly overpainting at **Soho & Winson Green,** which was renamed Winson Green in June 1965. There were many totems to repaint as the station boasted four platforms. Since 1999 much of the original route between **Birmingham Snow Hill** and **Wolverhampton Low Level** now forms form part of the West Midlands Metro line.

The NER had few irregularities but four distinct flange types were found, including the largest number of flat or unflanged totems and those with the very wide flange, denoted as **WF** in the database, which were unique to this region. These wide flanges were a full inch in depth and made the signs extremely robust, thereby deterring vandalism. Two odd totems were found at **Darlington** and **Wakefield Kirkgate,** where the reverse of the totem was enamelled in tangerine. Just four stations were fitted with the peculiar tangerine-flanged totems, as listed in Chapter 6.

Some totems at **South Shields** were uniquely double-sided! These were in addition to the regular HF design and were completely flat: this was not an easy item to display unless hung from chains so that both sides could be viewed.

A unique colour was used on **Twickenham** totems. The normal shade on a HF Southern totem would be dark green, but for some unknown reason, a peculiar shade of deep lime green was used. Only one example of an overpainted **Folkestone Junction** totem has ever been seen. This curiosity had been painted over a black flanged **Kenley** totem, which was clearly visible through the paint. The abbreviated and unusually stylized 'Jct' appendage is unique and hopefully, the owner will never be tempted to put paint stripper over it to reveal the former totem!

Both painted and overpainted/reused wooden totems were found at several SR locations; more than any other region. These were at **Appledore** and **Axminster**, with some at **Balcombe**, **Bromley South**, **Burgess Hill**, **Clandon**, **Holborn Viaduct**, **London Bridge**, **New Malden**, **Waterloo**, **West Croydon** and all those at **Wimbledon**. Overpainting was avoided in the ScR and NER. Whilst the ER did not seem to overpaint any totems, they did use **Bromley-By-Bow** vinyl stickers over **Bromley** totems on the ex-LT&SR station in East London, maybe to help confused passengers looking for **Bromley** in Kent! Different sized letters were used at three ER curiosities in a one-line arrangement at **Dore and Totley**, **Hopton on Sea** and **Saxham and Risby**. Only thirteen stations had the odd oversize lettering unique to the ER with letters half-an-inch higher than the standard 3-inch. This was a size not mentioned in the 1948 manufacturers' book *The Code of Instructions*. **Thetford** is just one example.

We mentioned 'lightweight' totems earlier; these were manufactured in a lighter grade steel. They were always FF and confined to the LMR, ER and SR. In addition to the LMR examples listed at the end of the Restoration Section, we have found evidence of these at **Braughing**, **Littleworth**, **Melton Constable**, **Narborough & Pentney**, **Peterborough East** and **Silvertown** in the ER. SR examples were found at **Wivelsfield** and **Walmer**. The FF **Reading General** below is unique and our research during the drafting of this new volume has unearthed the fact that these were mysteriously manufactured in aluminium. Two of our major contributors owned two different examples; one still had its bracket on the rear, plus the rods which were once attached to the platform canopy, so the provenance is irrefutable. The vast majority of **Reading General** totems are HF and forty have appeared in auction: the FF aluminium version has never appeared in auction. Many of the letters including the elongated 'D' and a curiously shaped 'G' differ from the HF version and the baseline of the letters is wavy.

The formation of BR in 1948 and the need for thousands of new totems to be manufactured inevitably caused some consternation, which may explain why some very odd looking totems appeared in 1948, perhaps preceding the *Code of Instructions* booklet. The early enamel WR examples from **Bath Spa** (below), **Helston** and **Kings Nympton** are unusual, but very collectable. The signs have wooden ends for mounting and rigidity: at 38in wide, they are also narrower than a standard totem.

4
The Eastern Region

Opening Comments

When nationalisation occurred on 1 January 1948, the Eastern Region (ER) was formed from the English LNER lines that existed pre-WWII. Of all the regions, the ER was most in need of post-war investment especially in and around London, along the East Coast Main Line (ECML) and on the former Great Central Line from Marylebone. The LNER had begun electrification, which was continued by the British Transport Commission. To focus major investment, the LNER in England was divided into the Eastern and North Eastern Regions.

The ER encompasses a vast area of England with hugely contrasting scenery, extensive rich farmland in the east, the former industrial heartland of South Yorkshire and the sparsely 'totemed' county of Lincolnshire. East Anglia has hundreds of miles of beautiful, often unspoilt, coastline and some of the prettiest villages to be found anywhere. Almost all the important routes funnel towards London, with its four main regional stations. Marylebone was the former GCR Headquarters serving Leicester, Nottingham and Sheffield. Further east is the majesty of **Kings Cross** with its main lines to **Peterborough**, Doncaster and much of Lincolnshire.

The final two termini, Liverpool Street and Fenchurch Street, close to the City of London, served much of East Anglia and the **Southend on Sea** areas respectively. Alan Young's opening map shows the extent of the network and the quartet opposite exemplifies totems from the region's extremities.

Of the 385 stations fitted with dark blue totems, we list 68 stations with no known survivors. This is the highest percentage (17.7%) in any of the six BR regions. In the 2002 book, we had 80 unknowns and since then, a further 10 stations have been discovered as having totems, so this chapter's database shows considerable change. Of the 14 English counties the ER covered, Essex has the largest number of the region's stations fitted with totems (94 with 26% unknown), contrasting with Huntingdonshire and Rutland with one example each and Bedfordshire with two.

Brief Regional History

Railways evolved in this region from the opening of the Sheffield & Rotherham Railway in 1838. By 1840, this had connected with the North Midland Railway's Leeds–Derby line, providing Yorkshire passengers with through trains to London, albeit via Birmingham and a lengthy 8-hour journey! The Midland Railway did not open a direct line from Derby to St. Pancras until 1868. The first passenger line in East Anglia was opened by the Eastern Counties Railway, with their temporary 1839 Devonshire Street (Shoreditch) station, providing a service to Romford using 5-foot-gauge track! The ECR adopted standard gauge from 1844. The Northern & Eastern Railway forged a route towards **Cambridge** from a junction with the ECR at **Stratford**. This opened in three stages: **Broxbourne** in 1840, **Bishops Stortford** in 1842 and **Cambridge** finally in 1845. The final section involved much earthwork and two tunnels at **Audley End**.

Another early company in East London was the London & Blackwall Railway who saw lucrative traffic on the River Thames being dominated by shipping companies. From Fenchurch Street (originally Minories), rope-hauled trains ran to the new terminus at Blackwall Pier from 1840. In 1849 steam haulage was permitted and, gradually, some traffic was taken away from the river, as dockers and day trippers frequented the short line. Its success was short-lived as parallel tram services lured passengers away and it closed to passengers in 1926.

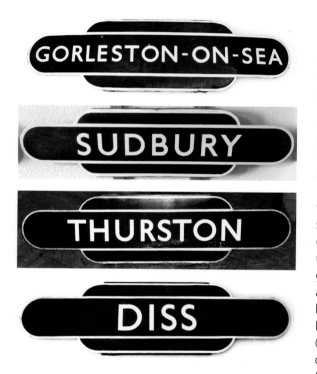

In 1844 the Yarmouth & Norwich Railway opened, giving rise to the seaside day trip. Between 1844 and 1849 various lines were built providing the missing links. The Eastern Union Railway opened the **Colchester** to **Ipswich** and **Bury-St-Edmunds** lines, followed by the all-important **Ipswich** to Norwich section in 1849. It was during this period that a Gauge Commission was set up to unify the different gauges in use. They decided unsurprisingly that standard gauge should be adopted for all UK lines, and this proved to be an expensive conversion for Brunel's Great Western Railway (GWR)! From 1846 to 1848, often referred to as the 'Railway Mania' years, the Midland opened the **Nottingham** to **Lincoln** line closely followed by **Peterborough** to **Stamford**. Both **Grimsby** to **Louth** and **Lincoln** to **Peterborough** were opened in 1848 by the Great Northern Railway (GNR).

The GNR's sights were firmly set on reaching London, which they did in 1850, using a temporary station at Maiden Lane north of **Kings Cross**. Planned by the GNR engineer George Turnbull, with detail design by Lewis Cubitt, a member of the famous Cubitt dynasty of builders, the great terminus opened in 1852; it is one of the most elegant of all the London termini. Between 2007 and 2012, the station underwent a £500 million refurbishment and a spectacular arched glazed roof was installed over a new concourse west of the train shed. The wonderful façade has been restored to its former glory (right hand picture) after decades of being partly hidden by unsightly smaller buildings, which had sprung up at the main entrance (left hand picture).

The wonderful frontage of Kings Cross with 1970s additions, and after restoration. *TSG library*

The section from **Peterborough** to **Retford** also opened in 1852, connecting with the GNR line from Doncaster that had opened three years earlier. The evolution and proliferation of lines, sometimes duplicated by rival companies, was often dictated by the movement of coal and freight to and from the collieries and ports. Between 1840 and 1850, some 4,600 miles of railway were built in the UK. The speeds attained were slow by today's standards, but the only alternatives were horse-drawn carriages along very poorly maintained roads.

Looking at Lincolnshire, the Manchester, Sheffield & Lincolnshire Railway was a dominant force in opening links to **Grimsby** and its giant docks complex, which subsequently evolved giving some 6 miles of quayside. Further dock building and the opening of Immingham Dock to handle mainly coal in 1912 was mostly driven by the railway companies' desire for increased revenue. Despite Lincolnshire's largely rural nature, some busy complex junctions evolved at **Lincoln**, **Spalding**, **Sleaford, Barnetby** and even **Louth** to cope with the rising volumes of holidaymakers and freight traffic.

Sadly, during the Beeching years, the county suffered from a dramatic contraction of its network and very large areas were cut off and became isolated. A train journey today from Cleethorpes to **Skegness** takes a ludicrous six hours or more! The direct East Lincolnshire line via **Louth** that closed in 1970 provided journey times of about a quarter of today's timings! Can this really be called progress?

South Yorkshire is renowned for being an industrial powerhouse and former mining stronghold. The spread of railways in this area during the Industrial Revolution was phenomenal, giving rise to belching chimneys, collieries galore and some superb backdrops for totems! Sheffield and **Chesterfield** were central

to the development and a link to Manchester was paramount to the expanding Sheffield, Ashton-under-Lyne and Manchester Railway (absorbed by the Manchester, Sheffield & Lincolnshire Railway in 1847). The mighty Pennines could not stand in the way of the railway navvies and the 3-mile long Woodhead Tunnel opened in 1845 after six years of toil and the loss of thirty men. A second bore opened in 1852 to cope with increasing traffic.

East Anglia witnessed a proliferation of minor companies, which were all swallowed up in 1862, with the exception of the M&GN, when the Great Eastern Railway (GER) was formed. Sadly, East Anglia was also a target of Beeching's axe, with numerous branch lines falling victim to the economic argument. The **King's Lynn** to **Hunstanton** line, liberally decked with totems and the through-route via **Swaffham** and Dereham to **Wymondham,** both succumbed, as did the branch lines to Wells-next-the-Sea and **Aldeburgh**. They were socially important, but that mattered not.

The through-route from **Shelford** to **Sudbury**, which provided a shortcut for many summertime holidaymakers from the Cambridge area visiting **Clacton on Sea** via **Haverhill**, was also severed. A large proportion of the stations on these routes, including the M&GN, had totem signs and the majority of them seemed to have survived. Real rarities are **Holbeach**, **Wisbech North** and **Fakenham East** and **West**. Early installation of

fluorescent lighting saw wholesale scrapping of totems in the mid- to late 1950s at **Cambridge**, **Bury-St-Edmunds**, **Newmarket** and **March**.

The GER Shenfield to **Southend-on-Sea Victoria** line opened in 1889, some thirty years after the London, Tilbury & Southend Railway (LTSR) reached the Essex resort via their line along the north bank of the Thames from Fenchurch Street via Tilbury.

There was considerable rivalry between the GER and the LT&SR for holiday traffic, prompting the LT&SR to build a faster link between **Barking** and **Pitsea**. This opened in stages from 1885 to 1888 to compete with the new 1889 GER line. These totems are very sought-after because many had short lives. Between 1956 and 1961, much modernisation and electrification occurred, when fluorescent lighting superseded our beloved totems. Only one **Wickford** totem (large letters) has been seen from the whole Shenfield to **Southend Victoria** line! A very rare **Westcliff on Sea** totem appeared in auction in 2018, with fluorescent lighting being installed there by 1957.

Eastern Region Totem Geography

Alan Young & Richard Furness

The hand-drawn chapter-opening map shows how randomly totems were dispersed, essentially revealing a three-way geographical split. South of a line drawn between Yarmouth and **Peterborough**, generous provision was afforded. North of a second line from the **Chesterfield**/Sheffield area to **Grimsby** was also well fitted, but the central area between these two lines had far fewer totems. The 1950-based map depicts the ER's almost-final boundaries, so the installation of totems began in earnest that year.

The ER wisely chose not to provide totems on unprofitable lines that were soon to close: branches to Framlingham, Laxfield, Thaxted, Tollesbury, Bardney to **Louth**. In addition, **Bishops Stortford** to Braintree & Bocking, **Bury-St-Edmunds** to **Thetford**, County School to **Wroxham**, **Heacham** to Wells-next-the-Sea, **St Albans Abbey** to **Hatfield**, **Tivetshall** to **Beccles**, and **Welwyn Garden City** to **Hertford North** were among the lines that closed before 1955. However, **Crouch End** and **Stroud Green** on the Alexandra Palace branch (closed 1954) in North London briefly had totems. The widespread closures robbed enthusiasts of sights similar to that at **Whittlesford** alongside. This station opened in 1845, but in 2007 it was renamed Whittlesford Parkway.

Rare **Whittlesford** totems have not yet been auctioned and one is shown above with an equally uncommon **Mellis** from Suffolk that has been auctioned just once, in 2013.

The Eastern Region is one of contrasting landscapes. Between the bustling capital city and the industrial area of South Yorkshire, formerly dominated by collieries and steelworks, are pretty English villages, vast fields of flowers and vegetables, and some

typically English communities. East Anglia has long stretches of beautiful often unspoilt but eroding coastline. Many towns still retain their former charm and places such as Southwold, Sheringham, Caister, Cromer and **Frinton on Sea** are still stuck in the past, thankfully. Anybody growing up in London during the 1960s would have most likely visited **Southend on Sea**, with beaches stretching several miles from **Leigh-on-Sea** to **Thorpe Bay**. The dark blue ER direction signs above would have directed you to your train after a day at the seaside.

The Eastern boasted three times as many stations fitted with totems as the NER, but still managed a poor fifth place in the regional league table. Several principal stations in the Eastern Region never carried totems, such as London's Liverpool Street and Fenchurch Street stations, Doncaster, Sheffield Midland and Victoria, all three Yarmouth

Top: Tilbury Riverside *in situ. Above:* Stratford *in situ. Jim Connor*

termini, Lowestoft Central and Norwich Thorpe. It might have been the early installation of electric strip lighting, which made totems unnecessary, though dark blue enamel running-in boards and various information and platform number signs were fitted.

Whereas the gaudier NER totems glowed in their very frequently gloomy industrial surroundings, the sober and more dignified dark blue ER totems were far less conspicuous in comparable settings, such as under the soot-encrusted awnings of **Blackhorse Road**, **New Southgate** or **Silvertown,** for example.

In the southern area, few London suburban stations were overlooked, yet many of them lost their totems by 1961, sometimes in connection with electrification,

when fluorescent strip lighting was installed bearing the station name. The London to **Southend** routes were cases in point, as were the **Hertford East** and Chingford branches, where several stations had fully flanged totems, which must have hung for no more than five or six years. Several have not been seen or heard of since removal.

Totems even appeared at unlikely, minor rural locations such as **Birdbrook** and all the other Colne Valley intermediate stations, some of which had superb names. We list **White Colne**, **Earls Colne**, **Sible & Castle Hedingham** or **Yeldham** as being desirable. The line remained independent until it became part of the LNER in 1923.

The main line stations from London to **King's Lynn** and Norwich (both routes) were almost entirely totemised, as was **Cambridge-Ipswich**. A few routes that survived into the 1960s had few totems, notably **Cambridge**-Mildenhall, **Wickford**-Southminster (still open) and **Cambridg**e-**Bedford**. The last-named is one of several routes inherited from the LMS, on which totems were scarce; others included Huntingdon East-Thrapston and the lines west of **Peterborough**, where there were joint interests; the LMR provided the train services, while the stations were operated by the ER.

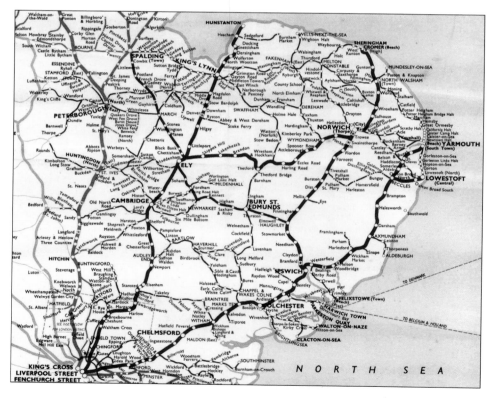

However, further north the ex-LMS **Nottingham-Lincoln St. Marks** line was lavished with totems and in London the **Crouch Hill-Barking** route was similarly favoured. On both these lines there was often the curious spectacle of ER totems displayed on distinctive LMS gas lamp standards. Totems from two stations on these lines are found below and all of them are fairly elusive.

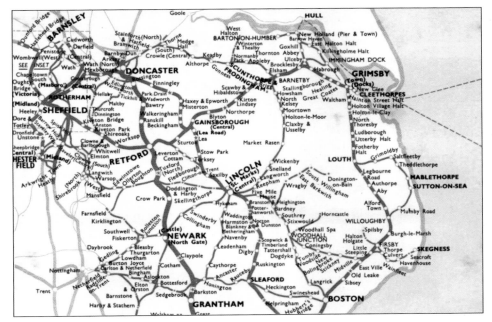

Going north from **Peterborough**, totems were thin on the ground, almost confined to town and junction stations. In the 78 miles from **Peterborough North** to **Grimsby** (via **Boston**) only 6 of the 28 intermediate stations had totems.

Similarly, **March** to Doncaster (96 miles) had 3, and on the ECML from **Peterborough** to Doncaster (80 miles) there were totems at only 4 intermediate stations. Almost all minor stations on these lines closed by 1962, so to deny them totems probably made economic sense.

Essendine, **Littleworth**, and **Kirton** were the only early closures on these lines to have carried totems. In this totem-poor area it is remarkable, as previously mentioned, that **Nottingham–Lincoln** was so well provided, and that the **Retford–Lincoln** intermediates at **Leverton**, **Cottam**, and **Torkesey** (closed as early as 1959) had totems, but Saxilby (still open) did not. (**Torkesey** was an inaccurate spelling of the village's name, **Torksey**).

The sprawling Midland & Great Northern network (**Leicester** and **Peterborough** to Cromer, Yarmouth and Norwich via **Melton Constable**) almost entirely closed to passengers in 1959, even before the Beeching review happened. The ER was not slow in recognising and severing unprofitable lines. Totems were limited to a few of the more significant M&GN stations such as **Holbeach**, **Sutton Bridge** and **Fakenham West** (though not South Lynn or Bourne) and, curiously, at the humble **Moulton** station.

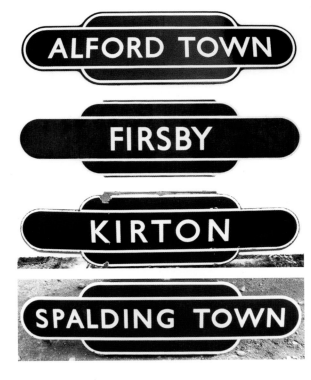

The industrialised belt from **Chesterfield**/Sheffield through Doncaster to **Grimsby** enjoyed a more generous allocation of totems than the zone to its immediate south. From **Chesterfield Midland** to **Grimsby**, for instance, totems were fitted at two-thirds of the stations. In this area totems hung only briefly at **Barrow Hill** and **Holmes,** the former being closed in 1954 and the latter in 1955. **Barrow Hill** was another peculiar 'joint interest' station, appearing only in the LMR timetable.

The picture below shows a real ER rarity *in situ,* as totems from **Wivenhoe** have not been seen since early removal. The station is on the *Sunshine Coast Line* that links **Colchester** to **Clacton on Sea**, **Frinton-on-Sea** and **Walton on Naze**. Stations at **Hythe** (to the west) and **Alresford** (to the east) also lost their totems around the same time. None from this trio are known survivors; what a shame that the area suffered badly.

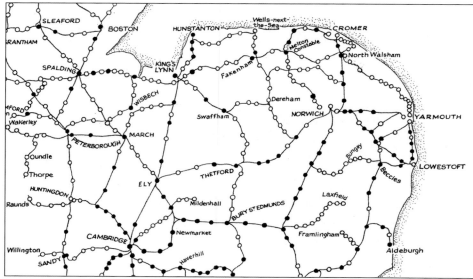

The map highlights the distribution of totems in the Eastern Region in Norfolk. Note how certain lines are almost 'totemless', **Bury-St-Edmunds** to **King's Lynn** via **Thetford** for example, whilst others are generously endowed, **Ipswich**–Norwich, with the two totems below the map being representative. The area surrounding Dereham was particularly barren, as was the coastal route from North Walsham to Yarmouth.

To counter this, there was a generous distribution in the NE London and Sheffield areas, along with certain Suffolk branch lines chosen to receive a healthy complement.

Many Eastern stations retained their totems long into the black-and-white corporate identity era. Totems were in evidence in numerous places in 1973, typically in Greater London and in North Lincolnshire. However, wholesale removal of totems began in earnest in 1974/5, but a few places seemed to be missed by the 'modernisers'. **Woodbridge** did not receive attention until about 1984, and **Goxhill** on the New Holland branch somehow gained the distinction of being the last station in Britain to succumb to the dreaded corporate identity takeover, as late as 1988.

County Feature: Lincolnshire

Lincolnshire is a large county of over 2,660 square miles, the second largest in England after Yorkshire but, in reality, it is three distinct areas. The northern steel mills and fishing ports in the Lindsey area contrast markedly with the fertile flower-growing area of Holland around The Wash. In the centre is the flat half-a-million acres of Kesteven and the historic city of **Lincoln**. It is a not a densely populated county, currently ranking 18th out of the 48 English shires. Reference to the database pages reveal that 37 stations throughout Lincolnshire were fitted with totems, a low number considering there were nearly 200 stations in the county in the 1950s. These were very unevenly spread with almost a third around the **Grimsby** and Humber area, and another 30% in the south around **Spalding**. The **Lincoln** area has further 20% of the total, leaving the rest of the county with just 8 stations which were totem-provided, all randomly spread. Lincolnshire totems are today highly prized by many collectors.

The 1957 map right shows that few railway lines (shown in black) were built in this county. The four main routes are: from the south through **Spalding**, **Boston** and **Louth** into **Grimsby**; from **Nottingham** through **Lincoln** into **Grimsby**; from Sheffield through **Gainsborough** into **Grimsby**; and from **Leeds** through Scunthorpe into **Grimsby** (what an important place that used to be with its huge fishing industry at that time).

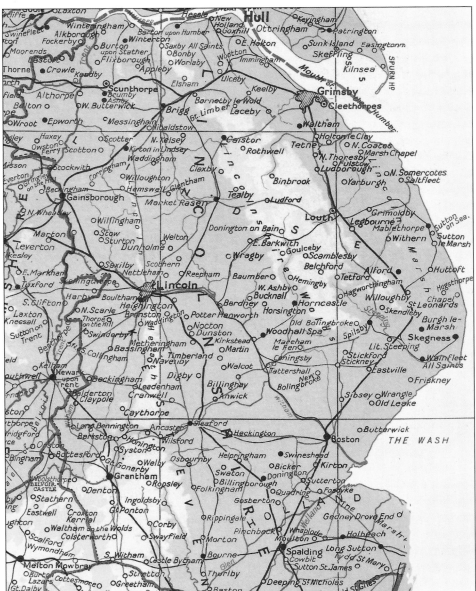

From these four cross-county lines, connections and branch lines fanned out to the many seaside towns along a long sandy coastline. This is far less busy today than in totem times, when the 'East Midlands invasions' took place from Easter to the end of the summer. The wonderful dark blue totems in bright summer sunshine must have been a sight to behold when first installed. It may be best to start our tour in the north and work south, maybe leaving the best till last?

The stations fitted with totems in the north of the county are **Althorpe**, **Appleby**, **Barnetby**, **Brigg**, **Crowle Central**, **Goxhill**, **Grimsby Docks**, **Grimsby Town**, **Habrough**, **New Holland Town** and **Stallingborough**, the last-named not having been seen or heard of since removal. The surprise omissions from the area are Cleethorpes and Scunthorpe. Why, for example, on the line in from Doncaster have totems at **Crowle**, **Althorpe**, **Appleby** and **Barnetby** and omit the far more important Scunthorpe in the middle? The wonderful names of Kirton Lindsey, Holton-le-Clay and Thornton Abbey would have made real collectors' items today and show that BR really did not realise the assets and potential they had, nor the resale values of those items they did make available; oh for a few more visionary George Dow's during that period!

Moving south away from fish docks, refineries and steel, we find the Lincolnshire Wolds, a line of limestone hills that rise to just over 500 feet. These were once tree-clad but have been tamed into farmland. Almost in the centre is **Lincoln**, built on a rock outcrop almost 200 feet above the River Witham; Roman *Lindum* was an elegant colonnaded city, and William the Conqueror founded Lincoln Castle in 1068.

Also topping the limestone ridge and alongside the castle is Lincoln Cathedral, a magnificent Early Gothic building, the construction of which had commenced in 1072. Throughout its history, the location and importance of the city has been enormous, and the Midland Railway built the first station here in 1846. Later the Great Northern opened their station named 'Lincoln' just to the north of the Midland's 'Lincoln' in 1850. That must have been confusing for passengers.

The ex-MR station became **Lincoln St. Marks** in September 1950 and on the same day the ex-GN Lincoln became **Lincoln Central**. Both stations were fitted with totems shortly thereafter and although St. Mark's station closed as late as 1986, the Central station went back to its original name of just Lincoln in 1991. Happily, totems from both stations survive. Above is the unusual layout from **Gainsborough Central**. The main letters seem too large for the layout

and a lower panel design would have been visually better. Alongside is the standard totem layout from **Swinderby**. In 2009, a large letter variant also passed through auction. Other totems in this part of the county are, **Hykeham**, **Market Rasen**, **Torkesey** and **Woodhall Junction.**

Torksey (note the correct village spelling compared to that on the totem) was a station on the line between **Lincoln** and **Retford**, which closed to passengers in 1959.

Moving east to the coast are more desirable names. **Mablethorpe** and **Skegness** shown above have regularly appeared in auction, but the same cannot be said for **Louth**, which has only been in auction once (2016). Recent photo evidence confirms the lettering here was larger than the regulation 3 inches, as is the lettering on the **Skegness** totem shown above. Other totems in this part of Lincolnshire are **Alford Town**, **Firsby**, **Sutton-on-Sea** and **Wainfleet** and all are known survivors. Of around 50 stations in this part of Lincolnshire, only 8 were fitted with totems.

In the south of the county, the real gems are to be found. These include the classics of **Grantham** (not known to have survived) **Stamford Town** (only in auction once in 2003), **Boston**, **Spalding Town** and **Holbeach,** all of which are rare. Therefore, collecting this quintet is next to impossible. The remaining 'Holland' totems are **Heckington**, **Kirton**, **Littleworth**, **Moulton**, **Sleaford** and **Sutton Bridge**. The picture opposite of **Heckington** *in situ* is a superbly composed photograph.

South Lincolnshire has some of the most fertile soil in Britain. The **Boston** to **Spalding** area is ablaze with colour each spring, rivalling, if not surpassing, the fabulous bulb fields of Holland in the Netherlands. It may not surprise readers that 65% of the total area for all bulbs in Great Britain is concentrated here. **Boston** and **Spalding** are both ex-GNR stations of 1848. **Boston** is more commonly associated with its American city cousin, but the name stems from Anglo-Saxon times (in reality, St. Botolph's Town). **Stamford** station, built by the Midland Railway in 1848, is an architectural masterpiece in a showpiece town. It held the totem name for just sixteen years (1950–1966). **Grantham** station (ex GNR from 1852) was stripped of totems early on: survivors are not known.

A superb Lincolnshire scene in July 1974. *Alan Young*

Essex: A Difficult County for Collectors

Reference to the totem statistics spreadsheet in the opening chapter shows Essex is the hardest county from which to collect totems. A total of 94 stations were fitted, but we have no survival data on 26 and another 17 have not appeared in auction; 10 of Essex's 94 'totemed' stations closed in the 1960s, 2 of which appear below.

The line from **Barking** to **Tilbury Riverside** forms a loop running along the industrial north-side of the River Thames, where very elusive totems once hung at **Dagenham Dock** (for the Ford's factory), **Rainham** and **Purfleet,** before reaching the busy port of Tilbury. Individual wagonload trains once dominated this scene, but Freightliner trains now rule. In 1912, the Midland Railway bought out the LT&SR from underneath the nose of the Great Eastern and, in 1923, the railway passed into LMS hands. At their peak, the LT&SR operated 26 stations: a pair of ex-LTSR totems appears below.

There is far more to the county than the media would like you to believe, and our focus on the county will concentrate on the more picturesque main lines and former branch lines, which once threaded their way through quintessentially English countryside. Numerous seaside resorts are still frequented by day-trippers. The map shows the railway system in 1956 before Dr. Beeching started to remove services. Essex fared better than the other East Anglian counties, with only the branch lines to **Maldon East**, Brightlingsea and Chapel & Wakes Colne to **Haverhill** being axed.

The line from Braintree to **Bishops Stortford** lost its passenger services in 1952 and the **Kelvedon** & Tollesbury Light Railway was closed to passengers in 1951. The majority of Essex lines were owned by the Great Eastern Railway, but the London Tilbury & Southend Railway (LT&SR) had a stronghold in the south of the county, operating from Fenchurch Street to **Shoeburyness**. Collecting totems from this line is infuriating, due to the relative ease of finding them from stations west of **Upminster Bridge** but great difficulty in finding them east of **Upminster** (with the exception of **Grays** and **Tilbury Town**). The database contains photos of some rare totems from this area.

1956 map of the County of Essex.

The major seaside resort for the area is **Southend-on-Sea**, and the first totem known to survive from any of the stations here **(Central)** was fiercely contested in 2006 at Kidlington; nothing else has appeared since. The photo below shows **Southend-on-Sea Victoria** station in 1954/55, with at least half-a-dozen totems mounted along this platform alone. There are three others, and all four platforms could take 12-coach trains bringing hordes of day-trippers from London throughout the year.

Along the coast we have further resorts at **Clacton on Sea**, **Frinton-on-Sea**, **Walton on Naze** and **Dovercourt Bay**. None of these are easy to obtain, with **Walton on Naze** not known, so collecting from the Essex coast represents quite a challenge, even for the most serious of collectors within our hobby.

The Chingford line also had several stations within the former county boundaries and the Liverpool Street to **Cambridge** main line has just four stations that stray into Essex at **Stansted**, **Elsenham** (junction for Thaxted), **Newport** and **Audley End** (junction for **Saffron Walden** closed 1964). We have included a photograph of a **Saffron Walden** survivor in the database pages. Beyond **Saffron Walden** was the former junction station of **Bartlow** (closed 1967) with its FF totems that have twice been auctioned.

Travelling further east, although **Haverhill** lies in Suffolk, it was the junction for the small branch line to Chapel & Wakes Colne known as the Colne Valley Railway, which retained its independence from the GER until 1923. The Colne Valley stretches from Great Yeldham in Colchester's neighbouring Braintree district, following the path of the River Colne through nearby villages. Two of these are shown above and the other stations of **Birdbrook**, **Sible & Castle Hedingham** and **White Colne** prove that Essex has some of the best names imaginable on its totems. The villages along this former route retain considerable charm and some still possess their former station buildings. It is a great pity Chapel & Wakes Colne was not endowed with dark blue totems.

Taking pride of place in the Colne Valley is the 346-metre long Chapel Viaduct. Its 32 arches make it the second largest brick-built structure in England. With the exception of **Halstead**, all these stations were very minor but were equipped with totems. Remarkably at least one example is known to survive from each station due to the foresight of one of our fellow collectors in 1962. He went along the line and officially obtained one from each station!

Nearby is **Manningtree**, a short walk to Flatford Mill, where John Constable painted his famous composition, *The Hay Wain,* and is the junction for the branch line to **Harwich Town**. No **Manningtree** totem has ever turned up due to early installation of fluorescent lighting. **Colchester** is equally elusive and is the junction for the line to **Clacton on Sea** and **Walton on Naze**. The intermediate stations of **St. Botolphs, Hythe, Wivenhoe, Alresford, Great Bentley** and **Weeley** all lost their totems early on and are enthusiastically sought-after. Curiously, **Thorpe-le-Soken, Kirby Cross** and **Frinton-on-Sea** do survive, but the terminus at **Walton on Naze** has yet to yield a surviving totem.

Heading towards London, we pass through lovely countryside with small villages such as **Kelvedon**, which retains many fine old buildings; it is the former junction for the line to Tollesbury. **Witham** once boasted two junctions: one to **Bishops Stortford**, now truncated to Braintree, and the other to **Maldon East**. This tragically closed in 1964, the folly and irony being that this is now one of largest towns in the county without a station. **Hatfield Peverel,** where only two totems are known to survive, then follows, before **Chelmsford**, the county town. The imposing station stands high on a curved viaduct. Only one totem from here has ever been in auction, that in 2019. The next station, **Ingatestone**, had nearly mint FF totems. This is because they were made and never used, having been found in a storeroom still wrapped in brown paper!

Shenfield is the junction for the line to Southend and the land of ludicrously elusive totems: **Billericay, Rayleigh, Rochford, Prittlewell** and **Southend-on-Sea Victoria** all had them and not one is known to survive due to being re-signed around 1955. This probably makes this the most difficult line in the UK to collect totems from. A curious lone outpost on the branch line to Southminster, namely **Burnham-on-Crouch,** was chosen for totem installation: a pleasant riverside location with much yachting activity. Due to sporadic installation between Shenfield and Liverpool Street, the task of collecting is ever-more frustrating, as just **Chadwell Heath** and **Manor Park** had them before we enter the London boundaries, further out today than in the totem years.

We close with rare images of **Chalkwell, Hythe** and **Wickford** totems *in situ*.

A brand new Wickham DMU for Southminster at Wickford on 8 December 1957.

Elusive Yorkshire 'Blues'

It might not be appreciated that Yorkshire stations were well endowed with Eastern Region blue totems. Our research shows 36 stations were signed this way, accounting for 26.4% of all the totems to be found in England's largest county. Many have few auction appearances and when they do surface, they are normally eagerly contested. We have no survival data on six of these (**Ecclesfield West**, **Elsecar and Hoyland**, **Oughty Bridge**, **Rotherham Central**, **Swinton Central** and **Woodhouse**). Totems from a further six stations are known to have survived but have not appeared in auction, and examples from eight more stations have appeared just once or twice. This amounts to 20 Yorkshire stations that are difficult or impossible to find, over 55% of the known ER Yorkshire stations. The database pages contain five of these 'rare blues', and an additional pair is shown below; neither has appeared in auction – thus far.

Alan Young's Sheffield area map shows the railway lines, then in southern West Riding, but now termed South Yorkshire after its creation in the 1972 Local Government Act. In view of the line duplication resulting from Victorian railway mania, it is not surprising that 20 of the 36 stations suffered closure, the first in 1955 (**Holmes**), the last in 1988 (**Rotherham Masborough**). **Deepcar**, **Dodworth**, **Oughty Bridge**, **Summer Lane**, **Wadsley Bridge**, **Wath Central** and **Wombwell Central** were all closed four years before Beeching's 1963 pruning. Amazingly totems were still *in situ* at **Wath Central** in 1970 and at **Summer Lane** in 1972, many years after closure. **Wadsley Bridge** was also kept open for years after closure to allow Sheffield Wednesday football specials to call.

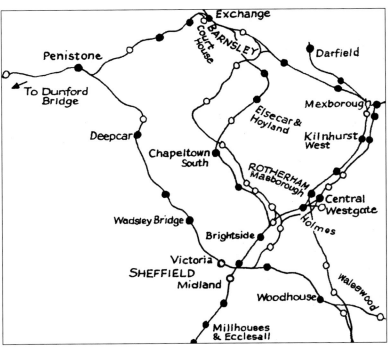

Elusive Yorkshire 'Blues': Two Sheffield area totems *in situ. The late John Mann*

The two photos of the 'wonky' **Kiveton Bridge** and **Kiveton Park** *in situ* were taken by Sheffield's John Mann in the 1960s; both totems have appeared just twice in auction. The quartet above all succumbed to closure in the same year (1968) when the Sheffield area was heavily targeted. Over the years, Sheffield has been hit hard, with **Attercliffe Road** (1995), **Brightside** (1995), **Heeley** (1968) and **Wadsley Bridge** (1959) all being casualties as passenger numbers steadily declined. The city's new tram system has revived the use of public transport considerably and as a result several of the outer suburban areas have been revitalised.

Sheffield Area Railway Clearing House map of 1912. *Wikipedia Commons*

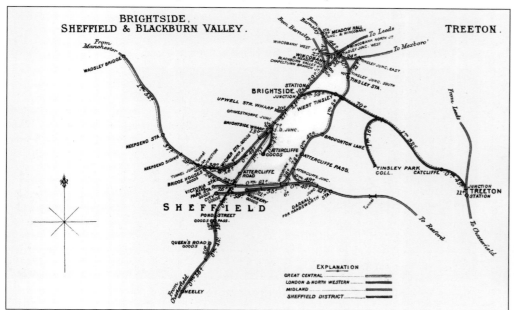

The preceding 1912 RCH map shows the railway layout in and around Sheffield in detail. Three major railway companies served the city, and it is amazing (and a great pity) that neither of the two main stations, Sheffield Midland (ex-MR) nor Sheffield Victoria (ex-GCR), were fitted with totems. Sheffield Victoria closed in 1970 and Midland was refurbished and enhanced in 2006 as a major interchange hub; the façade is superb.

The first tracks in the area were built by the Sheffield and Rotherham Railway, a route of just 5 miles that opened in 1838. It was later taken over and incorporated into the MR's development of the area. As Sheffield developed into a centre for steel production, railways were needed to support the growing heavy industry so that during Queen Victoria's reign, all the major steel mills were furnished with rail links. Sheffield cutlers were first recorded in the 13th century and, by 1692, the first steel-making facilities appeared. The steady growth of making steel fuelled a massive growth in population, rising from around 60,000 in 1801 to 577,000 by 1951. The city became a major railway junction, as the 1912 Clearing House map shows.

Travelling north towards **Barnsley** and **Rotherham**, coal was found in large quantities, a key ingredient in steel production. During the totem years, large amounts were moved around the area and the giant Tinsley Yard was a major freight hub.

Most South Yorkshire ER totems are difficult to find. Known but rare survivors include **Barnsley Exchange**, **Penistone** (with its larger letters), **Stainforth**, **Wath North** and **Wombwell West**. In addition, we might suggest **Chapeltown South**, **Conisbrough** and **Summer Lane** as real enhancements to any Yorkshire collection.

County Review of Eastern Region Totems

BEDFORDSHIRE

We begin the county review with an area not normally associated with dark blue totems. There were just two Bedfordshire stations so adorned; **Biggleswade** and **Sandy** have respectively appeared in auction 11 and 16 times to date.

Both these Bedfordshire stations lie on the ECML. The Great Northern built both of them in 1850. **Biggleswade** is 41 miles from **Kings Cross** and was rebuilt in 1901. **Sandy** station is 3 miles further north, and underwent major rebuilding in the 1970s.

Below: Sandy station before restoration. *Alan Young*

CAMBRIDGESHIRE

This county had quite a large contingent of ER blue totems, with 32 stations being fitted. Between 1962 and 1970, 14 of these closed. A small collage of closed station totems is presented below.

The database pages include six Cambridgeshire rarities, but in addition, **Chatteris**, **Foxton**, **Great Chesterford**, **Harston** and **Shelford** are not easy to come by. We have no survival data on **Cambridge**, **Ely**, **Linton**, **March** and **Newmarket**.

Above: Alan Young Right: Brian Matthews

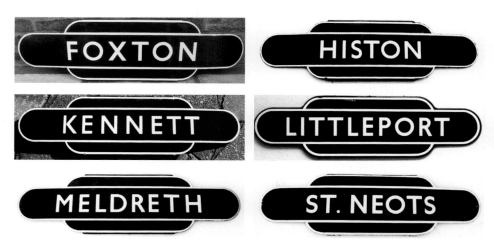

Chesterfield Midland. *Wikipedia Commons*

Totems from **Histon** (4 appearances) **Kennett** (5), **Littleport** (4), **Meldreth** (6), the 2L **Peterborough East** (4), **Six Mile Bottom** (4) and **Waterbeach** (1) are also difficult.

DERBYSHIRE

This is another county from which it is difficult to collect ER totems. Just 14 stations were fitted, and we have no survival data from 4 of these (**Langwith**, **Renishaw Central**, **Staveley Works** and **Whitwell**). In addition, **Heath** and **Shirebrook West** totems have not appeared in auction, with 6 others appearing just once or twice. The most common Derbyshire ER totem is **Dore and Totley**; that has only been auctioned 3 times, the last appearance being in 2010. On top of this, 12 of the 14 stations closed between 1954 and 1967. For these reasons it is very difficult to build a substantial collection of 'blue' Derbyshire totems.

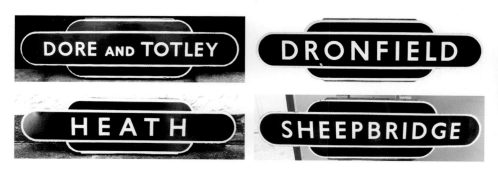

The two pictures above show rare totems *in situ*. **Heath** station was actually in the village of Holmewood, just south of **Chesterfield**; its location was just before the Great Chesterfield Loop, which ran between **Staveley Central** and Heath Junction on the former GCML. **Chesterfield Midland** station opened in 1840, but was re-sited further south in 1870. This was developed and rebuilt for a second time in 1963, but that was not the end of refurbishment. Most of the 1963 buildings were demolished in the late 1990s, shortly after privatisation. Both **Chesterfield Midland** and **Chesterfield Central** totems were HF, but the former featured a lower panel layout whilst the latter was two-line (*see* database pages 85 and 86). **Chesterfield Central** closed in 1963 and thereafter all services would be concentrated on the Midland station. Its track bed and former freight yards now form the basis of Chesterfield's inner ring road.

ESSEX

This county carried more dark blue totems than any other in the region. Many featured earlier in this chapter, but this section allows us to show a few more.

Notice in the sextet above the large letters featured on **Elm Park** and **Witham**, a feature unique to the Eastern Region – why should this be? **Elm Park** and **Mistley** are two of the few Essex totems that have appeared regularly in auction, contrasting with **West Ham (Manor Road)**, **White Notley** and **Witham** all with two each. As previously stated, Essex is a very difficult area to collect.

HERTFORDSHIRE

Of the 26 stations in Hertfordshire that carried ER blue, some of them with wonderful names, such as **Bishops Stortford**, **Brookmans Park**, **Sawbridgeworth**, **Waltham Cross** and **Welwyn Garden City**, we have no survival data on **Hertford North**, **New Barnet**, **Potters Bar** and **Rye House**, with 5 others known to have survived, but never having been in auction, including **Cheshunt** (shown alongside *in situ*), **Hitchin** and **Ware**. Therefore, as with the other the ER Home Counties, trying to collect totems from Hertfordshire is not that easy. The pair below have just one public appearance each, with those auctions being in 2001 and 2013 respectively.

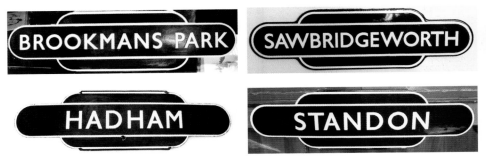

When the **Hertford East** branch from **Broxbourne** via **Ware** was electrified, **Buntingford** branch trains were reduced in both frequency and quality. The line was recommended for closure in Dr. Beeching's Report, and the passenger service was withdrawn in 1964, closing stations at **Hadham**, **Standon**, **Braughing** and **Buntingford**; goods services on the branch ceased a year later.

Cheshunt station, Hertfordshire, looking north in 1959.

Some of the **Welwyn Garden City** totems were made with a top flange only, as shown in the preceding photo. **Welwyn North** is not as common as its local 'brother' with just four public appearances; other rarities include **Letchworth** and **St. Margarets**.

Above: Stevenage old station, closed 1973. *Robert Joanes*

Left: March 1973. *Alan Young*

The old station at **Stevenage** was built in 1850, but a new British Rail station, closer to the New Town centre, replaced it in 1973. The picture above, therefore, is something of a rarity. Left is Alan Young's colourful photo of an **Oakleigh Park** totem still hanging proudly in March 1973.

HUNTINGDONSHIRE

Only **Somersham** carried totems in this county. It has appeared only once in auction, and that back in 2005. A photo is found on page 59.

LINCOLNSHIRE

There were 37 stations in Lincolnshire clothed in dark blue signage. From this list, 14 suffered closure, the earliest being 1959 (**Holbeach**, **Moulton**, **Sutton Bridge** and **Torksey**) and the last being 1986 (**Lincoln St. Marks**). Totems from **Grantham** and **Stallingborough** are not thought to have survived and in addition **Heckington** and **Holbeach** have no public auction appearances. The county was the subject of a major feature earlier in this chapter.

LONDON

There were 16 stations that carried dark blue London totems, but we have no evidence of the survival of 5 of these (**Bethnal Green**, **Clapton**, **Rectory Road**, **Stepney East** and **Stoke Newington**). Photographic evidence in our library confirms the existence of all these totems. With the exception of **Hackney Downs** and **Maryland,** examples of which are known, all the others have been publicly auctioned, the most common being **Harringay West** with 12 appearances to date.

London has suffered just 2 station closures: **Kings Cross York Road** in November 1976, (though it was open briefly in March 1977) and **Lea Bridge** in 1985. **Kings Cross York Road** was a single platform at the exit from the easternmost of the three Gasworks Tunnels just outside the main station. In 2007, the York Road tunnels were used by contractors working on the new St Pancras International station.

The **Bromley** totem shown above was modified slightly by the addition of a sticker reading **Bromley-by-Bow**. This totem is shown in our database pages and is also a great rarity. **Forest Gate** has been in auction five times, the last in 2020.

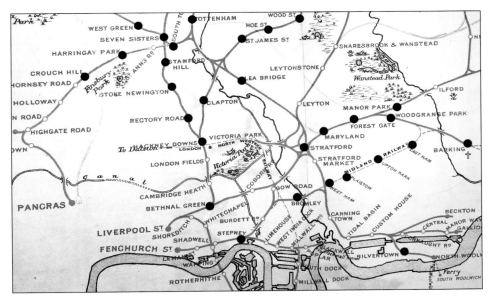

The GER map above shows the lines in north-east London, with totem stations shown as black dots. All the totems in this part of London vanished over a 10–15 year period. For many ER aficionados, THE dark blue totem to collect is Kings Cross York Road, and four of them are shown in the picture below left. The picture below right is of a **Harringay Park** totem dug up in 2003 during building work at the station. Between 1958 and 1991 it was renamed twice. Today the station is Harringay Green Lanes.

The much-damaged totem is shown partially restored alongside **Harringay West** in far better condition. This station opened as Harringay in 1885 but carried the totem name from June 1951 to May 1971, when it reverted to **Harringay**. **Lea Bridge** station is between **Stratford** and **Tottenham** Hale on the Lea Valley Line: it was closed between 1985 and 2016. **Stratford** opened in 1839, but has been transformed from its original size, with DLR services, Central and Jubilee underground lines, Eurostar, London Overground and National Rail, all used intensively during London's Olympics in 2012.

MIDDLESEX

Totems from 4 regions contributed to the Middlesex total of 75, but only 26 of these were ER. A total of 5 stations have been closed, 2 in 1954 (**Crouch End** and **Stroud Green**) and 3 in 1963 (**Noel Park**, **Palace Gates** and **West Green**). We currently have no survival data on **Bruce Grove**, **Enfield Chase**, **Silver Street**, **Stamford Hill** and **Stroud Green**. Only three others have not been in auction (**Bowes Park**, **Crews Hill**, **Lower Edmonton** and **White Hart Lane**).

This information means out of 22 survivors, 18 have been in auction, with **New Southgate** being the most common (37) followed by **Wood Green** (20), **Angel Road** (15) and **Brimsdown** (12); the remaining 14 have single-figure appearances. (**Bush Hill Park**, **Palmers Green**, **Seven Sisters** and **Winchmore Hill** have all appeared once).

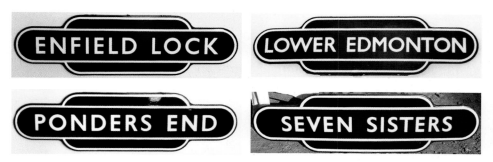

The preceding 6 totem photos depict a wonderful set of Middlesex totems. The database pages contain 5 other totem photographs with the number of auction appearances shown in parentheses after the name; **Bush Hill Park** (1), **Northumberland Pk**. (3), **Palmers Green** (1), **Tottenham** (3) and **White Hart Lane** (1).

ECML Totems *in situ* at New Southgate station, September 1973. *Alan Young*

New Southgate dates from 1850 but was substantially re-built in the 1970s. The station name changed five times with that on the totem only being borne from 1971.

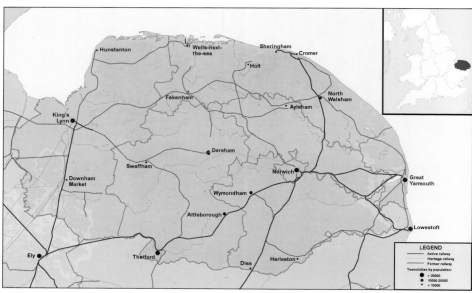

Wikipedia Commons

NORFOLK

This East Anglian county had 40 stations adorned with ER totems, but 20 of these were closed between 1959 and 1970. North Norfolk suffered particularly badly, with almost all cross-county routes being closed (*see* map above). **Fakenham**, **Hunstanton** and **Swaffham** are just 3 places to lose their links, as depicted by the red lines; 4 heritage lines are shown in yellow.

This quartet shows some of Norfolk's rarities, **West Runton** especially so.

Salhouse and Brandon Norfolk totems *in situ. Tim Clarke*

Three closures occurred in 1959 and two of them, **Drayton** and **Grimston Road,** are very recent discoveries; (**Fakenham West** also closed that year). The final closure occurred in 1970 when **Gorleston on Sea** was lost. In between, three or four closures occurred in 1964, 1966, 1968 and 1969. The only trunk lines remaining are Liverpool Street to **Kings Lynn** and Liverpool Street to Cromer and Sheringham via Norwich. In addition, the Norwich to **Ely** main line is equally important as a cross-country route, as is the **Ipswich** to **Ely** line via **Bury-St-Edmunds**, especially as a freight route from the port of Felixstowe to the North and the Midlands.

The running-in board (RIB) from Cromer is included below as the station itself was not fitted. It is most unusual to have such a large totem included in a RIB, but this sign is also shown because of the richness of the blue ER enamel, a rare survivor indeed.

Brandon and **Salhouse**, shown *in situ* in the 1970s, are both survivors. The former is a curiosity, because **Brandon** station is just within Norfolk, but the community it serves, on the Norwich to **Ely** line, is in Suffolk. The Grade II-listed station building was designed for the Eastern Counties Railway by the sculptor and architect John Thomas and completed in 1845. It is also well-known as a filming location for the TV series *Dad's Army*. (Thomas also worked on Buckingham Palace and the Palace of Westminster). **Salhouse** station, on the *Bittern Line* (Norwich to Sheringham), dates from 1874.

The two totems above have each appeared in auction four times and both stations are still open. These totems sit well together and are adjacent to each other on the Norwich to Great Yarmouth line, with the stations both serving the village of **Brundall**. **Reedham** and **Wroxham** are two more operational Norfolk stations.

Forncett and **Weybourne** below were closed in 1966 and 1964 respectively. The **Weybourne** totem seems to have taken rather a beating from the elements!

Of the 40 Norfolk totems only **Dersingham**, **Downham**, **Forncett**, **Haddiscoe**, **King's Lynn**, **Reedham** and **Wroxham** have appeared in auction 10 times or more and 29 of the Norfolk totems have appeared 5 times or fewer: Norfolk is also not easy.

NOTTINGHAMSHIRE

Like its neighbour Derbyshire, this county is not often thought of as being an Eastern Region county and yet 17 stations were clothed in ER blue. Of the those, 3 were

closed in 1959 (**Cottam**, **Leverton** and **Southwell**), with **Daybrook** and **Gedling** also losses in 1960. Nottinghamshire blue totems rarely come up for auction, the most common being **Collingham** and **Cottam** at just 5 showings each. We have no survival data for **Newark Castle**, **Newark Northgate** or **Southwell**. The database pages contain 4 county rarities and when these are added to the quartet left, it forms the core of Nottinghamshire 'rare birds'. The 4 have just 7 auction appearances between them, making county blue totems elusive.

Above: Daybrook in 1975. *John Ford*

The photo of **Daybrook** above was taken six years before closure, while **Collingham** right remains operational today. **Daybrook** is ex-GNR, opened in 1876, but closed due to subsidence in Mapperley tunnel to the east; **Collingham** is on the Nottingham to **Lincoln** line. **Cottam** closed in November 1959 but the line is open to freight serving the nearby Cottam power station. **Rolleston Junction** served the **Southwell** branch off the **Nottingham** to **Newark** line. Today the station is simply called Rolleston.

Right: Collingham 1974. *Alan Young*

RUTLAND

Just one set of ER totems hung in this the smallest of English counties. **Essendine** totems have not been seen or heard of since the station closed in 1959.

SUFFOLK

This beautiful county was home to 41 stations signed in ER blue. We have no information on the whereabouts or survival of totems from **Bury-St-Edmunds** (note the recently discovered hyphenated layout), **Orwell** or **St. Olaves**. Examples of totems from the other 38 stations have survived and have been in auction. Suffolk totems are generally uncommon, with only **Felixstowe Town** (17), **Finningham** (12), **Leiston** & **Somerleyton** (11 each) reaching double-figure auction appearances. Our database contains photos of 10 of these, indicating the rarity and desirability of Suffolk totems. Other totem rarities include the following four examples.

Suffolk is blessed with attractive countryside, a wonderful coast and picturesque villages scattered throughout the county, all famous for being quintessentially English. These include **Cavendish**, **Clare**, Earl Soham, Kersey, **Lavenham**, **Long Melford**, Polstead and **Somerleyton;** some were the subjects for wonderful 1950s BR posters. On the coast, **Woodbridge** and Thorpeness are quite superb to visit, but with the exception of **Somerleyton**, totems from this listing are not easy to acquire.

Notice the small '**and**' on the **Saxham and Risby** totem, a layout used for **Hopton on Sea** also in Suffolk. (Only **Dore and Totley**, a Derbyshire blue, had a similar layout). Suffolk fared badly when the cuts came. The county lost 20 of its stations, the majority being in 1966 and 1967, one of these being **Saxham and Risby**. The earliest closures came in 1959 (**Orwell** and **St. Olaves**); the last in 1970 (**Corton**, **Hopton on Sea** and **Lowestoft North**).

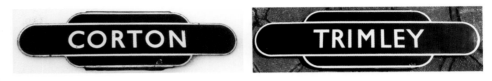

YORKSHIRE

This county, and particularly the area around Sheffield, was featured in more detail earlier in this chapter. Yorkshire was the subject of wholesale station closures between 1955 and 1995. Of the 36 stations with blue ER totems, only 14 remain open today. When BR was formed, Yorkshire had several duplicate routes, so rationalisation was inevitable. Furthermore, with the demise of both coal and steel industries in the area the railways became uneconomic to operate; these two factors were responsible for the severe pruning. The two stations, whose weather-beaten totems are presented first in the foursome right, closed in 1959, whilst stations represented by last two totems remain open. Seven stations were lost in 1959 and a further six suffered closure in 1968.

Station Name	County in 1956	Layout	Flange	Closed	Auction	Survived
ACLE	Norfolk		HF		•	•
ALDEBURGH	Suffolk		HF	1966	•	•
ALFORD TOWN	Lincolnshire		HF	1970		•
ALFORD TOWN	Lincolnshire		FF	1970	•	•
ALRESFORD	Essex		HF			
ALTHORPE	Lincolnshire		HF		•	•
ANGEL ROAD	Middlesex		FF		•	
APPLEBY	Lincolnshire		FF	1967	•	•
ATTERCLIFFE ROAD	Yorkshire		FF		•	•
ATTLEBOROUGH	Norfolk		HF		•	•
AUDLEY END	Essex		HF		•	•
BALDOCK	Hertfordshire		HF			
BARKING	Essex		HF			
BARNETBY	Lincolnshire		HF		•	•
BARNSLEY EXCHANGE	Yorkshire	2L	HF			•
BARNWELL JUNCTION	Cambridgeshire	2L	HF	1962	•	•
BARROW HILL	Derbyshire		HF	1954	•	•
BARTLOW	Essex		FF	1967	•	•
BEAUCHIEF	Yorkshire		HF	1961	•	•
BECCLES *large letters*	Suffolk		HF		•	•
BECONTREE	Essex		HF		•	•
BENFLEET	Essex		HF			
BENTLEY	Suffolk		FF	1966	•	•
BETHNAL GREEN	London		HF			
BIGGLESWADE	Bedfordshire		HF		•	•
BILLERICAY	Essex		HF			
BIRDBROOK	Essex		HF	1962	•	•
BISHOPS STORTFORD	Hertfordshire		HF		•	•
BLACKHORSE ROAD	Essex		HF		•	
BLEASBY	Nottinghamshire		HF		•	•
BOSTON	Lincolnshire		HF		•	•
BOWES PARK	Middlesex		HF			•

1L = one line: 2L = two line: LP = Lower panel

Station Name		County in 1956	Layout	Flange	Closed	Auction	Survived
BRAMPTON	still up in 1982	Suffolk		FF		•	•
BRANDON		Norfolk		HF		•	•
BRAUGHING		Hertfordshire		HF/FF	1964	•	•
BRIGG		Lincolnshire		FF		•	•
BRIGHTSIDE		Yorkshire		FF	1995		•
BRIMSDOWN		Middlesex		FF			
BROMLEY		London		HF		•	•
BROMLEY-BY-BOW	(sticker over Bromley)	London		HF		•	•
BROOKMANS PARK		Hertfordshire		HF		•	•
BROXBOURNE		Hertfordshire		HF		•	•
BRUCE GROVE		Middlesex		FF			
BRUNDALL		Norfolk		HF		•	•
BRUNDALL GARDENS HALT		Norfolk	LP	FF		•	•
BUNTINGFORD		Hertfordshire		HF	1964	•	•
BURES		Essex		HF		•	•
BURNHAM-ON-CROUCH		Essex		HF		•	•
BURNT MILL		Essex		FF			
BURSTON		Norfolk		HF	1966	•	•
BURTON JOYCE		Nottinghamshire		HF		•	•
BURY-ST-EDMUNDS		Suffolk		HF			
BUSH HILL PARK		Middlesex		HF		•	•
CAMBRIDGE		Cambridgeshire		HF			
CANTLEY		Norfolk		HF		•	•
CARLTON & NETHERFIELD		Nottinghamshire	LP	HF			
CAVENDISH		Suffolk		HF	1967	•	•
CHADWELL HEATH		Essex		HF			
CHALKWELL		Essex		HF			
CHAPELTOWN SOUTH		Yorkshire	2L	HF		•	•
CHATTERIS		Cambridgeshire		HF	1967	•	•
CHELMSFORD		Essex		HF		•	•
CHESHUNT		Hertfordshire		HF			•
CHESTERFIELD CENTRAL		Derbyshire	2L	HF	1963	•	•

1L = one line: 2L = two line: LP = Lower panel

Station Name		County in 1956	Layout	Flange	Closed	Auction	Survived
CHESTERFIELD MIDLAND		Derbyshire	LP	HF		•	•
CLACTON ON SEA		Essex	LP	HF			•
CLACTON ON SEA		Essex	1L	HF		•	•
CLAPTON		London		FF			
CLARE		Suffolk		HF	1967	•	•
COLCHESTER	large letters	Essex		HF			
COLLINGHAM		Nottinghamshire		HF		•	•
CONISBROUGH		Yorkshire		HF		•	•
CORTON		Suffolk		HF	1970	•	•
COTTAM		Nottinghamshire		FF	1959	•	•
CRESSING		Essex		HF		•	•
CREWS HILL		Middlesex		HF			•
CROUCH END		Middlesex		HF	1954	•	•
CROWLE CENTRAL		Lincolnshire	LP	HF		•	•
CUFFLEY		Hertfordshire		HF		•	•
DAGENHAM DOCK		Essex	1L	HF			
DAGENHAM EAST		Essex	1L	HF		•	•
DAGENHAM HEATHWAY		Essex	1L	HF		•	•
DARFIELD		Yorkshire		HF	1963	•	•
DARNALL		Yorkshire		HF/FF		•	•
DAYBROOK		Nottinghamshire		HF	1960	•	•
DEEPCAR		Yorkshire		HF	1959	•	•
DERBY ROAD		Suffolk		HF		•	•
DERSINGHAM		Norfolk		FF	1969	•	•
DISS	large letters	Norfolk		HF		•	•
DODWORTH		Yorkshire		HF	1959	•	•
DORE & TOTLEY		Derbyshire		HF		•	•
DORE AND TOTLEY	small 'and'	Derbyshire		HF		•	•
DOVERCOURT BAY		Essex		HF		•	•
DOWNHAM		Norfolk		HF/FF		•	•
DRONFIELD	*re-opened 1981	Derbyshire		HF	1967*	•	•
DRAYTON		Norfolk		HF	1959		
DULLINGHAM		Cambridgeshire		HF		•	•

1L = one line: 2L = two line: LP = Lower panel

Station Name		County in 1956	Layout	Flange	Closed	Auction	Survived
EARLS COLNE		Essex		HF	1962		•
EAST HAM		London		FF		•	•
EAST TILBURY		Essex		HF			
ECCLES ROAD		Norfolk		HF		•	•
ECCLESFIELD WEST		Yorkshire	2L	HF	1967		
ELM PARK	large letters	Essex		HF		•	•
ELMSWELL		Suffolk		HF		•	•
ELSECAR AND HOYLAND		Yorkshire	2L	HF			
ELSENHAM		Essex		FF		•	•
ELY		Cambridgeshire		HF			
EMERSON PARK HALT		Essex	1L	HF		•	•
ESSENDINE		Rutland		HF	1959		
FAKENHAM EAST		Norfolk	LP	HF	1964		•
FAKENHAM WEST		Norfolk	LP	HF	1959		
FELIXSTOWE BEACH		Suffolk	LP	HF	1967	•	•
FELIXSTOWE TOWN		Suffolk	1L	HF		•	•
FINNINGHAM		Suffolk		HF	1966	•	•
FIRSBY		Lincolnshire		HF	1970	•	•
FISKERTON		Nottinghamshire		HF		•	•
FLORDON		Norfolk		FF	1966	•	•
FORDHAM		Cambridgeshire		HF	1965		
FOREST GATE		London		HF		•	•
FORNCETT		Norfolk		FF	1966	•	•
FOXTON		Cambridgeshire		HF		•	•
FRINTON-ON-SEA		Essex		HF		•	•
FULBOURNE		Cambridgeshire		HF	1967	•	•
GAINSBOROUGH CENTRAL		Lincolnshire	2L	HF		•	•
GEDLING		Nottinghamshire		HF	1960	•	•
GLEMSFORD		Suffolk		HF	1967	•	•
GORLESTON-ON-SEA		Norfolk		HF	1970	•	•

1L = one line: 2L = two line: LP = Lower panel

Station Name	County in 1956	Layout	Flange	Closed	Auction	Survived
GOXHILL	Lincolnshire		HF		•	•
GRANTHAM	Lincolnshire		HF			
GRAYS	Essex		HF		•	•
GREAT BENTLEY	Essex		HF			
GREAT CHESTERFORD	Cambridgeshire		FF		•	•
GRIMSBY DOCKS	Lincolnshire		HF		•	•
GRIMSBY TOWN	Lincolnshire		HF		•	•
GRIMSTON ROAD	Norfolk		HF	1959		
HABROUGH	Lincolnshire		FF		•	•
HACKNEY DOWNS	London		HF			•
HADDISCOE	Norfolk		FF		•	•
HADHAM	Hertfordshire		HF	1964	•	•
HALESWORTH	Suffolk		HF		•	•
HALSTEAD	Essex		HF	1962		•
HARLING ROAD	Norfolk		FF		•	•
HARLOW some carried label 'Mill' in lower panel	Essex		HF			•
HARRINGAY (was Harringay West 1951-1971)	London		HF		•	•
HARRINGAY PARK	London	1L	HF		•	•
HARRINGAY WEST	London	LP	HF		•	•
(renamed from Harringay 1951)						
HARSTON	Cambridgeshire		FF	1963		•
HARWICH TOWN	Essex		HF		•	•
HATFIELD	Hertfordshire		HF		•	•
HATFIELD PEVEREL	Essex		HF			•
HAUGHLEY	Suffolk		HF	1967	•	•
HAVERHILL	Suffolk		HF	1967	•	•
HEACHAM	Norfolk		FF	1969	•	•
HEATH	Derbyshire		HF	1963		•
HECKINGTON	Lincolnshire		HF			•
HEELEY	Yorkshire		HF	1968	•	•
HERTFORD EAST	Hertfordshire	1L	HF		•	•
HERTFORD NORTH	Hertfordshire	1L	HF			•
HIGHAM	Suffolk		HF	1967	•	•

1L = one line: 2L = two line: LP = Lower panel

Station Name		County in 1956	Layout	Flange	Closed	Auction	Survived
HIGHAMS PARK		Essex		FF			•
HISTON		Cambridgeshire		HF	1970	•	•
HITCHIN		Hertfordshire		HF			•
HOE STREET		Essex		FF			
HOLBEACH		Lincolnshire		HF	1959		•
HOLMES	large letters	Yorkshire		HF	1955	•	•
HOLT	*heritage station open 1987	Norfolk		HF	1964*	•	•
HOPTON ON SEA	small 'on'	Suffolk		HF	1970	•	•
HORNCHURCH		Essex		HF			
HORNSEY		Middlesex		HF		•	•
HUNSTANTON		Norfolk		HF	1969	•	•
HYKEHAM		Lincolnshire		HF		•	•
HYTHE		Essex		HF			
INGATESTONE		Essex		FF		•	•
IPSWICH		Suffolk		HF		•	•
KELVEDON		Essex		FF		•	•
KENNETT		Cambridgeshire		HF		•	•
KILLAMARSH CENTRAL		Derbyshire	2L	HF	1963	•	•
KILNHURST CENTRAL		Yorkshire	LP	HF	1968	•	•
KILNHURST WEST		Yorkshire	LP	HF	1968	•	•
KINGS CROSS		London		HF		•	•
KINGS CROSS YORK ROAD		London	LP	FF	1977	•	•
KING'S LYNN		Norfolk		FF		•	•
KIRBY CROSS		Essex		HF		•	•
KIRTON		Lincolnshire		HF	1961	•	•
KIVETON BRIDGE		Yorkshire		FF		•	•
KIVETON PARK		Yorkshire		HF		•	•
KNEBWORTH		Hertfordshire		HF/FF		•	•
LAINDON		Essex		HF			
LANGWITH		Derbyshire		HF	1964		

1L = one line: 2L = two line: LP = Lower panel

Station Name		County in 1956	Layout	Flange	Closed	Auction	Survived
LAVENHAM		Suffolk		HF	1961	•	•
LEA BRIDGE	*new station 2016	London		HF/FF	1985*	•	•
LEIGH-ON-SEA		Essex		HF			
LEISTON		Suffolk		HF	1966	•	•
LETCHWORTH		Hertfordshire		HF			•
LEVERTON		Nottinghamshire		FF	1959	•	•
LEYTON MIDLAND RD.		Essex	LP	HF		•	•
LEYTONSTONE HIGH ROAD		Essex	LP	HF			•
LINCOLN CENTRAL		Lincolnshire	LP	HF		•	•
LINCOLN ST. MARKS		Lincolnshire		HF	1986	•	•
LINGWOOD		Norfolk		HF		•	•
LINTON		Cambridgeshire		HF	1967		
LITTLEPORT		Cambridgeshire		FF		•	•
LITTLEWORTH		Lincolnshire		FF	1961	•	•
LONG MELFORD		Suffolk		HF	1967	•	•
LONG STANTON		Cambridgeshire		HF	1970	•	•
LOUTH	large letters	Lincolnshire		HF	1970	•	•
LOWDHAM		Nottinghamshire		HF		•	•
LOWER EDMONTON		Middlesex		FF			•
LOWESTOFT NORTH		Norfolk	2L	HF	1970	•	•
MABLETHORPE		Lincolnshire		HF/FF	1970	•	•
MAGDALEN ROAD		Norfolk		FF	1968	•	•
MALDON EAST		Essex	LP	HF	1964		•
MANNINGTREE		Essex		HF			
MANOR PARK		Essex		HF		•	•
MARCH		Cambridgeshire		HF			
MARKET RASEN		Lincolnshire		HF		•	•
MARKS TEY		Essex		HF		•	•
MARYLAND		London		HF			
MELDRETH		Cambridgeshire		HF		•	•
MELLIS		Suffolk		HF	1966	•	•
MELTON CONSTABLE		Norfolk		FF	1964	•	•

1L = one line: 2L = two line: LP = Lower panel

Station Name	County in 1956	Layout	Flange	Closed	Auction	Survived
MEXBOROUGH	Yorkshire		HF		•	•
MILLHOUSES & ECCLESALL	Yorkshire	LP	HF	1968	•	•
MISTLEY	Essex		HF		•	•
MOULTON	Lincolnshire		HF	1959	•	•
NARBOROUGH AND PENTNEY	Norfolk	LP	FF	1968	•	•
NEEDHAM *re-opened as Needham Market 1971	Suffolk		FF	1967*	•	•
NEW BARNET	Hertfordshire		HF			
NEW HOLLAND TOWN	Lincolnshire	1L	HF			
NEW SOUTHGATE	Middlesex		HF		•	•
NEWARK CASTLE existence to confirm	Nottinghamshire	?	?			
NEWARK NORTHGATE	Nottinghamshire	2L	HF			
NEWMARKET	Cambridgeshire		HF			
NEWPORT	Essex		FF		•	•
NOEL PARK	Middlesex		HF	1963	•	•
NORTH WALSHAM MAIN	Norfolk	LP	HF		•	•
NORTHUMBERLAND PK.	Middlesex		FF		•	•
OAKINGTON	Cambridgeshire		HF	1970	•	•
OAKLEIGH PARK	Hertfordshire		HF			
OCKENDON	Essex		HF			•
ORWELL	Suffolk		HF	1959		
OUGHTY BRIDGE	Yorkshire		HF	1959		
OULTON BROAD NORTH	Norfolk	2L	HF		•	•
OULTON BROAD SOUTH	Norfolk	2L	FF		•	•
PALACE GATES	Middlesex		HF	1963	•	•
PALMERS GREEN	Middlesex		HF		•	•
PARKGATE & RAWMARSH	Yorkshire	LP	HF	1968	•	•
PENISTONE Large letters	Yorkshire		HF			•
PETERBOROUGH EAST	Cambridgeshire	LP	HF	1966	•	•
PETERBOROUGH EAST	Cambridgeshire	2L	FF	1966	•	•
PETERBOROUGH NORTH	Cambridgeshire	2L	HF		•	•

1L = one line: 2L = two line: LP = Lower panel

Station Name		County in 1956	Layout	Flange	Closed	Auction	Survived
PITSEA		Essex		HF			•
PLAISTOW		Essex		HF		•	•
PONDERS END		Middlesex		FF		•	•
POTTERS BAR		Hertfordshire		HF			
PRITTLEWELL		Essex		HF			
PURFLEET		Essex		HF			
RADCLIFFE ON TRENT	Lightweight letters	Nottinghamshire		HF		•	•
RAINHAM		Essex		HF			
RAYLEIGH	large letters	Essex		HF			
RECTORY ROAD		London		FF			
REEDHAM		Norfolk		HF		•	•
RENISHAW CENTRAL		Derbyshire	LP	HF	1963		•
RETFORD		Nottinghamshire		HF		•	•
ROCHFORD	large letters	Essex		HF			
ROLLESTON JUNCTION		Nottinghamshire	LP	HF		•	•
ROTHERHAM CENTRAL	*new station 1987	Yorkshire	?	HF	1966*		
ROTHERHAM MASBOROUGH		Yorkshire	LP	FF	1988	•	•
ROYDON		Essex		HF		•	•
RYE HOUSE		Hertfordshire		HF			
SAFFRON WALDEN		Essex		FF	1964	•	•
SALHOUSE		Norfolk		FF		•	•
SANDY		Bedfordshire		HF/FF		•	•
SAWBRIDGEWORTH		Hertfordshire		FF		•	•
SAXHAM AND RISBY	small 'and'	Suffolk		HF	1967	•	•
SAXMUNDHAM		Suffolk		HF/FF		•	•
SEVEN SISTERS		Middlesex		FF		•	•
SHEEPBRIDGE		Derbyshire		HF	1967	•	•
SHELFORD		Cambridgeshire		FF			
SHEPRETH		Cambridgeshire		HF		•	•
SHIREBROOK WEST		Derbyshire	LP	HF	1964		•
SHOEBURYNESS		Essex		HF			•

1L = one line: 2L = two line: LP = Lower panel

Station Name	County in 1956	Layout	Flange	Closed	Auction	Survived
SIBLE AND CASTLE HEDINGHAM	Essex	2L	HF	1962		•
SILVER STREET	Middlesex		FF			
SILVERTOWN	Essex		FF	2006	•	•
SIX MILE BOTTOM	Cambridgeshire		HF	1967	•	•
SKEGNESS large letters	Lincolnshire		HF		•	•
SLEAFORD	Lincolnshire		HF		•	•
SNETTISHAM	Norfolk		FF	1969	•	•
SOHAM	Cambridgeshire		HF	1965	•	•
SOMERLEYTON	Suffolk		HF		•	•
SOMERSHAM	Huntingdon		HF	1967	•	•
SOUTH TOTTENHAM	Middlesex		HF		•	•
SOUTHEND-ON-SEA CENTRAL	Essex	LP	HF		•	•
SOUTHEND-ON-SEA EAST	Essex	LP	HF			
SOUTHEND-ON-SEA VICTORIA	Essex	LP	HF			
SOUTHWELL	Nottinghamshire		HF	1959		
SPALDING TOWN	Lincolnshire		HF		•	•
ST. BOTOLPHS	Essex		HF			
ST. IVES	Cambridgeshire		HF	1970	•	•
ST. JAMES STREET	Essex		FF		•	•
ST. MARGARETS	Hertfordshire		HF			
ST. NEOTS	Cambridgeshire		HF		•	•
ST. OLAVES	Suffolk		HF	1959		
STAINFORTH	Yorkshire		HF			•
STALLINGBOROUGH	Lincolnshire		FF			
STAMFORD HILL	Middlesex		FF			
STAMFORD TOWN	Lincolnshire	2L	HF		•	•
STANDON	Hertfordshire		HF	1964	•	•
STANFORD-LE-HOPE	Essex		HF			
STANSTED	Essex		FF		•	•
STAVELEY CENTRAL	Derbyshire	LP	HF	1963	•	•
STAVELEY WORKS	Derbyshire	1L	HF	1963		
STEPNEY EAST renamed Limehouse 1987	London	1L	HF			
STEVENAGE	Hertfordshire		HF		•	•

1L = one line: 2L = two line: LP = Lower panel

Station Name	County in 1956	Layout	Flange	Closed	Auction	Survived
STOKE	Suffolk		HF	1967	•	•
STOKE NEWINGTON	London		FF			
STOWMARKET	Suffolk		HF		•	•
STRATFORD	London		FF		•	•
STROUD GREEN	Middlesex		HF	1954		
STURMER	Essex		HF	1967	•	•
SUDBURY	Suffolk		HF		•	•
SUMMER LANE _totems still up in 1972_	Yorkshire		HF	1959	•	•
SUTTON BRIDGE	Lincolnshire		HF	1959	•	•
SUTTON-ON-SEA	Lincolnshire		HF/FF	1970	•	•
SWAFFHAM	Norfolk		HF	1968		•
SWINDERBY	Lincolnshire		HF/FF		•	•
SWINTON CENTRAL	Yorkshire	LP?	HF	1957		
THETFORD _large letters_	Norfolk		HF		•	•
THORNE NORTH	Yorkshire		HF		•	•
THORNE SOUTH	Yorkshire		HF		•	•
THORPE BAY	Essex		HF			•
THORPE-LE-SOKEN	Essex		HF		•	•
THURGARTON	Nottinghamshire		HF		•	•
THURSTON	Suffolk		HF		•	•
TILBURY RIVERSIDE	Essex	LP	HF			
TILBURY TOWN	Essex		HF		•	•
TIVETSHALL	Norfolk		FF	1966	•	•
TORKESEY _actual village name is Torksey_	Lincolnshire		HF	1959	•	•
TOTTENHAM	Middlesex		HF		•	•
TRIMLEY	Suffolk		HF		•	•
UPMINSTER	Essex		HF			
UPMINSTER BRIDGE	Essex		HF		•	•
UPNEY	Essex		HF		•	•
UPTON PARK	Essex		HF		•	•
WADSLEY BRIDGE	Yorkshire		HF	1959	•	•

1L = one line: 2L = two line: LP = Lower panel

Station Name		County in 1956	Layout	Flange	Closed	Auction	Survived
WAINFLEET		Lincolnshire		HF		•	•
WALTHAM CROSS		Hertfordshire		HF		•	•
WALTHAMSTOW		Essex		HF		•	•
WALTON ON NAZE		Essex		HF			
WANSTEAD PARK		Essex		HF		•	•
WARE		Hertfordshire		HF			•
WATERBEACH		Cambridgeshire		FF		•	•
WATH CENTRAL	totems still up in 1970	Yorkshire	LP	HF	1959	•	•
WATH NORTH		Yorkshire	LP	HF	1968		•
WEELEY		Essex		HF			
WELWYN GARDEN CITY (some top flange only)		Hertfordshire		HF		•	•
WELWYN NORTH		Hertfordshire		HF		•	•
WEST GREEN		Middlesex		HF	1963	•	•
WEST HAM (MANOR ROAD)		Essex	LP	HF		•	•
WEST RUNTON		Norfolk		HF		•	•
WESTCLIFF ON SEA		Essex	LP	HF		•	•
WESTERFIELD		Suffolk		HF		•	•
WEYBOURNE	*heritage station open 1975	Norfolk		HF	1964*	•	•
WHITE COLNE		Essex		HF	1962		•
WHITE HART LANE		Middlesex		HF			•
WHITE NOTLEY		Essex		HF		•	•
WHITTLESEA		Cambridgeshire		HF		•	•
WHITTLESFORD		Cambridgeshire		FF			•
WHITWELL		Derbyshire		HF	1964		
WICKFORD	large letters	Essex		HF		•	•
WICKHAM MARKET		Suffolk		HF		•	•
WINCHMORE HILL		Middlesex		HF			•
WISBECH NORTH		Cambridgeshire	LP	HF	1959	•	•
WITHAM	large letters	Essex		HF		•	•
WIVENHOE		Essex		HF			
WOMBWELL CENTRAL		Yorkshire	LP	HF	1959	•	•
WOMBWELL WEST		Yorkshire	2L	HF			•
WOOD GREEN		Middlesex		HF		•	•

1L = one line: 2L = two line: LP = Lower panel

Station Name	County in 1956	Layout	Flange	Closed	Auction	Survived
WOOD STREET	Essex		FF		•	•
WOODBRIDGE	Suffolk		HF		•	•
WOODGRANGE PARK	Essex		HF		•	•
WOODHALL JUNCTION	Lincolnshire		FF	1970	•	•
WOODHOUSE	Yorkshire		HF			
WORSTEAD	Norfolk		HF		•	•
WORSTEAD	Norfolk		FF			
WRABNESS	Essex		HF		•	•
WROXHAM	Norfolk		HF/FF		•	•
WYMONDHAM	Norfolk		HF		•	•
YELDHAM	Essex		HF	1962		•

1L = one line: 2L = two line: LP = Lower panel

Other Eastern Region Collectables

5
The London Midland Region

Opening Comments

At formation on 1 January 1948, the London Midland Region (LMR) was based totally on former LMS routes in England and Wales. The LMS had services into Scotland, and these became part of the Scottish Region. The LMR headquarters was initially at Euston House, London, but in the 1960s it was moved to Stanier House in Birmingham, a huge purpose-built Brutalist-style office block in Holliday Street on the site of the former MR Goods Depot. It was ironic that the Euston Doric Arch was demolished (and the wonderful St Pancras was only narrowly saved). The LMR 'modernised' Euston station into an ugly faceless structure, while St Pancras is superbly restored.

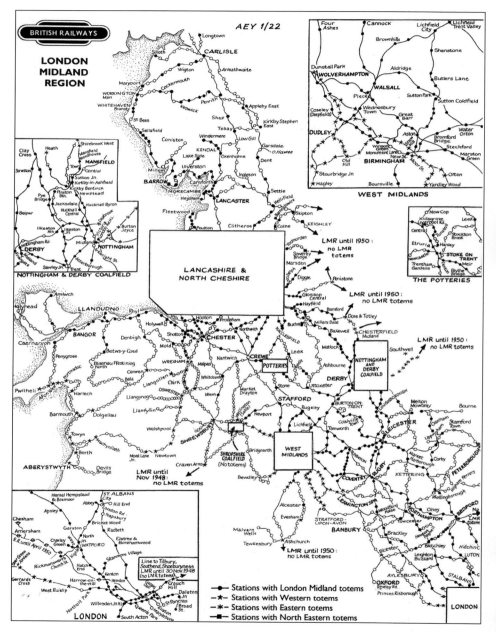

The LMS was the largest of the 'Big Four' in 1947. At 7,790 route miles it stretched from London to the Scottish Highlands, south to north, and from Essex to Anglesey, east to west. At formation in January 1948, the Scottish routes were hived off (ex-Caledonian at 1,170 miles, ex G&SWR at 499 miles and ex-Highland at 506 miles), leaving just less than 5,000 route miles in England and Wales. This included the route from Fenchurch Street to **Shoeburyness,** with a loop through **Tilbury,** which the Midland Railway had purchased in 1912 – maroon corporate colours in dark blue territory! This was soon rectified in 1949.

Brief Regional History

There is a rich railway heritage bound up in the LMR. Two of the most influential Victorian companies, the Midland Railway (MR) and the London & North Western Railway (LNWR), made strange partners in 1923 because, for over fifty years prior to that date, they were bitter enemies. Some fourteen other companies, most notably the Lancashire and Yorkshire (L&YR) and the Furness Railway (FR) were added to the LMS 'cocktail'. The four totems below are examples from each of these companies.

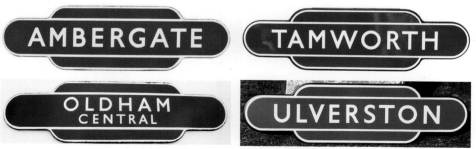

The LNWR was the heavyweight in this LMS 'cocktail' at 2,668 route miles, followed by the MR at 2,170 miles. In comparison, the FR was a mere 158 miles, but they helped develop Barrow Docks, an important terminal in years past for the export of iron ore, and today a crucial part of UK military shipbuilding.

The LMR's history dates right back to the Grand Junction Railway (1833–1846) who built the world's first trunk railway, covering the 82 miles from **Birmingham** to **Wolverhampton**, **Stafford**, Crewe and **Warrington**, where it joined the Liverpool & Manchester Railway line. In 1846 the GJR merged with London & Birmingham Railway (L&BR) and the Manchester & Birmingham to form the LNWR.

By 1838, the L&BR had opened the 112-mile long route from Euston to Curzon Street, so becoming the world's first inter-city line. At Curzon Street, adjacent platforms allowed passengers to change to the GJR for onward travel north. The line was engineered by Robert Stephenson, who routed it via **Rugby** and **Coventry** and into Birmingham; a quartet from the 16 station stops is depicted below.

Once the main lines were in place, branch lines were constructed, first to **Aylesbury** in 1839, **Rugby** to the East Midlands in 1840 and **Blisworth** across to **Peterborough** in 1845. Soon, the main southern components of what was to become the West Coast Main Line (WCML) were in place. The northern half was also built in sections, with **Wigan–Preston** line being opened by the North Union Railway in 1838. The Lancaster & Preston Junction Railway (L&PJR) opened the next section in 1840, and the final part in England (**Penrith** to **Carlisle**) was opened by the Lancaster & Carlisle Railway (L&CR) in 1846. All these 'minnows' were eventually absorbed into the LNWR, who quickly consolidated timetables and operations.

Records show that the northern route was controversial, avoiding some population centres and constructing steep gradients in place of a summit tunnel, the costs of which would have been enormous; **Carlisle** station costs fell mainly on the L&CR.

By the early 20th century, the Midland Railway (MR), headquartered in Derby, had grown to be one of Britain's largest railway companies. The lines, emanating from Derby and reaching London St. Pancras, Manchester, Birmingham, Carlisle, and on towards the south-west, such as **Gloucester Eastgate**, had been gained by acquisition and construction; the fabulous **Settle–Carlisle** line was built by the MR. As well as railways, the company operated ships from **Heysham** to Douglas, in the Isle of Man, and Belfast. They ran a prestigious chain of hotels at Bradford, Derby, Morecambe and St. Pancras. The word 'Midland' was all over their territory!

By the 1840s, the MR had taken over smaller companies in Nottinghamshire, Leicestershire and Derbyshire, giving access to lucrative coalfield freight revenues. Their long-term strategy was impeccable as **Derby** was at the junction of the two main routes from London to Scotland, by its connections to the L&BR in the south and to the north via the York and North Midland Railway, giving them initial control of London to Scotland routes and the North-east. Within twenty years they had consolidated further and their line into London ran through a gap in the Chiltern Hills via **Luton**. Sheffield soon gained a mainline station. After the building of the **Settle** and **Carlisle** line in the 1870s, the MR's final connection opened in 1894 between Sheffield and Manchester, via a branch at **Dore & Totley** to **Chinley**.

The MR had high engineering standards so when these were combined with strong LNWR practices, the resulting LMS had a sound technical base. However, the MR was not the only company operating in the north. The Lancashire & Yorkshire Railway (L&YR) developed a network of routes, including the linking of Manchester and Leeds via **Rochdale**, Hebden Bridge and **Dewsbury**.

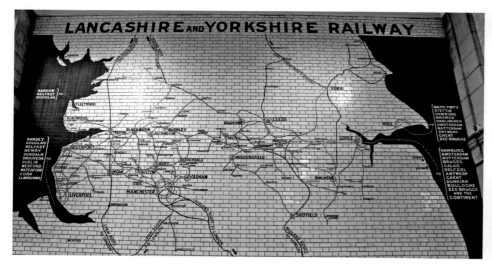

The final section, which included a mile-long tunnel near the summit north of **Littleborough**, was completed by 1841. There were many other routes, but no clear main lines; the large map at **Manchester Victoria** station (above) depicts the higgledy-piggledy network that linked Liverpool, Southport, Manchester, **Blackburn**, **Burnley**, **Bradford**, Leeds, Sheffield, Doncaster, **York** and Hull. Much of this was achieved between 1840 and 1850 and many of the stations that carried LMR totems were ex-L&YR. The L&YR amalgamated with the LNWR in 1922 and, a year later, both moved into the new LMS at grouping.

In the Manchester/Liverpool/Cheshire area, one of the larger companies in Victorian times was the Cheshire Lines Committee (CLC). Formed by the Great Northern (GNR) working closely with the Manchester, Sheffield and Lincolnshire

Railway, their aim was to counter LNWR growth in their areas. There are some wonderfully named CLC stations that carried totems, including the pair below.

Formed in 1865, the CLC expanded gradually developing commuter lines in Cheshire, South Lancashire and the Wirral, playing its part in the growth of the Lancashire coalfield and the Mersey Docks traffic. When the LMS formed in 1923, they remained outside but were incorporated in BR's LM Region. They had some wonderful stations, a trio of which was lost during the pruning of duplicate routes (**Liverpool Central**, **Manchester Central** and **Chester Northgate**).

In the northern section of the new LMR, two historic companies were included: the Furness Railway (FR), from north Lancashire and southern Westmorland, and the Cockermouth, Keswick and Penrith Railway (CK&PR), in and around the Lake District. The FR dates from 1844, carrying passengers from 1846. The CK&PR formed some twenty years later and used to operate the fabulous route along the shores of **Bassenthwaite Lake**. This became the A66 dual carriageway road. For years the station was much neglected, but, thankfully, it is now fully restored (see page 117).

The Mersey Railway had not joined the LMS in 1923 but was included in the new LMR in 1948. After trying steam locos inside the Mersey Tunnel, they were forced to adopt electric traction as early as 1903. At its peak around 1890 almost 10 million passengers travelled annually. The main line linked **Liverpool Central**, **James Street**, Hamilton Square, **Birkenhead Park**, **Birkenhead Central** and **Rock Ferry,** with links to other networks in the area. At the **James Street** and **Hamilton Square** stations, maroon roundels were found instead of 3-foot totems.

Lancaster and **Carlisle** (1846), then west to **Chester** and Holyhead (1848), east through **Bedford** and **Cambridg**e (1865) and south into Central and South Wales (1865 onwards). Desirable collectors' pieces from these expansions might include the following, two from England and two from Wales.

The LNWR described itself as Britain's 'Premier Line' and, as the UK's largest stock-holding company by the late-19th century, its revenue stream alone justified the title. It had many 'firsts': the first company to run a mail service, the first to use water troughs, and the first to consolidate locomotive building (at Crewe Works). There were two main lines, London Euston via Birmingham to the north, and Liverpool trans-Pennine to Leeds, but in addition there were secondary major routes to Derby, Nottingham, Peterborough and South Wales. At its peak, the LNWR ran 2,707 miles of services (including joint workings) and employed well over 100,000 people. The company had some impressive city stations, **Birmingham New Street**, **Leeds Central**, Liverpool Lime Street and **Manchester Exchange** for example. A 1964–67 rebuild ruined **New Street**, but Lime Street (1836) is a superb station, the world's oldest operational terminus.

The picture above shows **Liverpool James Street** station in June 1957. As well as roundels, there were unique totem panels at least 6 feet by 2 feet in size!

Throughout this short review, the LNWR keeps cropping up. During the Victorian years they developed right through England and Wales, to the consternation of any rivals – but especially the Midland. Their first major expansion was north towards

After WW2, as the LMS network was largely bankrupt, nationalisation was inevitable, but even so, the task in putting all the history, assets and liabilities together was daunting. This was not helped by disagreements within the BR's senior management, with the British Transport Commission (BTC) and the Railway Executive (RE) arguing on just about everything concerned with rail operations. Even the initial network was illogical (but historical), with LNER lines in North Wales and LMR lines in Essex. Within a year, Essex routes were transferred to the ER. The next major boundary change occurred in April 1950, when LMR tracks in South Wales and to the south-west of Birmingham went into the WR, lines in Lincolnshire and South Yorkshire went to the ER, the **Oxford** to **Cambridge** line was shared between the WR, LMR and ER and the LMR lost lines in West Yorkshire to the NER. In return, the LMR gained the GCR main line south of **Heath**, including all the stations, two of which appear below.

The next change happened in 1963, when services across the West Midlands were rationalised and many WR lines in the region's northern part were transferred into the LMR. The WR northern boundary became a line formed by stations **Craven Arms & Stokesay**, **Blackwell**, Milcote Halt, Aynho for Deddington and Aynho Park Platform. Within ten years the LMR had closed the former GWR main line as their route from **Birmingham New Street** to **Wolverhampton High Level** was electrified and upgraded.

Major loco sheds that moved into the region such as **Shrewsbury** (originally 84G then 89A) were given LMR shed codes (6D). Finally in 1974, the Chiltern Main Line from Marylebone through Banbury and into **Birmingham Moor Street** was also moved from the WR to the LMR. The *Beeching Report* had recommended image overhaul as well as line closures. As the totem installation was wound down, new corporate signage appeared and the romance of totems sadly waned. The LMR ceased to be an operating unit in its own right in the 1980s and was wound up at the end of 1992.

LMR Totem Geography
Alan Young & Richard Furness

The LMR had an extensive 4,993 route miles at its formation in 1948, based largely on LMS lines (minus those in Scotland) but the figure also included some joint routes, some of which it soon lost (the S&D went to the SR, and the M&GNR from Bourne became ER). This still left the LMR as a huge network, stretching to **Bristol**, **Carmarthen**, **Goole**, **Cambridge**, and **Shoeburyness**, its lines deeply penetrating into the Eastern, North Eastern and Western Regions. No maroon totems were fitted by the LMR on outlying lines that it lost up to April 1950. Because of the long-shaped network, as in this chapter's opening map, we have split the region into two sections to show totem detail.

The map that follows shows LMR lines from London to Crewe with maroon totems depicted as black-filled circles and WR stations with totems by stars. In January 1963, major boundary changes between the WR and LMR took place, with the WR losing over 100 stations that carried 'chocolate & creams'. After the changes, the existing totems were not removed and replaced, so for the last decade of their lives, many newly acquired LMR stations sported WR totems. The LMR did not install totems as quickly as the other regions but, surprisingly, did install totems at six of their stations which were early closures. This list includes **Aylesbury High Street**, **Golborne North**, **Rickmansworth Church Street**, **Stanmore Village**, **St Helen's Central** and **Towcester**, but only **Aylesbury High Street** is a known survivor (*in-situ* picture below) and none have yet appeared in auction.

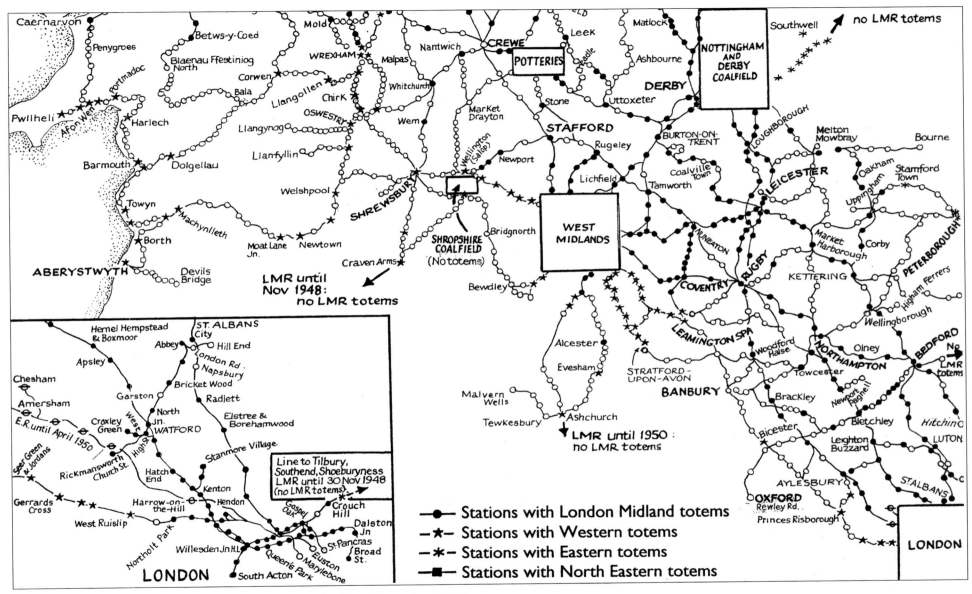

Southern section of BR's London Midland Region. *Map by Alan Young, June 2020*

Aylesbury High Street only carried this name from 23 September 1950 to 31 January 1953, so presumably the totems were just over two years old at closure. **Rickmansworth Church Street** totems had an even shorter life (1 July 1950 to 3 March 1952)! Other early LMR southern area closures included **Ampthill**, **Barton & Walton**, **Four Ashes** and **Oakley.**

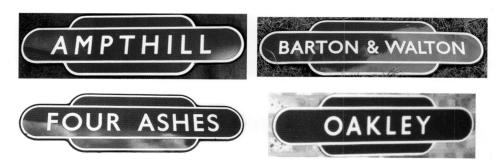

The slower pace of totem installation compared to other regions also meant the LMR adopted another quirk, the use of poster totems, a practice not used elsewhere. These were large posters with the totem logo in the centre. Research by a Totem Study Group (TSG) member showed that no fewer than 623 stations were intended to have posters, with lists of locations where they definitely existed. Enamel totems replaced many such items (e.g. **Aldridge** or **Cannock**) but posters probably survived until closure (vandals and elements permitting) as at Heapey, Brinscall, Withnell and Feniscowles between **Chorley** and **Cherry Tree.**

Aldridge and Cannock poster totems *in situ*, around 1959. *Clive Holden*

Most poster totems were in the northern part of the LMR, but we feel the enamel variants of those known in the southern area are so much nicer!

In the late 1950s, the LMR embarked on a more vigorous programme of totem installation, following the HF variants installed early in the LMR's tenure. The later variants were predominantly FF, but the LMR also used many face-drilled designs, far more than any other region, as illustrated by the Midlands pair below.

The LMR showered totems liberally along most main lines, including relatively minor stations, for example between Euston and Birmingham, and between St. Pancras, Nottingham/Derby and Manchester, but the map also shows lines where few totems appeared (**Towcester** to **Market Harborough** for example). Some notable LM main stations never had totems, including London (Euston, Marylebone and St. Pancras – but see page 351 for a recent discovery), Manchester (Piccadilly and Mayfield), Liverpool (Lime Street, Exchange and Central High Level), Nottingham Victoria, and Crewe.

In the West Midlands the LMR was very enthusiastic in fitting totems, providing them at all stations except Winson Green (closed 1957) and Monument Lane (1958); they even installed them at **Bromford Bridge**, an untimetabled racecourse station. **Smethwick Rolfe Street** received totems as late as June 1963 when renamed.

In the LMR's northern section map alongside, notice particularly the three competing routes from **Birmingham** to **Wolverhampton**. Outside this enlarged area, **Coventry–Nuneaton** also had a complete set of totem stations, including **Chilvers Coton** and **Daimler Halt**. It is worth noting that apart from Daimler, only **Canley, Leire and Rushcliffe** had 'Halt' totems, but others (e.g. **Upton-by-Chester, Hawarden Bridge** and **Newchurch**) had their totems without the word 'Halt' included.

The LMR's unwillingness to fit totems at halts extended to ex-LNWR 'motor stations' such as Bow Brickhill, Buckinghamshire, and Star Crossing, Flintshire. The LMR had 825 stations fitted with totems, substantially more than the other five regions. To this figure can be added the hundred or so acquired from the WR, some of which were the last the LMR removed: (WR Totems at **Smethwick West** and **Cradley Heath & Cradley** were in still proudly hanging in July 1979).

As in other regions, main urban centres tended to have many totem stations. The randomness of southern area installations extended northwards, where the greatest concentration of maroon totems occurred. The map on page 106 shows the Derby/Nottingham area and the North Wales Coast route were well provided, but the Potteries area was only around 50% fitted, with isolated examples at **Kidsgrove, Newcastle, Stoke on Trent**, some on the **Hanley** loop, and southwards towards **Blythe Bridge**; none appeared on the line to Leek (closed 1956). The Nottingham–Derby coalfield had a good supply, but with a few gaps, as on the **Pinxton South** branch, and none on the Shirebrook South line.

The North Wales Coast route affords collectors the chance to garner totems with some simply wonderful names. In travelling from **Chester General** to **Menai Bridge**, no fewer than 19 stations were fitted with totems out of a total of 23 along the line. If the branch to **Llandudno** via **Deganwy** is included, the totem count available rises to 21. This line contrasts with the limited totem supply on the Blaenau Ffestiniog North branch (only at **Dolgarrog**, and **Llanrwst & Trefriw** and **Betws-y-Coed**, but none at the terminus) and between Gaerwen and **Amlwch**. Only two are found on Anglesey (**Llangefni** and **Amlwch**, both closed in 1964) and recent photo evidence confirms Holyhead was not provided with totems as previously thought.

Few Settle & Carlisle stations had totems, only **Settle**, **Horton-in-Ribblesdale**, **Dent** and **Appleby West**, which seems a strange assortment. Some secondary lines also had an unpredictable distribution of totems. Between Chester, **Northwich** and Manchester minor stations at **Ashley** and **Mobberley** were fitted, but Cuddington, Delamere and Plumley were not, all suggesting there was no logic to the signage policy.

The Cumbrian Coast route likewise had a majority of totem stations (e.g. **Askam**, **Drigg**, **Seascale**) but some, which are still open, did not: Braystones, Green Road, Nethertown, St Bees, and Millom. This last-named was one of the more important stops, which had LMS hawkseyes *in situ* until 1973. **Skipton** to **Carnforth** also had many omissions, including Giggleswick: what a real pity! However other lines of limited importance had totems liberally provided, such as all the wonderfully named intermediates from the **Penrith** to **Keswick** route: **Blencow**, **Penruddock**, **Troutbeck**, and **Threlkeld** is quite a set.

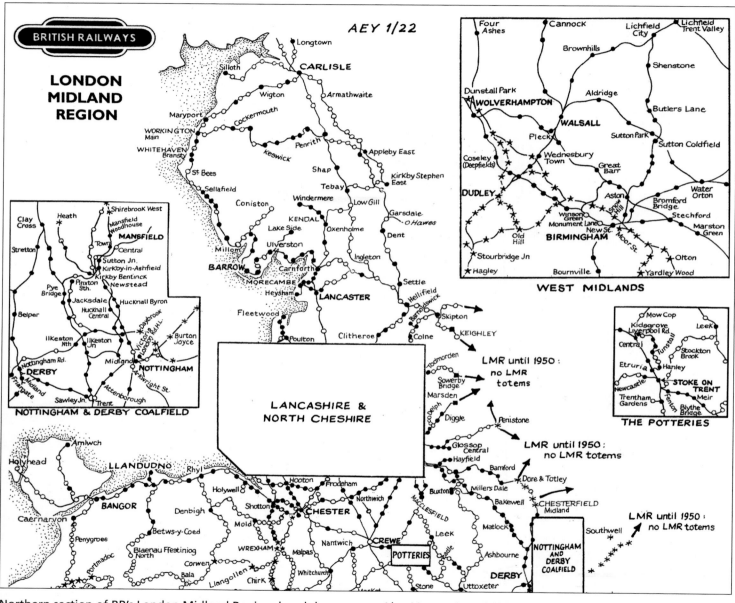

Northern section of BR's London Midland Region, hand drawn map. *Alan Young, June 2020*

Travels in the North Cheshire/Liverpool/Manchester Area

The map opposite of the northern-half of the LMR contained a large box covering Lancashire and North Cheshire. Below we show the detail, a plethora of lines and stations, seemingly inter-connecting every town via a haphazard series of Victorian-built routes. Anybody trying to collect a set from here is in for a quite a task!

For the first few months of BR's administration in 1948, the area's lines were divided between the London Midland and Eastern Regions, plus the Cheshire Lines Committee (CLC). The CLC was independent until 30 November 1948, so it was only then that such routes as Liverpool to Manchester via **Glazebrook**, **Altrincham and Bowdon** to **Chester** and the Southport (Lord Street) branch officially became LMR.

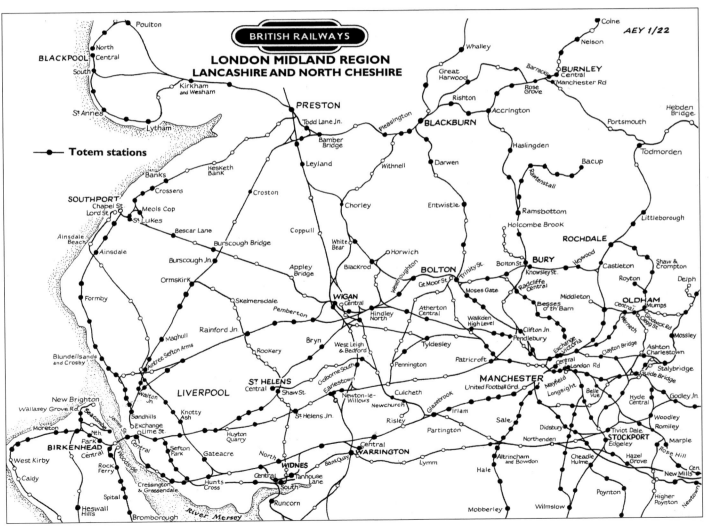

Northern section of BR's London Midland Region, hand drawn map.
Alan Young, June 2020

The ER's ex-Great Central system included the Woodhead route into **Manchester Central** via **Fallowfield**, as well as detached sections between Wigan Central/**St Helen's Central** and **Glazebrook**, plus the **Bidston** to Wrexham line: yes, for a short while the ER did extend into North Wales!

By 1950 the entire area was in the LMR. However, the ER continued to operate services up to 1959 in the Manchester area, including Manchester to Macclesfield via **Bollington**, and Stockport to Oldham via **Guide Bridge.**

On acquiring the ER routes, the LMR swiftly installed half-flanged totems at **St Helens Central** and at all stations from **Ashburys for Belle Vue** to **Glossop** and **Hadfield** (except, it seems, **Godley Junction**, which later had fully-flanged specimens). This was the longest succession of early-totem stations in Lancashire–North Cheshire, and it is possible that it was the LMR's way of imprinting its image on the ER-operated 1954-electrified Woodhead main line services.

Few other stations in the area had half-flanged totems. Some major stations were favoured, such as **Preston**, **Rochdale**, **Bury Bolton Street**, **Blackpool Central**, **Blackpool North** and **Blackpool South**.

Three ex-GWR/ MS joint stations (**Rock Ferry**, **Bebington & New Ferry**, and **Spital**) had half-flanged totems, as with four stations on the Liverpool Exchange to Southport Chapel Street line (**Sandhills**, **Marsh Lane and Strand Road**, **Ainsdale**, and **Hillside**). **Aughton Park** and its neighbour **Town Green & Aughton** received early totems as did **Lytham** and **Ansdell & Fairhaven**, but otherwise distribution appears random, as the map shows. Contrast Southport via **Formb**y to Liverpool, with **Ormskirk** via **St Helen's Shaw Street** to **Widnes South**. The two pictures of the area's *in-situ* totems below are absolutely nostalgic. **Upholland** was named Pimbo Lane until 1902.

Presumably on renaming in 1952, **Todd Lane Junction** (formerly Preston Junction) received totems; furthermore, **Reddish North** and **Reddish South** were renamed in 1951 and 1952 respectively, to identify the former LMS and LNER stations. **Golborne South** and **Golborne North** had been renamed in 1949 for the same reason. They must have received half-flanged totems, but none seem to have survived.

The likely widespread use of 'poster totems' in the area from 1950, mentioned on page 104, could explain the limited early use of enamel totems. By the late 1950s the LMR gained new enthusiasm for their installation, which, probably from 1957, were fully-flanged. Most of the area's stations were eventually fitted, many, as the database shows, being face-drilled. The **Blackburn-Rose Grove** loop closed in 1957, yet **Great Harwood** received these newer totems.

This Newchurch direction sign included the full name of the station.

Several other stations that closed before 1961, such as **Knotty Ash**, **Pendlebury** and **Sefton Park**, had totems, but generally the shorter-lived stations and lines were by-passed. Totems did not appear on the Holcombe Brook branch (closed 1952), Bolton Great Moor Street to **Worsley** and to Pennington (closed 1954), the Delph branch and **Greenfield** to Oldham (closed 1955), **Chorley** to **Cherry Tree**, **Blackrod** to **Hindley North**, and Liscard & Poulton on the **Seacombe** branch (all closed 1960). The Widnes South to **Timperley** line lasted until 1962, but stations lacked totems, unless they were installed on this line's **Warrington** Bank Quay platforms.

Some early closure of 'lineside' stations probably explains the absence of totems at such places as Lea Green, Collins Green, The Oaks and Baxenden. Some of the other stations never to receive totems were termini, with Middleton, Horwich, Birkenhead Woodside, and New Brighton being examples, perhaps less in need of them than through stations, though in hindsight, Birkenhead and New Brighton were somewhat unexpected omissions. One might also have expected the city termini of Liverpool Lime Street and Liverpool Exchange to have had totem signage.

None of the halts in this area carried totems, apart from **Newchurch**, where 'Halt' was omitted from the signs, but was included on the direction signs, as shown above. Untimetabled halts – the two at Risley, Chorley Royal Ordnance Factory, Longsight Yard, Mottram Yard, and [Manchester] United Football Ground – had no totems, though the last-named had enamel RIBs. Although **Old Trafford** and **Trafford Park** were fitted, Manchester United totems would probably have been the most popular collectors' item of all time! Both the totems below left are on many collectors' lists and are uncommon.

Elsewhere there were absences of totems that are difficult to explain. Between **Romiley** and **Macclesfield Central,** only **Rose Hill** and **Bollington** were considered worthy of totems. On the Southport to **Preston** line (closed 1964) the former electrified section to **Crossens** had totems, plus the next station, **Banks**, but the remaining six stations did not. It really is hard to decide if the LMR had a consistent policy, or whether signage was purely at the whim of local managers.

Of the Wigan to Southport intermediates, only **Burscough Bridge, Bescar Lane** (both open) and **St Lukes** (closed) had totems, but not the other five stations, which are all are still open. One of these, New Lane close to the Martin Mere bird sanctuary, had LMS hawkseye signs (and oil lamps) in place until 1974! Park (closed 1994), Upton, and Rufford (both still open) are also surprising omissions.

Some unconventional totems turned up in this area. Some of the totems at **Manchester Central** and **Sandhills** were 4 feet long (instead of the normal 36 inch), and the underground **Liverpool Central Low Level** station had only this type of sign. Another of the rare BR underground stations, **Liverpool James Street** had giant enamel signs, at least 6 feet long (*see* page 101). Some of the totems at **Mauldeth Road** and **Pleasington** were wooden, the latter in a non-Gill Sans condensed font.

Three unusually lettered but otherwise conventional totems belonged to this area. **Town Green & Aughton** was rendered in an unnecessarily small typeface; **Marsh Lane and Strand Road** for some reason required three lines of print, producing a rather clumsy effect; and some humorous character gave **Besses o' th' Barn** its unique appearance by use of lower-case typeface. The curious mixture of upper and lower letters produces a rather ungainly-looking totem. Nevertheless, it is extremely collectable and worthy of a larger image: (*see* also chapter 2 page 34).

Overall, the Lancashire-North Cheshire area was rich in totems, and many stations retained them well into the 1970s. Most stations at this time were caught in a 1950s time warp, complete with elegant Victorian buildings, gas lamps and totems. **Hindley North**, **Pemberton**, **Warrington Central** and **Wigan** Wallgate were splendid examples as the 1977 photograph below shows. **Upholland** even had oil lamps; however, the BR corporate identity addition to the original LMR running-in board, *'Alight here for Skelmersdale New Town'* was a little ironic!

Warrington Central in 1977. *Alan Young*

Two Wonderful Railway Journeys

The LMR has two of England's finest railway journeys, the famous 73-mile long **Settle** to **Carlisle** route and the Hope Valley line from Manchester to Sheffield. Train travel on both routes is extremely popular today after past threats of closure. The map below details the route and stations along the S&C. This historic line was constructed in the 1870s and has several notable tunnels and viaducts, such as the imposing Ribblehead Viaduct. **Dent** station is the highest in England and the climb to Ais Gill summit takes the line to 1,169 feet (356m) above sea level.

Wikipedia Commons

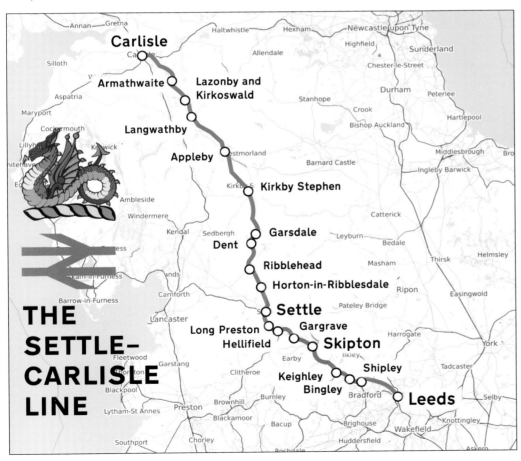

Of the eleven stations shown along the route, totems were only fitted at **Carlisle, Appleby West, Dent, Horton-in-Ribblesdale** (painted steel) and **Settle**. The line's classic pair is shown below, with **Carlisle** not an easy totem to find.

Settle station, ex-Midland Railway and also Grade-II listed, opened in 1876 as *Settle New* to distinguish itself from the nearby *Settle Old* (later Giggleswick) on the Leeds to Lancaster route. **Dent** station (opened 1877) is over 4 miles away from the village by road and is 1,150 feet (350m) above sea level. The buildings there, which are now privately owned, are available as holiday cottages and are Grade-II listed. The 1970s pictures below show two of the line's totems *in situ*.

The line was built by the MR, who in the expansive years of railway building, were locked in a bitter track access rights dispute with the LNWR. Construction by an army of 6,000 navvies was difficult and undertaken in harsh conditions; hundreds died as a result. BR earmarked the line for closure in the 1980s but it was subsequently saved. We are left with a wonderfully scenic route that is extremely popular with tourists and rail enthusiasts alike. Many steam-hauled specials, usually full, run over the route.

Construction began in 1869 and the line opened to freight in August 1875 and to passengers in May 1876. The line was engineered to express timetable standards by John Crossley and, as a result, gradients were kept at 1 in 100 or better. This meant a 16-mile (26km) climb from Settle to Blea Moor and along the whole line there are 22 viaducts and 14 tunnels, with spectacular views at every mile. The most notable is the 24-arch Ribblehead Viaduct which is 104ft (32m) high and 440 yards (402m) long. The swampy ground meant that the piers had to be sunk 25ft (8m) below the peat and set in concrete to provide a suitable foundation. Soon after crossing the viaduct, the line enters Blea Moor tunnel, 2,629yd (2,404m) long and 500ft (152m) below the moor, before emerging onto Dent Head Viaduct. The tunnel at Lazonby was constructed at the request of a local vicar as he did not want the railway to run past the vicarage! It is a great pity totems were not installed at Ribblehead and Garsdale.

The second memorable journey is on the Hope Valley line through Derbyshire's High Peak area between Sheffield and Manchester Piccadilly. The route is shown below, beginning in ER dark blue totem territory and after **Chinley**, an area bedecked with maroon totems that offered three routes into Manchester. This was also not an easy line to construct, climbing from **Grindleford** to beyond **Edale**.

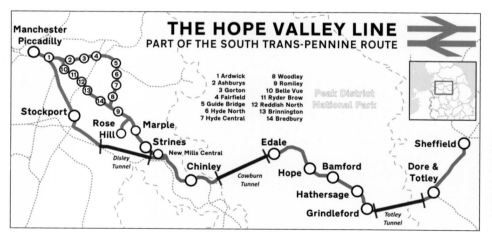

Top: Totley Tunnel. *Courtesy Derbyshire Heritage Above:* Enamel still *in situ*!

Even today, the Totley tunnel between **Dore & Totley** and **Grindleford** is the longest tunnel totally underground. Of course, the Channel Tunnel, and Severn Tunnel between Bristol and Cardiff, are both longer, but they pass below water. The Midland Railway built Totley tunnel as a rival route to the Woodhead Pass to the north.

The tunnel bore, started in 1888 and completed in 1892, is 3 miles 950 yards long and cut through rock containing powerful springs. It is straight throughout, with the exception of the outlet curve at **Grindleford**, where the work actually started. The station is not actually in Grindleford but is in the neighbouring village of Nether Padley.

The water springs made tunnelling extremely difficult and at times only 20 yards of progress was made in a week as the workings regularly filled with water. Tunnelling also began from the Sheffield end in early 1889 and when the bores met in October 1892, they were 5 inches apart laterally and only 2 inches out of level: the engineering surveyors had done a fantastic job. The complete Hope Valley line finally opened in November 1893 to goods traffic and later to passengers in June 1894.

The quartet above shows totems from along the line before we arrive at **Edale**, a real totem rarity and shown in the database pages. This is a popular destination today for hill walkers to Kinder Scout and the tiny hamlet boasted the luxury of a small station (opened June 1894). It is not far to Cowburn Tunnel (completed in 1891) passing under Colbourne Moor for 2 miles to emerge east of **Chinley**. The highest point on the whole Hope Valley route lies within the tunnel itself. The eastern side has a rising gradient of 1 in 100 and the western side has a falling grade of 1 in 150. It was the excellent condition of this part of the route that led to the controversial decision in 1970 to have Hope Valley as the preferred Sheffield to Manchester route, rather than the already electrified Woodhead line to the north.

This *in-situ* shot of **Hathersage** (right) dates from the early 1960s. Opened originally by the Dore & Chinley Rly in 1894, this station nestles amongst the hills and dales of this trans-Pennine route. The original timber buildings shown have been replaced and new masonry platforms appeared during the line's upgrading. Approaching 200 people per day now use this station, many being hill walkers.

Totems in Other London Midland Region Counties

The LMR included totems from nineteen English and four Welsh counties, based on the boundaries that existed in the 1950s and 60s. This final chapter section looks at rarities and desirable items from each county to aid the many totem collectors.

ANGLESEY

The LMR only fitted two stations with totems on this island, those at **Amlwch** and **Llangefni** and both closed in 1964. This pair has also appeared twice each in auction (2011 and 2012 respectively) so are fairly uncommon items. Our 2002 book listed Holyhead as also being fitted, but our photographic evidence now confirms this was not the case.

BEDFORDSHIRE

Collectors have a choice of 19 different stations fitted with totems to seek out, with some being quite common (**Leagrave** or **Flitwick**) and others quite rare (**Bedford Midland Road** or **Oakley**). The *RCH Book of Stations* shows there were 44 stations across Bedfordshire, so less than half were given totems and of these, almost 50% have closed: a quartet of uncommon totems follows.

Most of the totems fitted in Bedfordshire were the later fully flanged types, the exceptions being **Dunstable North** and **Luton Bute Street**.

Henlow Camp, on the **Hitchin** to **Bedford** line, opened in 1857 as Henlow, but with the establishment of RAF Henlow at the end of WWI, and its subsequent development, the name was changed to that shown on the totem in 1933. There was another RAF base at nearby **Cardington**, also on the same line. This closed on 1 January 1962 and both stations were lost. **Millbrook** station serves the villages of Marston Moreteine and Millbrook. Opened in 1846 as Marston, four name changes followed until it received its totem name in July 1910.

BUCKINGHAMSHIRE

This county contained totems from both Western and London Midland Regions. There were 16 stations fitted with maroon totems and all are known to have survived, but **Aylesbury High Street** and **Calvert** have not yet appeared in auction. The two most common totems are **Aylesbury Town** and **Leighton Buzzard**, with rarities being **Bletchley**, **Finmere** and **Olney**. Only four Buckinghamshire stations carried HF totems, the rest being the later FF design.

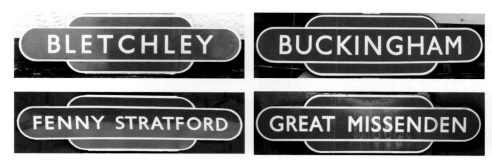

Buckinghamshire has a long and proud railway history as the first sections of the two London–Birmingham main line passed through the county and the Metropolitan Railway (Met) developed the first underground mass transit system when it opened in London in 1863 and eventually was extended through Buckinghamshire via Chesham, Amersham and Aylesbury. It was the Met who coined the term 'Metroland'. The zenith was reached in 1920s, when five companies ran services (the GCR, GWR, LNWR and LSWR plus the Met up to 1922 and the 'Big Four' plus the Met after 1923). The

Beeching era saw the closure of the former GCR main line north of Aylesbury and most of the 'Varsity Line' closed in 1967, (**Bletchley** to **Bedford** remaining open) even though the axing was not part of the Beeching plans. Almost all other surviving stations, branches and connecting lines in the north of the county were also closed to passengers. Most lines in the south survived, being busy London commuter routes, and new stations subsequently opened at Milton Keynes Central to serve the new town on the West Coast Main Line (1982); and at Haddenham & Thame Parkway (1987).

Today most of the county services are operated by Chiltern Railways and in 2010 they opened Aylesbury Vale Parkway 2 miles northwest of Aylesbury. Fast commuter trains now run from **Oxford** to Marylebone via **High Wycombe**, **Princes Risborough** and a new **Bicester** chord.

The picture above shows three rare **Winslow** totems *in situ* on a disused section of the *'Varsity Line'* in the north of the county. Houses cover much of this site today, but the platforms survive in very poor condition. There are plans to re-open **Winslow** on a new site sometime in the next five years.

CAERNARVONSHIRE

This North Wales County was one of the thirteen historic counties of Wales and is represented by eleven stations that carried LMR totems. All have survived and all have appeared in auction. **Llandudno Junction** and **Caernarvon** are the two most common, with **Betws-y-Coed** and **Dolgarrog** being the two rarest: a **Betws-y-Coed** totem appears in the database.

The main county railway operating companies were the Cambrian, GWR and LNWR, plus many former mineral and slate industry narrow gauge lines that, since closure, have re-invented themselves as tourist attractions. Additionally, there is the fabulous Snowdon Mountain Railway, so railway journeys in the county are truly spectacular.

The main line from Crewe to Holyhead traverses the coastal area of the county with stations at **Menai Bridge**, **Bangor**, **Llanfairfechan**, **Penmaenmawr**, **Conway** and **Llandudno Junction** in the county, plus **Deganwy** on the branch to **Llandudno,** and **Caernarvon** on the branch from **Menai Bridge** that closed in January 1970. It was temporarily re-opened to freight following a disastrous fire that destroyed the famous Britannia tubular bridge across the Menai Straits in May 1970. It eventually closed to all operations at the end of January 1972. It used to be a midway stop between **Bangor** and **Afon Wen**, but this line was a victim of the Beeching axe in December 1964. Happily, a new railway station in the town opened in 1997 when the narrow gauge Welsh Highland line was fully opened between **Portmadoc** and Caernarfon (the new correct Welsh spelling for the town) and from there visitors can walk directly to the fabulous castle that dominates the town.

Menai Bridge station closed in February 1966, when the line down to **Caernarvon** was reduced to single track. It had opened in October 1858 but was too close to **Bangor** being just 2 miles (3.2kms) away. There used to be four platforms, two for each line and two which formed an Island platform. The main station building was a large brick building with a brick waiting shelter on the island platform.

CHESHIRE

This county had totems installed on a whopping 93 stations, but no information exists on totems from **Birkenhead Central**, **Green Lane**, **Hyde Junction**, **Macclesfield Central**, **Mollington**, **Mouldsworth**, **Neston South**, **Northwich**, **Runcorn**, and **Seacombe**. However, photographic evidence does confirm they were installed, an example being shown below for **Runcorn** station. Records show 61 stations were closed in Cheshire during the 20th century and of this number, 14 carried totems. Most became redundant in the 1960s but **Upton-by-Chester** was closed in January 1984. (The word 'halt' was dropped from the station name in 1968, but was never on the totem). Cheshire totems range from the quite common (**Leasowe** or **Meols**) to the ultra-rare (**Dukinfield Central**, **Gatley** or **Newton for Hyde**) with more in the database: **Hartford**, **Heswall Hills**, **Hyde North** and **Sale** are also rather uncommon.

Railways first came to Cheshire in September 1840 with the opening of the 14½ miles from Chester to Birkenhead and the 20-mile stretch from Chester to Crewe. Liverpool was already a very important port and connections from the Wirral, Chester and beyond drove the rapid building of the line. The Crewe and Chester line was developed more with an eye on the Irish traffic, especially the mail, just as Telford's A5 Holyhead Road had done in earlier times. Hopes of Inter-Rail connectivity were beginning to grow and with the later Chester-Holyhead Railway becoming a reality by 1850, this otherwise rural main line became paramount to railway growth. Nevertheless, many independent railway companies were developing the Cheshire network in the early 1840s and it grew exponentially, because greater speed was more attractive than the use of the slower canals to towns and ports such as **Ellesmere Port**. It did not last and 'Railway Mania' was over by 1852.

The database pages list all the Cheshire 'totemed' stations but for rarities and special names we might suggest **Belle Vue**, **Cheadle Heath**, **Chester General**, **Ellesmere Port**, **Macclesfield Hibel Road**, **Port Sunlight** and the newly discovered **Seacombe.** Several important collections currently exist based on the Chester/Macclesfield/Wirral area.

CUMBERLAND

We now come to a county whose totems are sought by quite a few collectors, so whenever these classic names appear in auction, let the bidding commence! Our records show 25 Cumberland stations carried totems and 24 have survived (and **Corkickle** has just been confirmed as having totems but no survivors): 23 of the 24 and all have appeared in auction (exception is **Maryport**, the coastal town and port). There are some quite superb names (and relative rarities), as shown by this quartet.

The classic Cumberland station is Carlisle Citadel (named just **Carlisle** from 1948). It is Grade II listed with a quite beautifully designed exterior, the work of William Tite. At its zenith, seven separate railway companies used the station and it was a hive of activity. Only two totems have ever appeared in public auctions and its trio of engine sheds makes it a magnet for serious collectors. Equally magical is **Bassenthwaite Lake** on the now closed line between **Keswick** and **Cockermouth**. Other County rarities include **Blencow**, **Cockermouth**, **Harrington**, **Longtown**, **Silloth** and **Troutbeck**.

The closed route between **Penrith** and **Workington** was a quite superb train journey, passing through the beautiful Lakeland fells and along the shores of Bassenthwaite. Of the ten stations from **Penrith** to **Cockermouth**, eight were fitted with totems. The line west of Keswick closed in 1966 followed by the **Penrith** to **Keswick** section six years later. The former trackbed forms part of the rebuilt A66 and the lovely station at **Bassenthwaite Lake** was badly neglected for years but is now completely restored.

Bass Lake photos courtesy Guy Wilson/David Robinson, Cumbrian Railways Association

DENBIGHSHIRE

Only four stations in this North Wales County carried totems. Of the four, **Colwyn Bay** is very common, appearing more than 30 times in public auction, but we have no information about **Denbigh**, which is not thought to have survived. However, we do have a wonderful shot of this 'rare bird' *in situ* around 1960. Built in 1860, the Tudor-Gothic style buildings were constructed in limestone with attractive detailing

in freestone, including some first-floor accommodation for the station master: it was closed in April 1962 and the only remains on the site are a few sections of platform edge.

The superbly named pair of **Abergele and Pensarn** and **Llanrwst & Trefriw** have both been in public auction eight and nine times respectively.

DERBYSHIRE

A total of 72 Derbyshire stations were adorned with totems, 58 of them LMR maroon and 14 ER dark blue, with each of the latter grouping appearing far less often in auction than their LMR counterparts. LMR totems not yet appearing in auction include **Borrowash, Doe Hill** (a very recent discovery) and **Hayfield**; those auctioned just once or twice include **Birch Vale, Cromford, Derby Nottingham**

Road, **Draycott and Breaston**, **Edale**, **Furness Vale**, **Hadfield**, **Tibshelf Town** and **Whatstandwell**.

Derbyshire railway history is very closely aligned with the history of the Midland Railway. In 1839 the North Midland Railway, Midland Counties Railway and Derby & Birmingham Railway set up workshops at the back of Derby station, as railway lines started to spread across the county (and country) like a spider's web. On 30 May 1839 the line from Derby to Nottingham opened with the Birmingham line following on 5 August. The line north, through **Chesterfield** to near **Rotherham**, opened in 1840.

These three companies merged to form the MR in 1844, but despite its nationwide expansion, the Midland kept its headquarters in **Derby**, making the town one of the most important UK railway centres. The MR reached **Matlock** in 1849, transforming the prosperity of the town and bringing tourism to nearby **Matlock Bath**, and in 1863 it reached **Buxton**.

During the 1960s, 24 of Derbyshire's LMR-totemed stations were closed, but three, **Ilkeston North**, **Repton & Willington** and **Tutbury** have since re-opened. Many of the closures occurred in 1967, when fourteen stations were lost.

For those collectors who like a lot of letters for their money, Derbyshire has many to offer including the superb sextet below: the trio of **Chapel-en-le-Frith Central**, **Derby Friargate** and **Peak Forest for Peak Dale** are especially collectable.

FLINTSHIRE

There were thirty five stations in Flintshire at the peak of operations but today only nine remain open. The county had a surprisingly high number of 18 stations that carried totems, with 'surprisingly' being used because of the relatively low population served (in 2017 it was just over 155,000): there are no large centres of population, with only **Flint** and **Mold** being main towns. Cheshire lies to the east, Denbighshire to the West and Wrexham (formerly Flintshire) to the south.

A good proportion of Flintshire's totems were found on the North Wales Coast route westwards from Chester. However from our database list, **Bagillt**, **Connahs Quay**, **Holywell Junction**, **Mostyn** and **Queensferry** were all closed in 1966.

Saltney Ferry (Mold Junction) is technically on the North Wales route, but for all practical purposes was on the **Chester** to **Denbigh** branch as only this route saw station stops. It was an early closure (1962) when **Mold** station was also closed. There are no remains today of either station and no totems appear to have survived. There are some relative rarities (**Hope Village** with two appearances and **Hawarden** with five) contrasting with **Hawarden Bridge** (30) and **Prestatyn** (34). There is one unusual totem, that from **Cefn-y-Bedd** which features small lettering, one of only a handful of totems on the BR network with this characteristic. In addition there is the story about **Shotton Low Level** which closed in 1966. It re-opened in August 1972 as part of the station complex redevelopment and the suffix 'Low Level' was added only in 1999! The **High Level** station had a two-line layout but curiously, **Low Level** was single line.

HERTFORDSHIRE

This Home County had 47 'totemed' stations, twenty-six of them ER blue and twenty-one carrying LMR maroon. Photos of six LMR totems appear in the database pages and this short section gives the chance to suggest other Hertfordshire LMR collectables. There are some multi-lettered totems (top pair below) and some others have appeared in auction only once. All are known to have survived, save for **Rickmansworth Church Street**, which closed to passengers in March 1952, but remained open to freight until 1967. The buildings were demolished in 1974.

In June 2005 we learned via GWRA Pershore that a **Hemel Hempstead & Boxmoor** totem had been overpainted as **Cricklewood** – and upside down! The three photos left show the unusual sequence, including the partial cleaning and a **Hemel Hempstead** was finally auctioned. (It has appeared eight times in public auction). The original overpaint was additionally non standard Gill Sans as discussed in chapter 2.

Two other overpainted examples exist in Hertfordshire. Some **Radlett** totems were overpainted on **Caledonian Road & Barnsbury** (a Middlesex totem) and some **St Albans City** totems were overpainted on **Cheddington** (a Buckinghamshire totem).

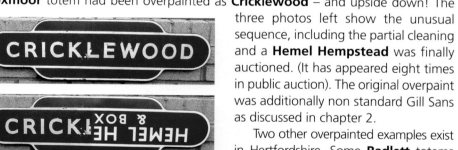

One other curiosity in Hertfordshire was the selection available from **Watford**. Five separate types were fitted, four of them conventional size plus 4 feet examples from **Watford High Street**. Although the rarity in the quartet, the normal sized **Watford North** appears in the database; below we show the whole set together.

Notice on the modern map below that **Watford High Street** station is on the London Overground line alongside the WCML. The **Watford West** branch closed in 2002 and the main station **Watford Junction** and **Watford North** lie away from the town.

Wikipedia Commons

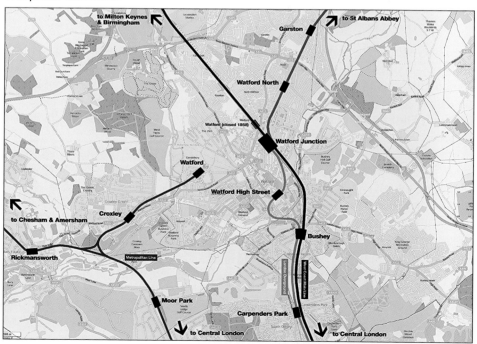

The map also includes three further local Hertfordshire totems, **Bushey & Oxhey**, **Carpenders Park** and **Croxley Green** (closed 2003).

LANCASHIRE

We now come to the real 'heavyweight' totem area on the whole of BR's national network. There were far more totems in Lancashire that any other British county and more than twice the number of stations fitted in the complete NER region! A total of 271 stations were adorned with maroon totems. With so many to choose from, this section will concentrate on historicals, rarities and desirables. The database pages contain photographs of 34 of Lancashire's gems, but there are many others to comment upon here. We have no survival information on 20 of the 271 stations, second only to Essex and a whopping 90 Lancs stations were closed due to economic rationalisation. Some names are pure Lancashire, as in the pair below.

Though even the world's first railway operated between **Stockton** and **Darlington**, a possibly more significant event took place at **Rainhill** Lancashire in October 1829, when the famous locomotive trials saw Stephenson's *'Rocket'* as the winner. This went on to power the new Liverpool to Manchester railway, the world's first inter-city service. From Castlefield, Manchester, the route ran via **Eccles**, Chat Moss, Newton and **Huyton** to **Edge Hill** where a 1.2 mile tunnel (2km) ran down to the docks.

The photo right shows a station on this famous route, that at **Earlestown** near St Helens; the **Earlestown** totem in situ is shown to the right of the 'Black Five' entering the station, which is the junction for the line down to **Warrington** Bank Quay.

In addition to those items that have not yet appeared in auction, nine stations have appeared only once (**Ainsdale**, **Bromley Cross**, **Clitheroe**, **Knotty Ash**, **Mersey Road & Aigburth**, **Pendleton**, **Trafford Park**, **Whitefield** and **Wilpshire**). These are the real Lancashire rarities. They are followed by a further 25 stations whose totems have appeared twice or three times, **Eccles** and **Tyldesley** for example, so despite the huge number of 'Red Rose' totems to collect, there are many great rarities for the county.

Oxford Road. This last named station sits on a Grade II listed viaduct and English Heritage describes it as a *"building of outstanding architectural quality and technological interest; one of the most dramatic stations in England"*. It is the second busiest station in the Manchester area, serving the Universities as well as lines from Piccadilly. Below is a 1960s photograph of a proud **Oxford Road** totem *in situ*.

Those totems appearing two or three times only in auction include the group above.

When it comes to collectables, this is personal taste, but there are some quite superb names and stations to choose from. Around Liverpool, we suggest **Aintree Sefton Arms**, **Blundellsands and Crosby** or **Seaforth & Litherland**. For the Manchester area, we like **Daisy Hill**, **Knott Mill and Deansgate**, and especially **Manchester Victoria.**

Further north the two totems from **Lancaster** are very collectable (**Castle** and **Green Ayre**), **Morecambe Euston Road** fits the bill as do the hyphenated **Bolton-le-Sands** or

Tim Clarke

LEICESTERSHIRE

This is a county where many totem aficionados and avid collectors reside: it is represented by 39 maroon totems. However, the closure of the Great Central Main Line (GCML – from Marylebone via Leicester and Nottingham to Sheffield and Manchester) hit the county hard and the database shows that of the 39 stations, no fewer than 31 were lost during the closure years. The most common totems are **Ashby-de-la-Zouch** (17 appearances), **Market Harborough** (17) and **Moira** (20), contrasting with **Quorn & Woodhouse**, **Saxby** and **Whetstone** (all zero). The photo alongside of a **Quorn &**

Woodhouse hanging proudly *in situ* is a real rarity and this station is now part of the Great Central Heritage Line (**Loughborough** to **Leicester**), the world's only double track heritage main line. Leicestershire has some quite superb names as evidenced by the set above.

The LMR database pages contain eight of Leicestershire's rarer totems, but in addition to these, eight other totems have appeared three times or fewer in public auctions (**Ashby Magna**, **Countesthorpe**, **Croft**, **East Langton**, **Elmesthorpe**, **Hinckley**, **Leire Halt** and **Lutterworth**). Overall Leicestershire is not an easy place on which to base a sizeable collection and relatively few totems from the county appear each year for auction. **Leicester London Road** is the city's main station. It was renamed simply as Leicester in 1969, when **Leicester Central** station on the GCML was closed.

LONDON

In contrast to Leicestershire, London's 17 stations bedecked with maroon signage saw only four closures; **Dalston Junction** re-opened in 2010. Research on Willesden Junction High Level station confirmed that it carried totems saying simply **Willesden Junction**; additionally, **Hampstead Heath** and **Kentish Town West** have not been seen in auction. Examples of 4-foot totems were found at **Broad Street** and **Willesden Junction** and the database pages contain photos of the four most desirable London maroon totems, including **Highbury & Islington** and **West End Lane**. Both **Finchley Road & Frognal** or **South Hampstead** are also collectable.

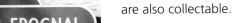

MIDDLESEX

From London, it is a short train ride to our next county, Middlesex. This contained 28 stations fitted with maroon signage. In our county list, we have no information on **Stanmore Village** and there have been no auction appearances thus far for **Belmont**, **Harlesden**, **Mill Hill Broadway** or **South Acton**, all 'rare birds' indeed!

Everton Cup final in 1968. The 1914 Clearing House map below shows lines and stations in the Wembley area.

In 1978 **Wembley Hill** was renamed Wembley Complex and renamed again in 1987 as Wembley Stadium. **Wembley Central** was heavily redeveloped in 2008 as the main interchange for Wembley on the WCML. Totems from the station have

The county is the home of English football at Wembley and four stations carried the name, **North Wembley**, **Wembley Central**, **Wembley Hill** and **Wembley Stadium**. This last-named is a curiosity, as shown alongside. These items were overpainted on **Watford Junction**, with the station closing after the West Brom v

appeared just once, the same number of times as **Wembley Stadium**, the station totem has appeared only once in public auction. **North Wembley** is the most common of the quartet (nine auction appearances).

Middlesex rarities include the quartet below, (a combined twelve appearances). The **Harrow & Wealdstone** totem is the 4-foot variant, rarer than the conventional size.

Wikipedia Commons

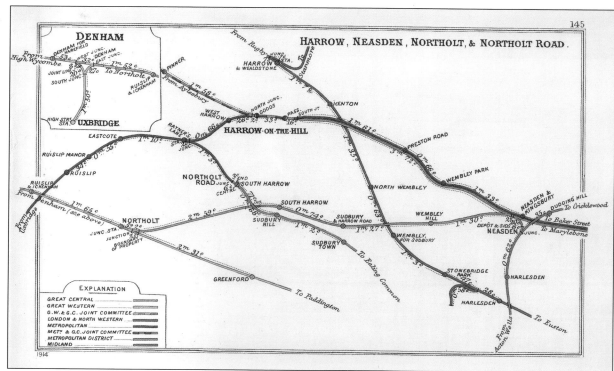

NORTHAMPTONSHIRE

Like its neighbour Leicestershire, this county lost most of its totemed stations, following the closure of the GCML. Only **Kettering**, **Long Buckby** and **Northampton Castle** are today's survivors from the original 20 stations that carried totems. Consequently, this county's totems are relatively uncommon, though three, **Blisworth**, **Long Buckby** and **Wellingborough Midland Road,** have approaching 50 appearances between them. We currently have no survival data on **Wellingborough London Road** or **Towcester** and additionally, **Charwelton** and **Glendon & Rushden** have not appeared publically. **Brackley**, **Helmdon** and **Roade** are also not at all common, registering just one appearance each.

Two other names on many shopping lists both feature ampersands as shown below.

NOTTINGHAMSHIRE

Station closures continued north into Nottinghamshire during the 1960s, though our listings show all maroon totems the county possessed have survived. There were 32 LMR stations of which 28 are closures. Only **Attenborough**, **Beeston**, **Newstead** and **Nottingham Midland** are open today. In addition 17 dark blue ER totems were displayed on Nottinghamshire stations. The database pages include photos of the rarer LMR totems, **East Leake**, **Jacksdale**, **Kimberley**, **London Road High Level**, **Ruddington** and **Stapleford**, while **Awsworth**, **Hucknall Byron**, **Kegworth** and **Trowell** have a combined total of 21 auction appearances.

The delightfully named octet above would enhance any Nottinghamshire collection.

RUTLAND

The tiny county of Rutland possessed five stations carrying maroon totems. All have survived and have appeared in auction. Four stations closed in 1966 and only **Oakham** remains open. Right is a lovely photo of **Seaton** totems *in situ* on the last day of operation, 6 June 1966. In the background is the impressive Welland Viaduct on the **Kettering** to **Melton Mowbray** line.

The Welland Viaduct is an 82-arch bridge with each span 40 ft, making the viaduct 1286 yards long (1,175m). It was constructed in 1880, with in excess of 16 million bricks and is still in use today having completely re-opened in 2009. Three railway companies had a presence in the county during the early construction years, the MR, the LNWR and the GNR. Of the two totems above, **Ashwell** (opened 1848) and **Luffenham** (opened 1848) were both ex-MR.

SHROPSHIRE

Five stations in Shropshire carried maroon, in a county far more populated by the WR's chocolate and cream. These five were on the **Wellington** to **Stafford** route and the **Shrewsbury** to Crewe route. The rarest totem is **Trench Crossing** (shown on database page 140) and the most common is **Whitchurch**. The top two both closed in 1964, when the **Stafford** line was considered superfluous.

The bottom two totems were on the **Shrewsbury** to Crewe line and the stations remain open. **Donnington** and **Newport** (both opened 1849) are ex-LNWR stations, as are **Wem** and **Whitchurch**, when they opened in 1858. **Wellington (Salop)** was a joint GWR/LNWR administered station that carried chocolate and cream, but many LMS engines, *'Jubilees'* and *'Black Fives'* were seen alongside *'Castles'* and *'Halls'*.

STAFFORDSHIRE

This county boasted a heavy concentration of 64 stations fitted with maroon signage. Of these, 38 were closed during the late 1950s and the 1960s, but happily three from the list have re-opened (**Cannock**, **Hednesford** and **Rugeley Town**). We have no survival information on **Albion**, **Armitage** and **Brindley Heath**, all relatively early closures, but we do have a picture of **Albion** *in situ*.

Albion was opened by the LNWR in 1852 to serve the town of Oldbury in the West Midlands. **Armitage** was in the Trent Valley, but like **Albion,** it was closed in 1960. **Brindley Heath** was on the Chase Line, between **Hednesford** and **Rugeley Town**. It closed to all traffic in 1959. Other Staffordshire rarities include **Bescot**, **Leek**, **Pleck** and **Wolverhampton High Level**, with no auction appearances between them followed by **Blythe Bridge**, **Burton-on-Trent**, **Coseley (Deepfields)**, **Oakamoor**, **Stoke on Trent**, **Tipton Owen Street** and **Willenhall** with one appearance each: **Darlaston** and **Stoke on Trent** have two appearances. At the opposite end of the scale, we have **Tamworth** (24 appearances), **Lichfield City** (23), **Lichfield Trent Valley** (20) and **Rugeley Trent Valley** (18).

Staffordshire has a long and proud railway history, beginning with the Grand Junction Railway in 1833, followed by the North Staffordshire in 1845 and the LNWR in 1846. Both **Stafford** and **Stoke on Trent** were major hubs, but as industry declined, rail services were cut, with the Potteries area in particular being devastated. **Stone** was closed in 2004 (but re-opened in 2008) and **Etruria** closed in 2005. The quartet right was lost from the Stoke area during the savage cutbacks. Some other routes such as that through **Uttoxeter**, only just survived the economy drive.

The database pages contain pictures of 14 county rarities, but in addition there are a couple of delightfully named stations that carried totems, as depicted below.

WARWICKSHIRE

This county is represented by 51 stations with maroon signage. Seventeen stations have closed, nearly half in the first wave of cuts in 1965, with the other half being lost in 1968. There was one early closure, **Brandon & Wolston** in 1960 and in addition, totems from four stations have not appeared in auction (**Coventry**, **Daimler Halt**, **Penns**, **Polesworth** and **Rugby Midland**); **Rugby Central** (closed in 1969) is shown in the picture below, confirming that FF totems were also installed here.

Warwickshire totems appear at regular intervals, with **Nuneaton** very common (59 appearances), **Barnt Green** (24) and **Erdington** and **Kings Norton** (21 each) being fairly easy to obtain. (Note: Nuneaton's two stations, **Abbey Street** and **Trent Valley**, both carried the name **Nuneaton**). Other Warwickshire desirables include **Birmingham New Street**, **Hawkesbury Lane** (page 143), **Tile Hill** and **Vauxhall & Duddeston**.

Relative rarities include **Atherstone**, **Bournville**, **Hampton in Arden**, **Marston Gree**n, **Shustoke and Stechford** , plus seven photographs included in the database pages.

WESTMORLAND

This beautiful county contains some of the most wonderful English scenery to be seen by rail. It is traversed by parts of the WCML and the Settle & Carlisle routes, with a branch into **Windermere**. Just thirteen stations here carried totems, half of which were closed in the 1960s. There are some evocative names as the quartet below illustrates. **Ambleside Pier** had a very large enamel sign (alongside).

WORCESTERSHIRE

Only one station in Worcester carried maroon, **Oldbury & Bromford Lane**, which is a fairly common totem. In 1983 it was completely rebuilt and renamed Sandwell and Dudley: it is used now by one million people annually.

YORKSHIRE

The final county in this series of reviews is Yorkshire, where twelve stations were fitted with LMR signage. Of the 12, seven closed, so that only **Greenfield**, **Hellifield**, **Settle**, **Skipton** and **Todmorden** survived. We have no data on **Newsholme** (closed 1957) and **Earby**'s wooden totems have not been in auction.

Two totems below from the climb through the Southern Fells are always contested. Examples from all thirteen stations have survived, all appearing in public auctions.

Station Name	County in 1956	Layout	Flange	Closed	Auction	Survived
ABERGELE AND PENSARN	Denbighshire	2L	FF		•	•
ACCRINGTON	Lancashire		FF		•	•
ACTON BRIDGE	Cheshire		FF		•	•
ACTON CENTRAL	Middlesex		HF		•	•
ADDERLEY PARK **	Warwickshire		FF		•	•
ADLINGTON	Cheshire		FF		•	•
ADLINGTON	Lancashire		FF		•	•
AINSDALE	Lancashire		HF		•	•
AINTREE SEFTON ARMS	Lancashire	2L	HF		•	•
ALBION	Staffordshire		HF	1960		
ALDERLEY EDGE	Cheshire		FF		•	•
ALDRIDGE	Staffordshire		FF	1965	•	•
ALFRETON & SOUTH NORMANTON ** *open 1973	Derbyshire	2L	FF	1967*	•	•
ALLERTON *new Liverpool South Parkway 2006	Lancashire		FF	2005*	•	•
ALREWAS **	Staffordshire		FF	1965	•	•
ALSAGER	Cheshire		FF		•	•
ALTHORP PARK	Northamptonshire		FF	1960	•	•
ALTON TOWERS	Staffordshire		HF	1965	•	•
ALTRINCHAM AND BOWDON	Cheshire	2L	FF		•	•
AMBERGATE	Derbyshire		FF		•	•
AMLWCH	Anglesey		FF	1964	•	•
AMPTHILL	Bedfordshire		FF	1959	•	•
ANSDELL & FAIRHAVEN	Lancashire		HF		•	•
APPLEBY EAST	Westmorland	1L	HF	1962	•	•
APPLEBY WEST	Westmorland	1L	HF		•	•
APSLEY	Hertfordshire		HF		•	•
ARDWICK	Lancashire		HF		•	•
ARLEY & FILLONGLEY	Leicestershire	2L	FF	1960		•
ARMITAGE	Staffordshire		HF	1960		
ARNSIDE	Westmorland		FF		•	•
ASHBURYS	Lancashire		FF		•	•
ASHBURYS ** face drilled version	Lancashire		FF			•
ASHBURYS FOR BELLE VUE	Lancashire	2L	HF		•	•
ASHBY MAGNA	Leicestershire		FF	1969	•	•
ASHBY-DE-LA-ZOUCH **	Leicestershire		FF	1964	•	•
ASHLEY	Cheshire		FF		•	•

** = some totems face drilled   1L = one line: 2L = two line: LP = Lower panel

Station Name		County in 1956	Layout	Flange	Closed	Auction	Survived
ASHTON CHARLESTOWN **		Lancashire	2L	FF		•	•
ASHWELL		Rutland		FF	1966	•	•
ASKAM **		Lancashire		FF		•	•
ASPATRIA **		Cumberland		FF		•	•
ASTON		Warwickshire		FF		•	•
ATHERSTONE		Warwickshire		FF		•	•
ATHERTON CENTRAL		Lancashire	2L	FF		•	•
ATTENBOROUGH **		Nottinghamshire		FF		•	•
AUGHTON PARK		Lancashire		HF		•	•
AWSWORTH	also BR made fibreglass version	Nottinghamshire		HF/FF	1964	•	•
AYLESBURY HIGH STREET		Buckinghamshire	1L	HF	1953		•
AYLESBURY TOWN		Buckinghamshire	1L	FF		•	•
BACUP		Lancashire		FF	1966	•	•
BAGILLT		Flintshire		FF	1966	•	•
BAGWORTH		Leicestershire		FF	1964	•	•
BAKEWELL **		Derbyshire		FF	1967	•	•
BAMBER BRIDGE		Lancashire		FF		•	•
BAMBER BRIDGE**	face drilled version	Lancashire		FF			•
BAMFORD		Derbyshire		FF		•	•
BANGOR		Caernarvonshire		FF		•	•
BANK HALL		Lancashire		FF		•	•
BANKS		Lancashire		FF	1964		•
BANKS **	face drilled version	Lancashire		FF	1964		•
BARE LANE		Lancashire		FF		•	•
BARE LANE **	face drilled version	Lancashire		FF			•
BARNOLDSWICK		Yorkshire		FF	1965	•	•
BARNT GREEN		Warwickshire		FF		•	•
BARROW		Lancashire		FF		•	•
BARROW ON SOAR **	*re-opened 1994	Leicestershire		FF	1968*	•	•
BARTON & WALTON **		Staffordshire		FF	1958	•	•
BASFORD NORTH		Nottinghamshire		HF	1964	•	•
BASFORD VERNON		Nottinghamshire		HF	1967	•	•
BASSENTHWAITE LAKE **		Cumberland		FF	1966	•	•
BEBINGTON & NEW FERRY		Cheshire	2L	HF		•	•

** = some totems face drilled   1L = one line: 2L = two line: LP = Lower panel

Station Name	County in 1956	Layout	Flange	Closed	Auction	Survived
BRYN	Lancashire		FF		•	•
BUCKINGHAM	Buckinghamshire		FF		•	•
BUCKLEY JUNCTION	Flintshire	1L	FF		•	•
BULWELL COMMON	Nottinghamshire		FF	1963	•	•
BULWELL MARKET *re-opened 1994	Nottinghamshire		HF	1964*	•	•
BURN NAZE	Lancashire		FF	1970	•	•
BURNAGE	Cheshire		FF		•	•
BURNESIDE	Westmorland		FF		•	•
BURNLEY BARRACKS	Lancashire		FF		•	•
BURNLEY BARRACKS ** face drilled version	Lancashire		FF			
BURNLEY CENTRAL	Lancashire		FF		•	•
BURNLEY MANCHESTER RD re-opened 1986	Lancashire	2L	FF	1961*	•	•
BURSCOUGH BRIDGE	Lancashire		FF			
BURSCOUGH JUNCTION	Lancashire	2L	FF		•	•
BURTON-ON-TRENT	Staffordshire		HF		•	•
BURY BOLTON STREET *heritage stn 1987	Lancashire	1L	HF	1980*	•	•
BURY KNOWSLEY STREET	Lancashire	2L	FF	1970	•	•
BUSHEY & OXHEY	Hertfordshire	2L	FF		•	•
BUTLERS LANE	Staffordshire		FF		•	•
BUXTON	Derbyshire		HF		•	•
CAERNARVON	Caernarvonshire		HF	1970	•	•
CALEDONIAN ROAD & BARNSBURY	Middlesex	2L	FF		•	•
CALVERT	Buckinghamshire		FF	1963		•
CAMDEN ROAD	London		HF		•	•
CANLEY HALT **	Warwickshire		FF		•	•
CANNOCK *re-opened 1989	Staffordshire		FF	1965*	•	•
CANONBURY	London		FF		•	•
CAPENHURST	Cheshire		FF		•	•
CARDINGTON	Bedfordshire		FF	1962	•	•
CARK & CARTMEL **	Lancashire		FF		•	•
CARLISLE	Cumberland		HF		•	•
CARNFORTH	Lancashire		FF		•	•
CARPENDERS PARK **	Hertfordshire		HF/Flat		•	•
CASTLE BROMWICH	Warwickshire		HF	1968	•	•

** = some totems face drilled   1L = one line: 2L = two line: LP = Lower panel

Station Name	County in 1956	Layout	Flange	Closed	Auction	Survived
CASTLETHORPE	Buckinghamshire		FF	1964	•	•
CASTLETON	Lancashire		FF		•	•
CEFN-Y-BEDD small letters	Flintshire		FF		•	•
CHAPEL-EN-LE-FRITH CENTRAL	Derbyshire	LP	FF	1967	•	•
CHAPEL-EN-LE-FRITH SOUTH	Derbyshire	2L	FF		•	•
CHARWELTON **	Northamptonshire		FF	1963		•
CHASSEN ROAD	Lancashire		FF		•	•
CHATBURN	Lancashire		FF	1962	•	•
CHEADLE HEATH	Cheshire		FF	1967		•
CHEADLE HULME	Cheshire		FF		•	•
CHEDDINGTON	Buckinghamshire		FF		•	•
CHELFORD	Cheshire		FF		•	•
CHERRY TREE **	Lancashire		FF		•	•
CHESTER GENERAL	Cheshire	1L	HF		•	•
CHESTER NORTHGATE	Cheshire	2L	HF	1969	•	•
CHESTER ROAD	Warwickshire		FF		•	•
CHILVERS COTON	Warwickshire		FF	1965	•	•
CHINLEY	Derbyshire		HF/FF		•	•
CHORLEY Some o/p on Burscough Bridge	Lancashire		FF		•	•
CHORLTON-CUM-HARDY	Lancashire		FF*	1967	•	•
CHORLTON-CUM-HARDY ** face drilled version	Lancashire		FF*	1967		•
CHURCH AND OSWALDTWISTLE **	Lancashire	2L	FF*		•	•
CHURCHTOWN	Lancashire		FF	1964	•	•
CLAY CROSS	Derbyshire		FF	1967	•	•
CLAYTON BRIDGE **	Lancashire		FF	1968	•	•
CLIFTON JUNCTION	Lancashire		HF		•	•
CLITHEROE * reopened 1994	Lancashire		FF	1962*	•	•
CLOUGH FOLD	Lancashire		HF	1966	•	•
CLOUGH FOLD ** face drilled version	Lancashire		FF	1966		•
CLUBMOOR	Lancashire		FF	1960		
COALVILLE TOWN	Leicestershire		HF	1964	•	•
COCKERMOUTH	Cumberland		FF	1966	•	•
CODNOR PARK & IRONVILLE	Derbyshire	2L	FF	1967	•	•
COLESHILL *re-opened 2007	Warwickshire		FF	1968 *	•	•
COLNE	Lancashire		HF/FF		•	•
COLWYN BAY	Denbighshire		FF		•	•

** = some totems face drilled   1L = one line: 2L = two line: LP = Lower panel

Station Name		County in 1956	Layout	Flange	Closed	Auction	Survived
CONGLETON		Cheshire		HF			
CONGLETON **	face drilled version	Cheshire		FF		•	•
CONNAHS QUAY		Flintshire		FF		•	•
CONNAHS QUAY **	face drilled version	Flintshire		FF	1966	•	•
CONWAY **	*re-opened 1987	Caernarvonshire		FF	1966	•	•
CORBY	small letters *re-opened 2009	Northamptonshire		FF	1966*	•	•
CORKICKLE		Cumberland		FF			
COSELEY (DEEPFIELDS)		Staffordshire	2L	HF			
COUNDON ROAD		Warwickshire		FF	1965	•	•
COUNTESTHORPE		Leicestershire		FF	1962	•	•
COVENTRY		Warwickshire		HF			
CRESSINGTON & GRASSENDALE **		Lancashire	2L	FF**	1972	•	•
CRICKLEWOOD """		Middlesex		FF		•	•
CROFT		Leicestershire		FF	1968	•	•
CROMFORD		Derbyshire		FF		•	•
CROSSENS		Lancashire		FF	1964	•	•
CROSTON		Lancashire		FF		•	•
CROUCH HILL		London		HF		•	•
CROXLEY GREEN		Hertfordshire		FF	2003	•	•
CRUMPSALL re-opened 1991		Lancashire		FF		•	•
CULCHETH		Lancashire		FF	1964	•	•
DAIMLER HALT		Warwickshire		FF	1965		•
DAISY HILL		Lancashire		FF		•	•
DALSTON		Cumberland		FF		•	•
DALSTON JUNCTION	*new stn 2010	London	1L	FF	1986*	•	•
DALTON		Lancashire		FF		•	•
DANE ROAD	*new tramway re-opened 1992	Cheshire		FF	1991*	•	•
DARLASTON		Staffordshire		FF	1965	•	•
DARLEY DALE	*heritage stn. open 1991	Derbyshire		FF	1967*	•	•
DARLEY DALE **	face drilled version	Derbyshire		FF	1967*	•	•
DARWEN		Lancashire		FF		•	•
DAVENPORT		Cheshire		FF		•	•
DEAN LANE		Lancashire		FF		•	•
DEGANWY		Caernarvonshire		FF		•	•

"""Some Cricklewood were overpainted on Hemel Hempstead & Boxmoor (see page 120).

** = some totems face drilled   1L = one line: 2L = two line: LP = Lower panel

Station Name	County in 1956	Layout	Flange	Closed	Auction	Survived
DENBIGH	Denbighshire		FF	1962		
DENT ** +o/p on Burnley Central *reopened 1986	Yorkshire		FF	1970*	•	•
DENTON	Lancashire		FF		•	•
DERBY FRIARGATE	Derbyshire	1L	HF	1964	•	•
DERBY MIDLAND	Derbyshire	1L	HF/FF		•	•
DERBY NOTTINGHAM ROAD	Derbyshire	2L	FF	1967	•	•
DESBOROUGH & ROTHWELL **	Northamptonshire	2L	FF	1968	•	•
DESFORD **	Leicestershire		FF	1964	•	•
DIDSBURY	Lancashire		FF	1967	•	•
DIGGLE	Yorkshire		FF	1968	•	•
DINTING	Derbyshire		HF		•	•
DISLEY	Cheshire		HF		•	•
DITTON JUNCTION	Lancashire	1L	FF	1994	•	•
DOE HILL New discovery	Derbyshire		FF	1960		
DOLGARROG	Caernarvonshire		FF		•	•
DONNINGTON	Shropshire		FF	1964	•	•
DRAYCOTT & BREASTON	Derbyshire	2L	FF	1966	•	•
DRIGG **	Cumberland		FF		•	•
DROYLSDEN	Lancashire		FF	1968		
DUDLEY PORT	Staffordshire		HF/FF		•	•
DUFFIELD **	Derbyshire		FF		•	•
DUKINFIELD CENTRAL	Cheshire	LP	HF	1959		•
DUNSTABLE NORTH	Bedfordshire	1L	HF	1965	•	•
EARBY wooden totem	Yorkshire		wood	1970		•
EARLESTOWN	Lancashire		FF		•	•
EAST DIDSBURY	Lancashire		FF		•	•
EAST LANGTON	Leicestershire		FF	1968	•	•
EAST LEAKE	Nottinghamshire		FF	1969	•	•
ECCLES	Lancashire		HF		•	•
ECCLESTON PARK	Lancashire		FF		•	•
EDALE	Derbyshire		FF		•	•
EDGE HILL **	Lancashire		FF		•	•
EGGINTON JUNCTION	Derbyshire	1L	FF	1962	•	•
ELLESMERE PORT	Cheshire		FF		•	•
ELMESTHORPE	Leicestershire		FF	1968	•	•

** = some totems face drilled

1L = one line: 2L = two line: LP = Lower panel

Station Name	County in 1956	Layout	Flange	Closed	Auction	Survived
ELSTREE & BOREHAMWOOD	Hertfordshire	2L	HF		•	•
ENTWISTLE	Lancashire		FF		•	•
ERDINGTON **	Warwickshire		FF		•	•
ETRURIA	Staffordshire		FF	2005	•	•
ETTINGSHALL ROAD & BILSTON	Staffordshire	2L	FF	1964	•	•
EWOOD BRIDGE	Lancashire		FF	1972	•	•
FAILSWORTH	Lancashire		FF		•	•
FAIRFIELD FOR DROYLESDEN	Lancashire	2L	HF		•	•
FALLOWFIELD	Lancashire		FF	1958		
FARINGTON	Lancashire		FF	1960		
FARNWORTH AND HALSHAW MOOR	Lancashire	2L	FF		•	•
FAZAKERLEY	Lancashire		FF		•	•
FENNY STRATFORD	Buckinghamshire		HF		•	•
FENTON	Staffordshire		FF	1961	•	•
FINCHLEY ROAD & FROGNAL	London		HF		•	•
FINMERE also wooden totems	Buckinghamshire		FF	1963	•	•
FLEETWOOD **	Lancashire		FF	1966	•	•
FLINT	Flintshire		FF		•	•
FLITWICK **	Bedfordshire		FF		•	•
FLIXTON **	Lancashire		FF		•	•
FOLESHILL	Warwickshire		FF	1965	•	•
FORMBY	Lancashire		FF		•	•
FOUR ASHES **	Staffordshire		FF	1959	•	•
FOUR OAKS	Warwickshire		FF		•	•
FOXFIELD **	Lancashire		FF		•	•
FRESHFIELD **	Lancashire		FF		•	•
FRODSHAM **	Cheshire		FF		•	•
FURNESS VALE **	Derbyshire		FF		•	•
GARSTON Replaced by Liverpool Parkway South	Lancashire		FF	2006	•	•
GARSWOOD **	Lancashire		FF		•	•
GATEACRE	Lancashire		FF	1972	•	•
GATLEY	Cheshire		FF		•	•
GLAZEBROOK	Lancashire		FF		•	•
GLENDON & RUSHTON	Northamptonshire	2L	FF	1960		•

** = some totems face drilled   1L = one line: 2L = two line: LP = Lower panel

Station Name	County in 1956	Layout	Flange	Closed	Auction	Survived
GLOSSOP CENTRAL	Derbyshire	1L	HF		•	•
GODLEY JUNCTION	Cheshire	1L	FF		•	•
GOLBORNE NORTH	Lancashire	1L	?	1952		
GOLBORNE SOUTH	Lancashire	1L	?	1961		
GOOSTREY	Cheshire		FF		•	•
GORTON AND OPENSHAW	Lancashire	2L	HF		•	•
GOSPEL OAK **	London		FF		•	•
GRANGE-OVER-SANDS	Lancashire		FF		•	•
GRAVELLY HILL	Warwickshire		FF		•	•
GREAT BARR	Warwickshire		FF		•	•
GREAT BRIDGE NORTH	Staffordshire	1L	FF	1964	•	•
GREAT HARWOOD **	Lancashire		FF	1957	•	•
GREAT LONGSTONE **	Derbyshire		FF	1962	•	•
GREAT MISSENDEN	Buckinghamshire		FF		•	•
GREEN LANE	Cheshire		HF			
GREENFIELD	Yorkshire		FF		•	•
GRESLEY	Derbyshire		FF	1964	•	•
GRETTON	Northamptonshire		FF	1966	•	•
GRINDLEFORD **	Derbyshire		FF		•	•
GUIDE BRIDGE	Lancashire		HF		•	•
HADFIELD New discovery	Derbyshire		HF		•	•
HALE	Lancashire		FF		•	•
HALL ROAD	Lancashire		FF		•	•
HAMMERWICH	Staffordshire		FF	1965	•	
HAMPSTEAD HEATH	London		FF			•
HAMPTON IN ARDEN **	Warwickshire		FF		•	•
HANDFORTH	Cheshire		FF		•	•
HANLEY	Staffordshire		FF	1964	•	•
HAPTON	Lancashire		FF		•	•
HARLESDEN	Middlesex		HF			•
HARLINGTON	Bedfordshire		FF		•	•
HARPENDEN CENTRAL	Hertfordshire	1L	HF/FF		•	•
HARPENDEN EAST	Hertfordshire	1L	HF	1965	•	•
HARRINGTON	Cumberland		FF		•	•
HARROW & WEALDSTONE	Middlesex	2L	HF		•	•

** = some totems face drilled   1L = one line: 2L = two line: LP = Lower panel

Station Name		County in 1956	Layout	Flange	Closed	Auction	Survived
HARROW & WEALDSTONE	4' totem	Middlesex		FF		•	•
HARTFORD		Cheshire		FF		•	•
HARTFORD & GREENBANK		Cheshire	2L	FF		•	•
HASLINGDEN		Lancashire		FF	1960	•	•
HATCH END		Middlesex		FF		•	•
HATHERN		Nottinghamshire		FF	1960	•	•
HATHERSAGE		Derbyshire		FF		•	•
HAWARDEN		Flintshire		HF		•	•
HAWARDEN BRIDGE		Flintshire		HF/FF		•	•
HAWKESBURY LANE **		Warwickshire		FF	1965	•	•
HAYFIELD		Derbyshire		FF	1970	•	•
HAZEL GROVE **		Cheshire		FF		•	•
HEADSTONE LANE		Middlesex		FF		•	•
HEALD GREEN		Cheshire		HF/FF		•	•
HEATON CHAPEL & HEATON MOOR		Lancashire	2L	HF/FF		•	•
HEATON MERSEY		Lancashire		FF	1961		•
HEATON PARK **		Lancashire		FF		•	•
HEDNESFORD	*re-opened 1989	Staffordshire		FF	1965*	•	•
HELLIFIELD		Yorkshire		FF		•	•
HELMDON **		Northamptonshire		FF	1963	•	•
HELMSHORE **		Lancashire		FF	1966	•	•
HELSBY		Cheshire		FF		•	•
HEMEL HEMPSTEAD & BOXMOOR		Hertfordshire	2L	FF		•	•
HENDON		Middlesex		FF		•	•
HENLOW CAMP		Bedfordshire		FF	1962	•	•
HESKETH PARK		Lancashire		HF	1964	•	•
HEST BANK **		Lancashire		FF	1969	•	•
HESWALL HILLS		Cheshire		FF		•	•
HEYSHAM	*re-opened 1987	Lancashire		FF	1975*	•	•
HEYWOOD	*heritage station 2003	Lancashire		FF	1970 *	•	•
HIGHBURY & ISLINGTON ""		London		HF/Flat		•	•
HIGHTOWN		Lancashire		FF		•	•
HILLSIDE		Lancashire		HF		•	•
HINCKLEY		Leicestershire		FF		•	•
HINDLEY NORTH		Lancashire		FF		•	•
HINDLEY SOUTH		Lancashire		FF	1964	•	•

""Highbury & Islington HF totem has condensed Gill Sans lettering, while the flat version shown above does not.

** = some totems face drilled | 1L = one line: 2L = two line: LP = Lower panel

Station Name		County in 1956	Layout	Flange	Closed	Auction	Survived
HOLLINWOOD		Lancashire		FF		•	•
HOLMES CHAPEL		Cheshire		FF		•	•
HOLYWELL JUNCTION		Flintshire	1L	FF	1966	•	•
HOOTON		Cheshire		HF		•	•
HOPE		Derbyshire		FF		•	•
HOPE VILLAGE		Flintshire		FF		•	•
HORTON-IN-RIBBLESDALE	*re-opened 1986	Yorkshire		Steel	1970*	•	•
HOUGH GREEN		Lancashire		HF/FF		•	•
HOYLAKE		Cheshire		FF		•	•
HUCKNALL BYRON	*re-opened 1993	Nottinghamshire		HF	1964	•	•
HUCKNALL CENTRAL **		Nottinghamshire	1L	FF	1963	•	•
HUMBERSTONE ROAD		Leicestershire		FF	1968	•	•
HUNCOAT		Lancashire		FF		•	•
HUNTS CROSS **		Lancashire		FF		•	•
HUYTON		Lancashire		FF		•	•
HYDE CENTRAL		Cheshire	1L	FF		•	•
HYDE JUNCTION	renamed Hyde North in 1951	Cheshire	1L	HF			
HYDE NORTH		Cheshire	1L	HF			•
HYDE NORTH		Cheshire	1L	FF		•	•
ILKESTON JUNCTION	*re-opened 2017	Derbyshire	2L	FF	1967*	•	•
ILKESTON NORTH		Derbyshire	2L	HF	1964	•	•
INCE		Lancashire		HF			•
INCE **	face drilled version	Lancashire		FF		•	•
IRCHESTER		Northamptonshire		FF	1960	•	•
IRLAM **		Lancashire		FF		•	•
JACKSDALE		Nottinghamshire		HF	1963	•	•
KEARSLEY		Lancashire		HF			•
KEARSLEY		Lancashire		FF		•	•
KEGWORTH		Nottinghamshire		FF	1968	•	•
KENDAL		Westmorland		FF		•	•
KENILWORTH	*re-opened 2018	Warwickshire		FF	1965*	•	•
KENSAL GREEN		Middlesex		HF		•	•
KENSAL RISE		Middlesex		HF		•	•

** = some totems face drilled   1L = one line: 2L = two line: LP = Lower panel

Station Name	County in 1956	Layout	Flange	Closed	Auction	Survived
KENTISH TOWN	London	1L	HF		•	•
KENTISH TOWN WEST *re-opened 1981	London	2L	HF	1971*		•
KENTON	Middlesex		HF		•	•
KENTS BANK **	Lancashire		FF		•	•
KESWICK ** face drilled version not in auction	Cumberland		FF	1972	•	•
KETTERING	Northamptonshire		FF		•	•
KIBWORTH	Leicestershire		FF	1968	•	•
KIDSGROVE CENTRAL	Staffordshire	1L	FF		•	•
KIDSGROVE LIVERPOOL ROAD	Staffordshire	2L	FF	1964	•	•
KILBURN HIGH ROAD	Middlesex		HF		•	•
KILSBY & CRICK	Northamptonshire		FF	1960	•	•
KIMBERLEY	Nottinghamshire		FF	1964	•	•
KINGS LANGLEY & ABBOTS LANGLEY	Hertfordshire	2L	HF		•	•
KINGS NORTON **	Warwickshire		FF		•	•
KINGSBURY	Warwickshire		FF	1968	•	•
KIRBY MUXLOE	Leicestershire		FF	1964	•	•
KIRKBY	Lancashire		FF		•	•
KIRKBY BENTINCK	Nottinghamshire		FF	1963	•	•
KIRKBY IN FURNESS	Lancashire		FF		•	•
KIRKBY STEPHEN EAST	Westmorland	1L	HF	1962	•	•
KIRKBY IN ASHFIELD	Nottinghamshire		FF	1965	•	•
KIRKDALE **	Lancashire		FF		•	•
KIRKHAM AND WESHAM	Lancashire	2L	FF		•	•
KNOTT MILL AND DEANSGATE	Lancashire	2L	FF		•	•
KNOTTY ASH	Lancashire		FF	1960	•	•
KNUTSFORD **	Cheshire		FF		•	•
LAKE SIDE *heritage station 1973	Lancashire		FF	1965*	•	•
LANCASTER CASTLE	Lancashire	1L	HF		•	•
LANCASTER GREEN AYRE	Lancashire	2L	HF	1966	•	•
LANGLEY MILL & EASTWOOD *re-opened 1986	Nottinghamshire	2L	FF	1967*	•	•
LAYTON	Lancashire		FF		•	•
LEA HALL ** face drilled version in auction	Warwickshire		FF		•	•
LEAGRAVE	Bedfordshire		FF		•	•
LEASOWE	Cheshire		FF		•	•
LEDSHAM	Cheshire		FF	1959		•

** = some totems face drilled   1L = one line: 2L = two line: LP = Lower panel

Station Name	County in 1956	Layout	Flange	Closed	Auction	Survived
LEEK	Staffordshire		FF	1965		•
LEICESTER CENTRAL	Leicestershire	1L	FF	1969	•	•
LEICESTER LONDON ROAD ^some flat poster types	Leicestershire	2L	HF^		•	•
LEIGH **	Lancashire		FF	1969	•	•
LEIGHTON BUZZARD	Buckinghamshire		FF		•	•
LEIRE HALT	Leicestershire		FF	1962	•	•
LEVENSHULME	Lancashire		FF		•	•
LEVENSHULME NORTH New discovery	Lancashire	2L	HF			
LEYLAND	Lancashire		FF		•	•
LICHFIELD	Staffordshire		FF		•	•
LICHFIELD CITY	Staffordshire	1L	FF		•	•
LICHFIELD TRENT VALLEY	Staffordshire	2L/LP	FF		•	•
LIDLINGTON	Bedfordshire		FF		•	•
LINBY	Nottinghamshire		FF	1964	•	•
LITTLE SUTTON	Cheshire		FF		•	•
LITTLEBOROUGH **	Lancashire		FF		•	•
LIVERPOOL CENTRAL LOW LEVEL	Lancashire	2L	4' only		•	•
LIVERPOOL JAMES STREET Large Totem	Lancashire	1L	Flat			
LLANDUDNO	Caernarvonshire		HF		•	•
LLANDUDNO JUNCTION	Caernarvonshire	1L	FF		•	•
LLANFAIRFECHAN **	Caernarvonshire		FF		•	•
LLANGEFNI	Anglesey		FF	1964	•	•
LLANWRST & TREFRIW	Denbighshire		FF		•	•
LONDON ROAD HIGH LEVEL	Nottinghamshire	2L	FF	1967	•	•
LONG BUCKBY	Northamptonshire		FF		•	•
LONG EATON (renamed from Sawley Junction)	Derbyshire		FF	1967	•	•
LONGPORT	Staffordshire		FF		•	•
LONGPORT ** face drilled version	Staffordshire		FF			•
LONGSIGHT FOR BELLE VUE	Lancashire	2L	HF	1958		•
LONGTON ** ^also some poster header totems	Staffordshire		FF^		•	•
LONGTOWN	Cumberland		FF	1969	•	•
LOSTOCK GRALAM	Cheshire		FF		•	•
LOSTOCK HALL	Lancashire		FF	1969	•	•
LOSTOCK JUNCTION ** *re-opened 1988	Lancashire	1L	FF	1966*	•	•
LOUGHBOROUGH *heritage station 1974	Leicestershire		FF	1969*	•	•
LOUGHBOROUGH MIDLAND	Leicestershire	2L	HF		•	•

** = some totems face drilled   1L = one line: 2L = two line: LP = Lower panel

Station Name		County in 1956	Layout	Flange	Closed	Auction	Survived
LOWER DARWEN		Lancashire		FF	1958		•
LUFFENHAM		Rutland		FF	1966	•	•
LUTON BUTE STREET		Bedfordshire	1L	HF	1965	•	•
LUTON MIDLAND ROAD		Bedfordshire	1L/2L	HF/FF		•	•
LUTTERWORTH		Leicestershire		FF	1969	•	•
LYTHAM		Lancashire		HF		•	•
MACCLESFIELD		Cheshire		FF		•	•
MACCLESFIELD CENTRAL		Cheshire	2L	HF		•	•
MACCLESFIELD HIBEL ROAD		Cheshire	2L	HF	1960	•	•
MAGHULL		Lancashire		FF		•	•
MANCHESTER CENTRAL	+ 4' totems 2L	Lancashire	1L	FF*	1969	•	•
MANCHESTER EXCHANGE **		Lancashire	2L	FF	1969	•	•
MANCHESTER LONDON ROAD^	renamed 1960 New discovery	Lancashire	2L	HF			
MANCHESTER VICTORIA		Lancashire	2L	FF		•	•
MANOR ROAD		Cheshire		FF		•	•
MANSFIELD TOWN	*re-opened 1995	Nottinghamshire		HF	1964*	•	•
MANSFIELD WOODHOUSE	*re-opened 1995	Nottinghamshire		FF	1964*	•	•
MANTON **		Rutland		FF	1966	•	•
MARKET HARBOROUGH **		Leicestershire		FF		•	•
MARPLE		Cheshire		FF		•	•
MARSH LANE AND STRAND ROAD		Lancashire	3L	HF		•	•
MARSTON GREEN **	Drilled version in auction	Warwickshire		FF		•	•
MARYPORT		Cumberland		FF			•
MATLOCK		Derbyshire		FF		•	•
MATLOCK BATH **	*re-opened 1972	Derbyshire		FF	1967*	•	•
MAULDETH ROAD	+ some wooden totems	Lancashire		FF		•	•
MEIR		Staffordshire		FF	1966	•	•
MELTON MOWBRAY		Leicestershire		FF		•	•
MENAI BRIDGE		Caernarvonshire		FF	1966	•	•
MEOLS		Cheshire		FF		•	•
MEOLS COP		Lancashire		FF		•	•
MERSEY ROAD & AIGBURTH **		Lancashire	2L	FF	1972	•	•
MIDDLETON JUNCTION		Lancashire	2L	FF	1966	•	•
MILES PLATTING **		Lancashire		FF		•	•
MILL HILL		Lancashire		FF		•	•

^MANCHESTER LONDON ROAD was heavily rebuilt from 1958 to 1962 and was re-named Manchester Piccadilly. Totems not carried after the re-build.

** = some totems face drilled   1L = one line: 2L = two line: LP = Lower panel

Station Name	County in 1956	Layout	Flange	Closed	Auction	Survived
MILL HILL BROADWAY	Middlesex	1L	FF			•
MILLBROOK	Bedfordshire		FF		•	•
MILLERS DALE	Derbyshire		FF	1967	•	•
MILNROW **	Lancashire		FF		•	•
MILNTHORPE	Westmoreland		FF	1968	•	•
MOBBERLEY	Cheshire		FF		•	•
MOIRA	Leicestershire		FF	1964	•	•
MOLD	Flintshire		FF	1962		
MOLLINGTON	Cheshire		FF	1960		
MONTON GREEN	Lancashire		HF	1969	•	•
MOORSIDE AND WARDLEY	Lancashire	2L	FF		•	•
MORECAMBE EUSTON ROAD	Lancashire	2L	HF	1963	•	•
MORECAMBE PROMENADE *new station 1994	Lancashire	2L	HF	1994*		•
MORETON	Cheshire		HF		•	•
MOSES GATE **	Lancashire		FF		•	•
MOSSLEY	Lancashire		FF		•	•
MOSSLEY HILL	Lancashire		FF		•	•
MOSTON	Lancashire		FF		•	•
MOSTYN	Flintshire		FF	1966	•	•
MOULDSWORTH	Cheshire		HF			
NANTWICH	Cheshire		FF		•	•
NARBOROUGH *re-opened 1970	Leicestershire		FF	1968*	•	•
NAVIGATION ROAD	Cheshire		FF		•	•
NELSON **	Lancashire		FF		•	•
NESTON NORTH	Cheshire	1L	HF		•	•
NESTON SOUTH	Cheshire	1L	HF			
NEW BASFORD	Nottinghamshire		FF	1964	•	•
NEW HEY	Lancashire		FF		•	•
NEW MILLS CENTRAL	Derbyshire	1L	FF		•	•
NEW MILLS NEWTOWN	Derbyshire	2L	HF		•	•
NEWCASTLE **	Staffordshire		FF	1964	•	•
NEWCHAPEL & GOLDENHILL	Staffordshire	2L	FF	1964	•	•
NEWCHURCH last in auction 1965	Lancashire		FF	1964	•	•
NEWPORT	Shropshire		FF	1964	•	•
NEWSHOLME	Yorkshire		FF	1957		

** = some totems face drilled   1L = one line: 2L = two line: LP = Lower panel

Station Name		County in 1956	Layout	Flange	Closed	Auction	Survived
NEWSTEAD **		Nottinghamshire		FF		•	•
NEWTON FOR HYDE	New discovery	Cheshire	2L	HF			•
NEWTON HEATH		Lancashire		FF	1966	•	•
NEWTON-LE-WILLOWS		Lancashire		HF		•	•
NORMACOT		Staffordshire		FF	1964	•	•
NORTH WEMBLEY		Middlesex		HF		•	•
NORTHAMPTON BRIDGE STREET		Northamptonshire	2L	FF	1964	•	•
NORTHAMPTON CASTLE		Northamptonshire	2L	FF		•	•
NORTHFIELD		Warwickshire		FF		•	•
NORTHOLT PARK		Middlesex		FF		•	•
NORTHWICH **		Cheshire		FF			
NOTTINGHAM MIDLAND		Nottinghamshire	1L	HF			
NUNEATON **		Warwickshire		FF		•	•
OAKAMOOR		Staffordshire		FF	1965	•	•
OAKHAM		Rutland		FF		•	•
OAKLEY		Bedfordshire		FF	1958	•	•
OLD DALBY		Leicestershire		FF	1966	•	•
OLD ROAN		Lancashire		FF		•	•
OLD TRAFFORD	renamed 1992	Lancashire		FF		•	•
OLDBURY & BROMFORD LANE		Worcestershire	2L	FF		•	•
OLDHAM CENTRAL **		Lancashire	2L	FF	1966	•	•
OLDHAM MUMPS		Lancashire		FF		•	
OLDHAM WERNETH		Lancashire		FF			
OLNEY		Buckinghamshire		FF	1962	•	•
ORMSKIRK **		Lancashire		FF		•	•
ORRELL		Lancashire		FF			
ORRELL PARK		Lancashire		FF		•	•
OXENHOLME		Westmorland		FF		•	•
OXFORD ROAD **		Lancashire		FF		•	•
PADGATE		Lancashire		FF		•	•
PADIHAM	New discovery	Lancashire		FF	1957		
PARK STREET & FROGMORE		Hertfordshire	2L	FF		•	•

** = some totems face drilled   1L = one line: 2L = two line: LP = Lower panel

Station Name	County in 1956	Layout	Flange	Closed	Auction	Survived
PARTINGTON	Cheshire		FF	1964	•	•
PATRICROFT	Lancashire		FF		•	•
PEAK FOREST FOR PEAK DALE	Derbyshire	LP	FF	1967	•	•
PEAR TREE & NORMANTON *re-opened 1976	Derbyshire	2L	FF	1968*	•	•
PELSALL	Staffordshire		FF	1965		•
PEMBERTON	Lancashire		FF			•
PENDLEBURY	Lancashire		FF	1960		•
PENDLETON	Lancashire		FF	1966	•	
PENDLETON BROAD STREET **	Lancashire	2L	FF	1998	•	•
PENKRIDGE **	Staffordshire		FF		•	•
PENMAENMAWR	Caernarvonshire		FF		•	•
PENNS	Warwickshire		FF	1965	•	•
PENRITH	Cumberland		FF		•	•
PENRUDDOCK	Cumberland		FF	1972	•	•
PERRY BARR **	Warwickshire		FF		•	•
PIDDINGTON	Northamptonshire		FF	1962	•	•
PINXTON SOUTH	Nottinghamshire	1L	HF	1963	•	•
PITTS HILL	Staffordshire		FF	1964	•	•
PLEASINGTON + some painted wood	Lancashire		FF			•
PLECK	Staffordshire		FF?	1958		•
POLESWORTH **	Warwickshire		FF		•	•
PORT SUNLIGHT	Cheshire		FF		•	•
POULTON	Lancashire		FF		•	•
POYNTON	Cheshire		FF		•	•
PRESCOT	Lancashire		FF		•	•
PRESTATYN	Flintshire		HF		•	•
PRESTBURY	Cheshire		FF		•	•
PRESTON +* flat poster board header type	Lancashire		HF*		•	•
PRESTON ROAD renamed Rice Lane in 1984	Lancashire		FF		•	•
PRESTWICH **	Lancashire		FF		•	•
PRIMROSE HILL	London		HF	1991	•	•
PYE BRIDGE	Nottinghamshire		FF	1967	•	•
QUEENS PARK 4' totems only	Middlesex		FF		•	•
QUEENSFERRY	Flintshire		FF	1966	•	•
QUORN & WOODHOUSE *heritage stn 1974	Leicestershire	1L	FF	1963*		•

** = some totems face drilled   1L = one line: 2L = two line: LP = Lower panel

Station Name	County in 1956	Layout	Flange	Closed	Auction	Survived
RADCLIFFE BLACK LANE **	Lancashire	2L	FF	1970		•
RADCLIFFE CENTRAL	Lancashire		FF		•	•
RADFORD **	Nottinghamshire		FF	1964	•	•
RADLETT some o/p on Caledonian Road	Hertfordshire		HF			
RADWAY GREEN	Cheshire		FF	1966	•	•
RAINFORD JUNCTION	Lancashire	1L	FF		•	•
RAINHILL	Lancashire		FF		•	•
RAMSBOTTOM *heritage station 1987	Lancashire		FF	1972*	•	•
RAVENGLASS **	Cumberland		FF		•	•
RAWTENSTALL *new heritage stn 1992	Lancashire		FF	1972*	•	•
REDDISH NORTH	Lancashire	1L	HF		•	•
REDDISH SOUTH	Lancashire	1L	HF		•	•
REPTON & WILLINGTON *re-opened 1994	Derbyshire	2L	FF	1968*	•	•
RHYL	Flintshire		HF/FF		•	•
RICKMANSWORTH CHURCH STREET	Hertfordshire	2L	HF	1952		
RIDGMONT	Bedfordshire		FF		•	•
RISHTON	Lancashire		FF		•	•
ROADE	Northamptonshire		HF	1964	•	•
ROBY **	Lancashire		FF		•	•
ROCHDALE	Lancashire		HF		•	•
ROCK FERRY	Cheshire		HF		•	•
ROMILEY	Cheshire		FF		•	•
ROOSE **	Lancashire		FF		•	•
ROSE GROVE	Lancashire		FF		•	•
ROSE HILL	Cheshire		FF		•	•
ROWSLEY **	Derbyshire		FF	1967	•	•
ROYTON	Lancashire		FF	1966	•	•
ROYTON JUNCTION	Lancashire	1L	FF		•	•
RUDDINGTON	Nottinghamshire		FF	1963	•	•
RUGBY CENTRAL also FF o/p variant not in auction	Warwickshire	1L	HF	1969	•	
RUGBY MIDLAND	Warwickshire	1L	HF			
RUGELEY TOWN *re-opened 1997	Staffordshire	1L	FF	1965*	•	•
RUGELEY TRENT VALLEY	Staffordshire	2L	FF		•	•
RUNCORN	Cheshire		FF			
RUSHCLIFFE HALT *re-opened 2000	Nottinghamshire	1L	FF	1963*	•	•

** = some totems face drilled	1L = one line: 2L = two line: LP = Lower panel

Station Name	County in 1956	Layout	Flange	Closed	Auction	Survived
SADDLEWORTH	Yorkshire		FF	1968	•	•
SALE	Cheshire		FF		•	•
SALFORD **	Lancashire		HF/FF		•	•
SALTLEY	Warwickshire		FF	1968	•	•
SALTNEY FERRY (MOLD JUNCTION)	Flintshire	2L	FF?	1962		
SALWICK **	Lancashire		FF		•	•
SANDBACH	Cheshire		FF		•	•
SANDHILLS also 4' totems FF	Lancashire		HF/FF		•	•
SANKEY **	Lancashire		FF		•	•
SAWLEY JUNCTION (renamed Long Eaton)	Derbyshire	1L	FF		•	•
SAXBY	Leicestershire		FF	1961		
SCALE HALL	Lancashire		FF	1966	•	•
SEACOMBE new discovery	Cheshire		HF	1960		
SEAFORTH & LITHERLAND **	Lancashire	2L	FF		•	•
SEALAND	Flintshire		FF	1968	•	•
SEASCALE	Cumberland		FF		•	•
SEATON	Rutland		FF	1966	•	•
SEFTON PARK	Lancashire		FF	1960		•
SELLAFIELD	Cumberland		FF		•	•
SELLY OAK	Warwickshire		FF		•	•
SETTLE	Yorkshire		FF		•	•
SHAP **	Westmorland		FF	1968	•	•
SHARNBROOK	Bedfordshire		FF	1960	•	•
SHAW & CROMPTON **	Lancashire		FF		•	•
SHEFFORD	Bedfordshire		FF	1962	•	•
SHENSTONE	Staffordshire		FF		•	•
SHOTTON HIGH LEVEL	Flintshire	2L	FF		•	•
SHOTTON LOW LEVEL *re-opened 1972	Flintshire	1L	HF	1966 *	•	•
SHUSTOKE	Warwickshire		FF	1968	•	•
SILEBY *re-opened 1994	Leicestershire		FF	1968*	•	•
SILECROFT	Cumberland		FF		•	•
SILLOTH	Cumberland		FF	1964	•	•
SILLOTH ** face drilled version	Cumberland		FF	1964		•
SILVERDALE	Lancashire		FF		•	•
SKIPTON	Yorkshire		FF		•	•
SMETHWICK ROLFE STREET	Staffordshire	2L	FF		•	•
** = some totems face drilled			1L = one line: 2L = two line: LP = Lower panel			

Station Name	County in 1956	Layout	Flange	Closed	Auction	Survived
SMITHY BRIDGE *re-opened 1985	Lancashire		HF	1960*		
SOUTH ACTON	Middlesex		FF			•
SOUTH HAMPSTEAD	London		HF		•	•
SOUTH KENTON *(+4' totems FF)	Middlesex		FF*		•	•
SPITAL	Cheshire		HF		•	•
SPON LANE	Staffordshire		FF	1964	•	•
SPONDON **	Derbyshire		FF			
SQUIRES GATE	Lancashire		FF			
ST. ALBANS ABBEY	Hertfordshire		FF		•	•
ST. ALBANS CITY some o/p on Cheddington	Hertfordshire		HF/FF		•	•
ST. ANNES	Lancashire		FF		•	•
ST. HELENS CENTRAL	Lancashire	2L	HF	1952		
ST. HELENS JUNCTION	Lancashire	2L	FF		•	•
ST. HELENS SHAW STREET	Lancashire	2L	FF?			
ST. LUKES **	Lancashire		FF	1968	•	•
ST. MICHAELS	Lancashire		FF		•	•
ST PANCRAS New discovery poster header type 52in long	London		Flat		•	•
STACKSTEADS	Lancashire		FF	1966		•
STAFFORD	Staffordshire		FF		•	•
STALYBRIDGE	Lancashire		FF		•	•
STANLOW & THORNTON	Cheshire		FF		•	•
STANMORE VILLAGE	Middlesex		HF	1952		
STANTON GATE	Derbyshire		FF	1967	•	•
STAPLEFORD	Nottinghamshire		FF	1967	•	•
STAVELEY	Westmorland		HF			•
STECHFORD	Warwickshire		HF		•	•
STOCKINGFORD	Warwickshire		FF	1968	•	•
STOCKPORT EDGELEY	Cheshire	2L	FF		•	•
STOCKPORT TIVIOT DALE	Lancashire	2L	FF	1967	•	•
STOKE MANDEVILLE	Buckinghamshire		FF		•	•
STOKE-ON-TRENT	Staffordshire		HF		•	•
STONE *re-opened 2008	Staffordshire		FF	2004*	•	•
STONEBRIDGE PARK	Middlesex		HF		•	•
STREETLY	Staffordshire		FF	1965	•	•
STRETFORD	Lancashire		FF		•	•
STRETTON	Derbyshire		FF	1961	•	•
STRINES **	Derbyshire		FF		•	•

** = some totems face drilled   1L = one line: 2L = two line: LP = Lower panel

Station Name	County in 1956	Layout	Flange	Closed	Auction	Survived
STUBBINS	Lancashire		FF	1972	•	•
STYAL	Cheshire		FF		•	•
SUDBURY	Staffordshire		FF	1966	•	•
SUDBURY & HARROW ROAD	Middlesex	2L	FF		•	•
SUDBURY HILL HARROW	Middlesex	LP	FF		•	•
SUMMERSEAT *heritage station open 1987	Lancashire		FF	1972*	•	•
SUTTON COLDFIELD	Warwickshire		FF		•	•
SUTTON JUNCTION **	Nottinghamshire	1L	FF	1964	•	•
SUTTON PARK	Warwickshire		FF	1965	•	•
SWINTON	Lancashire		HF		•	•
SYSTON *re-opened 1994	Leicestershire		FF	1968*	•	•
TAMWORTH	Staffordshire		FF		•	•
TANHOUSE LANE	Lancashire		FF	1964	•	•
TEBAY	Westmorland		FF	1968	•	•
THATTO HEATH **	Lancashire		FF		•	•
THORNTON-CLEVELEYS	Lancashire		HF	1970	•	•
THRELKELD **	Cumberland		FF	1972	•	•
TIBSHELF TOWN ** FF version in auction	Derbyshire		FF	1963	•	•
TILE HILL ** Face drilled version in auction	Warwickshire		FF		•	•
TIMPERLEY	Cheshire		FF		•	•
TIPTON OWEN STREET	Staffordshire	2L	HF		•	•
TODD LANE JUNCTION	Lancashire	LP	HF	1968	•	•
TODMORDEN	Yorkshire		HF/FF		•	•
TOWCESTER	Northamptonshire		HF	1952		
TOWN GREEN & AUGHTON small letters	Lancashire	2L	HF			•
TRAFFORD PARK	Lancashire		FF		•	•
TRENCH CROSSING	Shropshire		FF	1964	•	•
TRENT rectangular enamel poster header type	Derbyshire		Flat	1968	•	•
TRENTHAM	Staffordshire		FF	1964	•	•
TRING	Hertfordshire		FF		•	•
TROUTBECK **	Cumberland		FF	1972	•	•
TROWELL	Nottinghamshire		FF	1967	•	•
TUNSTALL	Staffordshire		FF	1964	•	•
TURVEY	Bedfordshire		FF	1962	•	•
TUTBURY *re-opened 1989	Derbyshire		FF	1966*	•	•

** = some totems face drilled   1L = one line: 2L = two line: LP = Lower panel

Station Name		County in 1956	Layout	Flange	Closed	Auction	Survived
TYLDESLEY		Lancashire		FF	1969	•	•
ULLESTHORPE		Leicestershire		FF	1962	•	•
ULVERSTON		Lancashire		FF		•	•
UPHOLLAND		Lancashire		FF		•	•
UPTON-BY-CHESTER		Cheshire		FF	1984	•	•
URMSTON		Lancashire		FF		•	•
UTTOXETER		Staffordshire		FF		•	•
VAUXHALL & DUDDESTON		Warwickshire	2L	FF		•	•
WALKDEN HIGH LEVEL		Lancashire	2L	FF		•	•
WALLESEY GROVE ROAD		Cheshire	2L/LP	FF		•	•
WALLESEY VILLAGE		Cheshire	1L	FF		•	•
WALSALL		Staffordshire		FF		•	•
WALTON JUNCTION **		Lancashire	1L	FF		•	•
WARBRECK	New discovery	Lancashire		HF?	1960		
WARCOP		Westmorland		FF	1962	•	•
WARRINGTON		Lancashire		FF		•	•
WARRINGTON CENTRAL		Lancashire	2L	FF		•	•
WARWICK ROAD		Lancashire		FF		•	•
WATER ORTON		Warwickshire		FF		•	•
WATERFOOT		Lancashire		FF	1966	•	•
WATERLOO		Lancashire		FF		•	•
WATFORD HIGH STREET	*(+4' totems FF)	Hertfordshire	2L*	FF		•	•
WATFORD JUNCTION		Hertfordshire	1L	HF		•	•
WATFORD NORTH		Hertfordshire	1L	HF		•	•
WATFORD WEST		Hertfordshire	1L	HF	2002	•	•
WAVERTREE		Lancashire		HF	1958		•
WEDNESBURY TOWN		Staffordshire		FF	1964	•	•
WELFORD & KILWORTH		Leicestershire	2L	FF		•	•
WELLINGBOROUGH MIDLAND ROAD		Northamptonshire	2L	HF	1964	•	•
WEM		Shropshire		FF		•	•
WEMBLEY CENTRAL	re-developed 2008	Middlesex		HF		•	•
WEMBLEY HILL	named Wembley Complex 1978	Middlesex		FF		•	•

** = some totems face drilled   1L = one line: 2L = two line: LP = Lower panel

Station Name		County in 1956	Layout	Flange	Closed	Auction	Survived
WEMBLEY STADIUM	o/p on Watford Junction	Middlesex		HF	1969	•	•
WENDOVER		Buckinghamshire		FF		•	•
WEST ALLERTON		Lancashire		FF		•	•
WEST DERBY		Lancashire		FF	1960		
WEST END LANE		London		HF		•	•
WEST HAMPSTEAD MIDLAND		London	1L	HF		•	•
WESTHOUGHTON **		Lancashire		FF		•	•
WESTHOUSES & BLACKWELL		Derbyshire	2L	FF	1967	•	•
WHALEY BRIDGE		Derbyshire		FF		•	•
WHALLEY	*re-opened 1994	Lancashire		FF	1962*		
WHATSTANDWELL **		Derbyshire		FF		•	•
WHETSTONE		Leicestershire		FF	1963		•
WHITACRE		Warwickshire		FF	1968	•	•
WHITCHURCH **		Shropshire		FF		•	•
WHITEFIELD		Lancashire		FF		•	•
WHITEHAVEN BRANSTY		Cumberland	2L	FF		•	•
WIDNES	New discovery	Lancashire		FF			•
WIDNES CENTRAL		Lancashire	LP	FF	1964	•	•
WIDNES NORTH		Lancashire	2L	FF		•	•
WIDNES SOUTH		Lancashire	2L	FF	1962		
WIGAN		Lancashire		FF		•	•
WIGSTON GLEN PARVA		Leicestershire	2L	FF	1968	•	•
WIGSTON MAGNA		Leicestershire	1L	FF	1968	•	•
WIGSTON SOUTH		Leicestershire	1L	FF	1962	•	•
WIGTON		Cumberland		FF		•	•
WILLENHALL		Staffordshire		FF	1965	•	•
WILLESDEN JUNCTION	+ *4 ft totems 1 line	London	2L	FF*	1962	•	•
WILMSLOW		Cheshire		HF/FF		•	•
WILNECOTE		Warwickshire		FF		•	•
WILPSHIRE		Lancashire		HF		•	•
WINDERMERE		Westmoreland		HF		•	•
WINGFIELD		Derbyshire		FF	1967	•	•
WINSFORD		Cheshire		FF		•	•
WINSLOW **		Buckinghamshire		FF	1968	•	•
WITHINGTON & WEST DIDSBURY	New discovery	Lancashire	2L	FF			

** = some totems face drilled   1L = one line: 2L = two line: LP = Lower panel

Station Name		County in 1956	Layout	Flange	Closed	Auction	Survived
WITTON **		Warwickshire		FF		•	•
WOBURN SANDS **		Bedfordshire		FF		•	•
WOLVERHAMPTON HIGH LEVEL		Staffordshire	2L	HF			•
WOLVERTON		Buckinghamshire		HF		•	•
WOODFORD HALSE		Northamptonshire		FF	1966	•	•
WOODLANDS ROAD		Lancashire		FF		•	•
WOODLEY **		Cheshire		FF		•	•
WORKINGTON MAIN		Cumberland	2L	HF		•	•
WYLDE GREEN		Warwickshire		FF		•	•
WYRE DOCK		Lancashire		FF	1976		•
WYRE DOCK **	face drilled version	Lancashire		FF	1976	•	•
WYRLEY & CHESLYN HAY		Staffordshire	.	FF	1965	•	•

** = some totems face drilled   1L = one line: 2L = two line: LP = Lower panel

Other London Midland Region Collectables

6
The North Eastern Region

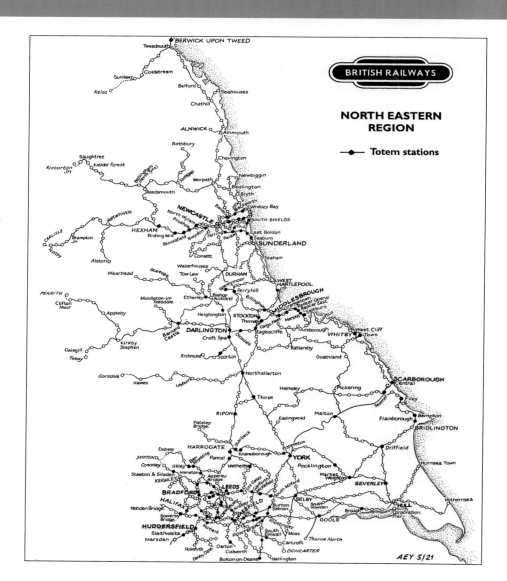

Opening Comments

The North Eastern Region (NER) is by far the smallest of the six BR Regions that came into being on 1 January 1948. Although covering a large area of England, it had only 116 stations that carried totems, 45% of the number in the whole of Lancashire for example, and slightly less than the total that were fitted in Lanarkshire. However, its size is more than countered by its importance in railway history, as it is the birthplace of world rail travel. Following on from Durham and Northumberland's early network of coal-mining waggonways using horse traction on rails, steam locomotives were first developed here. This proved to be an invention that transformed the way peopled travelled and goods were moved. In 1825 the world's first regular-service steam railway opened between **Stockton** and **Darlington**, based on the engineering prowess of George Stephenson. Other local pioneers included his son Robert, Timothy Hackworth, William Hedley and George Hudson, the first railway magnate.

The BR(NER) was the near-direct post-nationalisation descendant of the North Eastern Railway, which had amalgamated with some smaller companies to form the LNER in 1923. The BR network, from the Humber Estuary to Scottish Border, was based on former LNER lines, plus just fewer than 100 miles of ex-NBR lines (Border area, Wansbeck/Rothbury, plus Silloth) for a few months. In 1950, in a major boundary redrawing, it gained those former LMS lines that lay in present-day West and North Yorkshire. In 1967 it was disbanded and merged with the Eastern Region, so it was in existence for less than twenty years!

Darlington's superb trainshed interior in the 1890s.

However, it was not just engineering expertise that was present in the region. Some of the region's stations are superb, Newcastle Central being the supreme example. The NER inherited this from the York, Newcastle & Berwick Railway (YN&BR). It then built other fine stations at Alnwick, **Darlington Bank Top**, Gateshead East, Hull Paragon, Middlesbrough, **Stockton**, Sunderland, Tynemouth and **York**. From this list, Alnwick is a second-hand book warehouse, Gateshead East is largely demolished, and the original Tynemouth is part of the Metro, but the rest are in use, though in refurbished or rebuilt status following WWII air raids.

Above is a photograph of superb **Darlington** station, which opened in July 1887.

Brief Regional History

The NER, incorporated in 1854, was formed from several constituent companies that had sprung up during the early years of the area's railway development. One of the most important of these was the YN&BR, itself formed in 1847 from several smaller companies that began in 1842. As well as building Newcastle Central, the YN&BR also constructed the High Level Tyne Bridge and the Royal Border Bridge at Berwick. They were a very progressive company with enormous vision.

The vision was that of George Hudson, who controlled several railway companies, and he saw the immense possibility of building and controlling a railway between London and Edinburgh. As well as the YN&BR, he ran the York & North Midland Railway (Y&NMR), a company he planned to form a major part of his north–south railway. The Y&NMR included most of the railways in the area bounded by **York**, **Whitby**, Hull and **Leeds,** and these strategic links allowed London to be reached via the Great Northern. Two ex-Y&NMR station totems are shown below.

One of the oldest Y&NMR routes was the Whitby & Pickering Railway of 1836, engineered by **North Wylam**-born George Stephenson and absorbed in 1845. Another key component of the NER was the Leeds Northern Railway (LNR), originally the Leeds and Thirsk Railway, which provided lines between **Leeds**, **Harrogate**, **Ripon**, **Thirsk**, **Northallerton** and **Stockton**. In 1845 the L&TR received permission to construct a line from Leeds to Thirsk, part of which opened in 1848, but problems building Bramhope Tunnel (3,761 yards – 3,439m) between Horsforth and the Arthington Viaduct, delayed trains operating into Leeds until 1849. Today, sections of the former LNR line form the *Harrogate Line* between **Leeds** and **Harrogate**, and the **Northallerton** to **Stockton** line. The final and smallest component was the **Malton** to **Driffield** line, absorbed in 1854.

The next big development occurred in 1862, when the NER absorbed the Newcastle & Carlisle plus the Hull & Holderness Railway companies. A pair of N&CR totems appears above. **Blaydon** and **Stocksfield** both opened in 1835.

A year later the NER absorbed the Stockton & Darlington, followed by other Durham independents. It had also taken over Hartlepool Dock in 1857 and added West Hartlepool Harbour & Railway shortly afterwards. The present East Coast Main Line (ECML) between Durham and Newcastle was opened in 1868, followed by Doncaster to **York** via **Selby** in 1871 and the Sunderland to **West Hartlepool** in 1905. The bulk of the future North Eastern Region network was then in place.

In rural Northumberland, the North British Railway was an interloper, opening Riccarton Junction to **Hexham** (1862), Reedsmouth to Morpeth (1865) and Scotsgap to Rothbury (1870).

Apart from the North British presence in the far north, the only other 'invader' of NER territory was the Hull & Barnsley, established by Hull businessmen to try to break the NER monopoly. The H&B line opened in 1885, running from Hull's Alexandra Dock in the east and from Neptune Street and Dairycoates Goods yards in the west, to join at a large junction at West Springbank and on towards Barnsley. Its city terminus was Hull Cannon Street, (opened 1885, closed 1924). However, this remained as a freight depot until 1968, but has since been demolished. The NER finally absorbed the H&B in 1922, just before the formation of the 'Big Four'. Right is a quartet of totems from former NER stations.

At its zenith, the NER ran on 4,990 miles of track, including lines in Scotland, Cumberland and Westmorland, but with many acquisitions and duplicated routes, some rationalisation had to take place. Befitting the successor to the Stockton & Darlington Railway, the NER had a reputation for innovation. It was a pioneer in architectural and design matters, and in electrification. In its final days it also began the collection that became the Railway Museum at York, now the National Railway Museum, so rail aficionados and collectors have a great deal for which to thank the NER. It was also the first railway company in the world to appoint a full-time salaried architect to work with its chief engineer in constructing railway facilities, including stations, hotels and other buildings; accounting for their superb stations.

On the formation of the LNER in 1923, the NER was its largest route mileage contributor (1,864 miles out of a total of 6,590). They also contributed thirteen electric locomotives, having started traction developments back in 1905.

Other companies forming the amalgamation included the Great Central, the Great Eastern, the Great Northern, Great North of Scotland and the North British. Because some of these companies offered competing routes and facilities, slimming down of the system was inevitable. The LMS also offered services into West Yorkshire with their infrastructure. An example of change occurred in Leeds, where Central, New and Wellington stations all existed in close proximity. The latter two stations were combined as **Leeds City,** with **Leeds Central** (which was a joint GNR, LNWR, L&YR and NER station), eventually closing in 1967. Alongside the totem right is the hawkseye sign that preceded it. Tangerine was the colour used in some areas by the LNER (the Leeds City hawkseye for example) and BR's NER retained it in 1948.

There were other prominent examples of two stations in the same town for rival companies, affording collectors great chances to display pairs together. Bradford had **Bradford Exchange** (ex-L&YR/GNR and closed 1973) and **Bradford Forster Square** (ex-MR). Dewsbury had **Dewsbury Central** (ex-GNR and closed 1964) and **Dewsbury Wellington Road** (ex-LNWR) and Wakefield had **Wakefield Kirkgate** (ex-L&YR) and **Wakefield Westgate** (ex-GNR). The two Bradford totems are 2-line, both from Dewsbury are lower panel, but the two Wakefield totems have different layouts.

LNER developments, innovation and investment were continued, based in part on the NER's good revenue streams from freight, especially coal, as well as the appointment of Nigel Gresley as Chief Mechanical Engineer. He held the post for much of the LNER's existence and his 'big engines policy' produced some of the UK's finest locomotives, including the A4 4-6-2 *Mallard,* the fastest steam loco on record.

New marshalling yards were built at Hull and Whitemoor in Cambridgeshire and the line from Sheffield to Manchester was electrified. Then in 1929, Gill Sans was chosen as the LNER's standard typeface and soon it appeared on every facet of the company's identity, from locomotive nameplates and hand-painted and enamel station signage to printed restaurant car menus, timetables and advertising posters. A slightly modified Gill Sans was retained by BR in 1949, so most totems displayed in this book sport this style. The font was the railways' official typeface until British Rail replaced it in the mid-1960s with Rail Alphabet. Further details on the railway fonts used on station signage can be found in Chapter 2.

Middlesbrough station after a 1942 air raid destroyed the Victorian trainshed roof.

Everything in the north-east was running well until, in 1939, WWII broke out. The industrial heartlands of Tyneside, Wearside and Teesside suffered constant raids from enemy aircraft throughout the war. In one of those raids Middlesbrough's wonderful glass and iron station roof was destroyed. Hull, Newcastle, Sunderland and **York** were other key targets. Once hostilities ceased, the north-east's industrial sector became a major contributor to the British recovery. At **Billingham** there were extensive ICI chemical plants producing plastics, but following company restructuring, most of the facilities were sold. Other locations sporting totems in the area include **Heighington**, **Croft Spa** and **West Hartlepool,** all of which are collectable and not particularly common.

The wartime beating taken by Britain forced the Transport Act of 1947 to be passed, putting the pre-war 'Big Four' into public ownership. At the planning stage there were to have been five regions, but at the eleventh hour the Eastern Region was broken in two, with the ER taking 2,836 route miles and a North Eastern Region consisting of 1,823 miles, almost a 'throwback' arrangement to the area's pre-grouping management. The most important of the region's routes was the northernmost portion of the ECML running from north of Doncaster to Marshall Meadows on the Scottish border. The NER was bisected by two important cross-country routes. In the south, the eastern section of the trans-Pennine route ran from Marsden via **Huddersfield**, **Leeds**, **Garforth**, **Selby** and **Brough** into Hull and the important Newcastle–**Carlisle** route traversed the northern sector.

Other network routes, largely originating from the former North Eastern Railway, connected to the major lines throughout the 1950s, including the counties of Durham and Northumberland, plus the East and North Ridings of Yorkshire.

The conurbations of Tyneside, Wearside and Teesside contained a high density of lines, carrying not only suburban passenger traffic, but also large volumes of freight generated by the coal, steel and chemical industries of the area. There were also branch lines of rural character, particularly in the more remote parts of Durham and Northumberland, as well as in the Yorkshire Dales and Moors. Some of these closed in the early BR years (e.g. Wensleydale), but further cuts were accelerated by Beeching and subsequent economic reviews. Yorkshire was especially 'pruned' with more than 30% of totem stations being closed, including the quartet shown below.

The relative scarcity of stations fitted with totems reflects the BR NER policy not to embark on a major signage programme. Compared with the SR, the NER had relatively few stations with long platforms, so the numbers of totems required was low. What is interesting, however, is the high number of survivors (97.5%), with only **Northallerton, Seaburn** and **Whitby West Cliff** totems being currently unknown. This is by far the highest percentage of survivors in any of the six regions. Of the known survivors, only eight have not appeared in auction, including the pair above.

Totem Geography
Alan Young

The North East corner of England is an area combining dramatic history (aside from the development of railways) with abundant natural beauty, classic castles, cathedrals and bastions of industry. Much of the coast is peppered with historic sites and the rugged city of Durham has always been a great seat of learning. Much of the western boundary follows the Pennine Chain, and the eastern coastal area contains stations whose totems are very desirable, e.g. **Scarborough Central**.

For reasons that are not entirely clear, the NE region was allocated tangerine, a colour disliked by some, but accepted and enjoyed by those of us whose first encounter with railway stations was in the North East in the 1950s or '60s. The earliest flat and HF totems were usually of a mid-tangerine or a brownish-orange colour. Unfortunately, these older totems might simply have weathered and lost their original colour and sheen, and some are believed to have been discoloured by fire or burial after removal from their station. Some totems at stations on the south bank of the Tees (as at **Cargo Fleet**, **Grangetown** or **Redcar East**) were damaged and bleached by noxious gas emissions from neighbouring factories (*see* map).

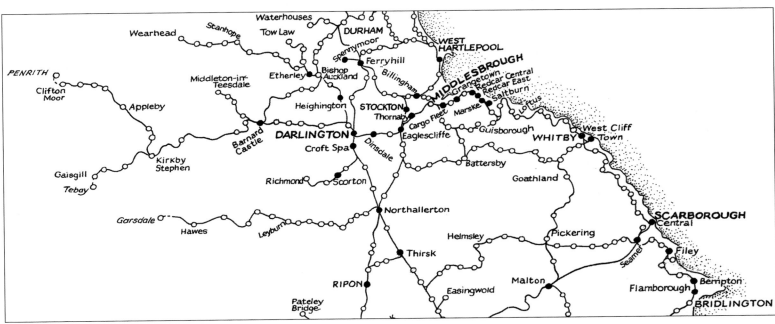

By 1955 it seems that white letters on tangerine were thought to be insufficiently legible and black-edged lettering was introduced. This feature continued on FF totems, with a matching black flange. Some of these totems (as at **Knaresborough**, **Marske** and **Poppleton**) had a strong reddish hue. Totems installed after 1960 reverted to lettering without the black edge, and **Garforth**, **Pontefract**, **Prudhoe** and **Redcar East** totems were all manufactured with tangerine flanges.

At nationalisation, in 1948, station signs of various origins and vintage were already in place. Many of these remained *in situ* until stations closed, or even two decades later, after the NE region had been absorbed into the ER. The NE inherited not only station signage from the LNER, but from the LMS when some West Riding lines were added in 1950 and, in addition, some pre-grouping signs.

For instance, at High Field, a russet NER running-in board was on display in 1976, over 20 years after the station's closure! GNR boards, mounted on stanchions with distinctive ball finials, were still in place after closure at Beeston. The survival of the L&YR nameboards and other signage contributed to Hebden Bridge acquiring Grade-II-listed status, so it is possible to admire these boards today in one of Britain's most appealing stations.

The two B&W photos bottom left show **North Wylam** and **Dinsdale** *in situ*, the second-named being a totem that has not appeared in auction. If we look at totems installed in the north central sector of the NE region, the foregoing map shows a concentration around Wearside, scattered items along the Yorkshire Coast and a few on the ECML. BR's signage policy appears random, and the NER was much less inclined to use totems than the other five regions, with a mere 116 stations being fitted. Only a handful of village stations had them: **Bempton**, **Burton Salmon**, **Croft Spa**, **Flamborough**, **North Wylam**, **Pannal**, **Poppleton**, **Riding Mill**, **Seamer**, **Scorton**, **South Milford** and **Stocksfield** were among the privileged few. The quartet below shows some wonderful items, but note the range of tangerine shades.

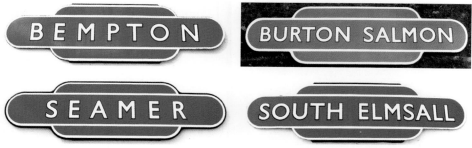

While the ScR provided totems at the most diminutive of their stations, such as **Rutherford**, the NER did not. To emphasise this difference, the ScR installed totems at just over 53% of the approximately 960 stations it possessed in 1948. However, of the 650 or so stations open in 1948 that would become part of NER when its boundaries were fixed, under 20% of all stations received totems. The two maps that follow for the southern area around Leeds and the northern section around Newcastle show the same haphazard distribution. Some lines that survived into the mid-1960s were devoid of totems, such as Hull to Hornsea and Withernsea (18 stations at closure), Bishop Auckland to Sunderland (14 stations, including the termini and Durham), and the Blyth/Newbiggin system (10 stations). Why **Darlington**, **York**, **Huddersfield**, and both of the major **Leeds**, **Bradford**, **Wakefield** and **Dewsbury** stations received totems, while Hull and Newcastle did not, is equally strange.

North Wylam *in situ*.

Dinsdale *in situ* (very rare totem).

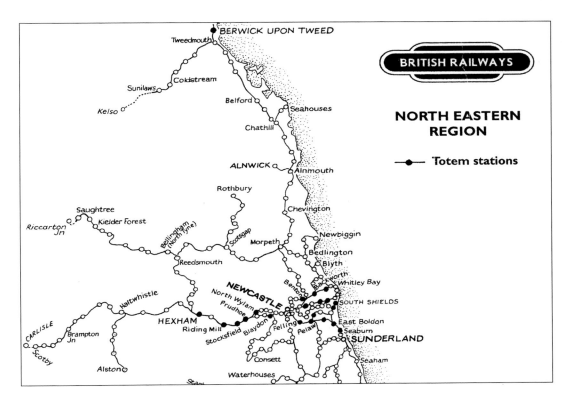

Teesside, with the notable exceptions of Middlesbrough and South Bank, was amply supplied with totems, and there was a little cluster in the environs of **Harrogate**, including **Pannal** and **Starbeck**. There was one notable curiosity in **Spennymoor**. Although closed to regular passenger traffic in 1952, at least one totem was still in place ten years later. These were probably installed after official closure, for the benefit of passengers using occasional excursion trains.

It would have seemed logical when a station was re-signed with totems that complementary enamel RIBs would be simultaneously installed. However, this was not always the case. **Stocksfield** received totems by 1955, but its wooden LNER boards were not replaced with NE specimens until sometime later. Conversely the Coast Circle stations via Wallsend were all fitted with NE boards in about 1959 yet LNER lamp plates continued to be displayed at most of the stations until 1971 or later. **Prudhoe**, **Hebburn** and **High Shields** appear to have received totems and boards at the same time, probably in 1961/2. Whilst many stations never received totems, some received them twice over!

A change in the station name could explain this. Darlington's earlier HF signs read **Darlington Bank Top** whilst later FF types lacked the suffix, simply displaying **Darlington**. Similarly, **Halifax Town** received abbreviated **Halifax** totems after 1961, whilst **Moorthorpe and South Kirkby** totems were replaced with ones reading simply **Moorthorpe**. The change from the two-line to single-line design seemed to produce a more pleasing and more easily readable totem.

The ECML had no totem stations for 90 miles between **Ferryhill** and **Berwick upon Tweed,** as illustrated above, making **Berwick** a very lonely totem outpost indeed!

In the Tyne & Wear area there seems to have been no pattern in totem-fitting. Between Newcastle and Sunderland the stations (except the termini, Gateshead and Monkwearmouth) received totems at different times. On the **South Shields** branch, Jarrow and Tyne Dock were omitted. On the Newcastle–Coast circle (via Wallsend) **Benton**, the line's only gas-lit station in BR days, had totems from an early date, followed by **West Monkseaton**. When fluorescent lighting replaced gas at **Benton**, the totems disappeared, but at about the same time totems were fitted at **Backworth, Howdon-on-Tyne, Percy Main** and **Walker Gate**; quite why these stations were favoured is unclear.

In the southern area of West Yorkshire, a smaller totem concentration than may have been expected was provided. The map below shows this area's distribution.

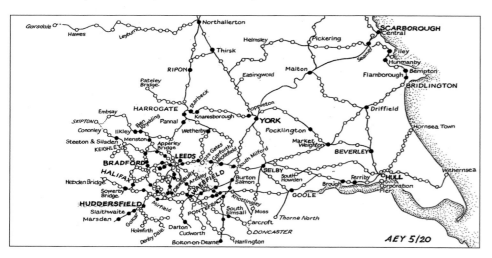

Notice how many stations did not have totems fitted, even though this was a busy commuter area and tangerine station signs would also have been useful for visitors. The southernmost installation was **Bolton on Dearne** and on the line into Hull we find **Brough**, the most common regional totem with 40 auction appearances: **Micklefield** and **Apperley Bridge** are both delightful names.

A more detailed look at railways, stations and history in the **Leeds/Bradford** area is included in a feature article in the next section of this chapter. This shows the involvement of competing railway companies in the Victorian and Edwardian years, before mergers and rationalisation of services took place.

The process of totem removal was apparently as haphazard as their installation had been. Early removals generally occurred when stations closed – **Whitby West Cliff** (closed 1961) was among the earliest, though, as noted earlier, **Benton** lost them when electric lighting was installed, and **York's** totems disappeared under the same circumstances. Totem removal began in earnest in the early 1970s. The Tyne-Wear area was attended to in 1971/2; the **Harrogate** area's totems had gone by mid-1973, and by 1975 Teesside, the Newcastle–**Carlisle** line, and most of Yorkshire had been stripped of totems. **Whitby Town** still had them in 1976.

By 1979 tangerine totems had almost disappeared. A couple of specimens remained fixed to walls at **Walker Gate** and **Howdon-on-Tyne** until that year, no doubt because staff had instructions to remove them with the old lamp posts, and they were not noticed. At **Percy Main** it may be assumed that a virtuous employee stored the totems when the LNER lamps were removed in 1971 because they re-appeared on the new lamp posts, where they remained until the station closed in 1980; it was then converted into a Metro stop. **Driffield** was possibly the only other station to keep its totems until 1978/9.

Rails Around Leeds/Bradford

Over the years there have been many line closures in West Yorkshire and not many of the stations that were fitted with totems remain today. As the NER had the least number of stations fitted anyway, this makes West Yorkshire a prized area to collect from. The pre-grouping map that follows shows that at that time there was rivalry (as well as co-operation) between four companies for passenger business.

The Great Northern (shown in green), the London & North Western (shown in black), the Midland (shown in red) and the North Eastern (orange) all had lines running in the Leeds/Bradford environs. From this map, collectors can also realize just how

many stations there were in the Greater Leeds/Bradford area and yet only a minority were provided with totems. Railway records show there are 39 disused stations in the Leeds area, but many were not fitted with totems and there are currently 15 stations still open for passenger traffic. For Bradford, the corresponding figures are 27 (including small halts) and 16. In addition, heritage stations exist on the popular Keighley and Worth Valley Railway. It is therefore readily apparent that this area of West Yorkshire had a great reliance on rail transportation from the earliest years. Right are a quartet of Leeds/Bradford area totems.

Leeds has undergone something of a recent renaissance. Of the northern English cities, it has some of the most wonderful architecture: the 1858 Town Hall, the restored 1870s Victorian Arcades (Thornton's, the Grand and the magnificent County), the Grand Opera House and now modern apartments in place of once-derelict warehouses. The stations were built above and alongside the River Aire and have undergone major rebuilds since first opening in the 1840s.

Befitting its terminus status, **Leeds Central** was built in 1848 on an elevated site west of City Square by the LNWR but it was always a joint GN/L&Y/LNWR and NE station (as the map alongside shows). It cost around half-a-million pounds to build at that time (a huge sum today). There were major goods facilities and sheds to the North West, one for each of the four companies sharing the station. Sadly, when the lines around Leeds were rationalised it was obvious that the operationally more difficult **Central** station would be sacrificed; this happened on 1 May 1967. Today, few reminders of this bastion of steam remain, but architecturally, it did not possess a particularly appealing appearance.

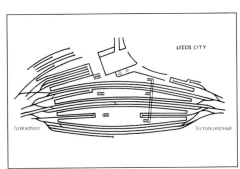

Leeds station complex in the 1960s.

The name was based on Bradford's world-famous wool exchange located nearby. In its 1920s heyday, the station served routes to **Wakefield Westgate** via **Ardsley** and through to **King's Cross**, **Wakefield Kirkgate** via **Batley** and Ossett, Keighley & **Halifax** via Queensbury, **Mirfield** on the Spen Valley Line to **Cleckheaton** and to **Leeds** via the **Pudsey** loop. These, however, had either been severely cut or closed by the end of 1966, victims of 1960s' economics.

Leeds City has an interesting but short 29-year history. It is a relatively new joint ex-LMS/LNER station (1938) ironically replacing the former Leeds New station (ex-LNWR/NER) of 1869 and the former Leeds Wellington station (what a totem that would have made) from 1850. They were almost next to each other and were initially linked and renamed **Leeds City**. In 1967 further consolidation took place under the BR modernisation scheme and the suffix 'City' was dropped.

Bradford also has two main stations, **Exchange** and **Forster Square**, but unlike Leeds, both have survived. The first Exchange station was jointly opened by the L&YR and GNR in 1850. The railway station was completely rebuilt on the same site in 1880 with ten bay platforms and two arched trainshed roofs. It was a wonderful looking station, constructed of wide wrought iron spans resting on plain stone walls, with classical Corinthian-style columns down the centre (below).

Bradford Exchange in 1912. *Courtesy Disused-Stations.org.uk*

By 1973 **Exchange** was deemed too large and was moved south to a new smaller station, part of an enlarged transportation hub for the city and this was renamed Bradford Interchange. It was rebuilt again in 2001 with enhanced local bus and long-distance coach facilities. The old site was subsequently redeveloped as Bradford's Legal Quarter with the Crown, Magistrate and Coroner courts, plus office suites.

The second station is **Bradford Forster Square**, whose totem has appeared only once in auction (January 2002) around the time we were completing our last totem book. The station today operates electric train services to **Skipton** (Airedale Line), to **Ilkley** (Wharfedale Line) and the main line between **Bradford** and **Leeds**. It was not as architecturally pleasing as **Exchange**, with a rather non-descript entrance, shown in the 1930s photo below, and a spacious but less expansive trainshed depicted above right in the 1870s photograph. It was opened by the L&BR in 1846, but following acquisition by the Midland Railway, the original structure was rebuilt in 1853 and

Below and above right: Exterior and interior of Bradford Forster Square station.

named Bradford Midland. It was rebuilt again in the 1890s, incorporating a Midland Hotel alongside. Initially, it was known as Market Street station, though this was never official. However, in 1924, the name **Bradford Forster Square** was coined, and the station has kept this designation to this day.

Because of Bradford's industrial atmosphere, some totems became a little faded, depending on where they were placed on the station. Below are four **Bradford** totems. Notice the variations in colour in the three **Exchange** totems and the richer colour of the **Forster Square** totem, but all are exceptionally collectable.

The old **Forster Square** was truncated in 1990, when a new facility was built on the western side of the former station. This new station has three platforms, two of which (Platforms 1 & 2) are able to accommodate intercity trains. Electrification in 1994 allows ECML expresses from London to travel directly to the city. Today only part of the screen arcade that fronted the 1890 station and the Midland Hotel remain and happily 2 million people use the station annually.

Other Totems in the Three NER Counties

The final section of this chapter presents a short review by county, to aid collectors in their local searches. Durham, Northumberland and the three Yorkshire Ridings make up the region's geography, though some Cumberland and Westmorland stations, also allocated to the NER, never received them.

DURHAM

The county has a mixture of mining, farming and heavy railway heritage, with the latter especially noteworthy in the southeast of the county, in **Darlington**, Shildon and **Stockton**. In the centre of the city of Durham, the cathedral and castle are UNESCO-designated World Heritage Sites.

Durham is a fine, ancient, ecclesiastical city dominated by the cathedral and castle on a bend in the River Wear. The ECML serves the city, approaching from the south on a spectacular Victorian viaduct high above the city, affording superb views. Totems were not fitted here but tangerine lamp tablets were. Below is a **Ferryhill** totem from a station south of Durham on the ECML that closed in 1967.

There were 22 stations in County Durham sporting totems, 8 of which were closed. **Spennymoor** was first in 1952 and the last were **Felling**, **High Shields** and **Pelaw** in 1979. None of these are common totems with a combined 12 appearances in auction between them. Other rarities include **Croft Spa,** and **Heighington** (6 appearances between them), with **Boldon Colliery**, **Darlington Bank Top**, **Dinsdale** and **Seaburn** not appearing in public at all – so far!

The database pages for this chapter contain some real County Durham gems, **Barnard Castle**, **Darlington Bank Top**, **Etherley**, **Pelaw** and **Spennymoor**, with only 10 auction appearances between them. What a shame totems weren't installed at Bishop Auckland, Chester-le-Street, or Washington! Finally, we show a wonderfully named almost mint tangerine County Durham totem to finish.

NORTHUMBERLAND

Only twelve stations in England's northernmost county were fitted with totems, with all except **Berwick Upon Tweed**, being in the south of the county. It is England's sixth largest county by area, which makes the totem dearth even more stark. A third of the twelve stations were closed, but two of these, **Benton** and **West Monkseaton** re-opened in 1980 as part of the new Metro light rail system. (They are on the line from Longbenton to Whitley Bay).

In terms of railway history, Northumberland ranks first, as the great pioneering engineer George Stephenson was born at Wylam in 1781. As well as Stephenson, Northumberland has a special place in history, being one of the first areas to develop waggonways, where timber rails were laid on the ground to facilitate the movement of coal. By the 18th century waggonways covered the Newcastle area.

Travelling by train west from Newcastle we have a superb journey through 'totemed' stations. In sequence these are **Blaydon** on the south loop and **North Wylam** on the north loop. These join at **Prudhoe** then the line snakes west through Stocksfield and **Riding Mill** to **Hexham**. It is a great pity Haltwhistle was not chosen to carry totems before the line enters Cumberland.

Alan Young's geographical review earlier in this chapter looked at totem fittings in the Newcastle area, commenting on simultaneous removal and installation at stations around the city. There are some very collectable totems in this part of the BR network, and we might suggest **Backworth**, **Howdon-on-Tyne**, **North Wylam**, **Percy Main**, **Walker Gate** and **West Hartlepool** as being especially collectable for the area's aficionados.

In September 2003, Alan Young reported: 'I was disappointed that **Benton** was detotemised (1961/2) when its ornate gas lamps were displaced by fluorescent strip lighting, but encouraged that totems were installed, at about the same time, at a random collection of 'Coast Circle' stations: **Walker Gate, Howdon-on-Tyne, Percy Main** and **Backworth**. I think the totems at **North Wylam, Riding Mill, Hebburn** and **High Shields** also date from 1961/2, as do the tangerine-flanged ones at **Prudhoe**. Closure removed **Barnard Castle, Etherley**, and **North Wylam** totems, and at **Billingham** a new station was constructed and the old one with totems closed.

'However in 1971–74 most totems disappeared on Tyneside. At **Percy Main** they were removed then re-fixed to new lamp posts. The gang sent to strip other Coast Circle stations of totems failed to spot some that were fixed to buildings at **Howdon-on-Tyne** and **Walker Gate**. These totems remained in place until 1979 and **Percy Main** finally lost its totems in 1980.' All this means many Northumberland and north Durham totems had a very short life, possibly accounting for the excellent condition of some of them in private collections today.

Looking at the county as a whole, anything from Northumberland is not easy to collect, even though examples from all the stations have survived. None of the 12 totems have made double-digit auction appearances, and over half have been auctioned less than 5 times. Difficult totems to find include **Riding Mill** (0), **Howdon-on-Tyne** (2), **Benton** (4), **Berwick upon Tweed** (3) and **Percy Main** (5), together with **Hexham** and **Prudhoe** (4 auctions each).

Lying on the Anglo-Scottish border, Northumberland has been the site of battles for centuries and, as a result, has a high number of fine castles. These include Alnwick, Bamburgh, Dunstanburgh, Newcastle and Warkworth. Indeed, Bamburgh is the historic capital of Northumberland. The gem on the county's railway system has to be the beautiful curved trainshed at Newcastle Central. This fabulous station was designed by John Dobson and dates from the late 1840s. Though upgraded and modernised several times, it has retained nearly all the original features, character and beauty, but sadly no totems were fitted!

and **Pocklington.** The area has few lines, the main ones being **Selby-Market Weighton-Driffield**, Hull-**Beverley-Driffield** and **Beverley-Market Weighton-York**. Alan Young's Bempton photo is shown below.

The main Trans-Pennine line runs along the north bank of the Humber from Hull to **Selby** and on to **Leeds. Market Weighton**, with just 2 auction appearances and **Flamborough also** with 2, are rare totems. In contrast, **Brough** and **Goole** are commonly available with 66 appearances between them. During the preparation of this book, it was confirmed that Ferriby did not carry totems.

EAST RIDING OF YORKSHIRE

The East Riding's landscape consists of a crescent of low chalk hills, the Yorkshire Wolds, flanked by the low-lying fertile Holderness Plain and the Vale of York. The Humber Estuary and North Sea mark its eastern and southern limits. There are few large settlements and no industrial centres (apart from Hull). The area is administered from **Beverley**, an ancient market and ecclesiastical town. In totem terms this was home to **Bempton, Brough, Driffield, Flamborough, Goole, Market Weighton**

NORTH RIDING OF YORKSHIRE

Now we come to an area of real totem interest and a source of some desirable 'tangerines', including **Malton, Harrogate, Knaresborough, Ripon, Saltburn, Scarborough, Whitby** and **York**. It was recently confirmed that Hunmanby, listed in the 2002 book, also did not carry totems

A **Scarborough Central** totem is on many collectors' shopping lists. These totems come in three designs, a wide flange (WF), plus HF and FD variants. The suffix '**Central**' appears in the lower panel on all designs, as shown right for the WF (top) and HF (bottom) types, but none of the variants carry black-edged lettering.

Alf Miles' photograph right shows a marked colour variation between the two **Scarborough** totems, but also documents a difference from the more traditional tangerine of a **Darlington** totem.

In his Totem Study Group article in 2004, Alf reported: 'Scarborough totems were always dark, no matter which design. In fact, some of them almost border on a shade of red.' The Harrogate alongside is an example. Below, a pair of HF totems hang proudly in February 1957 as D49 *Shire* No. 62710 *Lincolnshire* is about to depart.

Scarborough totems have been in auction 13 times, (12 HF and 1 flat FD in 2007). Although the survival of most North Riding totems is confirmed, we have no data as to whether **Northallerton** or **Whitby West Cliff** totems escaped the clearance gangs' skips. Photographic evidence proves these stations were fitted, but none have been seen since removal. At **Northallerton**, the early use of fluorescent lights almost certainly accounts for their scarcity. **Whitby West Cliff** closed in 1961, but the flange and layout detail has been verified from the rare photograph below.

WEST RIDING OF YORKSHIRE

Earlier in the chapter, the article *Rails around Leeds/Bradford* covered many of the former West Riding totemed stations but this short review gives a chance to show a few more.

In addition to the locations previously discussed, other Yorkshire towns with stations carrying totems include **Batley**, **Brighouse**, **Castleford (**both **Central** and **Cutsyke)**, **Dewsbury**, **Halifax**, **Heckmondwike**, **Mirfield**, **Pontefract**, **Pudsey**, **Slaithwaite**, **Selby** and **Wetherby**.

Examples from almost all West Riding stations that were totem-provided have survived. During our research, we used photo evidence to confirm that Golcar (closed 1968) and Marsden (still open), both on the route from **Huddersfield** to **Stalybridge**, were not fitted. All the survivors have appeared in auction, but a few are not common: **Pontefract Monkhill** has 1 appearance, **Pudsey Lowtown** has 2 and **Darton** (south of **Wakefield Kirkgate**) has 4. The savage economic cuts of the 1960s resulted in the closure of a high number of stations. **Brighouse**, on the Calder Valley line west of **Leeds**, was lost in 1970, but happily was re-opened in 2000. Today, the station is well-used again by over 400,000 passengers annually.

Aficionados, who collect Yorkshire totems , have 82 known 'tangerines', plus 12 maroon items from the far west of the county and 36 'dark blues' from around the Sheffield area to display, taking Yorkshire to third in the county list of total number of stations known to have been 'totemised'. We close with two photos showing **Northallerton** totems in 1955 and **Whitby Town** totems in 1976 *in situ*.

Alan Young

Station Name		County in 1956	Layout	Flange	Closed	Auction	Survived
APPERLEY BRIDGE	*re-opened 2015	Yorkshire		FF	1965*	•	•
ARDSLEY		Yorkshire		HF	1964	•	•
ARMLEY MOOR ^^		Yorkshire		HF	1966	•	•
BACKWORTH		Northumberland		FF	1977	•	•
BARNARD CASTLE		Durham		HF/FF	1964	•	•
BATLEY	*face drilled	Yorkshire		HF/Flat*		•	•
BEMPTON ^^		Yorkshire		HF		•	•
BEN RHYDDING ^^	face drilled	Yorkshire		Flat		•	•
BENTON	*re-opened 1980	Northumberland		HF	1978*	•	•
BERWICK UPON TWEED ^^		Northumberland	2L	FF		•	•
BEVERLEY ^^	face drilled	Yorkshire		Flat		•	•
BILLINGHAM		Durham		FF		•	•
BLAYDON		Durham		HF		•	•
BOLDON COLLIERY	named Brockley Whins 1991	Durham		FF			•
BOLTON ON DEARNE	Flat totem not in auction	Yorkshire	1L	HF/flat		•	•
BRADFORD EXCHANGE^^	*Interchange in 1983	Yorkshire	2L	FF	1973*	•	•
BRADFORD FORSTER SQUARE ^^		Yorkshire	2L	HF		•	•
BRIGHOUSE	*re-opened 2000	Yorkshire		FF	1970*	•	•
BROUGH ^^		Yorkshire		HF		•	•
BROUGH	face drilled non-standard shape & letters	Yorkshire		Flat		•	•
BURTON SALMON ^^		Yorkshire		HF/WF	1959	•	•
CARGO FLEET		Yorkshire		HF/FF	1989	•	•
CASTLEFORD CENTRAL	*face drilled	Yorkshire	LP	HF/Flat*		•	•
CASTLEFORD CUTSYKE		Yorkshire	LP	HF	1968	•	•
CLECKHEATON CENTRAL ^^		Yorkshire	2L	HF/WF	1965	•	•
CROFT SPA ^^		Durham		HF	1969	•	•
CROFT SPA ^^		Durham		WF	1969	•	•
CROSS GATES		Yorkshire		HF		•	•
CROSS GATES	face drilled version	Yorkshire		Flat		•	•
DARLINGTON		Durham		FF		•	•

^^ = black edged lettering   WF = Wide flange   RF = reduced flange width   1L = one line: 2L = two line: LP = lower panel

Station Name		County in 1956	Layout	Flange	Closed	Auction	Survived
DARLINGTON BANK TOP		Durham	LP	HF			•
DARTON ^^		Yorkshire		FF		•	•
DEWSBURY CENTRAL ^^	face drilled	Yorkshire	LP	Flat	1964	•	•
DEWSBURY WELLINGTON ROAD		Yorkshire	LP	HF		•	•
DEWSBURY WELLINGTON ROAD ^^		Yorkshire	LP	FF		•	•
DINSDALE		Durham		HF			•
DRIFFIELD		Yorkshire		HF		•	•
EAGLESCLIFFE ^^	*face drilled	Durham		FF/Flat*		•	•
EAST BOLDON		Durham		FF			•
ETHERLEY		Durham		HF	1965	•	•
FEATHERSTONE	*re-opened 1992	Yorkshire		FF/WF	1967*	•	•
FELLING ^^		Durham		HF	1979	•	•
FERRYBRIDGE ^^	also HF	Yorkshire		FF/WF	1965	•	•
FERRYHILL		Durham		HF	1967	•	•
FILEY ^^		Yorkshire		WF		•	•
FLAMBOROUGH ^^	WF version not in auction	Yorkshire		HF/WF	1970	•	•
GARFORTH	orange flange	Yorkshire		FF		•	•
GOOLE		Yorkshire		HF		•	•
GRANGETOWN ^^		Yorkshire		FF		•	•
HALIFAX	*face drilled name from 1961	Yorkshire		FF/RF*		•	•
HALIFAX TOWN	name carried until 1961	Yorkshire	1L	HF		•	•
HALIFAX TOWN	face drilled version	Yorkshire	1L	Flat			•
HARROGATE		Yorkshire		HF		•	•
HEBBURN	*re-opened 1984 (Metro)	Durham		FF	1981*	•	•
HECKMONDWIKE		Yorkshire		FF	1965	•	•
HEIGHINGTON	face drilled	Durham		Flat		•	•
HEXHAM ^^		Northumberland		HF		•	•
HIGH SHIELDS		Durham		FF	1981	•	•

^^ = black edged lettering   WF = Wide flange   RF = reduced flange width   1L = one line: 2L = two line: LP = lower panel

Station Name		County in 1956	Layout	Flange	Closed	Auction	Survived
HOWDON-ON-TYNE	*re-opened 1982 (Metro)	Northumberland		FF	1980*	•	•
HUDDERSFIELD ^^		Yorkshire		HF/FF		•	•
ILKLEY ^^		Yorkshire		FF		•	•
KNARESBOROUGH ^^		Yorkshire		FF		•	•
LEEDS CENTRAL	some face drilled	Yorkshire	1L	HF/Flat	1967	•	•
LEEDS CITY		Yorkshire	1L	HF		•	•
MALTON ^^		Yorkshire		HF/WF		•	•
MARKET WEIGHTON		Yorkshire		HF	1965	•	•
MARSKE ^^		Yorkshire		FF		•	•
MENSTON ^^		Yorkshire		HF/WF		•	•
MICKLEFIELD ^^		Yorkshire		FF		•	•
MIRFIELD		Yorkshire		HF		•	•
MOORTHORPE		Yorkshire		FF		•	•
MOORTHORPE AND SOUTH KIRKBY ^^		Yorkshire	2L	FF		•	•
MORLEY LOW ^^		Yorkshire		HF/WF		•	•
MORLEY TOP ^^	face drilled	Yorkshire		Flat	1961	•	•
NEWLAY & HORSFORTH ^^		Yorkshire		HF/WF	1965	•	•
NORMANTON		Yorkshire		FF		•	•
NORTHALLERTON		Yorkshire		HF			
NORTH WYLAM		Northumberland		FF	1968	•	•
PANNAL		Yorkshire		HF		•	•
PELAW ^^		Durham		FF	1979	•	•
PELAW ^^		Durham		HF	1979		
PERCY MAIN	*re-opened 1982 (Metro)	Northumberland		FF	1980*	•	•
POCKLINGTON		Yorkshire		HF	1965	•	•
PONTEFRACT	orange flange	Yorkshire		FF		•	•

^^ = black edged lettering   WF = Wide flange   RF = reduced flange width   1L = one line: 2L = two line: LP = lower panel

Station Name		County in 1956	Layout	Flange	Closed	Auction	Survived
PONTEFRACT BAGHILL	*face drilled	Yorkshire	LP	HF/Flat*		•	•
PONTEFRACT MONKHILL	face drilled	Yorkshire	LP	Flat		•	•
PONTEFRACT TANSHELF	+face drilled *open 1992	Yorkshire	LP	HF/Flat+	1967*	•	•
POPPLETON ^^		Yorkshire		FF		•	•
PRUDHOE	orange flange	Northumberland		FF		•	•
PUDSEY GREENSIDE ^^	face drilled	Yorkshire	LP	Flat	1964	•	•
PUDSEY LOWTOWN ^^	face drilled	Yorkshire	LP	Flat	1964	•	•
REDCAR CENTRAL^^	some face drilled	Yorkshire	1L	FF		•	•
REDCAR EAST	orange flange	Yorkshire	1L	FF		•	•
RIDING MILL		Northumberland		FF			•
RIPON		Yorkshire		HF	1967	•	•
SALTBURN ^^		Yorkshire		FF		•	•
SCARBOROUGH CENTRAL	WF not in auction	Yorkshire	LP	HF/WF		•	•
SCARBOROUGH CENTRAL	face drilled	Yorkshire	LP	Flat		•	•
SCORTON ^^		Yorkshire		FF/WF	1969	•	•
SEABURN		Durham		HF			
SEAMER ^^		Yorkshire		FF		•	•
SELBY		Yorkshire		HF			•
SHIPLEY		Yorkshire		HF		•	•
SLAITHWAITE ^^	*re-opened 1982	Yorkshire		HF/WF	1968*	•	•
SOUTH ELMSALL ^^	FF totem not in auction	Yorkshire		HF/FF		•	•
SOUTH MILFORD ^^		Yorkshire		FF		•	•
SOUTH SHIELDS		Durham		HF/2side		•	•
SOWERBY BRIDGE		Yorkshire		HF		•	•
SPENNYMOOR ^^	still up in 1963	Durham		FF	1952	•	•
STANNINGLEY	*face drilled	Yorkshire		HF/Flat*	1968	•	•
STARBECK	face drilled	Yorkshire		Flat		•	•
STEETON & SILSDEN ^^	*re-opened 1990	Yorkshire		HF	1965*	•	•
STOCKSFIELD ^^		Northumberland		HF/WF		•	•
STOCKTON ^^		Durham		FF		•	•

^^ = black edged lettering   WF = Wide flange   RF = reduced flange width   1L = one line: 2L = two line: LP = lower panel

Station Name		County in 1956	Layout	Flange	Closed	Auction	Survived
THIRSK		Yorkshire		HF		•	•
THIRSK	face drilled version	Yorkshire		Flat			•
THORNABY ^^		Yorkshire		FF		•	•
WAKEFIELD KIRKGATE ^^		Yorkshire	2L	HF/WF		•	•
WAKEFIELD WESTGATE		Yorkshire	LP	HF		•	•
WALKER GATE	*re-opened 1982 (Metro)	Northumberland		FF	1980*	•	•
WEST HARTLEPOOL		Durham		FF		•	•
WEST MONKSEATON	*re-opened 1980	Northumberland		HF	1979*	•	•
WETHERBY ^^		Yorkshire		HF	1964	•	•
WHITBY TOWN ^^	also HF	Yorkshire		FF/WF		•	•
WHITBY WEST CLIFF		Yorkshire	LP	WF	1961		
YORK ^^		Yorkshire		HF/FF		•	•

^^ = black edged lettering   WF = Wide flange   RF = reduced flange width   1L = one line: 2L = two line: LP = lower panel

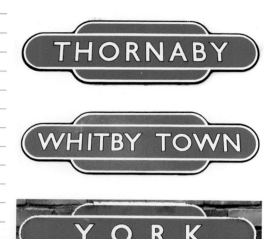

Other North Eastern Region Collectables

7
The Scottish Region

Opening Comments

The Scottish Region covered the whole of Scotland, the only one of the six regions to cover a whole country within Great Britain. It was formed from those LMS and LNER routes in Scotland that existed on 31 December 1947. With 3,625 miles of track, the new ScR was almost the same size as the Western Region, representing 19% of total British Railways mileage. The ScR was also different to the other regions due to the variety of shipping inherited by BR and, in addition, hosted five of the highest railway summits and two underground railways with steam power; not one mile of the ScR track was electrified! The Scottish railway-owned ships soon became the responsibility of the Railway Executive. The ScR's main routes were Burnmouth and northwards on the East Coast Main Line, the Caledonian, Callander & Oban Lines, the Inverness to **Wick line**, the Waverley line (**Carlisle** to Edinburgh), the Highland line to Inverness, the GSWR line via **Dumfries** and the main Glasgow to Edinburgh line.

During the Beeching era, Scottish stations were ravaged, suffering the highest closure percentage of all the regions, with the most occurring in 1965 and 1966. Fife, for example, saw 65% of the stations closed, Banffshire saw 90% closed and in Aberdeenshire 95% were dispensed with. Several of the smaller counties such as Kirkcudbright, Peebles and Roxburghshire saw total closures. However, in recent years ScotRail, BR's successor, has re-opened more of these stations than the other five regions. The importance of low-usage routes have been more recognised north of the border than in the rest of Great Britain. Sadly, however, these stations no longer carry the light blue that characterised all Scottish stations that were fitted with totems. Two iconic closed examples are presented below and overleaf are three of these *in situ* in the 1960s. Note the ornate lamp standard from the former Ayrshire GSWR railway at **Auchinleck**.

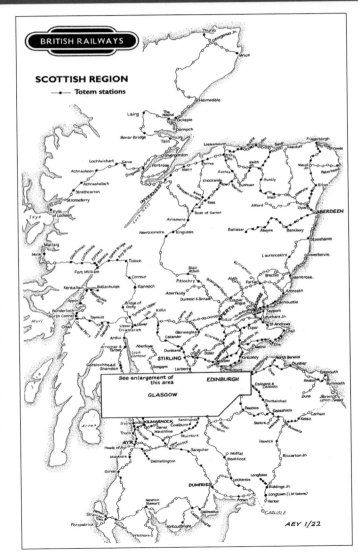

175

Scotland has had in the past an extensive railway network, with links across the country, connections to England, local commuter links to the major cities (some of which were electrified by BR) and freight. As of 2018, the total route length of the rail network in Scotland is 1,752 miles (2,819 km), of which 441 miles (709 km) is electrified and there are 359 operational stations. During the peak years of totem installation, 492 Scottish stations were adorned in ex-Caledonian blue.

History of BR's Scottish Region

In 1923 at grouping, both the LMS and LNER took over smaller Scottish companies that operated on a largely regional basis. The physical geography of Scotland was mainly responsible for the areas in which these constituent companies operated. Railways started in the south and gradually spread north, with the first passenger railway being the Kilmarnock and Troon. This began in 1812 with horse-drawn traction but, in 1841, the plateway was converted and it subsequently became part of the Glasgow and South Western Railway (GSWR). This covered Ayrshire, Dumfries-shire, Kirkcudbright and Renfrewshire. There are some interestingly named totems to collect from here.

The GSWR was formed in 1850 on the merger of two earlier and smaller regional companies. At that time **Paisley**, **Greenock**, **Kilmarnock**, **Ardrossan**, **Dumfries**, **Ayr** and down to Gretna were stations on the network. With the Caledonian Railways' (CR) agreement they also reached **Carlisle**. By 1875, tracks to **Girvan**, **Newton Stewart**, **Stranraer** and **Kirkcudbright** had been added.

Scottish Region totems *in situ*: Auchinleck, Ayrshire, and Callander, Perthshire, in the 1960s.

In 1876, Glasgow St Enoch station was opened, and trains began to run directly from there to London. The station was universally regarded as architecturally magnificent, and in 1879 the accompanying St Enoch Hotel, the largest in Scotland, opened. Sadly, the station was not fitted with totems during the BR years (what a collectable that would have been) and tragically it was closed in 1966, despite widespread protests, and then demolished in 1977. The station clock was saved and now resides in **Cumbernauld** town centre. On a happier note, the equally impressive St Enoch Centre now occupies the site of the old station, and the old subway station entrance, built in wonderfully coloured stone, can be seen outside.

Around the Glasgow area, the Caledonian Railway (CR) was an early railway rival company. The CR was formed in the early 19th century with the objective of providing a link between English railways and Glasgow. It progressively extended its network and reached the cities of Edinburgh and Aberdeen. It developed a dense network of branch lines in the greater Glasgow area and became one of Scotland's most powerful operators, with 1,115 miles of track at the 1923 grouping.

They operated in Angus, Argyllshire, Dumfries-shire, Kincardineshire, Lanarkshire, Midlothian, Stirlingshire, Perthshire and some parts of Aberdeenshire. At its zenith the CR ran over 330 stations, including those right and **Dunblane**, Perthshire.

The wording 'Scottish Central Raily' on the iron lamp post is intriguing. On checking official records, the data shows that the station was indeed opened by the Scottish Central Railway in 1848, but this company then merged with the Caledonian in July 1865. Some reference books list **Dunblane** as ex-CR, but the lamppost is far earlier.

The most important pioneering route was the main line between **Carlisle** and **Beattock** (via **Ecclefechan** and **Lockerbie**), which opened in September 1847, but the entire through route to Glasgow from **Carstairs** was not operational until February 1848. Therefore, through an agreement with the LNWR, a continuous railway route between Glasgow and London existed for the first time from that year. Their Glasgow station was the Townhead terminus of the Glasgow, Garnkirk and Coatbridge Railway, which the Caledonian had leased from January 1847. The line into Edinburgh from **Carstairs** via **Auchengray** opened in April 1848 completing the western links between London and Scotland's two most important cities.

For twenty years after 1847, the CR tried to build a more suitable Glasgow terminus. Finally in 1875 an Act was obtained to build a bridge crossing the Clyde, allowing their South Side route into the city centre. The new four-track railway bridge crossing the river was built by Sir William Arrol & Company, opening on 1 October 1878. The bridge gave access to the new Glasgow Central eight-platform station, opened in December 1879; a ninth platform was added in 1889. The years 1901 to 1906 a saw major expansion, when the platforms were lengthened and four more were added on the west side via a parallel second river crossing, carrying eight more tracks.

Moving northwards, the CR gained access to **Perth**, via **Cumbernauld**, **Stirling** and **Gleneagles** and, via a series of amalgamations and takeovers, reached Aberdeen by 1866. The Caledonian now had what it had wanted from the outset: control of an extensive network of lines covering a considerable territorial area in southern and central Scotland. Parliamentary regulators became increasingly uncomfortable with monopolies of this kind, and when the North British Railway protested, they were given access to much of the Caledonian's northern system.

On the western side, the purchase of the Callander & Oban Railway gave the CR a route to the Highlands and they extended to **Ballachulish** by 1903. The 'totemed' stations on the line included **Balquhidder**, **Dalmally**, **Loch Awe, Benderloch** and **Appin**. The eastern section of the line from **Dunblane** closed in 1965, but the western part is open today as part of the West Highland Line from **Crianlarich**.

A very rare Loch Awe totem *in situ* in Argyllshire in the 1960s.

The North British Railway (NBR) locked horns with the CR on many occasions during the Victorian years of 'railway mania'. The NBR linked to the English railway system on the East Coast and their main line from **Berwick** to Edinburgh is a mainstay of today's modern network. They operated in the Scottish counties of Berwickshire, Roxburgh, Selkirk, Peebles, Dumfries-shire, Midlothian, Lanarkshire, Stirling, Fife, Kinross, Clackmannanshire, Argyllshire and Inverness-shire. By 1922 its routes extended to 1,378 miles and it became part of the LNER at grouping. At that time, it ran 650 stations; totem examples from four of these are shown below.

The map shows the complete Scottish network in 1923. From it, readers can appreciate the competition there was between the CR and NBR. Alongside the map is Tim Clarke's rare shot of a **Kinghorn** totem *in situ*. This station in Fife was opened in 1847 by the Edinburgh & Northern Railway, before absorption into the NBR in 1877.

The NBR, formed in 1844, was based in Edinburgh and two years after formation, they had driven their line south to **Berwick-upon-Tweed**. Like the CR, they quickly expanded geographically, to put in place a fine network. They eventually expanded west to **Carlisle** and made operating agreements with the Midland Railway, which proved beneficial to both companies. They also built tracks from Edinburgh to **Perth** and **Dundee** and were responsible for constructing the first Tay Bridge, which later collapsed during a storm in 1879 with great loss of life. During the Tay Bridge's rebuilding (from 1883 to 1887), they also constructed the Forth Bridge (from 1882 to 1890) and this UNESCO World Heritage listed structure transformed their network north of Edinburgh.

It is not commonly appreciated that the NBR was a major coal carrier, indeed the largest in Scotland and only bettered in Great Britain by the NER, MR, GWR and LNWR. Many collieries were situated within their network, especially Lanarkshire, and the station totems left are also the names of four coal mines that the NBR served.

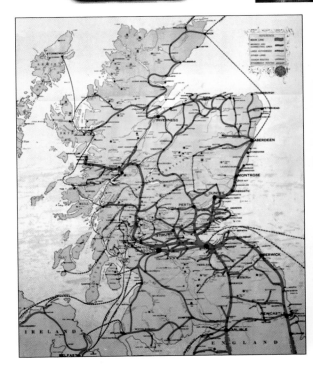

By the end of the 19th century, the NBR had sponsored the West Highland Line, linking Glasgow to the fishing ports at Oban and Mallaig, via **Crianlarich** and **Fort William**. Oban is just over 100 miles from Glasgow and Mallaig just more than 164 miles, a journey that takes around five hours. The line has some wonderfully collectable totems, evidenced by the quartet above. Interestingly, three of the four termini were not fitted with totems (the exception is **Fort William**) and later in this chapter, a focus article features much more of the line and its totems. It is considered by many to be the most scenic railway journey in the world and is hugely popular today.

The NBR grew to become Scotland's largest railway and the second largest constituent of the LNER when it was formed in 1923. Only the NER was larger within the LNER: examples of two more of their station totems appear below.

In addition to the two collectable totems bottom left column, they also had **Achnasheen**, **Blair Atholl** and Stromeferry within their portfolio of stations. Most ex-NBR station totems are highly desirable and form the basis of some eminent private collections.

The HR first opened the line from Inverness to **Nairn** in 1855, before extending it further east to **Elgin** in 1858. The main line from **Perth** to Inverness took much longer, eventually being completed in 1898. There are ten stations along the 118 mile route, with two of them shown *in situ* above. Other stations where totems were fitted are **Newtonmore**, **Kingussie** and **Aviemore**. There are two significant climbs on the route, Drumochter summit between **Blair Atholl** and Dalwhinnie and Slochd Summit between Carrbridge and Inverness. The former has severe gradients in both directions; a summit of 1,480 feet (452m) is the UK's highest. Slochd is equally testing with gradients of 1 in 60 to a summit of 1,315 feet (401m).

The Highland Railway (HR) was one of the two smaller railways that served the North of Scotland. With 506 route miles at the time of grouping, the network and its associated assets formed part of the LMS within the 'Big Four'. The HR was based in Inverness and served the counties of Caithness, Morayshire, Nairn, Perthshire and Ross & Cromarty. The world-famous line between **Dingwall** and the **Kyle of Lochalsh** (the Kyle Line) was one of their major routes, together with **Perth** to Inverness and the line to the far north of Scotland terminating at **Thurso** and **Wick**.

During the network's development, branch lines were built to Aberfeldy, Dornoch, Fortrose and Lybster, and once the HR had been grouped within the LMS, these remained open. Indeed, the LMS was generally fairly kind to railways in Scotland but this was certainly not the case once BR took over in 1948. All these aforementioned branches were early casualties as economics over-rode social and local need; even the HR main line from **Aviemore** to **Forres** was a casualty.

Happily, sections have re-opened as the Strathspey Railway; the line had some classic totems, **Boat of Garten**, **Broomhill** and **Grantown-on-Spey West**. The section northwards to **Forres** is now the Dava Way, a 23-mile walking and cycle track that follows the HR line on the original trackbed.

The mention of northern Scotland brings us to the final main component of early Scottish Region history. This was the Great North of Scotland Railway (GNSR), the smallest of the main five and not, as the name implies, covering a large area. They only operated trains in Aberdeenshire, Banffshire and Morayshire. At the 1923 grouping, their routes only amounted to 334½ miles. However, despite this, there are some very collectable totems within their network. A small classic collage is presented alongside, but almost any GNSR station totem is most Scottish collectors' aim.

Although the railway was formed in 1845, it did not carry its first passengers until 1854, between **Kittybrewster** and **Huntly,** a 39-mile journey. Other totem stations en-route were **Insch** and **Kennethmont,** with five other stations not fitted in the BR era. The line was single-track with the provision of passing loops.

The GNSR developed during the Victorian era, building lines to **Fraserburgh** (with a branch to **Peterhead**), Macduff (via Turriff), Banff and Portsoy (via **Tillynaught**), Lossiemouth (via **Elgin**) and **Boat of Garten** (via Craigellachie). However, their most famous branch line ran between Aberdeen and **Ballater** along the Dee Valley, allowing the Royal Family easy access to their summer residence at Balmoral. The line had some desirable intermediate station totems, at **Aboyne**, **Banchory, Cambus O'May, Crathes, Dess, Dinnet, Glassel, Lumphanan** and **Torphins.** Maybe they provisioned most of the stations to inform the VIP travellers!

Royal Deeside stations at Banchory and Cambus O'May, in the 1960s.

In the 1860s, financial difficulties affected nearly all the railways in the area, with many of the small ones succumbing. The GNSR survived, albeit almost bankrupt, and it was several years before they were able to invest again. The arrival of William Ferguson as Chairman and William Moffatt as General Manager brought renewed energy to the GNSR; some lines were doubled, new locos and rolling stock purchased and a new line was constructed along the Moray coast from Portsoy to **Elgin**.

The old engine works at **Kittybrewster** was replaced in 1902 with an enlarged facility at Inverurie and this remained in operation until 1969. The GNSR also owned three famous hotels, one at Cruden Bay and two in Aberdeen; they were one of the first railway companies to add a supporting bus network to their transport operations. In 1923, the GNSR passed into the LNER, and slowly many company functions moved south to Edinburgh. Two branch lines closed in the 1930s, Cruden Bay and Oldmeldrum, and the Macduff Branch in 1951, but the death knell for all remaining branch lines came with Dr. Beeching's 1963 report.

During the years of the LMS and LNER stewardship, these two at first competed and finally began to collaborate in the 1930s; some classic joint posters were issued from 1935. In some areas, passenger usage was low and additionally there was little freight revenue, mainly fish from the coastal ports, and whisky from the many distilleries.

When the Second World War broke out, English cities (and stations) suffered very badly, so much of Scotland's rolling stock was used south of the border to cover railway losses. During the war years, all railway equipment was utilised almost to breaking point, so by 1945, it was obvious things had to change. This happened on 1 January 1948 when Scotland's railways came together as a single region. Once funds became available, the area around Glasgow was electrified from 1960 onwards, following the introduction of DMUs in the 1950s. They widely advertised their 'Blue Trains', and services in Glasgow and its suburbs saw real improvement.

Scotland's network suffered many line closures during the 1960s and 70s, including important lines such as the 'Waverley Route' and the Fife Coast Line. In recent years, ScotRail has really begun to invest and many stations, as listed in our enlarged database, have re-opened and the electrification of Scotland's lines continues.

Scottish Totem Geography
Alan Young & Richard Furness

After the London Midland and Southern Regions, Scotland was most generously endowed with totems: these Caledonian blue nameplates appeared at 492 stations. Most stations in the Lowlands area carried totems, so it is easier to comment on those that did not. Remarkable omissions were Edinburgh's Waverley and Princes Street stations, and the four Glasgow city centre termini of Buchanan Street, Central, Queen Street and St. Enoch were similarly overlooked. However, at **Queen Street Low Level**, the through platforms were furnished with 4-foot totems.

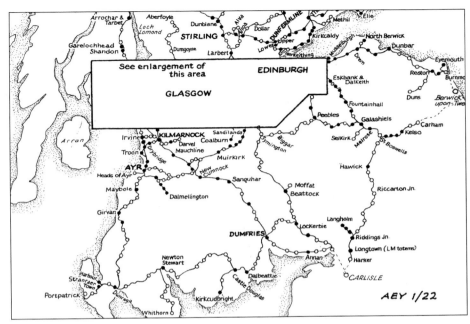

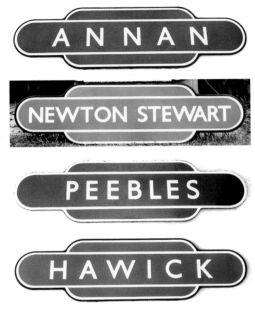

At the southernmost end of the Waverley line, **Longtown** (Cumberland) passed from ScR to LMR in the late 1950s, and maroon totems were installed. **Riddings Junction** (in Cumberland, but curiously remaining ScR) plus the three **Langholm** branch stations also received totems, and the branches to **Kelso** and **Peebles** were generously supplied, some with wonderful names (**Maxton, Rutherford, Roxburgh, Clovenfords, Walkerburn, Cardrona, Eddleston, Pomathorn, Rosslynlee, Rosewell and Hawthornden** and **Bonnyrigg**).

The two photographs below show two of these *in situ*. **Roxburgh** totems are also quite rare, though there are known survivors. Mark Williams' shot of **Rutherford** is quite a rarity, as we have no information on totem survival there.

The map above shows railway lines in the southern part of Scotland. The area between Glasgow and Edinburgh appears later in the chapter with a feature focus on collecting suburban totems (there are many to choose from!). The hill ranges of the Southern Uplands were a barrier to railway routes, with only three routes through. Consequently, Southwest Scotland was not well provided with totems, even with three lines. **Carlisle-Carstairs** had totems only at **Beattock, Lockerbie,** and (strangely) **Ecclefechan. Carlisle-Kilmarnock** was a bit more fortunate. North of the Solway Firth, only principal **Carlisle-Stranraer Town** and **Harbour** stations carried totems, plus **Dalbeattie, Castle Douglas, Newton Stewart, Dunragit** (junction for **Ayr**) and the **Kirkcudbright** branch terminus. **Ayr** to **Stranraer** was also given short measure, but stations on the busier northern-half of the 'Waverley Line' (**Carlisle**–Edinburgh via **Hawick**) had totems (including the classic Scottish names of **Eskbank and Dalkeith** or **Heriot**), even little-used **Tynehead** was fitted. Further south, St. Boswells and Riccarton Junction retained LNER lamp tablets until closure in 1969.

Roxburgh Junction and Rutherford *circa* 1960. *Mark Williams*

The vast majority of stations in the Lowlands area between Glasgow and Edinburgh carried totems, as the Central Belt map on page 187 shows. The first stops out of Buchanan Street, St. Rollox, Robroyston and Stepps, had no totems and other unlucky Glasgow area stations were Back o' Loch Halt, Bellahouston (closed 1954), Crow Road, Partick West and Possil. Garscadden, opened in 1960 when the route was electrified, had named strip lighting rather than totems, and we assume that the new Hyndland station (opened on the same day, also with strip lighting) also did not carry totems.

Away from Glasgow a few more stations were overlooked, including both the pier stations at Ardrossan, Fairlie Pier and Greenock Prince's Pier. Several stations on both **Ayr-Paisley Gilmour Street** lines, most of the Darvel branch, and all three **Coalburn** branch stations, had no totems. Edinburgh's local stations were lavished with totems, but beyond the city there were none at North Queensferry and Newtongrange. A quartet of Central Belt totems above.

Moving north of the industrial Glasgow–Edinburgh belt, Fife had a splendid array of totems, including all East Neuk line stations such as **Largo**, **Kilconquhar**, **St Monance**, **Pittenweem**, **Anstruther**, **Crail** and **St. Andrews** – some fine names! However, in Clackmannanshire and Kinross-shire the **Alloa-Kinross Junction** line survived until 1964, but intermediate stations received no totems, denying us such gems as Dollar, Rumbling Bridge and Crook of Devon. Further north, the Comrie 'branch' from Crieff Junction to Crieff, only had totems installed at **Tullibardine**, not an obvious location, especially with none being furnished at the terminus.

The West Highland Line (**Dumbarton–Fort William–** Mallaig) received totems relatively early, most stations carrying half-flanged specimens. **Corrour**, remote and little used, had the later fully-flanged type. Many stations on the **Stirling-Oban** line had totems, though not Killin Junction and the Killin branch terminus.

The **Ballachulish** branch had totems installed at **North Connel**, **Benderloch**, **Appin**, **Kentallen**, **Ballachulish Ferry** and the **Ballachulish** terminus, but three other stations en-route were overlooked. The **Perth**-Inverness main line was curiously 'totem-poor'. Only **Perth**, **Pitlochry**, **Blair Atholl**, **Newtonmore**, **Kingussie** and **Aviemore** on the 118-mile journey had totems installed. Sadly, Inverness never carried totems. East of **Perth**, Errol survived the 1956 purge but retained only LMS 'hawkseye' signs until closure in 1986. **Dundee Tay Bridge** and the **Tayport** branch carried totems, as did most main line stations to **Montrose**. These included **Golf Street Halt** and **Balmossie Halt,** opened 1960 and 1962 respectively, which received wooden totems.

These are presented in the column opposite and look distinctly odd, not being Caledonian Blue, but they blend well with the snow! They were however originally blue-and-white before being overpainted. No other late-opened halts had totems. Except for Dee Street and Rosslynlee Hospital they were modest affairs, without formal platforms: Imperial Cottages,opened 1959, on the Speyside line was an example.

In Northeast Scotland there was enthusiastic totem-fitting on the **Fraserburgh** and **Ballater** branches, including minor stations such as **Arnage** and **Cambus O'May**; the latter was a halt, but the totems did not carry the suffix. **Calderpark**, **Carfin** and **Woodhall** also lacked 'Halt' on their totems. The **Peterhead** branch had totems installed only at the terminus (Abbey of Deer Platform would have made a fabulous totem), but the St. Combs branch never received them.

Between Inverness and Aberdeen provision was patchy, generally favouring the more important stations such as **Nairn**, **Elgin**, **Forres** and **Keith,** both **Junction** and **Town**, but also lesser stations such as **Allanfearn**, **Cornhill** and **Kittybrewster**. Somewhat strange omissions were Inverurie (still with LNER lamp tablets in 1978), Cullen, Dufftown, Craigellachie, and particularly Aberdeen.

North of Inverness totems were few. About half of the **Kyle of Lochalsh** line had them, mainly half-flanged at intermediate stations, but fully-flanged at the terminus. The Inverness–**Wick/Thurso** line lost twenty intermediate stations (plus the Dornoch branch) in 1960, but of these casualties, only **The Mound** definitely had totems. **Wick** and **Thurso** were isolated outposts of totem installation, and some major intermediate stations, including **Dingwall**, **Tain** and **Lairg** were fitted with them. However, Brora, Helmsdale & Georgemas Junction, where the lines split for **Thurso** and **Wick**, were thought unworthy for totem provision.

The **Arbroath–Forfar**, Dundee East–**Forfar**, Dundee West-Alyth Jn lines and branches to Blairgowrie and Methil lasted until 1955. In addition, there was a purge of 'roadside' stations between **Stirling** and Aberdeen in 1955/6. A map showing only stations that survived beyond 1956 would indicate the enthusiasm that the ScR had for fitting totems. A few of the early closures had totems: **Calderpark,** opened 1951, and its neighbour **Uddingston West**, closed in 1955; the closure of **Airdrie**-Edinburgh (1956) relieved **Armadale** of totems. Much of this occurred before the more savage cuts as a result of the 1963 Beeching Review.

Totems and *in-situ* pictures from the far north of Scotland.

There were numerous closures before 1956, including the Whithorn, Holehouse–**Muirkirk**, **Ladybank–Mawcarse** and **Peebles**–Symington lines (1950). The following year saw the demise of branches to Aberfoyle, Alyth, Barnton, Brocketsbrae, Duns, Inverbervie, Kilsyth, Macduff, Penicuik, Polton, Selkirk, Whiteinch (Victoria Park) and Wilsontown. In addition, the **Ayr-Muirkirk**, **Balquhidder**-Comrie, Crieff–**Perth**, **Blairhill**–Bothwell and Newburgh–St. Fort lines closed, all with low passenger load factors, but of huge local social importance. The Brechin, **Dumfries–Lockerbie**, **Hamilton**–Bothwell, Kirriemuir and Leith Central lines closed in 1952, the Moffat and Alva branches two years later in 1954.

When the 1960s closures came, they were indeed savage, with Aberdeenshire losing all but **Huntly** and **Insch** out of 27 stations fitted, and similarly Morayshire had just 2 survivors from 15 stations, **Elgin** and **Forres**. Many stations kept their totems into the late 1970s, when journeys to **Kyle of Lochalsh**, **Wick**, Mallaig or Oban, from Glasgow to Edinburgh via **Shotts**, or Glasgow to **Ayr** were delights for totem-spotting. Although the re-branding of Scotland's railway into ScotRail has improved the image and the services in Scotland, sadly in the 1980s the management 'discovered' some stations still carried old-fashioned totems; by 1986 all were gone!

Collecting Theme: The Glasgow Suburbs

Glasgow has undoubtedly one of the most fascinating railway systems of any major UK city; despite the 1960s closures, it has remained largely intact. For collectors, the abundance of surviving totems has left a great legacy for future generations to recall the true heyday when we enjoyed the thrill of imposing termini, complex junctions and engine sheds. From the hustle and bustle of the city, it is just a short jaunt to some of the most special scenery found anywhere; the bonus is the train can take you there!

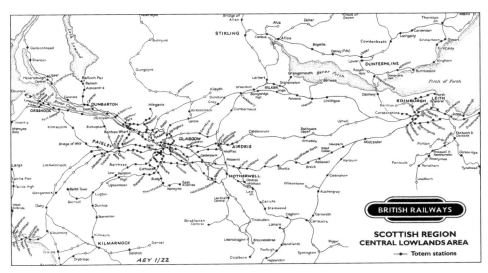

Map of the complex Glasgow suburban network. *Alan Young*

Dark foreboding tenement blocks used to surround the city centre, built between 1840 and 1920 to address the exponential rise in the city's population as industry rapidly grew. The railway system to serve these residents was hugely expensive to build, as much of it was in cuttings and tunnels as the picture of **High Street** shows. Though not fitted with totems, the photo of the abandoned Botanic Gardens station shows how dark and gloomy some of these stations must have been. A Glasgow suburban collection is very hard to complete and would be large. Just look how many stations there were on the route map alongside. Fortunately for us, most of these stations had totems provided, and many lasted *in situ* into the late 1970s and early '80s, though by that time most were in a sorry state.

The map above shows the complexity of the Glasgow network and how liberal the policy was for installing totems on many of the lines. Totemed stations are denoted by black circles and stations not fitted by white circles. Note the density of lines to the south and the number of stations not fitted north of **Kirkintilloch**. Lanarkshire had 120 stations where totems were installed. In addition, Renfrewshire had 37 and Dunbartonshire had 33. The City of Glasgow itself had more than 60 stations within its boundaries, but the only two totems carrying the name were **Glasgow Cross** and **Port Glasgow**. The Clyde had some of Britain's greatest shipbuilding yards and heavy industry on its banks, whilst further west the myriad of islands kept a thriving fleet of vessels in fulltime employment. Loch Lomond lies to the north, serviced by the 1960 electrified branch to **Balloch Pier**. This station closed in 1986.

Glasgow suburban stations in the 1960s: High Street (L) and Botanic Gardens (R).

Upon removal, some totems found their way into collectors' hands via local sales, but hundreds headed south in guards' brake vans to Euston's Collectors Corner (CC). Our research has found that CC also sent their road van to Glasgow on several occasions to be filled up with light blue enamel signs. **High Street** station (above left) was one such station where the signs ended up on the walls at Coburg Street.

However, **Duke Street, High Street** and some of their inner city neighbours had received the unwelcome attention of stone-throwing youths, as an early Collectors' Corner picture above left clearly shows. Alongside is an image of a slightly more cared for totem, though still bearing the evidence of stone-throwers' attention on the face. Many visitors to CC may recall that some of the ScR signs offered were more chips than enamel and these would hang on the walls for several months before being sold at knock-down prices.

Despite the gloomy industrial landscape and cramped city housing, one aspect of collecting from this area is the rather attractive names that appeared on many totems. From the large area list, we may choose **Alexandra Parade**, **Burnside, Crossmyloof, Easterhouse, Dalmuir Riverside**, **Fort Matilda**, **Kings Park**, **Mount Florida**, **Scotstounhill** and **Yoker Ferry**, to name but a few. However, at the opposite end of the scale, there were some equally unattractive names, if readers care to study a map of the entire system in some detail!

Engine sheds are a great magnet for many railwayana collectors: **Motherwell** (66B) and **Corkerhill** (67A) survive as totems. **Springburn** totems survive in good numbers, a reminder of the nearby works and Eastfield (65A) engine sheds. The former **Cowlairs** station, serving Glasgow's sprawling workshops, closed in 1964.

Our research shows that a **Cowlairs** totem could be seen in the shunters cabin after the station's demise; but only one (perhaps the same one) has ever appeared in auction. The other famous shed-serving Central station and the freight yards surrounding the south of the city was Polmadie (66A), home to *Coronation's*, *Royal Scot's* and *Jubilee's* in its heyday. Four other shed names appear on totems, **Parkhead Stadium** (65C), **Yoker High** (65G), **Helensburgh** (65H) and **Hamilton Central** (66C).

Two superb Glasgow stations: St Enoch (L) now demolished and Central (R) still operational.

The pre-grouping companies tried very hard to outdo each other when it came to building their Glasgow termini: these were magnificent structures and two have stood the test of time. Central Station copes admirably with all the traffic from the south, whilst Queen Street (HL and LL) sends trains to Edinburgh, Inverness and the West Highlands. The steep incline out of **Queen Street** through **Cowlairs** was a notorious challenge for engine crews, but a truly magnificent sight for steam photographers. The other two major city termini were St. Enoch (GSWR) and Buchanan Street (CR), which were both closed in 1966. Although Central and St. Enoch never carried totems, their architecture deserves inclusion. The pre-grouping duplication also applied to routes. Some have closed, but several others were kept open.

The former Caledonian line from **Partick West** to **Dumbarton East** on the north bank of the Clyde only closed after the North British line running parallel to the north was electrified in 1964. This was a shame, as the CR line always appeared to be the more interesting of the two, being just a few hundred yards from the riverside industrial landscape and workers bustling to and fro. Bearing in mind that this line closed in 1964, it is amazing that so many totems from this area have survived: great Scottish names such as **Scotstoun East**, **Kilbowie**, **Old Kilpatrick** (one was still in situ in the early 1970s) and **Dalmuir Riverside**.

Freight has played an important role in the formation of the Glasgow railway system and a huge number of small branches once formed an intricate network of lines around the former **Airdrie** coalfields to the east of the city. Ravenscraig's major steelworks opened in 1956 and provided thousands of local jobs until its demise. There were no less than 4 shunting yards within the complex handling dozens of trains every day. The major yard at nearby **Mossend** (station closed 1962) is still busy today, and much of Scotland's Freightliner traffic is handled at Coatbridge: we have yet to see a surviving **Coatbridge Central** totem. It is possible to collect certain complete lines, but as with all goals, there are major obstacles.

Consider the line out to **East Kilbride,** for example. It is a mystery that **Hairmyres** totems were still hanging in 1974, but none have ever been through auction and we only know of only one survivor! Similarly, on the **High Street** to **Coatbridge Sunnyside** line, **Shettleston** is a rare totem. An almost impossible task is the former line through the centre of Glasgow from **Anderston Cross** to **Carmyle** via **Bridgeton Cross** and **Tollcross**, as intermediate stations **Glasgow Cross**, **Bridgeton Cross** and **Parkhead Stadium** are all not thought to have any survivors and **Tollcross** is believed to have just one.

It is noticeable that Glasgow suburban totems generally do not make the higher prices at auction, even when rarities such as **Renfrew Fulbar Street** or **Renfrew South** are offered. These days, it may be true to say that there are more Scottish totems south of the border than in their former homeland! We know of collections in Scotland, but Caledonian blue totems have a very strong appeal to collectors all over the country. Consequently, there are some very fine Scottish collections in England.

A Wonderful Railway Journey: Scotland's West Highland Line

One of the world's most amazing railway journeys is between Glasgow and the west coast ports of Oban and Mallaig. It is considered by many to be the most scenic journey available anywhere, with interest from start to finish. It is a side of Scotland that can only be seen through a carriage window, a scenic journey that takes you from the city's bustle, north along the west coast, through the Loch Lomond & Trossachs National Park. The line splits at **Crianlarich**, carrying you past beautiful Loch Awe to Oban, or travelling north across Rannoch Moor through remote highland wilderness and on to **Fort William** and ultimately Mallaig.

The line was built in 1894 by the West Highland Railway Company, but in 1908 it was absorbed into NBR's network. It is 123 miles from Glasgow Queen Street to **Fort William** and a further 41 miles to Mallaig. The shorter route from Glasgow to Oban is 102 miles. The first stop out of Glasgow is **Dalmuir Park** (now just Dalmuir), then **Dumbarton Central** before arrival in **Helensburgh Upper**. At this point, railway enthusiasts may notice that there are no signals, but boards that say 'Obtain token before proceeding' on the single-track line. Most of the signalling on the West Highland Line is controlled via radio from the signal box at **Banavie** station. However, some of the lines around **Fort William** are still semaphore-controlled. The next stop is **Garelochhead**, where the Faslane nuclear submarine base can be seen.

The next pretty section is along Loch Long before the train reaches **Arrochar and Tarbet**, (photo showing totem *in situ* in 1977 alongside) followed by **Ardlui**, where the up train waits for the down train to pass. At 51 miles from Glasgow, the station is halfway to Oban. The next stop is **Crianlarich**, where the train splits in two, one part for Oban and the other for Mallaig; the suffix '**Upper**' was added in 1953.

Travelling on the Oban branch, the first stop is Tyndrum Lower (no totems here) before arrival at **Dalmally**. Kilchurn Castle lies between **Dalmally** and **Loch Awe**, the next stop. If totems had been fitted at the small station at Falls of Cruachan these would be very highly prized, but we have to go to the following station at **Taynuilt** before they reappear. From here, beautiful Loch Etive can be seen on the right. **Connel Ferry** is the penultimate stop before arriving at Oban.

Arrochar and Tarbet totem *in situ*, in 1977. *Dawlish Museum*

On journeying north from **Crianlarich** to **Fort William**, the first stop is **Tyndrum Upper** (curiously fitted while Lower was not) before we reach **Bridge of Orchy**, a station that carried collectable Scottish totems. From here it is bleakness all the way as we first stop at **Rannoch** and then **Corrour**, Britain's highest and most remote station. At 1,347 feet above sea level, the station is 9 miles from the nearest public road, serving only the Corrour Estate and the Loch Ossian Youth Hostel.

Rannoch and Corrour totems *in situ* on the bleak Highland moors.

A wonderful Inverness-shire shot from the 1960s of Tulloch station signal box plus totem.

Rannoch Moor itself extends to more than 50 square miles and the mainly boggy ground, with major peat deposits, posed real obstacles to the line's construction. The solution was to build it on thousands of tons of brushwood and tree roots, plus earth and ash to form a floating mattress. The climate in winter can be extremely harsh. Much of the western part lies within the Ben Nevis and Glencoe Scenic Areas and from a carriage window its vastness can be admired in comfort. The station, shown above, opened in August 1894, as an island platform with a passing loop.

Following **Corrour**, the train soon arrives in **Tulloch** followed by **Roy Bridge** and then **Spean Bridge,** a quartet of very desirable items**.** The atmospheric photo top right shows the **Tulloch** station signal box, but the lamp has seen better days, as at Corrour!

Fort William is just 20 miles distant, but on the way beautiful Monessie Gorge, subject of the famous BR(ScR) Cuneo poster, can be seen on the left-hand side of the train. The original station at **Fort William** opened in 1894, but was closed in June 1975, when the present station was built slightly further east. The former site, alongside the Loch Linnhe ferry dock, is now occupied by the A82 town by-pass. The new concrete-built station looks nothing like the old brick-built station with its turret tower and double-arch entrance, but today's station is used by around 160,000 passengers annually.

The train reverses at **Fort William** before heading out to **Banavie** and then **Corpach** along the shores of Loch Eil. Many consider this the best part because after passing Loch Eil and **Locheilside**, the train passes over the iconic **Glenfinnan** viaduct at the head of Loch Shiel, before entering the station. This viaduct, a 21-arch curved concrete structure built by Robert McAlpine between 1897 and October 1898, is one of Britain's most photographed bridges.

Banavie and **Corpach** are around a mile apart, and only a couple of miles outside **Fort William**, whilst **Glenfinnan** is about 17 miles distant. It is only another 25 miles before we reach journey's end at Mallaig. The intermediate stations for this last sector are Lochailort, Beasdale, Arisaig and **Morar**, with only this penultimate stop being fitted with totems. At Arisaig, passengers can catch ferries across to the islands of Eigg and Muck. From Mallaig there are ferries across to the Isle of Skye so, with its multiple connections, this line really is the 'Iron Road to the Isles'. From Glasgow to Oban takes about three hours and up to Mallaig takes around five-and-a-half hours. This short review closes with a couple of historic sights en-route.

Banavie and Taynuilt totems *in situ* in the 1970s. *Tim Clarke*

Regional Focus:
Totems from the Edinburgh Area

Scotland's capital has a rich railway history and its stations carried some of the most collectable names on their totems. It is a great pity Waverley Station was not provided for, sitting as it does in a valley between the famous Princes Street and the 18th-century New Town area with its superb architecture, and the even more famous castle sitting high above the city guarding the medieval Old Town, the Royal Mile down to the Palace of Holyrood and St. Giles Cathedral. The views of the station from the castle and the North Bridge that crosses the station are breath-taking.

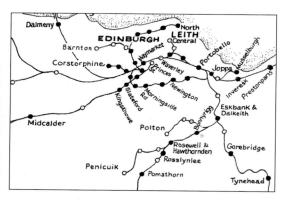

Stations around Edinburgh map. *Alan Young*

The map left shows the centre of Edinburgh was served by two other stations, Princes Street and **Haymarket**, the only one fitted with totems. Other suburban stations, however, were fitted, so collectors have some wonderful names to acquire. There were more than 20 stations in the city and central areas and a further 10–12 in the suburbs. **Corstorphine, Eskbank and Dalkeith, Morningside Road, Portobello** and **Rosewell and Hawthornden** are just a handful of the many collectables we might select, but almost anything marked on the map would form the basis of a great totem collection. The first known survivor from **Leith North** only surfaced in 2021.

In 1962, thirteen stations were closed, and we have no data on many of these. They included **Blackford Hill**, **Craigleith**, **Craiglockhart**, **Duddingston & Craigmillar**, **East Pilton**, **Gorgie East** and **Murrayfield**. It is suspected that once the stations closed, they were quickly stripped and nobody had the chance to save anything. It is a great pity, as **Murrayfield** particularly would be most desirable today and **Duddingston & Craigmillar** is a quite superb 2-line collectable. Fortunately, totems from some other stations closed in the 1960s have survived and two are shown below.

Abbeyhill closed in September 1964, along with **Piershill**, **Portobello**, **Joppa** and **Musselburgh** stations, when the Musselburgh branch service was withdrawn. **Pinkhill** served Edinburgh Zoo and east **Corstorphine**. Services were provided by trains on the Corstorphine Branch, which closed in 1968. That year there were those two closures and the following year saw a further six. The two totems below were 1964 closures, when the seven stations were lost.

Morningside Road is an elusive totem, with no public appearances, but we know of at least one survivor. The photo far right shows at least two *in situ* in the spring of 1962. Notice the well-kept gardens, so typical of stations of that era in most parts of Britain. There were not many passengers to catch the local service that morning.

Such passenger levels were typical of many small and suburban stations throughout Britain in the 1960s, hastening their demise, but notice how clean the DMU is! In contrast, the station at **Eskbank and Dalkeith** looks forlorn in the shot below left from 1969 with all the ScR signage still in place. This was on the Waverley Route south to **Carlisle** and when this was cut, many communities were isolated. Stations which closed in Midlothian that carried totems include **Gorebridge**, **Tynehead**, **Heriot**, **Fountainhall** and **Stow**; the Waverley collection above is one to savour!

Far left: Eskbank and Dalkeith just after closure.

Left: Morningside Road just before closure.

Portobello *in situ* in 1958.

Bonnyrigg *in situ* 1960.

The two pictures above show elusive Edinburgh area totems *in situ*. **Portobello** is east of the city and was originally not included in Dr. Beeching's list of stations earmarked for the axe. Sadly, it was later added and duly closed on 7 September 1964; totems have been auctioned three times. **Bonnyrigg** totems are real rarities, with no known survivors. The station, on the **Peebles** loop from **Eskbank and Dalkeith**, closed in 1962, but the goods facilities remained open until 1965.

The collage left presents totems from Midlothian stations closed in the 1960s. All of these are not that easy to find: the least rare of the quartet is **Tynehead**, on the Waverley Route. **Balgreen Halt**, on the **Corstorphine** branch, had two types of totem: standard letters and the much rarer smaller-lettered layout (as in **Balgreen Halt** left). **Cobbinshaw** was an ex-CR station on the Edinburgh–Carstairs line. It opened in 1848 but closed in April 1966. **Inveresk** is east of Edinburgh and was an ex-NBR station that closed in 1964: five totems from the station have appeared in auction.

Review of Scottish Totems by County

This final section of the chapter gives us the chance to examine the spread of totems by county and comment on rarity and availability for those collectors wishing to acquire totems based on location.

ABERDEENSHIRE

This county suffered serious pruning during the BR years as stations were closed all over Aberdeenshire. Only **Huntly** and **Insch** of the stations fitted with totems survived the axe. Overall, 113 stations have been closed, of which 27 carried totems. Happily, examples from all the installed stations have survived; **Cambus O'May**, **Dyce** and **Rathen** have not appeared in auction, but examples are known, so this quartet represents the real rarities. Furthermore, we have included pictures of six of the Aberdeenshire prized totems in our database pages, including the very rare **Rathen**, **Logierieve** which has appeared just once, and **Peterhead** that has been auctioned twice (1993 and 1997). In addition the four totems left are relatively 'rare birds'.

The county is blessed with classic names, and we might list **Auchnagatt**, **Ballater**, **Fraserburgh** and **Kittybrewster** amongst these. In terms of installed flange types, Aberdeenshire had a high percentage of fully flanged totems (almost 63%) an indication that many totems from the county were made and fitted in the late 1950s and early 1960s. If this is the case, then many were only on public display at the stations for a few years – what a waste, but good for totem collectors!

ANGUS

At its zenith, Angus had 57 stations of which 47 are closed, 8 are open and 2 have been made into heritage stations: Brechin and Bridge of Dun. Only 9 from this list were afforded the worthiness to carry totems, and of these, 2 were closed in 1967 and 2 more were only fitted with wooden totems (*see* page 185). (These 2 wooden specimens have only been seen 3 times)

Dundee Tay Bridge is a well-known station, built in 1878 as part of the Tay Bridge project. Totems from here are looked upon as Scottish classics, but surprisingly, 15 of them have appeared in auctions. Part of the station was demolished in the 1960s to make way for bridge upgrades and in 2018 a completely new £38 million building now serves the Scottish city. **Forfar** is an early station dating from 1848, whose totems have appeared 11 times; it is an ex-Caledonian station.

Tim Clarke

Montrose, shown *in situ* below, is the most readily available Angus totem (29 times in auction), but totems from **Monifeith** have not been seen since removal. **Arbroath** is also difficult to obtain, survivors are known but no auction sightings, and **Carnoustie,** with 4 appearances (2012 and 2019) is desirable but elusive. The wonderfully named **Broughty Ferry** (5 appearances) is also not easy to find.

ARGYLLSHIRE

Totems from any of the 11 stations that carried them would grace any Scottish collection. There are quite superb names, **Loch Awe**, **Ballachulish** and **North Connel** among them, all very hard to find. **Taynuilt** with 11 and **Kentallen** with 10 auction appearances are the most common, but the remainder are somewhat elusive. A simply magical trio follows.

Loch Awe station was opened on 1 July 1880 by the Callander and Oban Railway when it opened the **Dalmally** to Oban line. The station closed on 1 November 1965, but reopened on 10 May 1985, using only one of the two original platforms; the second one is disused (*see* photo on page 178). At least two totem survivors are known, with a first auction appearance occurring in February 2021. The database pages include photographs of other Argyllshire totems from **Ballachulish Ferry**, **Benderloch** and **Bridge of Orchy**: all these places in a quite beautiful part of the UK.

AYRSHIRE

This county was peppered with railway stations, 68 to be precise, at the peak of the railway system. Of these, 38 stations were fitted, providing Ayrshire passengers with plenty of information as to where they were. In the 1960s, 19 stations closed, 11 of these in 1964 and 1965. There are 14 Ayrshire stations where we have no information regarding the existence survivors, including the newly discovered **Stewarton**. It seems when stations were closed, they were quickly cleared, examples being **Ardrossan Town**, **Hollybush** and **Mauchline**.

Of those known to have survived, several have not appeared in auction, **Dalmellington**, **Kilmarnock**, and **South Beach** amongst them. Three of the quartet shown right have appeared 5 times, with West Kilbride having 6, but other rare items include **Ayr**, **Largs**, **Newton-on-Ayr** (shown *in situ* below) and **Waterside**.

Ayrshire totems *in situ. Tim Clarke*

BANFFSHIRE

Just one station, **Keith Junction**, survived the 1960s cull of Banff's totemed stations. On a happier note, this is one of the few Scottish Shires where totem examples from all stations fitted have survived and all have been in sold in public auctions. However, anybody trying to collect a complete set may find this quite difficult as none of the totems are readily available, apart from **Keith Junction,** which has been sold 15 times in public sales. The rare totems are **Portessie**, seen just once in 2017, **Glenbarry** and **Grange** (3 appearances each), **Cornhill**, **Keith Town**, **Portknockie** and **Tillynaught** (all 4 each).

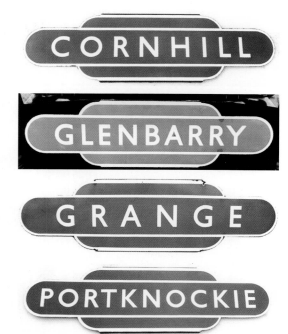

BERWICKSHIRE

Only three stations in Berwickshire were fitted with totems. All three were closed, **Ayton** and **Eyemouth** in 1962 and **Reston** in 1964. We have no information on the of survival of the two earliest closures, but we can include a rare photo of an **Ayton** totem *in situ* on a lean-to waiting room. **Reston** has been auctioned twice, the last time in 2013, so this is quite a rarity.

CAITHNESS

Just two stations were graced with totems in Scotland's most north-easterly railway county. Both **Thurso** and **Wick** totems have survived, along with the stations, which are still operational. A **Thurso** totem has appeared just once in auction, in 2017, while **Wick** has been seen five times, most recently in 2015.

    Thurso is the most northerly station on the British network, with co-ordinates 58.5900°N and 3.5278°W. It was opened by the Sutherland and Caithness in 1874. They also opened **Wick** station on the same day in 1874; the station is the second most-northerly and is slightly east of **Thurso** (58.44 16°N and 3.0975°W). The pair right would look stunning in a Scottish collection.

CLACKMANNANSHIRE

This is a small county, ranking 30th out of the 33 Scottish shires by area and 29th by population. There are just two stations that carried totems, both were closed in 1968, though **Alloa** re-opened in 2008. Totem examples from both stations have survived and have been in auction, **Alloa** 9 times and **Cambus** 10 times.

CUMBERLAND

Although very much in an English county, the station at **Riddings Junction** carried Caledonian blue totems! It

was intended as the junction for the **Langholm** branch and did not actually serve any of the local villages, which were miles away. The tiny hamlet of Moat was the nearest community.

DUMFRIES-SHIRE

Twelve stations carried totems in this southern Scottish county. Seven of these were closed in the 1960s and **Beattock** station was closed in 1972. The station at **Sanquhar** closed in 1965 but was re-opened in 1994. With the exceptions of **Beattock** (26 appearances) and **Dumfries** (23), totems from the county are fairly hard to come by, with no data at all on **Eastriggs** and **Gilnockie**.

Canonbie has 3 auction appearances and **Thornhill** 4. The Scottish database pages contain photographs of totems from **Ecclefechan** (3 times in auction) and **Langholm** just 1.

DUNBARTONSHIRE

The county lies on the north bank of the River Clyde to the west of the City of Glasgow. It is an important commuter area for the city and has a good railway network, 33 stations of which were fitted with totems. Of this total only 9 were closed: 5 in 1964 (**Dalmuir Riverside**, **Kilbowie**, **Kirkintilloch**, **Old Kilpatrick** and **Shandon**), 2 in 1967 (**Castlecary** and **Dullatur**) and 2 in the late 1980s (**Balloch Central** and **Balloch Pier**). We have no information about **Kirkintilloch** and **Westerton**, but fine quartet of Dunbartonshire totems that have survived appears right.

The left-hand picture above shows not one, but two **Balloch Pier** totems proudly hanging in this 1960s image. This former terminus station (viewed from the buffer stops in the right-hand picture), located at the southern end of Loch Lomond, was perfectly situated for pleasure boats to come alongside the single platform. Despite early 1960s electrification, passenger traffic to the pier was only seasonal and therefore uneconomic in the eyes of BR managers; it sadly closed in 1986, depriving summer travellers of an easy way to reach the Loch. The totems were of a very early design, being only 9½ inches in height instead of the usual 10 inches. They were allegedly thrown into the loch after being taken down, hence very few survivors!

Some Dunbartonshire totems are very elusive. **Drumry** has been in auction once, in 2001; **Cardross** last appeared in 2008. Three other single appearance totems are included in the database pages, these being **Balloch Pier**, **Castlecary** and **Dalmuir Riverside**. We close with another county quartet.

EAST LOTHIAN

Just seven stations in East Lothian were favoured with totems, and of these, two (**East Fortune** and **East Linton**) were closed in 1964.

Dunbar, on the ECML, had totems removed quickly and it would appear all were lost. Saved examples of all other East Lothian totems exist and all have been auctioned, the most common being **Prestonpans** 13 times and **Drem** 15 times. Some plastic totems were also made for **Prestonpans** and the photo below shows them *in situ*. A photo of a **North Berwick** totem is found in the database pages.

FIFE (THE KINGDOM OF FIFE)

This county, on the north side of the Firth of Forth, may only rank 13th in area but it is 3rd in population behind Glasgow and Edinburgh. Consequently, the county was favoured with 36 stations carrying totems, of which 22 suffered closure. There are really choice names to collect, so we might suggest **Anstruther**, **Cameron Bridge**, **Dunfermline** (**Upper** and **Lower**), **Dysart**, **Guard Bridge**, **Inverkeithing**, **Newport-on-Tay** (**East** and **West**) and **St. Andrews**.

We knew of one substantial collection based on Fife and the two photos below show just part of this before dispersal. Rare items include **Aberdour** and, **Crail** (1 appearance each), **Dysart** (3), **Elie** (5), **Guard Bridge** (5), **Kilconquhar** (2), **Kirkcaldy** (3), **Ladybank** (5), **Leuchars Junction** (5), **Pittenweem** (2), **St Monance** (2) and **Springfield** (5). There is only **Bogside** (closed 1958) where we have no information. In 1933, this was named Bogside (Fife) to avoid confusion with north Ayrshire's similarly-named station. **Lundin Links** and **Oakley (Fife)** have not been in auction.

Lundin Links and Largo totems *in situ. Both photos CineRail*

INVERNESS-SHIRE

Many regard this county as the epitome of Scotland, because of the scenery and its history. It is the nation's largest shire (4,211 sq. miles), but with only 1.4% of the population. These four totems are pure Scotland.

Inverness-shire is the second largest county in the UK as a whole after Yorkshire. It borders Ross-shire to the north, Nairnshire, Moray, Banffshire and Aberdeenshire to the east, and Perthshire and Argyllshire to the south. The inland section encompasses much of the famed Scottish Highlands, whilst the Great Glen bisects it in two. Ben Nevis, east of **Fort William**, is the UK's highest mountain. Collecting totems from here has always been popular, but difficult. Of the 19 stations fitted, totems from **Corpach** and **Morar** have survived but have not been auctioned and 6 others (**Banavie**, **Corrour**, **Locheilside**, **Nethy Bridge**, **Roy Bridge** and **Tulloch**) have appeared once. Highly-prized **Glenfinnan** has been auctioned 3 times, the last time in 2011.

In railway terms, the Kingdom of Fife is one of notable contrasts. Being surrounded by water on three sides gives stunning scenery in many places, whilst the inland areas used to contain much industry including several coalfields. **Dunfermline** is the old capital of Scotland and packed with history. The area suffered from many line closures in the 1960s. The most lamentable were the branch line from **Wormit**, south of the River Tay to **Tayport** and sections of the coastal route from **Leuchars Junction** to **Thornton Junction** (1965); the remainder closed four years later. The train journey today along the coast through **Aberdour** with its sandy beaches, **Burntisland**, **Kinghorn** and **Kirkcaldy,** where fine views across to Edinburgh can be gained on a clear day and inland to **Markinch** and **Ladybank**, is still one of great enjoyment. The Fife totem pinnacle has to be **St. Andrews**, the home of golf, and a fine university. There is always a keen contest when this totem comes up for auction, 5 times thus far. Work is underway to re-open the **Thornton Junction** to **Leven** 5-mile branch line, due for completion in 2024.

We have no information at all on the survival of totems from **Dalcross** (closed 1965), but not all Inverness-shire totems are elusive. **Aviemore** and **Kingussie** both have 32 appearances, **Newtonmore** 25, **Fort William** 14 and **Boat of Garten** 11, make it just 5 from the 19 available examples with double-figured sales. The database pages contain photographs of five of the rarest Inverness-shire totems. A reconstructed station at **Broomhill** was re-opened in 2002 by the Strathspey Railway as its eastern terminus, after being closed for 37 years. The **Fort William** totem is considered by many collectors to be a Scottish classic.

KINCARDINESHIRE

Just four stations make up the 'totemed' population of this county's railway network. Three of these have closed, but examples from all four stations have survived and all have been in auction. Roughly triangular in shape, Kincardineshire consists of the largely flat Strathmore area running parallel with the coast, and a hillier, forested landscape further inland, the prelude to the Grampian Mountains. The Edinburgh to Aberdeen railway line runs parallel to the coast and through the towns of **Laurencekirk** and **Stonehaven**. The former re-opened in 2009. The Royal Deeside branch line criss-crossed the border with Aberdeenshire and included the totem stations at **Banchory** and **Crathes**.

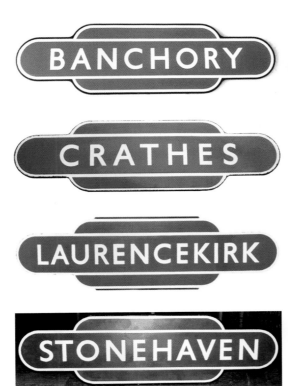

KINROSS-SHIRE

There were just three stations in Kinross-shire carrying totems and all are closed today. **Milnathort** has not been in auction, but **Kinross Junction** (7 appearances) and **Mawcarse** (11 times) have.

KIRKCUDBRIGHT-SHIRE

This county also has just three stations that carried totems, but those from **Kirkcudbright** have disappeared without trace – so far! Happily, totems from the other two stations, **Castle Douglas** and **Dalbeattie** have survived and been publically auctioned, though just once and twice respectively.

LANARKSHIRE

This is the real 'heavyweight' of stations adorned with totems in Scotland. Collectors have 117 different names to obtain, but we have no survival information from 25 of these, so completing the set is virtually impossible. In this list of 'lost' totems there are some wonderful names, **Bridgeton Cross**, **Clydebank Riverside**, **Coatbridge Central**, **Glasgow Cross**, **Maxwell Park**, **Parkhead Stadium**, **Strathaven Central** and **Yoker Ferry**. Lanarkshire totems seem to be less desirable than many other counties, but with names such as **Auchengray**, **Mount Florida** or **Whiteinch Riverside** surviving, this we find this difficult to understand.

Of the 92 stations whose totems have survived, several are uncommon. We can list the following with just one appearance each: **Ballieston, Bridgeton Central, Cardonald, Carnwath, Coalburn, Cowlairs, Douglas West, East Kilbride, Easterhouse, Hamilton West, Holytown, Langside, Law Junction, Maryhill Central, Maryhill Park, Mossend, Pollokshaws West** and **Ponfeigh**. Curiously, considering their rarity, several of these do not feature in a list of sought-after totems and the majority have not made high auction returns. Even the lovely-named **Charing Cross** or **Queen's Park** have not reached dizzy heights. Some totems remained *in situ* into the 1980s, as shown below.

The Glasgow suburbs in 1982: a Crosshill totem still clings to its fitting! *Alan Young*

The earlier section on Glasgow suburban totems allowed us to show many of the city's collectables and the database contains 15 of the county's rarer items. We recently confirmed that Clarkston on the Bathgate line was not fitted (*see* note on page 204).

MIDLOTHIAN

Although Midlothian ranked 24th by area in the 1950s, it was favoured with the installation of totems on 43 stations. Sadly, closures amounted to 77% of this number, so by the end of the 1960s, only 10 stations remained open. Three of the closures have since re-opened when part of the northern section of the Waverley Route was re-built in 2015.

As in Glasgow, when totems were removed, examples from 11 stations do not seem to have survived, just 28% of the Midlothian stations listed in the database pages. In addition to the 11 non-survivors, totems from another 4 stations have not appeared in auction: **Morningside Road, Newington, Rosewell and Hawthornden** and **Rosslynlee**. Photographs of 5 further rarities, **Addiewell** with 2 appearances, **Harburn**, 2, **Joppa**, 5, **Kingsknowe**, 5, **Merchiston**, 1, **Newington**, 0, and **Newpark**, 1, are found in the database pages. All these facts make collecting a set from Midlothian virtually impossible and assembling a large collection of 20 or more is also rather difficult.

The following two 1950s photos opposite top show rare Midlothian totems *in situ*. Five totems were installed at **Rosslynlee**, one being on the station building and the other four being fixed to the platform fence. We know of at least one survivor.

Rosslynlee *in situ* in 1958. *D. Martin*

Pomathorn *in situ* in the1950s.
TSG library

Pomathorn carried the LNER running in board 'Pomathorn for Penicuik' in the early 1950s prior to resigning. Interestingly, the BR timetable for September 1953 uses the name Pomathorn 'Halt' as it was unstaffed at that time. However, two totems were installed under the station canopy and can be clearly seen 'end-on' on the top right-hand corner. Sadly, we do not currently believe that any have survived.

The quartet right shows the final four Midlothian gems. **Breich** is on the Edinburgh–Glasgow via **Shotts** line, 21 miles west of the Capital. It was the second-least-used station in Scotland in 2018 with just 342 passengers! **Heriot** is an ex-NBR station on the Waverley route and was closed in 1969. **Slateford** is on the Glasgow–Edinburgh via **Shotts** line, and **West Calder** on the Edinburgh to **Carstairs** electrified line.

MORAYSHIRE

Morayshire had just 13 stations that carried totems, some with superb names. Of the 13 stations only **Elgin** and **Forres** survive today; 7 stations were closed in 1965 and 6 in 1968. Photographs of 5 of the rarer Morayshire totems are included in the database pages, with a small selection right. We list **Ballindalloch, Elgin, Grantown-on-Spey West, Longmorn** and **Spey Bay** as being real collectables; the hyphenated LP **Grantown-on-Spey West** is rather special.

The Morayshire rarities are **Ballindalloch** with 2 appearances, the last in 2009; **Garmouth,** 2; **Knockando,** 3; and **Calcots** and **Longmorn** with 4 each. Examples of all Morayshire totems are known to exist, with Urquhart having just one public appearance.

NAIRNSHIRE

Just **Nairn** station carried totems and this is one of the most common Scottish signs with 46 auction appearances: this is over four times the number that were actually fitted to the station!

PEEBLES-SHIRE

This small southern Scottish county had just four stations carrying totems, **Eddleston, Innerleithen, Peebles** and **Walkerburn**. All the stations were closed in 1962, and we have no survival data on two of these. Both **Peebles** and **Innerleithen** have been auctioned twice, in 2006 and 2007 respectively; they are elusive totems. **Innerleithen** totems were installed on the platform fence beneath the gas lamps. A rare photograph of an FF **Eddleston** totem *in situ* in the late 1950s follows. **Walkerburn** station, located south of the town, possessed at least 4 totems, all of them attached to the platform fence.

PERTHSHIRE

This beautiful county is Scotland's fourth largest, with some of the most classic Caledonian blue totems to collect from the 19 stations that once carried them. Examples of Perthshire totems from all the 19 stations have survived and all have been in auction. Collecting a complete set is therefore possibly the easiest of all the Scottish counties, though still tricky! Two of the classics appear below, although **Gleneagles** is a common sight: 17 times in auction.

Perthshire is a county of contrasts, ranging from rich agricultural soils in the south and east to the high mountains of the Southern Grampians in the north. The rather attractive but small city of **Perth** lines the banks of the River Tay. Given its location, **Perth** was perfectly placed to become a key transport centre with the coming of the railways; the first station was built there in 1848. The county rarities are **Blair Atholl,** 3 appearances; **Crianlarich Lower** and **Upper,** 2 each; **Perth,** 4; **Rannoch,** 1; **Strathyre,** 3; **Tullibardine,** 2, and **Tyndrum Upper,** 5. We did say there are some quite superb names from Perthshire!

Three stations closed in 1964, a further six in 1965 and one in 1967. This leaves **Blair Atholl**, **Crianlarich Upper**, **Dunblane**, **Gleneagles**, **Perth**, **Pitlochry**, **Rannoch** and **Tyndrum Upper** still operational today.

RENFREWSHIRE

This is another county where closures and rapid re-signing means we have many gaps in our database, with 7 of the 36 stations fitted having no known survivors – so far. Some of these have wonderful names, **Bishopton**, **Greenock Lynedoch**, and **Paisley Gilmour Street** to name just three. Totems at Clarkston & Stamperland station carried the name **Clarkston**. Of the known survivors, **Fort Matilda**, **Greenock Central**, **Inverkip**, **Paisley Abercorn** and **Thornliebank** have yet to make auction appearances, so collecting Renfrewshire totem is exceptionally testing. In 1951, Renfrewshire ranked 28th by area. It lies to the west of Glasgow on the southern bank of the River Clyde and is home to Glasgow's International Airport.

These totems are two more of Renfrewshire's rarities. **Gourock** opened in 1889 and is the terminus of today's Inverclyde line. It has been in auction twice, the last time in 2000. The first station in Neilston opened in 1855 as Crofthead but was re-named after the town in 1868. It closed in May 1870, but subsequently re-opened in 1871. It eventually took the totem name of **Neilston Low** in January 1953 but was finally closed in 1966. Though the station is long gone, the line through it remains open.

A trio of rare Greenock Central totems in *situ. TSG library*

ROSS & CROMARTY

Just nine stations in this county carried totems, and rather surprisingly all the stations escaped the economic axe and are operational today. One of these lines is the wonderful journey between **Dingwall** and the **Kyle of Lochalsh**. Many of the county's station totems are on collectors' wants lists.

The photos below left show the totem at the top and an *in-situ* picture of the station beneath. **Achnashellach,** opened in 1870, is on the Kyle line and in 2018 only 840 passengers used the station. **Bonar Bridge**, an ex-Highland railway station from 1864, is on the Far North Line from Inverness. It was renamed Ardgay in 1977.

The **Kyle of Lochalsh** line is one of Britain's finest and attracts travellers from all over the world; a totem from here is very highly prized. The sequence of stations from **Dingwall** is **Garve**, **Lochluichart**, Achanalt, **Achnasheen**, **Achnashellach**, **Strathcarron**, Attadale, Stromeferry, Duncraig, Plockton, Duirinish and the **Kyle of Lochalsh** (*see* page 46). Any of these totems are extremely desirable, with **Dingwall** being the most common, 11 appearances. **Achnashellach** and **Strathcarron**, the rarest; both have no appearances in auction. The line is 63-miles long, built in three sections, Inverness to **Dingwall** in 1864, **Dingwall** to Stromeferry in 1870, and the **Kyle of Lochalsh** extension in 1897. BR wanted to close the line in 1970, but a vigorous local campaign ensured this did not happen and in recent years more than 60,000 passengers use the line annually.

ROXBURGHSHIRE

There are six different stations that carried totems in Roxburgh, all of them being closed in the 1960s. Four closed in 1964 (**Kelso**, **Maxton**, **Roxburgh** and **Rutherford**) and two closed in 1969 (**Hawick** and **Melrose**) With the exception of **Hawick**, Roxburghshire totems are not at all easy to find, with **Rutherford** not known to have any survivors following closure. The colour picture overleaf of a **Roxburgh** totem *in situ* is itself quite a rarity.

The two *in-situ* pictures above and left show a lovely Scottish lamp at **Kelso**, and part of one at **Roxburgh**. This latter totem has survived but has not been seen in auction. **Kelso,** 3 auctions, and **Maxton,** 7, are also not easy to find.

SELKIRK

There are just two totemed stations in this county, **Galashiels**, which has survived, and **Clovenfords**, which has not. The first-named is a common totem from a station that closed in 1969 but was re-opened in 2015.

The two Selkirkshire totems are shown here *in situ circa* 1960 at **Galashiels**, below left, and **Clovenfords**, above. There are no lamps, so the two totems are just fixed to the fence!

STIRLINGSHIRE

Examples of totems from all 11 Stirlingshire totemed stations have survived and have been in auction, so collecting a complete set is entirely possible. **Stirling** is one of the most common Scottish totems, having been sold 51 times! **Grangemouth**, on the other hand, has been in auction just once. **Bridge of Allan** is possibly the nicest name, while **Larbert** is possibly not so collectable. A small selection below is representative of the totem names available.

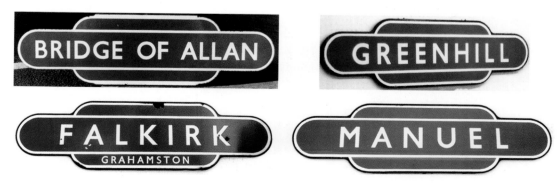

Stirlingshire is *Braveheart* territory and the three famous battles sites in the fight for independence are at Stirling Bridge, 1297; Falkirk, 1298, and Bannockburn, 1314. The quite majestic castle dominates the City of Stirling, while nearby the National Wallace Monument, built on Abbey Craig, looks down over the Forth Valley. **Camelon** is a suburb of Falkirk. The station opened in 1850 as Camelon, was closed in September 1967, and in 1903 it was renamed Falkirk (Camelon), but this name was never carried on the totems. The two totems together above therefore represent Scotland's battles for independence against the repressive King Edward I.

SUTHERLAND

This north-western county possessed just three stations that carried totems. In the totem era, it ranked fifth-largest by area, but the last census gave a population of less than 13,000. Totem examples from all the stations, **Golspie**, **Lairg** and **The Mound**, have survived and have all been in auction. Tim Clarke's photos below show the buildings and totems *in situ* at **Lairg** in the 1970s.

Sutherland totems *in situ*. Tim Clarke

Sutherland has some of the most dramatic scenery in the whole of Europe, especially on its western fringe where the mountains meet the sea, but miles from the railway!

The Far North line runs through Sutherland between Inverness and **Thurso/Wick**. Much of it is single track traversing the 167 miles of the route from Inverness to two outposts. It was built between 1862 and 1874, and was earmarked for closure by Beeching in the 1960s; local pressure meant this was rejected. Dornoch is the county town, but its railway station closed in 1960. Today it is a cafe!

WEST LOTHIAN

Scotland's third-smallest shire had just four stations adorned with totems, **Armadale**, **Dalmeny**, **Fauldhouse North** and **Linlithgow**. Although one of these appears elsewhere in this volume, it is worth showing all four together for the first time in a railway-related book.

West Lothian lies on the southern shore of the Firth of Forth and is predominantly rural, although there were extensive coal, iron, and shale oil mining operations in the 19th and 20th centuries. The old county town was the royal burgh of Linlithgow, which gave the shire is old name of Linlithgowshire, but the largest community is now the new town of Livingston. Stations such as **Addiewell** and **Breich** that were listed as Midlothian during the totem years are now classed as West Lothian, following area boundary changes.

Fauldhouse North is by far the most common of the quartet with 23 public appearances and **Armadale** is the least common with just 5, the last in 2011.

WIGTOWNSHIRE

Scotland's most south-westerly shire has only four stations that carried totems. Totem examples from all four have survived and have all been in auction. Recent research has confirmed that New Luce, listed in the 2002 book, was not fitted. In the 19th century it was called West Galloway and today is administered as part of Dumfries & Galloway. The county town used to be Wigtown but in 1890, when the County Council was created, it moved to Stranraer. Both the stations, **Stranraer Harbour** and **Stranraer Town,** carried totems, along with **Dunragit** and **Newton Stewart**. Collecting totems from here is far from easy, with all 5 stations having just 15 auction appearances in total. **Stranraer Harbour** is the rarest with just 2 appearances, the last being in 2008, and **Newton Stewart** the most common, but with just 6 auction sales. Only **Stranraer Harbour** station is open today.

Chapter Closure

Since our 2002 book appeared, a great deal of new information has been uncovered. As a result, this chapter is greatly expanded from the ten pages published in the *BR Book of Totems*. Scotland suffered badly from cuts and closures but in recent years, rail ridership has increased markedly and ScotRail have opened many of the old stations, as well as building new ones. Of the 492 stations adorned with totems, this chapter contains 238 different examples, 48% of all stations fitted. Our research finds that 419 Scottish stations have totem examples that have survived, so this chapter contains 58% of all the surviving examples, with many not appearing in print before.

Collecting Scottish totems is the hobby of many of our fellow enthusiasts and there are some quite wonderful names available. A top three might include **Kyle of Lochalsh**, **Boat of Garten** and **Dundee Tay Bridge**, but everybody has their own ideas. We close with a remarkable picture of eight foot BR totems which were installed at **Haymarket** station; one of these is currently on display at Mangapps Museum in Essex!

Left: Stranraer Harbour railway station. *Wikipedia Commons*

Station Name	County in 1956	Layout	Flange	Closed	Auction	Survived
ABBEYHILL	Midlothian		FF	1964	•	•
ABERDOUR	Fife		FF		•	•
ABERLOUR	Banffshire		FF	1965	•	•
ABOYNE	Aberdeenshire		FF	1966	•	•
ACHNASHEEN	Ross & Cromarty		HF		•	•
ACHNASHELLACH	Ross & Cromarty		HF			
ADDIEWELL	Midlothian		FF		•	•
AIRDRIE	Lanarkshire		FF		•	•
ALEXANDRA PARADE	Lanarkshire	1L	FF		•	•
ALEXANDRIA	Dunbartonshire		FF		•	•
ALLANFEARN	Inverness-shire		FF	1965	•	•
ALLOA *re-opened 2008	Clackmannanshire		HF	1968*	•	•
ANDERSTON CROSS *new Anderston station 1979	Lanarkshire		HF	1959*	•	•
ANNAN	Dumfries-shire		FF		•	•
ANNIESLAND	Lanarkshire		FF		•	•
ANSTRUTHER	Fife		FF	1965	•	•
APPIN	Argyllshire		FF	1966	•	•
ARBROATH	Angus		HF			•
ARDLUI	Dunbartonshire		HF		•	•
ARDROSSAN TOWN *re-opened 1987	Ayrshire	1L	HF	1968*	•	•
ARMADALE *re-opened and re-sited 2011	West Lothian		HF	1956 *		•
ARROCHAR AND TARBET	Dunbartonshire	1L	HF		•	•
AUCHENGRAY	Lanarkshire		FF	1966	•	•
AUCHINLECK *re-opened 1984	Ayrshire		HF	1965*		
AUCHNAGATT	Aberdeenshire		FF	1965	•	•
AVIEMORE	Inverness-shire		HF		•	•
AYR	Ayrshire		FF		•	•
AYTON New discovery	Berwickshire		FF	1962		
BAILLIESTON *re-opened 1993	Lanarkshire		FF	1964*	•	•
BALGREEN HALT some with reduced sized letters	Midlothian	1L	HF	1968	•	•
BALLACHULISH	Argyllshire		FF	1966		•
BALLACHULISH FERRY	Argyllshire		HF	1966		•
BALLATER	Aberdeenshire		FF	1966	•	•

1L = one line: 2L = two line: LP = lower panel

Station Name		County in 1956	Layout	Flange	Closed	Auction	Survived
BALLINDALLOCH		Morayshire		FF	1965	•	•
BALLOCH CENTRAL	replaced by Balloch 1988	Dunbartonshire	LP	HF	1988	•	•
BALLOCH PIER	early 9.5" high totem	Dunbartonshire		HF	1986	•	•
BALMOSSIE HALT	opened 1962 wooden only	Angus	1L	Wood		•	•
BALQUHIDDER		Perthshire		HF	1965	•	•
BANAVIE		Inverness-shire		HF		•	•
BANCHORY		Kincardineshire		FF	1965	•	•
BARASSIE		Ayrshire		FF		•	•
BARNHILL		Lanarkshire		FF		•	•
BARRHEAD		Renfrewshire		HF		•	•
BARRMILL		Ayrshire		HF	1964		
BEARSDEN		Dunbartonshire		FF		•	•
BEATTOCK		Dumfries-shire		HF/FF	1972	•	•
BEITH TOWN		Ayrshire		HF	1962		
BELLGROVE		Lanarkshire		FF		•	•
BELLSHILL		Lanarkshire		FF		•	•
BENDERLOCH		Argyllshire		FF	1966	•	•
BISHOPBRIGGS		Lanarkshire		HF		•	•
BISHOPTON		Renfrewshire		FF			
BLACKFORD HILL		Midlothian		FF	1962		
BLAIR ATHOLL		Perthshire		HF		•	•
BLAIRHILL		Lanarkshire		FF		•	•
BLANTYRE		Lanarkshire		HF		•	•
BOAT OF GARTEN	*Heritage station from 2002	Inverness		FF	1965*	•	•
BOGSIDE		Fife		HF	1967		
BOGSTON		Renfrewshire		HF			
BONAR BRIDGE		Ross & Cromarty		FF		•	•
BONNYBRIDGE HIGH		Stirlingshire	LP	HF	1967	•	•
BONNYRIGG		Midlothian		FF	1962*		
BOWLING		Dunbartonshire		FF		•	•
BRAIDWOOD		Lanarkshire		FF	1962		
BREICH		Midlothian		FF		•	•
BRIDGE OF ALLAN	*new station open 1985	Stirlingshire		HF	1965	•	•
BRIDGE OF EARN		Perthshire		FF	1964	•	•
BRIDGE OF ORCHY		Argyllshire		HF		•	•

1L = one line: 2L = two line: LP = lower panel

Station Name	County in 1956	Layout	Flange	Closed	Auction	Survived
BRIDGE OF WEIR	Renfrewshire		FF	1983	•	•
BRIDGETON CENTRAL	Lanarkshire		FF		•	•
BRIDGETON CROSS *open as Bridgeton 1979	Lanarkshire		FF	1964*		
BROOMHILL *re-opened 2002 by Strathspey Rly	Inverness-shire		FF	1965*	•	•
BROUGHTY FERRY	Angus		HF		•	•
BRUCKLAY	Aberdeenshire		HF	1965	•	
BURNSIDE	Lanarkshire		FF			•
BURNTISLAND	Fife		FF		•	•
BUSBY	Lanarkshire		FF			•
CALCOTS	Morayshire		HF	1968	•	•
CALDERPARK	Lanarkshire		HF	1955		
CALLANDER	Perthshire		FF	1965	•	•
CAMBUS	Clackmannanshire		FF	1968		•
CAMBUSLANG	Lanarkshire		HF/FF		•	•
CAMBUS O'MAY	Aberdeenshire		FF	1966		•
CAMELON *new station 1994	Stirlingshire		FF	1967*	•	•
CAMERON BRIDGE	Fife		FF	1969		
CANONBIE	Dumfries-shire		FF	1964		
CARDENDEN	Fife		FF		•	•
CARDONALD	Lanarkshire		FF		•	•
CARDROSS	Dunbartonshire		FF		•	•
CARFIN	Lanarkshire		FF		•	•
CARLUKE	Lanarkshire		FF		•	•
CARMYLE *re-opened 1993	Lanarkshire		HF	1964*	•	•
CARNOUSTIE	Angus		FF		•	•
CARNTYNE	Lanarkshire		FF		•	•
CARNWATH	Lanarkshire		HF	1966	•	•
CARRON	Morayshire		FF	1965	•	•
CARSTAIRS	Lanarkshire		HF		•	•
CARTSDYKE	Renfrewshire		HF			
CASTLECARY	Dunbartonshire		FF	1967	•	•
CASTLE DOUGLAS	Kirkcudbrightshire		FF	1965	•	•
CATHCART	Lanarkshire		HF		•	•

1L = one line: 2L = two line: LP = lower panel

Station Name		County in 1956	Layout	Flange	Closed	Auction	Survived
CHARING CROSS		Lanarkshire		FF		•	•
CLARKSTON	(see page 204)	Renfrewshire		FF		•	•
CLEGHORN		Lanarkshire		FF	1965	•	•
CLELAND		Lanarkshire		HF/FF		•	•
CLOVENFORDS		Selkirk		FF	1962		
CLYDEBANK CENTRAL		Lanarkshire	LP	FF		•	•
CLYDEBANK EAST	New discovery	Lanarkshire	LP		1959		
CLYDEBANK RIVERSIDE		Lanarkshire	LP	FF	1964		
COALBURN		Lanarkshire		HF	1965	•	•
COATBRIDGE CENTRAL		Lanarkshire	LP	?			
COATBRIDGE SUNNYSIDE		Lanarkshire	LP	FF		•	•
COATDYKE		Lanarkshire		FF		•	•
COBBINSHAW		Midlothian		FF	1966	•	•
CONNEL FERRY		Argyllshire		HF		•	•
CORKERHILL	*re-opened 1990	Lanarkshire		HF	1983*	•	•
CORNHILL		Banffshire		HF	1968	•	•
CORPACH		Inverness-shire		HF			•
CORROUR		Inverness-shire		FF		•	•
CORSTORPHINE		Midlothian		FF	1968	•	•
COUPAR ANGUS		Perthshire		FF	1967	•	•
COWDENBEATH		Fife		FF		•	•
COWLAIRS		Lanarkshire		HF	1964	•	•
CRAIGENDORAN		Dunbartonshire		FF		•	•
CRAIGLEITH		Midlothian		?	1962		
CRAIGLOCKHART		Midlothian		FF	1962		
CRAIL		Fife		FF	1965	•	•
CRATHES		Kincardineshire		FF	1966	•	•
CRIANLARICH LOWER		Perthshire	LP	FF	1965	•	•
CRIANLARICH UPPER		Perthshire	LP	FF		•	•
CROFTFOOT		Lanarkshire		HF			•
CROOKSTON	*re-opened 1990	Lanarkshire		HF	1983*	•	•
CROSSHILL		Lanarkshire		HF		•	
CROSSMYLOOF		Lanarkshire		HF			•
CROY		Dunbartonshire		HF		•	•

1L = one line: 2L = two line: LP = lower panel

Station Name	County in 1956	Layout	Flange	Closed	Auction	Survived
CULTER	Aberdeenshire		FF	1966	•	•
CULTS	Aberdeenshire		FF	1966	•	•
CUMBERLAND STREET	Lanarkshire	1L	FF	1966	•	•
CUMBERNAULD	Dunbartonshire		FF		•	•
CUMNOCK	Ayrshire		HF	1965		•
CUPAR	Fife		HF		•	•
DALBEATTIE	Kirkcudbrightshire		FF	1965	•	
DALCROSS	Inverness		FF	1965		
DALMALLY	Argyllshire		FF		•	•
DALMARNOCK *re-opened 1979 refurbished 2013	Lanarkshire		HF	1964*		•
DALMARNOCK *re-opened 1979 refurbished 2013	Lanarkshire		FF	1964*	•	•
DALMELLINGTON	Ayrshire		HF	1964		•
DALMENY	West Lothian		HF		•	•
DALMUIR PARK	Dunbartonshire	1L	HF/FF		•	•
DALMUIR RIVERSIDE	Dunbartonshire	LP	FF	1964	•	•
DALREOCH	Dunbartonshire		HF			•
DALRY	Ayrshire		HF		•	•
DALRY ROAD	Midlothian		HF	1962	•	
DESS	Aberdeenshire		FF	1966	•	•
DINGWALL	Ross & Cromarty		FF		•	•
DINNET	Aberdeenshire		FF	1966	•	•
DOUGLAS WEST	Lanarkshire	1L	FF	1964	•	•
DOUNE	Perthshire		HF	1965	•	•
DREM	East Lothian		FF		•	•
DRUMCHAPEL	Lanarkshire		FF			•
DRUMPARK	Lanarkshire		FF	1964	•	•
DRUMRY	Dunbartonshire		HF		•	•
DRYBRIDGE	Ayrshire		?	1969		
DUDDINGSTON & CRAIGMILLAR	Midlothian	2L	HF	1962		•
DUKE STREET	Lanarkshire		FF			•
DULLATUR	Dunbartonshire		HF	1967	•	•
DUMBARTON CENTRAL	Dunbartonshire	LP	HF		•	•
DUMBARTON EAST	Dunbartonshire	LP	HF		•	•
DUMFRIES	Dumfries-shire		HF/FF		•	•
DUNBAR New discovery	East Lothian		FF			

1L = one line: 2L = two line: LP = lower panel

Station Name	County in 1956	Layout	Flange	Closed	Auction	Survived
DUNBLANE	Perthshire		HF		•	•
DUNDEE TAY BRIDGE	Angus	LP	HF		•	•
DUNFERMLINE LOWER	Fife	1L	HF		•	•
DUNFERMLINE UPPER	Fife	1L	FF	1968	•	•
DUNLOP *re-opened 1967; expanded 2009	Ayrshire		HF	1966*		
DUNRAGIT	Wigtownshire		HF	1965	•	
DYSART	Fife		FF	1969	•	•
EASTERHOUSE	Lanarkshire		FF		•	•
EAST FORTUNE	East Lothian		FF	1964	•	•
EAST KILBRIDE	Lanarkshire		FF		•	•
EAST LINTON	East Lothian		FF	1964	•	•
EAST PILTON	Midlothian		HF	1962		
EASTRIGGS	Dumfries-shire		FF	1965		
ECCLEFECHAN	Dumfries-shire		HF	1960	•	•
EDDLESTON	Peebles-shire		FF	1962		
EGLINTON STREET	Lanarkshire		HF	1965	•	•
ELDERSLIE	Renfrewshire		FF	1966	•	•
ELGIN	Morayshire		FF		•	•
ELIE	Fife		FF	1965	•	•
ELLON	Aberdeenshire		FF	1965	•	•
ESKBANK AND DALKEITH *re-opened 2015	Midlothian	1L	FF	1969*	•	•
EYEMOUTH	Berwickshire		FF	1962		
FAIRLIE HIGH	Ayrshire	LP	HF		•	•
FALKIRK GRAHAMSTON	Stirlingshire	LP	FF		•	•
FALKIRK HIGH	Stirlingshire	LP	HF		•	•
FAULDHOUSE NORTH	West Lothian	LP	HF		•	•
FLEMINGTON	Lanarkshire		FF	1965	•	•
FORFAR	Angus		FF	1967	•	•
FORRES alignment re-located 2017	Morayshire		HF		•	•
FORT MATILDA	Renfrewshire		HF			•
FORT WILLIAM station re-located 1975	Inverness-shire		HF		•	
FOUNTAINHALL	Midlothian		FF	1969	•	•
FRASERBURGH	Aberdeenshire		FF	1965	•	•

1L = one line: 2L = two line: LP = lower panel

Station Name		County in 1956	Layout	Flange	Closed	Auction	Survived
GAILES	New discovery	Ayrshire		FF	1967		
GALASHIELS	*re-opened 2015	Selkirk		HF	1969*	•	•
GALSTON		Ayrshire		HF	1964		
GARELOCHHEAD		Dunbartonshire		HF		•	•
GARMOUTH		Morayshire		HF	1968	•	•
GARNKIRK		Lanarkshire		FF	1960		
GARROWHILL		Lanarkshire		FF		•	•
GARTCOSH	*re-opened 2005	Lanarkshire		FF	1962*		
GARTLY		Aberdeenshire		FF	1968	•	•
GARVE		Ross & Cromarty		HF		•	•
GIFFNOCK		Renfrewshire		FF		•	•
GILNOCKIE		Dumfries-shire		FF	1964		
GIRVAN	also plastic	Ayrshire		HF		•	•
GLASGOW CROSS		Lanarkshire		HF	1964		
GLASSEL		Aberdeenshire		FF	1966	•	•
GLENBARRY		Banffshire		HF	1968	•	•
GLENEAGLES		Perthshire		HF		•	•
GLENFARG		Perthshire		FF	1964	•	•
GLENFINNAN		Inverness-shire		HF		•	•
GLENGARNOCK		Ayrshire		FF		•	•
GOLF STREET HALT	opened 1961 wooden only	Angus	1L	Wood		•	•
GOLSPIE		Sutherland		FF		•	•
GOREBRIDGE	*new station 2015	Midlothian		FF	1969*	•	•
GORGIE EAST		Midlothian		HF	1962		
GOUROCK		Renfrewshire		HF			
GRANGE		Banffshire		HF	1968	•	•
GRANGEMOUTH		Stirlingshire		FF	1968	•	•
GRANTON ROAD		Midlothian		FF	1962		
GRANTOWN-ON-SPEY EAST		Inverness-shire	LP	FF	1965	•	•
GRANTOWN-ON-SPEY WEST		Morayshire	LP	FF	1965	•	•
GREENHILL		Stirlingshire		FF	1966	•	•
GREENOCK CENTRAL		Renfrewshire	LP	HF			•
GREENOCK LYNEDOCH	New discovery	Renfrewshire	1L	HF	1959		
GREENOCK WEST		Renfrewshire	1L	FF		•	•
GUARD BRIDGE		Fife		FF	1965	•	•

1L = one line: 2L = two line: LP = lower panel

Station Name	County in 1956	Layout	Flange	Closed	Auction	Survived
HAIRMYRES	Lanarkshire		FF			•
HAMILTON CENTRAL	Lanarkshire	1L	FF		•	•
HAMILTON WEST	Lanarkshire		FF		•	•
HAPPENDON	Lanarkshire		FF	1964		
HARBURN	Midlothian		FF	1966	•	•
HARTWOOD	Lanarkshire		HF		•	•
HAWICK	Roxburghshire		FF	1969	•	•
HAWKHEAD *re-opened 1991	Renfrewshire		HF	1966*	•	•
HAYMARKET	Midlothian		HF		•	•
HELENSBURGH CENTRAL	Dunbartonshire	LP	HF			•
HELENSBURGH UPPER	Dunbartonshire	LP	HF		•	•
HERIOT	Midlothian		FF	1969	•	•
HIGH STREET	Lanarkshire		FF		•	•
HILLFOOT	Dunbartonshire		FF		•	•
HILLINGTON EAST	Lanarkshire	1L	FF		•	•
HILLINGTON WEST	Lanarkshire	1L	FF			
HOLLYBUSH	Ayrshire		HF	1964		
HOLYTOWN	Lanarkshire		FF		•	•
HOUSTON & CROSSLEE	Renfrewshire		HF		•	•
HUNTLY	Aberdeenshire		HF		•	•
IBROX	Lanarkshire		FF	1967	•	•
INCHES	Lanarkshire		FF	1964		
INNERLEITHEN	Peebles-shire		FF	1962	•	•
INSCH	Aberdeenshire		FF		•	•
INVERESK	Midlothian		FF	1964	•	•
INVERKEITHING	Fife		FF		•	•
INVERKIP	Renfrewshire		FF			•
IRVINE	Ayrshire		HF/FF		•	•
JOHNSTONE HIGH	Renfrewshire	1L	HF		•	•
JOPPA	Midlothian		FF	1964	•	•
JORDANHILL	Lanarkshire		HF		•	•
KEITH JUNCTION	Banffshire	1L	FF		•	•

1L = one line: 2L = two line: LP = lower panel

Station Name		County in 1956	Layout	Flange	Closed	Auction	Survived
KEITH TOWN		Banffshire		HF	1968	•	•
KELSO		Roxburghshire		FF	1964	•	•
KELVIN HALL	formerly Partick Central: named 1959	Lanarkshire		FF	1964		
KENNETHMONT		Aberdeenshire		FF	1968	•	•
KENNISHEAD		Lanarkshire		HF			
KENTALLEN		Argyllshire		FF	1966	•	•
KILBARCHAN	New discovery	Renfrewshire		FF	1966		•
KILBOWIE		Dunbartonshire		FF	1964		•
KILCONQUHAR		Fife		FF	1965	•	•
KILMACOLM		Renfrewshire		FF		•	•
KILMARNOCK		Ayrshire		HF			•
KILMAURS	*re-opened 1984	Ayrshire		HF	1966*		
KILPATRICK		Dunbartonshire		FF		•	
KILWINNING		Ayrshire		HF		•	•
KINGHORN		Fife		FF		•	•
KINGSKNOWE	*re-opened 1971	Midlothian		HF	1964*	•	•
KING'S PARK		Lanarkshire		HF/FF		•	•
KINGUSSIE		Inverness-shire		HF		•	•
KINLOSS		Morayshire		FF	1965	•	•
KINROSS JUNCTION		Kinross-shire	LP	FF	1970	•	•
KIRKCALDY		Fife		FF		•	•
KIRKCONNEL		Dumfries-shire		HF		•	•
KIRKCUDBRIGHT		Kirkcudbrightshire		FF	1965		•
KIRKHILL		Lanarkshire		HF			
KIRKINTILLOCH		Dunbartonshire		HF	1964		
KITTYBREWSTER		Aberdeenshire		FF	1968	•	•
KNOCK		Banffshire		HF	1968	•	•
KNOCKANDO		Morayshire		FF	1965	•	•
KYLE OF LOCHALSH		Ross & Cromarty		FF		•	•
LADYBANK		Fife		HF		•	•
LAIRG		Sutherland		FF		•	•
LANARK		Lanarkshire		FF		•	•
LANGBANK		Renfrewshire		FF			

1L = one line: 2L = two line: LP = lower panel

Station Name	County in 1956	Layout	Flange	Closed	Auction	Survived
LANGHOLM	Dumfries-shire		FF	1964	•	•
LANGLOAN	Lanarkshire		HF	1964		
LANGSIDE	Lanarkshire		HF		•	•
LARBERT	Stirlingshire		HF/FF		•	•
LARGO	Fife		FF	1965	•	•
LARGS	Ayrshire		HF		•	•
LARKHALL CENTRAL *re-opened as Larkhall 2005	Lanarkshire	1L	HF	1965*	•	•
LAURENCEKIRK *re-opened 2009	Kincardineshire		HF	1967*	•	•
LAW JUNCTION	Lanarkshire		HF	1965	•	•
LEITH NORTH	Midlothian		FF	1962		•
LENZIE	Lanarkshire		HF		•	•
LEUCHARS JUNCTION	Fife	1L	HF		•	•
LEVEN	Fife		FF	1965	•	•
LINLITHGOW	West Lothian		FF		•	•
LOCH AWE *re-opened 1985	Argyllshire		FF	1965*	•	•
LOCHEILSIDE	Inverness-shire		HF		•	•
LOCHGELLY	Fife		FF		•	•
LOCHLUICHART	Ross & Cromarty		HF		•	•
LOCKERBIE	Dumfries-shire		HF		•	•
LOGIERIEVE	Aberdeenshire		HF	1965	•	•
LONGMORN	Morayshire		FF	1968	•	•
LONGNIDDRY	East Lothian		HF		•	•
LONMAY	Aberdeenshire		HF	1965	•	•
LUGTON	Ayrshire		HF	1966	•	•
LUIB	Perthshire		FF	1965	•	•
LUMPHANAN	Aberdeenshire		FF	1966	•	•
LUNDIN LINKS	Fife		FF	1965		•
MANUEL	Stirlingshire		FF	1967	•	•
MARKINCH	Fife		HF		•	•
MARYHILL CENTRAL	Lanarkshire	LP	HF	1964	•	•
MARYHILL PARK *re-opened as Maryhill 1993	Lanarkshire	LP	FF	1961*	•	•
MAUCHLINE	Ayrshire		HF	1965		
MAWCARSE	Kinross-shire		FF	1964	•	•
MAXTON	Roxburghshire		FF	1964	•	•

1L = one line: 2L = two line: LP = lower panel

7

Station Name		County in 1956	Layout	Flange	Closed	Auction	Survived
MAXWELL PARK		Lanarkshire		HF			
MAYBOLE		Ayrshire		HF		•	•
MELROSE		Roxburghshire		HF	1969	•	•
MERCHISTON		Midlothian		HF	1965	•	•
MIDCALDER		Midlothian		HF		•	•
MILLIKEN PARK	New discovery *re-opened 1989	Renfrewshire		HF	1966*	•	•
MILNATHORT		Kinross-shire		FF	1964		
MILNGAVIE		Dunbartonshire		FF		•	•
MONIFEITH		Angus		FF			
MONTROSE		Angus		FF		•	•
MORAR		Inverness-shire		HF			•
MORNINGSIDE ROAD		Midlothian		FF	1962		•
MOSSEND		Lanarkshire		FF	1962	•	•
MOSSPARK WEST	*re-opened as Mosspark 1990	Lanarkshire	1L	HF	1983*	•	•
MOTHERWELL		Lanarkshire		HF/FF		•	•
MOUNT FLORIDA		Lanarkshire		HF		•	•
MUIREND		Lanarkshire		HF		•	•
MUIRKIRK		Ayrshire		FF	1964	•	
MURRAYFIELD		Midlothian		HF	1962	•	
MUSSELBURGH	*new station 1988	Midlothian		FF	1964*	•	•
NAIRN		Nairn-shire		FF		•	•
NEILSTON HIGH		Renfrewshire	LP	FF		•	•
NEILSTON LOW		Renfrewshire	1L	HF	1966	•	•
NETHY BRIDGE		Inverness-shire		FF	1965	•	•
NEW CUMNOCK	*re-opened 1991	Ayrshire		HF	1965*	•	•
NEWHAVEN	restored as business park	Midlothian		FF	1962		
NEWINGTON		Midlothian		FF	1962		•
NEWMACHAR		Aberdeenshire		HF	1965	•	•
NEWPARK		Midlothian		HF		•	•
NEWPORT-ON-TAY EAST		Fife	1L	FF	1969	•	•
NEWPORT-ON-TAY WEST		Fife	1L	FF	1969	•	•
NEWTON		Lanarkshire		FF		•	•
NEWTONMORE		Inverness-shire		HF		•	•
NEWTON-ON-AYR		Ayrshire		HF		•	•

1L = one line: 2L = two line: LP = lower panel

Station Name	County in 1956	Layout	Flange	Closed	Auction	Survived
NEWTON STEWART	Wigtownshire		FF	1965	•	•
NITSHILL	Lanarkshire		FF		•	•
NORTH BERWICK	East Lothian		FF		•	•
NORTH CONNEL	Argyllshire		HF	1966		•
OAKLEY (FIFE)	Fife	LP	HF	1968		•
OLD KILPATRICK	Dunbartonshire		HF	1964	•	•
PAISLEY ABERCORN	Renfrewshire	LP	HF	1967		•
PAISLEY CANAL *open on new site 1990	Renfrewshire		FF	1983*	•	•
PAISLEY GILMOUR STREET	Renfrewshire	LP	HF			
PARK	Aberdeenshire		FF	1966	•	•
PARKHEAD STADIUM	Lanarkshire	LP	HF	1965		
PARTICK CENTRAL renamed Kelvin Hall 1959	Lanarkshire	1L	FF			
PARTICK HILL replaced by new Partick 1979	Lanarkshire		HF/FF	1979	•	•
PATNA	Ayrshire		HF	1964		
PATTERTON	Renfrewshire		FF		•	•
PEEBLES	Peebles-shire		FF	1962	•	•
PERTH	Perthshire		HF		•	•
PETERHEAD	Aberdeenshire		FF	1965	•	•
PIERSHILL	Midlothian		FF	1964	•	•
PINKHILL	Midlothian		FF	1968	•	•
PINMORE	Ayrshire		?	1965		
PITLOCHRY	Perthshire		HF		•	•
PITTENWEEM	Fife		FF	1965	•	•
POLLOKSHAWS EAST	Lanarkshire	1L	HF		•	•
POLLOKSHAWS WEST	Lanarkshire	LP	HF		•	•
POLLOKSHIELDS EAST	Lanarkshire	LP ?	HF			
POLLOKSHIELDS WEST	Lanarkshire	1L	HF		•	•
POLMONT	Stirlingshire		HF		•	•
POMATHORN New discovery	Midlothian		FF			
PONFEIGH	Lanarkshire		FF		•	•
PORTESSIE	Banffshire		HF	1968	•	•

1L = one line: 2L = two line: LP = lower panel

Station Name		County in 1956	Layout	Flange	Closed	Auction	Survived
PORT GLASGOW		Renfrewshire		HF		•	•
PORTKNOCKIE		Banffshire		HF	1968	•	•
PORTOBELLO		Midlothian		FF	1964	•	•
PRESTONPANS	also plastic variant	East Lothian		FF		•	•
PRESTWICK		Ayrshire		FF		•	•
QUEEN'S PARK		Lanarkshire		HF		•	•
QUEEN STREET (LL)	*(4'totems only)	Lanarkshire		FF*			
RANNOCH		Perthshire		HF		•	•
RATHEN		Aberdeenshire		HF	1965		•
RENFREW FULBAR STREET		Renfrewshire	1L	FF	1967	•	•
RENFREW SOUTH	New discovery	Renfrewshire		FF	1967	•	•
RENTON		Dunbartonshire		FF		•	•
RESTON		Berwickshire		FF	1964	•	•
RIDDINGS JUNCTION		Cumberland		FF	1964	•	•
ROSEWELL AND HAWTHORNDEN		Midlothian	2L	FF	1962		•
ROSSLYNLEE	New discovery	Midlothian		FF	1962		•
ROTHES		Morayshire		FF	1968	•	
ROXBURGH		Roxburghshire		FF	1964		•
ROY BRIDGE		Inverness-shire		HF		•	•
RUTHERFORD	New discovery	Roxburghshire		FF	1964		
RUTHERGLEN	re-located 1979	Lanarkshire		FF		•	•
SALTCOATS CENTRAL		Ayrshire	LP	HF		•	•
SANDILANDS		Lanarkshire		FF	1964		
SANQUHAR	*re-opened 1994	Dumfries-shire		HF	1965*	•	•
SCOTSTOUN EAST		Lanarkshire		FF	1964	•	•
SCOTSTOUNHILL		Lanarkshire		HF/FF		•	•
SHANDON		Dunbartonshire		HF	1964	•	•
SHAWLANDS		Lanarkshire		HF		•	•
SHETTLESTON		Lanarkshire		FF		•	•
SHIELDS ROAD		Lanarkshire		FF	1966	•	•
SHOTTS		Lanarkshire		HF			

1L = one line: 2L = two line: LP = lower panel

Station Name	County in 1956	Layout	Flange	Closed	Auction	Survived
SINCLAIRTOWN	Fife		FF	1969	•	•
SINGER	Dunbartonshire		HF/FF		•	•
SLATEFORD	Midlothian		HF		•	•
SOUTH BEACH	Ayrshire		FF			•
SPEAN BRIDGE	Inverness-shire		HF		•	•
SPEY BAY	Morayshire		HF	1968	•	•
SPRINGBURN	Lanarkshire		FF		•	•
SPRINGFIELD	Fife		HF		•	•
ST. ANDREWS	Fife		FF	1969	•	•
ST. MONANCE	Fife		FF	1965	•	•
STEVENSTON	Ayrshire		HF			•
STEWARTON New discovery: re-opened 1967	Ayrshire		HF	1966*		
STIRLING	Stirlingshire		HF		•	•
STONEHAVEN	Kincardineshire		FF		•	•
STOW *re-opened 2015	Midlothian		HF	1969*	•	•
STRANRAER HARBOUR	Wigtownshire	LP	HF		•	•
STRANRAER TOWN	Wigtownshire	LP	HF	1966	•	•
STRATHAVEN CENTRAL	Lanarkshire	LP	HF	1965		
STRATHBUNGO New discovery	Lanarkshire		HF?	1962		
STRATHCARRON	Ross & Cromarty		HF			•
STRATHYRE	Perthshire		FF	1965	•	•
STRICHEN	Aberdeenshire		HF	1965	•	•
TAIN	Ross & Cromarty		FF		•	•
TAYNUILT	Argyllshire		FF		•	•
TAYPORT	Fife		FF	1966	•	•
THE MOUND	Sutherland		HF	1960	•	•
THORNHILL	Dumfries-shire		FF	1965	•	•
THORNLIEBANK	Renfrewshire		FF			•
THORNTONHALL	Lanarkshire		FF		•	•
THORNTON JUNCTION	Fife	1L	HF	1969	•	•
THURSO	Caithness		FF		•	•
TILLYNAUGHT	Banffshire		HF	1968	•	•
TOLLCROSS	Lanarkshire		HF	1964		•
TORPHINS	Aberdeenshire		FF	1966	•	•

1L = one line: 2L = two line: LP = lower panel

Station Name	County in 1956	Layout	Flange	Closed	Auction	Survived
TROON	Ayrshire		HF/FF		•	•
TULLIBARDINE	Perthshire		FF	1964	•	•
TULLOCH	Inverness-shire		HF		•	•
TYNDRUM UPPER	Perthshire		HF		•	•
TYNEHEAD	Midlothian		FF	1969	•	•
UDDINGSTON CENTRAL	Lanarkshire	LP	FF		•	•
UDDINGSTON WEST	Lanarkshire	?	HF	1955		
UDNY	Aberdeenshire		HF	1965	•	•
UPPER GREENOCK	Renfrewshire		FF	1967	•	•
URQUHART	Morayshire		HF	1968	•	•
WALKERBURN	Peebles-shire		FF	1962		
WATERSIDE New discovery	Ayrshire		HF	1964	•	•
WEMYSS BAY	Renfrewshire		HF		•	•
WEST CALDER	Midlothian		FF		•	•
WESTERTON	Dunbartonshire		FF			
WEST KILBRIDE	Ayrshire		FF		•	•
WHITECRAIGS	Renfrewshire		FF		•	•
WHITEINCH RIVERSIDE	Lanarkshire	1L	FF	1964	•	•
WICK	Caithness		FF		•	•
WILLIAMWOOD	Renfrewshire		HF		•	•
WISHAW CENTRAL	Lanarkshire	1L	HF		•	•
WOODHALL	Renfrewshire		HF		•	•
WORMIT	Fife		FF	1969	•	•
YOKER FERRY	Lanarkshire	LP	FF	1964		
YOKER HIGH	Dunbartonshire		HF/FF		•	•

1L = one line: 2L = two line: LP = lower panel

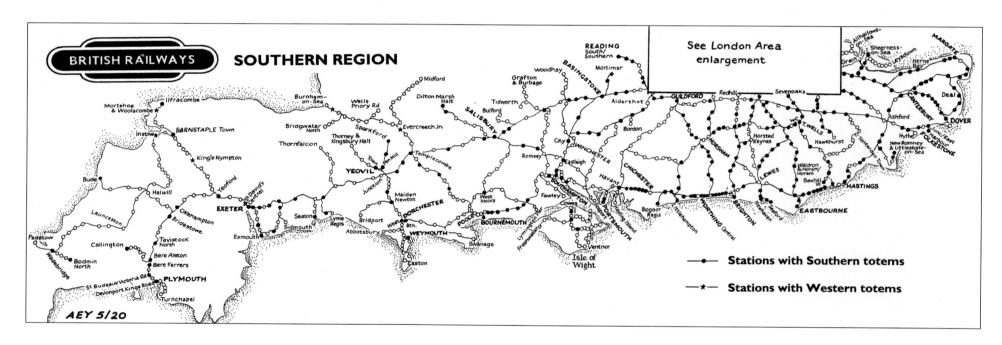

Opening Comments

This region covering London, the south-east and down into Cornwall lasted from 1948 to 1992, when wholesale changes took it out of public ownership. However, it had ceased to be an operating unit in its own right in the 1980s. Alan Young's opening regional map shows the concentration of stations around the region. The striking feature is just how many stations had totems fitted, over 50% in the London area, reducing as the tracks move further away from the capital. Based on the former Southern Railway colours, the familiar green totems were a welcome sight on 498 of the region's stations, as here at **Cowden**, near **Sevenoaks,** Kent.

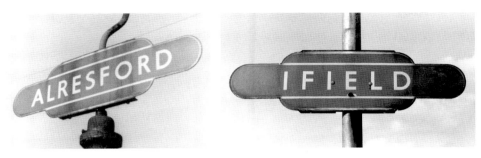

At inception, the SR inherited 2,156 miles of track and a system different from the other five regions. Electrification had commenced even before the formation of the SR (LSWR began in 1915 with **Waterloo–Wimbledon**) and by 1939 the Southern had amassed over 700 miles of third-rail electric track, around 30% of the lines operated, enabling profitable commuter routes to be well served. A series of reliable EMUs began to appear in 1933, when **London-Brighton** was upgraded. **London-Eastbourne** was added in 1935, **London–Portsmouth** in 1937, **London–Littlehampton**, plus **Portsmouth–Brighton** in 1938, then **London–Reading** and **London–Gillingham** in 1939.

Under the expert management of Sir Herbert Walker, the Southern became the railway company viewed by many as the nation's best, renowned for reliability and efficiency and building good revenues each year. During the 1930s, their passenger journeys rose by over 12 million, compared to a fall of 1 million on the other five regions using steam! When the SR appeared in 1948, it covered 14 English counties, from Kent in the east to Cornwall in the west, from Buckinghamshire in the north to the Isle of Wight (southern Hampshire) in the south.

Tim Clarke

Brief Regional History

The history of the Southern Region is very largely based on the history of the Southern Railway and its antecedent companies. In 1923, the London & South Western (LSWR), the combined South Eastern Railway and the London, Chatham and Dover Railway (SECR) together with the London Brighton & South Coast Railway (LBSCR) were all merged to form the Southern Railway. At grouping, these three companies ran more than 2,185 miles of routes. In addition, there were 56 miles of tracks on the Isle of Wight operated by three small associated companies. Below is a collage of totems, two each from the three main constituents of the former Southern Railway.

Ex-LSWR stations (top). Ex-SECR stations (centre) and ex-LBSCR stations (bottom).

One of the first lines in the region opened in 1830 between **Canterbury** and **Whitstable.** The adverse gradients meant using winding engines on the steep sections and locomotives where the gradients were more favourable. The largest of the early railways in the south of England was the LSWR, incorporated in 1838. It grew steadily, eventually reaching Plymouth, via **Salisbury** and **Exeter.** The LSWR opened their first main line in 1840 between London, actually Nine Elms, and Southampton, to Southampton Docks, via **Basingstoke** and **Winchester.**

This was quickly followed by London to **Brighton** in 1841 and the South Eastern Railway's line from Reigate, now Redhill, to **Dover** in 1844, as shown in the map right.

The onward branches to **Ilfracombe** and Padstow were a strange shape, due to the topography, and latterly attracted the name 'The Withered Arm' as decline

set in. Curiously, **Ilfracombe** had totems, but Padstow did not. As they came to the area after the GWR, the LSWR West Country services were not as successful as their rival's. The LSWR extended their first main line to Bournemouth Central, opened as Bournemouth East in 1885, and **Weymouth,** opened by the GWR in 1857, via Ringwood. **Bournemouth West** was opened in 1874 by the SDJR (MR and LSWR) and carried SR totems; Bournemouth Central only ever carried targets.

By 1899, the LSWR had an impressive network that connected all the major towns in Berkshire and Hampshire, including **Portsmouth** and **Reading.** Shipping from **Weymouth** and Southampton became significant, with passenger and freight services to the Channel Islands, the Isle of Wight and France.

By 1850 the Chiswick–**Brentford**-Hounslow loop was almost complete and by 1862, branch lines to Hampton Court, **Chertsey** and **Staines** to **Windsor** were in place, whilst **Wimbledon** was linked to **Epsom** and **Leatherhead.** A decade later and the LSWR's suburban network that we see today was largely in place. The Nine Elms station was never intended to be a permanent London terminal, so in 1845 the LSWR obtained powers to extend to a more central site at Waterloo Bridge by the road over the Thames; the name was changed to today's **Waterloo** in 1882. Early in

Southern railway lines in the mid-1840s. *Wikipedia Commons*

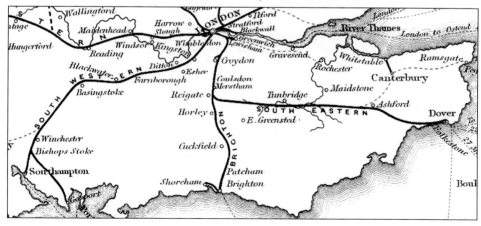

the 20th century, some lines were electrified. While the LSWR had been slower to adopt electric traction, it was the LB&SCR among the railways south of London that electrified some of its suburban lines, with the first opening on 1 December 1909. However, once Herbert Walker was made General Manager in 1912, the LSWR quickly followed suit, electrifying the **Waterloo** to **Wimbledon** line in 1915, the Hounslow and **Kingston** loops, the Shepperton branch, Hampton Court lines and associated branch, plus the new **Guildford** to Claygate line, and all complete by 1916. The new electric service was a considerable success, though there was some overcrowding as punctuality and reliability improved; people wanted to use the railway. The LSWR carried very little freight to generate revenue, so relied largely on its commuter and passenger income.

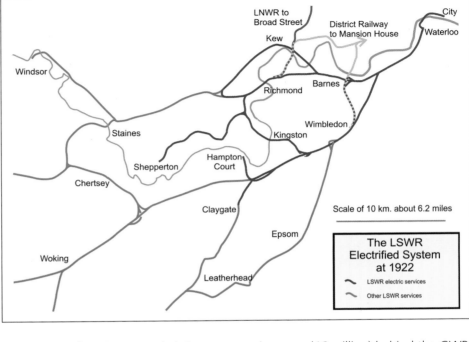

By 1921, the LSWR was sixth in passenger journeys (46 million) behind the GWR, Metropolitan, LNWR, MR and Great Eastern, but more importantly it was financially sound. Herbert Walker (later Sir Herbert Walker KCB) was an astute manager, and it was no surprise that he became the Southern Railway's first General Manager from 1923 to 1937. He was a Southern Railway Director until it was nationalised at the end of 1947. Among his many achievements, he appointed the talented Oliver Bulleid from the LNER as his Chief Mechanical Engineer. He was a good engineer but did not get the same levels of recognition as either Sir William Stanier or Sir Nigel Gresley.

The second largest company that was merged to form the Southern Railway was the South Eastern & Chatham Railway. This was an amalgamation, but not a legal merger, of two rival railways: the South Eastern and the London, Chatham & Dover, operating the important 76-mile link between London and the Port of **Dover**. In total it operated 637 route miles. Before 1899 the two companies had been bitter rivals, to the financial detriment of both. Between 1899 and 1923, they co-operated and had a monopoly of railway services in Kent and to the main Channel ports for ferries to France and Belgium. It therefore ran extensive passenger and commuter services to and from London termini, but also carried freight to the Channel ports. The SE&CR covered the whole of Kent, extending for a short distance into Sussex, all through Surrey and into Berkshire. In addition to **Dover,** it also serviced the ports of **Folkestone** (for Boulogne) and **Queenborough** (for Flushing) – *see* photo page 259.

The SER formed in 1836 to build the London to **Dover** route. Branch lines were later opened to **Tunbridge Wells**, **Hastings**, **Canterbury** and other places in Kent. The SER absorbed or leased other railways, some older than itself. Most of the routes were in Kent, East Sussex and the London suburbs, plus the long cross-country route from Redhill to **Reading**. The western boundary was defined by the lines from **Hastings** to **Tonbridge** and from Redhill into London, with spurs to **Bexhill**, to **Reading** and to Tattenham Corner. North of the Thames, the SECR extended into **Cannon Street**, St. Paul's (later called Blackfriars), **Holborn Viaduct**, **Charing Cross** and Victoria. Below, totems from two ex-SECR Kent stations hang proudly *in situ*. Interestingly, we have no current information on the survival of **Gravesend West** totems after closure in 1953.

All down the south side of the Thames from **London Bridge** to Port Victoria, the SECR served nearly every town and village between **Sheerness** and **Hastings**. Their former stations were liberally totem-signed, including the seaside towns of **Whitstable & Tankerton**, **Herne Bay**, **Birchington-on-Sea**, **Westgate-on-Sea**, **Margate**, **Broadstairs**, **Ramsgate**, **Sandwich**, **Deal**, **Walmer**, **Sandling for Hythe**, **Rye** and **West St. Leonards**.

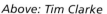

Above: Tim Clarke

Right: TSG Library

The main routes built by the SER included Redhill–**Tonbridge**-Ashford, 1842; Ashford–**Folkestone**, 1843; **Tonbridge–Tunbridge Wells Central**, 1845; Ashford–**Canterbury West**, 1846, and **Tunbridge Wells Central–Hastings**, 1851, but much of the early history documented fierce feuding with LBSCR to the west and the LCDR to the north. The arguments in Kent were especially bitter, particularly where competing routes were built to the same destinations. Many towns possessed two stations with regular services to multiple London termini: it was a recipe for poor financial stability.

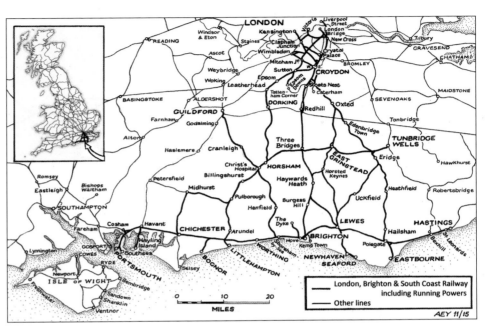

North Kent was LC&DR territory. The railway was created in August 1859, when the East Kent Railway changed its name. Its lines ran through London and northeast Kent to form a significant part of the Greater London commuter network, but it did not have a good punctuality record and its coaches were poor. The 1860s saw many lines and stations opened, including **Faversham–Canterbury**, **Canterbury–Dover**, **Meopham** and **Sole Street** stations (1861). In 1863, **Herne Bay** to **Margate** and **Broadstairs** opened and 1864 saw the City of London attained. Routes from Herne Hill to Blackfriars Bridge, 1864, and lines into the terminus at **Holborn Viaduct** were completed by 1874. By this time the LCDR had strong connections into London and linked with the GNR for onward northern journeys via the Snow Hill Tunnel. Their London–Dover Docks route was now more convenient than the rival SER's line.

The final company which formed part of the Southern Railway in 1923 was the London, Brighton and South Coast Railway (LBSCR), formed in 1846 from the merger of five small independent operators who covered much of Sussex and parts of Hampshire, Surrey and South London.

Its operational territory was triangular with the apex in

Central London, with **Hastings** and **Portsmouth** being the eastern and western extremities, as above in Alan Young's map. With 457 route miles, it was less than half the LSWR's size and a third smaller than the SECR. It did however link **Brighton**, **Eastbourne** and **Newhaven** to London and served the inland towns/cities of Chichester, Horsham, East Grinstead and Lewes. It jointly served **Croydon**, **Tunbridge Wells**, Dorking and **Guildford**. The London apex was a complex suburban network of lines between **Clapham Junction,** New Cross Gate and **East Croydon** (including **Norwood Junction** & **Wimbledon**) that emanated from **London Bridge** and Victoria as the map illustrates.

One of the LBSCR's original companies was the London & Croydon, who had their London terminus at **London Bridge**. A period of rapid expansion occurred between 1859 and 1865, when 177 route miles were added. This included lines in the West End and South London. The most important of these was the building of **Clapham Junction** in 1863 in partnership with the LSWR. Lines to **Uckfield** and **Seaford** were added around 1860 and soon branches to **Pulborough**, Petworth, **Littlehampton, Bognor Regis, Seaford** and Hayling Island appeared in the mid-1860s. It collaborated with the LSWR to develop lines in both Surrey and Sussex.

Following the opening of the branch from Lewes to **Newhaven Town**, the LBSCR then proceeded to develop a shorter cross-Channel London–Paris route via Dieppe, in direct competition with the SER's Dover–Calais and Folkestone–Boulogne routes. The LBSCR built its wharf and warehousing facilities on the east side of the river, along with **Newhaven Harbour** station. It funded the dredging of the Channel and other improvements to the harbour between 1850 and 1878, to enable it to be used by larger cross-Channel ferries. Although it was discontinued soon after inauguration, the service was reinstated in 1853 as it was the shortest route between the two capitals, but certainly not the quickest! In 1863 they and the Chemins de Fer de l'Ouest in France introduced an improved Newhaven–Dieppe ferry service.

As part of its expansion, the LB&SCR built a line from **Peckham Rye** roughly parallel to the main line, through **East Dulwich**, Tulse Hill, **Streatham** and **Mitcham Junction** to **Sutton** and **Epsom Downs**, which opened in October 1868. This came on the back of recovery from near bankruptcy a year before. From the 1870s onwards, the London suburban network they had developed enabled a sound financial base to be built and, over a 15-year period, revenues doubled, while operating costs were reduced. During its last 20 years, the LBSCR opened no new lines, but invested in improving its main line to both the **London Bridge** and Victoria terminals, together with the electrification of some of its London suburban lines.

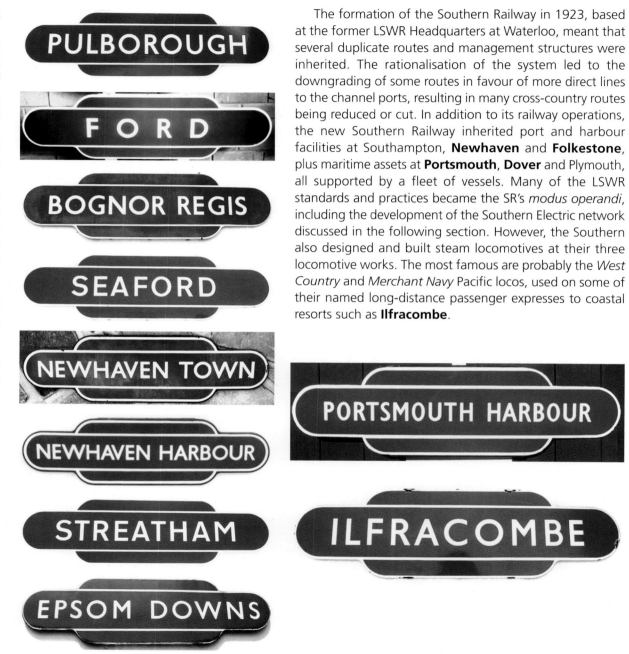

The formation of the Southern Railway in 1923, based at the former LSWR Headquarters at Waterloo, meant that several duplicate routes and management structures were inherited. The rationalisation of the system led to the downgrading of some routes in favour of more direct lines to the channel ports, resulting in many cross-country routes being reduced or cut. In addition to its railway operations, the new Southern Railway inherited port and harbour facilities at Southampton, **Newhaven** and **Folkestone**, plus maritime assets at **Portsmouth**, **Dover** and Plymouth, all supported by a fleet of vessels. Many of the LSWR standards and practices became the SR's *modus operandi*, including the development of the Southern Electric network discussed in the following section. However, the Southern also designed and built steam locomotives at their three locomotive works. The most famous are probably the *West Country* and *Merchant Navy* Pacific locos, used on some of their named long-distance passenger expresses to coastal resorts such as **Ilfracombe**.

These named expresses included the *Bournemouth Belle*, the *Golden Arrow* and the *Night Ferry* (London–Paris and Brussels) to the south and south-east. Passenger services to the West Country were dominated by lucrative summer holiday traffic with holidaymakers travelling by the *Atlantic Coast Express* or the *Devon Belle*. The south of England took a terrible beating during WWII, from both air-raid damage and from working the motive power hard during troop and munitions movements. The subsequent nationalisation was inevitable, even though the commuter traffic had cushioned the economic effects better than in some other parts of Britain.

Even before the Beeching closures of the 1960s were made, the Southern Region was constantly reviewing its financial position and was not afraid to close uneconomic routes. Under-used stations between East Grinstead and Lewes were closed, and most of the lines on the Isle of Wight were axed in the 1950s. When Beeching did look at the Southern Region, those lines closed included the *Cuckoo Line*, **Polegate** to **Eridge**; the *Cranleigh Line*, **Guildford** to Horsham; the *Steyning Line*, Horsham to Shoreham-by-Sea; plus the branches to **Bexhill West** and **New Romney and Littlestone-on-Sea**.

Sadly, during the economic review era, the named trains were discontinued and later the Snow Hill Tunnel (Blackfriars to Farringdon) was closed between 1969 and 1988 but it was refurbished and then reopened as part of the Thameslink Project.

Southern Electric

The Southern Region was different from the other five at the formation of British Railways in 1948. Developments using electric traction had begun in late Victorian times and the third rail low voltage system adopted by the LSWR for its initial surface electrification followed the system it used for its Waterloo & City underground line between Waterloo and Bank. This was the catalyst for the Southern Electric. By 1939 almost 700 miles, around 30% of the network, had been electrified. There was no other counterpart in Britain at that time, with the LMS being second at only 120 miles. The Southern's electrics became renowned for their reliability and frequency, serving an ever-growing passenger demand in the region. Alan Young's map shows the extent of London's Suburban network with a plethora of stations sporting green totems and underneath is a quartet of some of these stations.

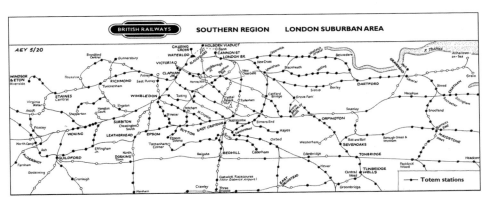

The big problem the Southern Railway had was having inherited different standards and systems to power their electric trains, legacies from their constituent companies. The LSWR had adopted their historic third rail 660 VDC, whereas the SECR had planned from 1919 to adopt three- and four-rail systems at +/- 1500VDC on the routes from **Charing Cross**, **Cannon Street**, **Holborn Viaduct** and Victoria London terminals on all routes to **Dartford, Addiscombe, Orpington, Hayes** and **Bromley North**. However, these schemes did not happen before the 1923 grouping. The LBSCR had used AEG to install a high voltage overhead system of 6666.66V at 25Hz, and by 1925 their system had reached **Coulsdon North** and **Sutton** from London. Therefore, the awkward position around 1920 was that there were three operating railway companies with three different electrification systems.

The significant LSWR presence in Southern's top management ensured that their 660VDC third-rail system would become the new regional standard, and all the subsequent investment and upgrades in electric trains worked to this directive. By 1928, the LBSCR overhead network had been converted to 660VDC third-rail standards. Metropolitan Vickers and British Thomson-Houston traction motors, control systems and lineside equipment were installed from 1929, but in 1935, English Electric traction equipment was adopted, a standard that lasted into the 1980s.

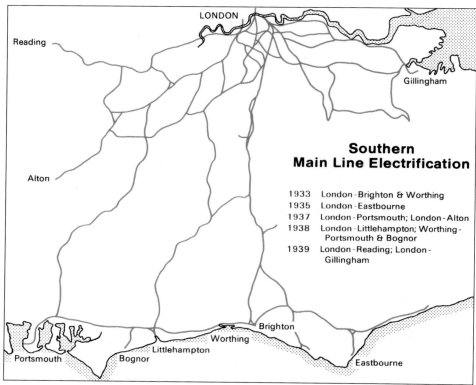

Southern Main Line Electrification

1933	London-Brighton & Worthing
1935	London-Eastbourne
1937	London-Portsmouth; London-Alton
1938	London-Littlehampton; Worthing-Portsmouth & Bognor
1939	London-Reading; London-Gillingham

The network just before the outbreak of WWII is shown above, but even then the Southern Railway had adopted a plan in November 1946 to convert all lines east of Portsmouth to third-rail electric traction, to be completed by 1955. This plan would have included several branch and secondary lines that were subsequently closed, such as the Bluebell and Steyning lines, following nationalisation. However, BR did press ahead with further electrification, the first of which was the North Kent Scheme. This extended the DC third rail beyond **Gillingham** and **Sevenoaks** to **Dover** in Phase 1 and to **Folkestone**, **Margate** and **Ramsgate** in Phase 2.

The electrification of the Bournemouth line was completed in 1967. This extended the third rail from Pirbright in Surrey. A push-pull system was operated for trains on the Bournemouth to **Weymouth** from 1968 to 1988, with a class 33/1 diesel replacing the electric train driving unit, which was detached at Bournemouth, to take the train over the non-electrified lines into **Weymouth**. In 1988 the whole line was finally electrified, and new electric class 442 electric units were introduced by Network SouthEast. In other parts of the network, electric trains were upgraded at regular intervals, ensuring that the network met with rising passenger expectations. Stations with totems on the South West Main Line are shown right.

Southern Region Totem Geography

Alan Young & Richard Furness

Unfairly dismissed by some critics as 'that tedious electric tramway south of the Thames', the Southern Region is actually fascinating for students of railway geography and totems. Its boundaries were incredibly unstable (*British Railways Station Totems,* Chapter 12). Until 1950 the region was virtually co-extensive with the old Southern Railway, but then the system west of Exeter was surrendered to the Western Region, only to be handed back to the Southern in 1958. It was finally returned to the WR in 1963, with this last boundary revision cutting the SR back almost to **Salisbury,** but with the **Bournemouth, Dorchester** and **Weymouth** route staying in the SR. The map that follows shows the large area given up by the

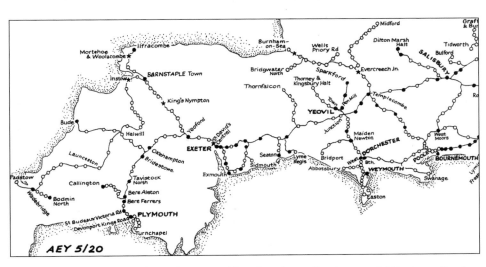

SR during these boundary changes. The Southern Region and Western Region crossed at Exeter, with North Cornwall and North Devon in SR hands; South Cornwall and South Devon were WR-managed.

The map above depicts the SR main line between **Exeter** & Plymouth via **Yeoford, Okehampton, Tavistock North, Bere Alston** & **St Budeaux Victoria Road**, a route heavily populated in the 1950s and 1960s with desirable totems. Today this line would be a welcome addition to the network, serving towns and communities long cut-off from the transport system and providing an alternative to the main Devon coastal line through **Dawlish**, which is often disrupted by very stormy weather, as in 2014.

Pre-nationalisation lamp nameplates of the GWR, LMS and LNER were quite unlike BR totems (*see* page 13). However, the SR's dark green 'targets' more closely resembled the BR

green totems; indeed, less discerning members of the travelling public might not even have spotted the difference. This could explain the retention of targets at numerous SR locations until the late-1970s, such as Penge East, Anerley, and particularly Bookham, which still had a splendid array of targets on the station in 1978.

The strange mixture of totems and targets at **Bingham Road, Coombe Road** and **Plumstead** at this late stage confirms the BR's tolerance of the SR target.

Totems never appeared on lines closed early by BR, including Easton–Melcombe Regis, closed 1952; Robertsbridge–**Headcorn**, Kent & East Sussex 1954; Petersfield–**Pulborough,** 1955; East Grinstead–Lewes, first closed 1955; Fareham–**Alton,** 1955; and the branches to Leysdown, 1950; Turnchapel, 1951; Ventnor West, 1952; Bulford, 1952; Bembridge, 1953; Freshwater, 1953; Gosport, 1953; Crystal Palace High Level, 1954; and Tidworth, 1955. A surprising exception was the **Gravesend West** branch, closed 1953, whose terminus had totems for a short time, but we have no record of any survivors. The Allhallows to Grain and Westerham branches survived until 1961, but had no totems, and none were fitted on the Fawley branch except for **Marchwood**. Elsewhere, in totem-rich areas, some short-lived stations (Margate East and Stonehall & Lydden Halt) were not fitted.

The London suburban area, East Sussex and Kent was one of the most fruitful zones for the totem hunter. Possibly the longest unbroken succession of totem-bearing stations was in this area: 40 of them on the rather convoluted route from **Charing Cross** via **Lower Sydenham**, **Riddlesdown** and **Eridge** to **Bexhill Central**.

Totem-free stations were the exception, and individual cases are generally difficult to explain. However, although the SR never shared the ER's enthusiasm for electric strip lighting carrying the station name, with Purley, South Croydon, Ashford, St Mary Cray and some other stations having this treatment, so they did not require totems. The Hampton Court and Chessington South branches were overlooked. Perhaps it was thought that the four stations on the latter branch, newly built in a startling modern style in 1938/9, featuring concrete awnings, electric strip lighting, and targets, were not ready for a refit. Other strange oversights were Norbury, Bexley, Shepperton and Tattenham Corner. By the early 1970s, hunting stations that had not yet suffered from corporate identity was not easy; targets rather than totems were found surprisingly close to the heart of London at Elephant & Castle, Denmark Hill, Herne Hill, East Brixton and Queen's Road Peckham. A particular curiosity was **East Putney**, staffed by the SR, served only by the District Line, but carrying totems until 1974!

The Sussex coast from **Brighton** to **Havant,** just into Hampshire, was well endowed with totems, only Holland Road Halt, Shoreham-by-Sea, West Worthing and especially Chichester being disappointments. Further west in Hampshire another sequence was **Brockenhurst** to **Boscombe**, including the western-most stations with the late Transport Medium style (**New Milton** and **Christchurch**), but moving further west, totems generally become the exception. Even the main **Waterloo–Portsmouth Harbour** line had nine successive stations between **Guildford** and **Havant** without totems, including Haslemere, Godalming, and Petersfield; all these had received corporate identity signs by 1976. There were other north–south routes

that had no totems at intermediate stations, including Winchester Chesil–**Newbury**, Romsey–Savernake (except **Horsebridge** and **Mottisfont**), and **West Moors–Salisbury**. These stations were well maintained and happily remained intact, adorned with Southern Railway fittings and signage until closure.

East Putney and Edenbridge Town totems *in situ. Tim Clarke*

Further west, we reach the Southern/Western frontier territory, where there was a general reluctance to install totems. About half of the **Salisbury–Exeter St David's** main line stations received them, but few other lines did. When the SR lost the S&D north of Cole to the WR in 1950, no totems had been fitted, but they were installed further south at **Templecombe** (main line), **Stalbridge**, **Shillingstone**, **Bournemouth West**, and at **Blandford Forum** (on the renaming from Blandford) in 1953. Only **Evercreech Junction, Bath Green Park** and **Highbridge**, in the northern section, received WR totems. SR totems appeared sparingly between **Weymouth** and **Castle Cary**, but were never used on the Bridport branch, north of **Yeovil Town**, or between Chard Junction and **Taunton**. Why the obscure **Combpyne** on the Lyme Regis branch was favoured with totems (or rather a totem) is a mystery.

West Country 'Greens' *in situ*:
Bere Alston (above) & Exton (right).
Tim Clarke (right)

In the Exeter area, they become still rarer. The SR fitted some HF totems west of Exeter, when **Devonport King's Road**, **Tavistock North**, **St Budeaux Victoria Road** and **Bodmin North** were renamed in September 1949, to distinguish them from their WR neighbours. Six months later the WR took control west of Exeter, but their own chocolate-and-cream totems appeared only at **King's Nympton**, **Instow** and **Mortehoe & Woolacombe**, before the Southern Region again resumed control.

In the short period of SR management between 1958 and 1963 the **Bude**, **Ilfracombe** and **Callington** termini, junctions at **Yeoford**, **Bere Alston**, **Okehampton** and **Wadebridge**, plus **Bere Ferrers**, **Barnstaple Town** and **Bridestowe** all gained totems. This rather parsimonious provision means that the four Cornish stations' totems are cherished by enthusiasts, in contrast to the lavish supply of London suburban specimens which are among the least expensive to collect.

Totems Along the Arun Valley
Tim Clarke

The ex-LBSCR Arun Valley line in West Sussex, with its projection north of Horsham into Surrey towards Dorking and **Leatherhead,** where it joins the ex-LSWR line from **Guildford**, is arguably one of the most picturesque and unspoilt lines remaining in the south of England. As well as passing through a largely rural area, its stations are, in general, remarkably complete. It was originally known, somewhat misleadingly as the '*Mid-Sussex*' line, and was electrified south of Dorking in 1938 using an up-rated 750 VDC system.

The Arun Valley Line was part of a network of lines radiating from Horsham, the principal town on the route, the others being the connection to the **Brighton** main line at **Three Bridges** – now the main route to London for all Arun Valley services – and the non-electrified branches to Shoreham-by-Sea and **Guildford,** both now closed. Another very minor branch line ran from **Pulborough** to Midhurst and beyond; this closed to passengers in 1954, although goods traffic lingered on until the 1960s. All these lines were well endowed with SR targets and/or totems. The only stations that were never fitted with either were Baynards, on the **Guildford** branch, and Fittleworth, on the **Pulborough** to Midhurst line.

Arun Valley area totems hanging proudly. *Tim Clarke*

Starting our totem journey at the northern end, **Leatherhead** was fitted with white-edged fully-flanged totems, using the later Transport Medium typeface and the lighter shade of green. Both Boxhill and Dorking North retained their SR targets until corporate image re-signing, so the next totems appeared at **Holmwood,** again with white full flanges, but this time dark green with conventional Gill Sans lettering.

Ockley & Capel totems were half-flanged, whilst those at **Warnham** were the same as **Leatherhead**, light green with white flanges and Transport Medium lettering. Nowadays, a change of train would be necessary at Horsham to continue our journey south, but in totem times a fast service in comfortable 4-COR units would continue through to the coast. Horsham's large and busy station was comprehensively rebuilt for the electrification and is a prime example of the Southern Railway's Art Deco 'Odeon' style.

Here there was a gap in totem provision – Horsham, Christ's Hospital and Billingshurst retaining their SR targets and no totems were ever made for these stations. They re-appeared at **Pulborough**, then at **Amberley** and **Arundel** until reaching Arundel Junction on the coast. All these three stations all had conventional dark-green white-flanged totems. As there were never any totems on the Midhurst branch, we return to Christ's Hospital, where we would have found a remarkable junction station in the middle of nowhere, with no fewer than seven platform faces, delightful LB&SCR buildings with extensive canopies on all platforms, and three signal boxes – two within station limits, and one just down the line at Itchingfield Junction.

Christ's Hospital was the junction for both the **Guildford** and Shoreham-by-Sea branches, alas both now just memories as railways, though both are now part of the 'Downs Link' footpath and cycleway. The station is still open, and much busier with passengers now than it ever was when the branches were still open, but it is a shadow of its former self with just two platforms remaining and a former waiting room in use as the ticket office.

Taking the double-track Shoreham branch first, totems were provided at all the stations except **Steyning**, ironically the principal station on the line! All were of the same variety, with **Southwater**, **West Grinstead**, **Partridge Green**, **Henfield** and **Bramber** all being conventional dark-green totems, with white full flanges. This was a busy line, which arguably should never have closed, and surely would not have done so if it had been electrified as planned. Before anybody shouts at us – yes, we know that a **Steyning** totem exists as shown on page 260, but we are pretty sure that these were never used.

Finally, we take the branch towards **Guildford**, a delightful single-track backwater that was only really busy at its northern end. Totems were fitted at all the stations on the branch with the exception of Baynards, which, as mentioned before, saw neither targets nor totems; this was unusual for the area. **Slinfold** and **Rudgwick** were both half-flanged, whilst **Cranleigh** and **Bramley & Wonersh** had dark-green totems with *black* full flanges, the only ones for some distance around. Whilst examples of all the totems mentioned above are known to have survived, none can really be classed as 'common', and indeed some are exceedingly rare. Of all the stations having totems or targets on the lines covered, the only stations where neither has survived are Petworth and Selham, on the Midhurst branch.

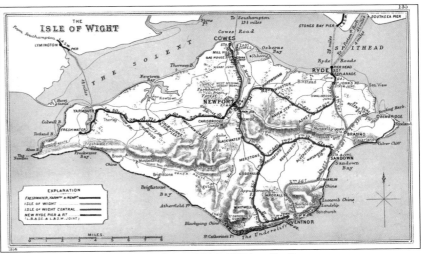

Railway Clearing House map from 1914. *Wikipedia Commons*

Area Focus: The Isle of Wight

The first railway on the Isle of Wight ran between Cowes and Newport; it opened in 1862 after three years of construction. Over the next forty years, more lines were built by different companies so that by 1901 more than 55 miles of track had been laid. They proved essential to the island economy acting both as links to the ferries at Yarmouth, Cowes and Ryde and also joining communities on the island at a time when roads were poor. The RCH map above shows the system's extent in 1914.

The 1923 grouping saw the lines fall under Southern Railway management, who then began a programme of upgrades; this included bringing locos from the former LSWR and LBSCR suburban fleets. Coaches and other rolling stock came from the LBSCR, LSWR and other former SR companies and improvements were made to both track and junction layouts. The short section of line from Brading to Sandown was double-tracked, with new passing loops and pointwork being added to give the network's services more operational flexibility.

Only three stations on the island were fitted with totems, **Merstone**, **Mill Hill** and **Newport**. Strangely, the Island's principal route, Ryde to Ventnor, never received totems at any of its stations. The likely reason is that the Southern Railway fitted targets to all stations on the line, including its short offshoot to Bembridge and all survived until closure or when replaced by BR corporate black-on-white signs. However, apart from these stations, targets were provided only at three other places on the Island – Freshwater, Yarmouth and Shide.

The major junction station at **Newport**, the Island's capital, had about twenty totems, all of the half-flanged variety and all seem to have been fitted at a very early stage. Presumably **Merstone's** status as a junction justified its inclusion as a station worthy of having totems fitted. Predictably, both totems and targets and enamel station signs from the Isle of Wight are all popular today with collectors. **Newport** totems exist in some quantity, and all three from **Mill Hill** also survive. Despite **Merstone** station being such an early closure (February 1956), one example is known to be safely in private hands. The fate of the other five is unknown.

The photo above shows two **Merstone** totems attached to the oil lamp standard in the foreground. Rather interestingly, the lamp standard is situated at ground level, adjacent to the level crossing. Normally totems are found on lamp standards on the platform, or attached to station building walls, so the photo depicts a less than usual location. The totems themselves are bracketed out to the side of the lamp post in the strange fashion favoured for island platforms on the Isle of Wight; such an arrangement is rarely found at other locations throughout the BR network.

There were just six totems at **Merstone,** the two in the photograph, and two fixed to each wall on either side of the island platform building under the canopy. The station was a very early closure in February 1956. The small but very busy station at **Mill Hill**, shown above left, which served the residential and industrial area of the sailing town of Cowes, had a grand total of three.

The Ryde to Shanklin line was earmarked for closure in Beeching's report, but was reprieved and electrified instead, using the third-rail DC system. Refurbished trains from the London Underground, classes 485 and 486, began to operate on the island in 1967. From 1990, these were replaced by class 483 units and soon a further upgrade under the auspices of South Western Railway, who run the island's network, will see new class 484 trains running from 2021 onwards. In 1971, the Isle of Wight Steam Railway began to operate on a section of the closed Ryde to Newport line and within twenty years the track was extended to more than 5 miles. Ryde Pier upgrades, funded by Network Rail will soon see the island's rail network firmly linked to the ferry services.

County Review of Totems in the Southern Region

The final section of this chapter presents a review of rarities and collectables arranged alphabetically by county to aid collectors in their local searches. Our database shows the SR had a presence in 13 English counties. The boundaries for this review are based on those existing in 1955, when for example, **Bournemouth** was in Hampshire not in Dorset, as it is today.

BERKSHIRE

A total of seven Berkshire stations carried green SR totems, and one of these, **Reading**, carried two different names, having been renamed from **Reading South** to **Reading (Southern)** in 1961. Totems with the former name have not appeared in auction and nothing is known about their whereabouts. The station closed in 1965. The county rarity is **Sandhurst Halt**, which has appeared just once in a public auction, in 2003. Some of these variants were overpainted on **Wraysbury** totems with non-standard Transport Medium lettering, as shown below.

Earley, **Mortimer** and **Winnersh Halt** have all appeared five times, contrasting with **Windsor & Eton Riverside** with 38 public appearances.

BUCKINGHAMSHIRE

There are only three totems from this county to collect. All are known to have survived and all have appeared in auction. Two are featured in the database pages 251 and 261, **Datchet** and **Sunnymeads**, and the third is **Wraysbury,** where some totems were enamelled all green, as shown below.

CORNWALL

This is an area of intense collectors' focus with only 4 stations fitted with totems; all were 1960s closures. Examples from each have survived and have been in auction. **Bodmin North**, **Bude**, **Callington** and **Wadebridge** have a combined total of only 15 auction appearances, so these are rare (and sought-after) 'greens'. Even though the database pages contain pictures of three of these, it is worth showing all four together below for the first time in a totem book. The rarity is **Callington**, with just 1 auction appearance: Sheffield Railwayana back in 1996.

Bodmin North was on the Bodmin to Wadebridge line and opened in 1834. It was given its totem name in 1949, to distinguish it from the town's GWR station, which then became Bodmin General. **Bodmin North** closed to passengers in 1967 and was later demolished. **Bude** station, opened in 1898, was the western terminus of the branch from **Okehampton**. After being recommended for closure by Beeching, it eventually did close in 1966: and now virtually nothing remains. The station at **Callington** was the terminus on the **Bere Alston** branch line, but Beeching's axe forced closure in 1966, except for the **Bere Alston** to Gunnislake section. **Wadebridge** station was one of the oldest in England, opening in 1834 and happily is still in use as the John Betjeman Centre, whilst the old goods shed is now the Betty Fisher Centre.

Bodmin North and Callington totems *in situ* around 1960. *TSG library*

DEVONSHIRE

This West Country county had 23 stations with green SR totems installed. All have survived, but four, **Bere Ferrers**, **Combpyne**, **Ottery St. Mary** and **St. James Park Halt,** have not appeared in auction. Most are real rarities, so pictures of ten Devon totems are included in the database pages. There are some wonderful local names, such as **Axminster**, **Budleigh Salterton**, **Okehampton** and **St. Budeaux Victoria Road** to name but four. Most Devonshire totems are uncommon with only **Exmouth,** 10, and **Ilfracombe,** 18, having appearances into double figures.

Notice the light green coloured **Okehampton** totem. The SR had only a handful of stations in their region adorned with this most attractive shade of green. Of the 23 stations that carried totems, 12 closed between 1964 and 1972: three have since been re-opened, with **Okehampton** re-opened in November 2021.

Bere Alston in situ. *Tim Clarke*

St. James Park Halt. *TSG library*

DORSET

This beautiful county had just 11 stations sporting Southern green. Totems from the county town are quite common: **Dorchester South** has 32 appearances, and **Dorchester West** 27. **Sherborne,** 24, and **Maiden Newton,** 19, are often readily available, but the remainder range from the quite difficult to find to the downright uncommon. **Evershot,** for example, has been seen just once in auction. We learned only recently at the end of 2020 that **Yetminster** carried totems, and a newly acquired photo appears in Chapter 10, The *In situ* Files, on page 330.

The most famous railway in the county was the S&D, running from **Bath Green Park** to **Bournemouth West**, with a branch from **Evercreech Junction** to Burnham-on-Sea and **Bridgwater**, very much chocolate-and-cream signage territory. The southern part of this line sported green totems, so items from **Blandford Forum**, **Shillingstone**, and **Stalbridge** are all particularly collectable. The first three named have a total of only 5 auction appearances between them, while **Templecombe** has been seen more than 20 times. In BR times, the S&D gained the dubious title of the 'slow and dirty', and famous though it was, it succumbed to Beeching's axe. Protests at its closure were widespread but to no avail and the loss in 1966, along with the former Great Central's main line, proved to be two high-profile casualties of business economics. The lovely station at **Shillingstone** is shown below.

Mike Rutter, North Dorset Railway Trust

HAMPSHIRE

This county was peppered with Southern 'greens', 42 of them to be precise, plus the three stations on the Isle of Wight previously discussed. While totems from the S&D's southern terminus at **Bournemouth West** are common, 48 appearances thus far, we have no survival information about **Hamble Halt**: additionally, **Alton** totems have yet to appear publicly. Furthermore, totems from **Andover**, **Dunbridg**e, **Itchen Abbas**, **Marchwood**, **Sway** and **Whitchurch North** have just 1 appearance each, and are widely considered as the county's rarities. The trio with **Marchwood** below are also rarities, with just 9 combined appearances.

Railways had crossed Hampshire by 1840, when the London and Southampton Railway opened the main line in sections between Nine Elms and Southampton; they changed their name to LSWR in 1839. The line passed through **Wimbledon**, Woking, **Basingstoke**, **Winchester** and **Eastleigh**. A quartet of the less common and quite desirable county totems appears below, including wonderfully named **Horsebridge**.

A Hamble Halt totem *in situ. Tim Clarke*

We close this short Hampshire review with a picture of **Hamble Halt** *in situ*. It is not known when the totems were removed but they have not been seen since and none are thought to have survived: for Hampshire collectors, this is a real shame.

KENT

This is the real 'heavyweight' of the Southern Region, with the second highest totem count behind Lancashire; amazingly 136 Kent stations were fitted with totems. An almost equal number carried targets, so travellers in the county were well informed as to which station the trains were stopping at.

These 6 Kent totems have just 5 combined appearances, so are real rarities. We have included a picture of the FF **Eden Park** below left, but it is the HF variant installed here that is the actual rarity. **High Brooms** and **Horsmonden** have not been seen in auction thus far. Indeed, looking through all the information in the database pages, readers can see several stations with a number of variants. In some cases, one variant is far less common than another from the same station. In addition to **Bromley South** and **Eden Park** variations, a far more striking example is **Chestfield & Swalecliffe Halt**: Here, the LP variant has 46 appearances but the FF 2L version has just 2. In Chapter 11, Tim Clarke explains the South-Eastern 10-car scheme, where platforms had to be extended at many stations to accommodate longer trains. These extensions carried a variety of totem designs, such as black-flange or half-flanged styles, while the rest of the station retained whatever signage had been installed prior to the extension's construction.

Several other uncommon totem pictures are found in the database and in total 12 totems have not been seen in public. In addition, we have no information about **Crayford.** There are some quite wonderful names, such as the preceding two 1960s pictures. Both these station names give collectors plenty of letters for their money!

The six Kent totems below depict some of the more unusual and longest named stations in the county, including the forementioned rare two-line **Chestfield & Swalecliffe Halt.** Notice the letter styles and totem layouts in this small selection of Kent collectables. This also highlights the three different shades of green the SR used during the manufacturing years. Who said SR totems were boring!

At the opposite end of the scale, the pair of totems above have 123 appearances between them, with **Margate,** 56, and **Minster Thanet,** 37, also readily available.

LONDON

Remarkably, London had 57 stations in the Southern Region that carried totems, more than most people might realise. Some are very rare with known survivors, but no auction appearances recorded for **Deptford** (BF version), the FF **Eltham Park,** the HF **Hither Green** and the wooden **Holborn Viaduct.** In addition, we have no survival information about totems from **Earlsfield,** but we have a photo.

Other Kent rarities include **Aylesham Halt,** 3 appearances; the BF **Barming,** 3; **Belvedere,** 4; **Cowden,** 2; **Folkestone Harbour** 2L, 1; **Goudhurst,** 3; **Gravesend Central,** 3; the HF **Marden,** 3; all green **Margate,** 2; **Northfleet,** 1; **Shepherds Well,** 3; **Sidcup,** 3; **Snodland,** 2; **Sturry,** 3; and the BF **West Wickham,** 2.

Earlsfield *in situ. Tim Clarke*

London Bridge *in situ. John Wells*

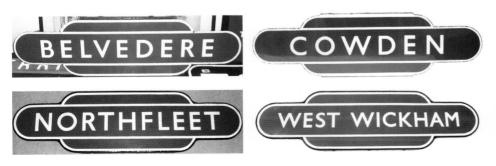

The main London stations carrying totems were **Cannon Street**, **Charing Cross,** **Holborn Viaduct**, **London Bridge** and **Waterloo:** Blackfriars and Victoria were not fitted. The busy **Clapham Junction** is one of the most common SR totems.

The preceding two pictures show the conventional 3-foot totem, which has appeared 73 times, alongside the all-green 4-foot totem, which has never been auctioned. The collage below shows totems that have appeared 3 times or less in auction and these represent London's rarities, in addition to those found in the database pages. The HF **Deptford** and **Hither Green** plus the FF **Eltham Park** are desirables, (HF design shown).

The photograph at the foot of the previous column shows a 3-foot conventional **Waterloo** totem with an all-green 6-foot variant above. This wooden item has not been in auction but the 3-foot totem has 8 public views. **Cannon Street** station had both large and small variants, again the large version not being auctioned. This was displayed outside the station. A selection of SR totems with desirable London names is presented below.

MIDDLESEX

Just 10 Middlesex stations were adorned with green totems. All are known to have survived and all have been in auction. The rarest is **Staines Central,** 2 appearances, followed by **Sunbury** with 4, then **Gunnersbury** and **Twickenham,** 5 each. The most common is **Brentford Central,** 25, with **Upper Halliford Halt** and **Whitton,** each appearing 11 times.

One of the most famous railways in the county was the Metropolitan, which served London from 1863 to 1933. Its main line headed north from the City's financial heart into what became the Middlesex suburbs, a classic case of railway influence.

SOMERSET

Almost anything SR from this county is desirable, as there were only 6 stations sporting the regional green signage. All are known survivors and each has appeared in auction. Five out of the six stations were closed in 1966, all victims of the savage economics of the time. Only **Yeovil Pen Mill**, a relatively common totem with 20

auction appearances, survived the Beeching reforms. Our database pages contain example photographs of half of Somerset's totems, with **Marston Magna**, **Milborne Port Halt** and **Sparkford** included. These have only 11 auction sales between them, the rarest being **Sparkford**. As well as this trio, the county is home to the collectable **Templecombe**, 22 appearances, which happily re-opened in 1983 and **Yeovil Town**, only 8 appearances, which was lost to history.

SURREY

The county had a heavy concentration of stations with green signage: exactly 100 were so adorned. It is also home to the most common auction totem, **Guildford** with 89 appearances. **Belmont**, **Farnham**, **Holmwood**, **Horsley** and **Wimbledon** have all not appeared publicly and with the 2L **Cobham and Stoke D'Abernon** and **East Croydon** just once. During 2020, much research was undertaken regarding **Wimbledon**. The final outcome was the scrutiny of several 1960s pictures of the station that show wooden totems mounted back-to-back. The backs of these signs were painted green and located on just a few platforms, mainly those serving the Underground. Most of **Wimbledon** station carried SR targets and these have been in auction 4 times. The two photos *in situ* that follow above right are real rarities.

Elusive Wimbledon totems *in situ* during the 1960s. *John Wells*

Other uncommon Surrey totems include **Addiscombe,** 3 appearances; **Ash,** 3; **Beddington Lane Halt,** 2; **Bramley & Wonersh,** 2; **Cranleigh,** 1; **Epsom,** 1; **Merstham,** 3; **Mitcham,** 2; **Morden Road Halt,** 2; **New Malden,** 3; **Norwood Junction,** 1; **Ockley & Capel,** 2; **Thornton Heath,** 3; **Waddon Marsh Halt,** 2; **Wanborough,** 2; **West Weybridg**e, 2; **Woldingham,** 2, and **Woodmansterne,** 1. SR totems are generally perceived to be common and readily available, but this list and discussion show that over 25% are fairly uncommon and some are extremely rare.

Some Surrey totems have been in auction many times: as well as **Guildford,** 89 appearances, the most common county items are **Ash Vale,** 27; **Bingham Road,** 32; **Carshalton,** 27; **Epsom Downs,** 31; **Ewell East,** 55; **Smitham,** 38; **Surbiton,** 37; and **West Croydon,** 38. Maybe it is numbers like these that have given the Southern Region its quite unfounded reputation for totem commonality.

SUSSEX

This is another SR county with a large number of stations sporting green totems. Though not as many as Surrey, there are 90 different examples to collect. We have no data at all regarding **Bexhill Central** and **Norman's Bay Halt,** whilst totems from **Hailsham, Heathfield, Mayfield, Steyning, Waldron and Horam, Winchelsea** and **Worthing Central** are known to have survived, but have not been seen in auction. Photographs of several of these are found in the database pages. In addition, all the totems shown below have been seen very infrequently in auction.

Surrey totems hang proudly at four stations. *Tim Clarke*

The small collage above shows a quartet of Surrey totems *in situ* towards the end of their era. The **Banstead** photograph (top left) can be dated exactly, as the Ryder Cup poster advertises the event held at Muirfield, Scotland in September 1973.

These six totems plus those in the list above, together with **Barnham, Bexhill West, Buxted, Hartfield, Haywards Heath, Horam, Lancing, Pevensey Bay Halt, Rudgwick, Three Oaks and Guestling Halt** and **Withyham** are Sussex collectables, a more than expected percentage of this county's totems.

246

Sussex fared quite badly regarding closures compared to its neighbour Surrey, losing 27 stations out of 90, compared to Surrey's 12 out of 100. Most of the closures came in 1965 and 1966. East Sussex lost 16 stations and West Sussex 11. The quartet below shows stations consigned to history in East Sussex.

The two totems below represent those lost in West Sussex. Other lost West Sussex station totems appear in the collage on the previous page, such as **Ardingly**, and in this chapter's database pages (e.g. **Slinfold** and **Steyning**). The two *in-situ* pictures that follow show totems proudly displayed in West and East Sussex before modernisation took away items we now prize. Finally, a fine six-totem collage is presented opposite.

WILTSHIRE

The final county that carried Southern Region totems is Wiltshire, with just 8 stations sporting the 'greens'. The cathedral city of **Salisbury** is by far the most common with 39 appearances, but all the others are not offered frequently for auction. **Dean,** 1; **Dilton Marsh Halt** and **Idmiston Halt,** both 2; **Warminster,** 5, and **Wilton South,** 6, all show the scarcity of SR Wiltshire totems.

In the second-half of the 1960s, the county lost half its 'totemed' stations, with **Idmiston Halt**, **Porton**, **Semley** and **Wilton South** all being closed. Happily, totem examples from all of the stations have survived and have appeared in auction.

Station Name	County in 1956	Layout	Flange	Closed	Auction	Survived
ABBEY WOOD	London		HF/FF		•	•
ADDISCOMBE	Surrey		BF	1997	•	•
ADDLESTONE	Surrey		HF		•	•
ADISHAM	Kent		FF		•	•
ALBANY PARK	Kent		HF/FF		•	•
ALDRINGTON HALT	Sussex	LP	FF		•	•
ALRESFORD *heritage station opened 1977	Hampshire		HF	1973*	•	•
ALTON + heritage station opened 1985	Hampshire		FF			•
AMBERLEY	Sussex		FF		•	•
ANDOVER "" o/p on Andover Junction	Hampshire		HF		•	•
ANDOVER JUNCTION renamed Andover in 1964	Hampshire	1L	HF		•	•
ANGMERING	Sussex		BF/FF		•	•
APPLEDORE wood only some all green	Kent		wood		•	•
ARDINGLY	Sussex		FF	1963	•	•
ARUNDEL	Sussex		FF		•	•
ASH	Surrey		HF/FF		•	•
ASH VALE	Surrey		FF		•	•
ASHURST	Kent		FF		•	•
AXMINSTER "" wood only	Devon		wood		•	•
AYLESFORD	Kent		FF		•	•
AYLESHAM HALT	Kent	LP	FF		•	•
BAGSHOT	Surrey		FF		•	•
BALCOMBE "" some wooden ""	Sussex		FF		•	•
BALHAM	London		BF		•	•
BANSTEAD ""	Surrey		FF		•	•
BARCOMBE MILLS	Sussex		HF/FF	1969	•	•
BARMING also BF	Kent		HF/FF		•	•
BARNEHURST ""	Kent		HF/FF "		•	•
BARNES	Surrey		HF		•	•
BARNES BRIDGE	Surrey		FF		•	•
BARNHAM	Sussex		BF		•	•
BARNSTAPLE TOWN	Devon	1L	FF	1970	•	•

"" = modified Gill Sans lettering used (termed Transport Medium) 1L = one line: 2L = two line: LP = lower panel

Station Name	County in 1956	Layout	Flange	Closed	Auction	Survived
BASINGSTOKE	Hampshire		HF			•
BAT AND BALL	Kent		HF		•	•
BATTERSEA PARK	London		HF			•
BEARSTED AND THURNAM	Kent	2L	FF		•	•
BECKENHAM HILL	London		FF		•	•
BEDDINGTON LANE HALT *re-opened 2000	Surrey	LP	FF	1997*	•	•
BEKESBOURNE	Kent		FF		•	•
BELLINGHAM	London		FF		•	•
BELMONT ""	Surrey		FF			•
BELTRING AND BRANBRIDGES HALT	Kent	2L	FF		•	•
BELVEDERE	Kent		HF		•	•
BENTLEY	Hampshire		FF		•	•
BERE ALSTON	Devon		FF		•	•
BERE FERRERS overpaint on Bingham Road	Devon		FF			•
BERWICK	Sussex		FF		•	•
BEXHILL CENTRAL	Sussex	1L	FF			•
BEXHILL WEST	Sussex	1L	FF	1964	•	•
BEXLEYHEATH	Kent		HF/FF		•	•
BINGHAM ROAD *re-opened 2000	Surrey		BF/FF	1983*	•	•
BIRCHINGTON-ON-SEA	Kent		FF		•	•
BISHOPSTONE	Sussex		FF		•	•
BLACKHEATH	London		HF		•	•
BLACKWATER	Hampshire		FF		•	•
BLANDFORD FORUM	Dorset		HF	1966	•	•
BODMIN NORTH	Cornwall		HF	1967	•	•
BOGNOR REGIS	Sussex		FF		•	•
BOROUGH GREEN AND WROTHAM	Kent	2L	FF		•	•
BOSCOMBE	Hampshire		HF	1965	•	•
BOSHAM	Sussex		FF		•	•
BOTLEY	Hampshire		BF/FF		•	•
BOURNEMOUTH WEST	Hampshire	1L	FF	1965		•
BRACKNELL	Berkshire		FF		•	•
BRAMBER	Sussex		FF	1966	•	•

"" = modified Gill Sans lettering used (termed Transport Medium)   1L = one line: 2L = two line: LP = lower panel

Station Name	County in 1956	Layout	Flange	Closed	Auction	Survived
BRAMLEY	Hampshire		FF		•	•
BRAMLEY & WONERSH	Surrey		BF	1965	•	•
BRENTFORD CENTRAL	Middlesex	1L	HF/FF		•	•
BRIDESTOWE	Devon		FF	1968	•	•
BRIGHTON	Sussex		FF		•	•
BRIXTON	London		FF		•	•
BROADSTAIRS	Kent		FF		•	•
BROCKENHURST	Hampshire		FF		•	•
BROCKLEY	London		FF		•	•
BROMLEY NORTH	Kent		HF		•	•
BROMLEY SOUTH some painted wood	Kent		FF		•	•
BROOKLAND HALT	Kent	1L	HF	1967		•
BUDE	Cornwall		FF	1966	•	•
BUDLEIGH SALTERTON	Devon		FF	1967	•	•
BURGESS HILL	Sussex		FF		•	•
BURGESS HILL	Sussex		wood			•
BUXTED (some o/p on Wraysbury BF)	Sussex		FF		•	•
BYFLEET AND NEW HAW	Surrey	2L	FF		•	•
CALLINGTON	Cornwall		FF	1966	•	•
CANNON STREET + large design variant	London		FF		•	•
CANTERBURY EAST	Kent	1L	FF		•	•
CANTERBURY WEST	Kent	1L	FF		•	•
CARSHALTON	Surrey		BF		•	•
CARSHALTON BEECHES	Surrey		FF		•	•
CATERHAM	Surrey		BF		•	•
CATFORD BRIDGE	London		BF/FF		•	•
CHARING CROSS also 5 foot FF version	London		BF		•	•
CHARLTON	London		HF		•	•
CHARTHAM	Kent		BF/FF		•	•
CHATHAM	Kent		BF/FF		•	•
CHEAM	Surrey		FF		•	•
CHELSFIELD	Kent		BF/FF		•	•
CHERTSEY	Surrey		HF/FF		•	•

"" = modified Gill Sans lettering used (termed Transport Medium)   1L = one line: 2L = two line: LP = lower panel

Station Name		County in 1956	Layout	Flange	Closed	Auction	Survived
CHESTFIELD & SWALECLIFFE HALT		Kent	LP	HF/FF		•	•
CHESTFIELD & SWALECLIFFE HALT		Kent	2L	FF		•	•
CHIPSTEAD		Surrey		BF		•	•
CHISLEHURST ""		Kent		FF		•	•
CHISLET COLLIERY HALT		Kent	LP	BF	1971	•	•
CHRISTCHURCH ""		Hampshire		FF		•	•
CLANDON	also wood	Surrey		HF/BF		•	•
CLAPHAM ""		London		FF		•	•
CLAPHAM JUNCTION	+ 4' totems FF	London		FF		•	•
CLOCK HOUSE		Kent		BF/FF		•	•
COBHAM & STOKE D'ABERNON		Surrey	1L	HF		•	•
COBHAM AND STOKE D'ABERNON ""		Surrey	2L	FF		•	•
COLLINGTON HALT		Sussex	1L	FF		•	•
COMBPYNE		Devon		FF	1965		•
COODEN BEACH		Sussex		HF/FF		•	•
COOMBE ROAD		Surrey		BF/FF	1983	•	•
COULSDON NORTH		Surrey		FF	1983	•	•
COULSDON SOUTH		Surrey		FF		•	•
COWDEN		Kent		HF		•	•
CRANBROOK		Kent		FF	1961		•
CRANLEIGH		Surrey		BF	1965	•	•
CRAYFORD		Kent		FF		•	•
CROWBOROUGH AND JARVIS BROOK		Sussex	LP	FF		•	•
CROWHURST		Sussex		FF		•	•
CUXTON		Kent		FF		•	•
DARTFORD		Kent		HF/FF		•	•
DATCHET		Buckinghamshire		FF		•	•
DEAL		Kent		FF		•	•
DEAN		Wiltshire		BF		•	•
DEEPDENE		Surrey		FF		•	•
DEPTFORD	also HF	London		BF/FF		•	•
DEVONPORT KINGS ROAD		Devon	LP	HF	1964	•	•

"" = modified Gill Sans lettering used (termed Transport Medium)   1L = one line: 2L = two line: LP = lower panel

Station Name	County in 1956	Layout	Flange	Closed	Auction	Survived
DILTON MARSH HALT	Wiltshire	LP	FF		•	•
DORCHESTER SOUTH	Dorset	1L	HF/FF		•	•
DORCHESTER WEST	Dorset	1L	FF		•	•
DORMANS	Surrey		FF		•	•
DOVER PRIORY	Kent		FF		•	•
DUMPTON PARK	Kent		FF		•	•
DUNBRIDGE	Hampshire		BF		•	•
DUNTON GREEN	Kent		BF/FF		•	•
DURRINGTON-ON-SEA ""	Sussex		FF		•	•
EARLEY	Berkshire		BF		•	•
EARLSFIELD *new discovery*	London		FF			
EARLSWOOD	Surrey		BF/FF		•	•
EAST CROYDON	Surrey		FF		•	•
EAST DULWICH	London		FF		•	•
EAST FARLEIGH	Kent		FF		•	•
EAST MALLING HALT	Kent	1L	FF		•	•
EAST MALLING HALT	Kent	LP	FF		•	•
EAST PUTNEY	London		FF		•	•
EAST WORTHING HALT	Sussex	LP	HF/FF		•	•
EASTBOURNE	Sussex		BF		•	•
EASTLEIGH	Hampshire		HF		•	
EDEN PARK	Kent		HF			•
EDEN PARK	Kent		BF		•	•
EDENBRIDGE	Kent		FF		•	•
EDENBRIDGE TOWN	Kent		FF		•	•
EFFINGHAM JUNCTION	Surrey	1L	FF		•	•
ELMERS END	Kent		BF		•	•
ELMSTEAD WOODS	Kent		HF/FF		•	•
ELTHAM PARK	London		HF/FF	1985	•	•
ELTHAM WELL HALL	London		HF/FF	1985	•	•
EMSWORTH	Hampshire		FF		•	•
EPSOM	Surrey		FF		•	•

"" = modified Gill Sans lettering used (termed Transport Medium)   1L = one line: 2L = two line: LP = lower panel

Station Name		County in 1956	Layout	Flange	Closed	Auction	Survived
EPSOM DOWNS		Surrey		FF		•	•
ERIDGE		Sussex		FF		•	•
ERITH		Kent		HF/FF			•
ESHER ""		Surrey		FF		•	•
EVERSHOT		Dorset		FF	1966	•	•
EWELL EAST		Surrey		FF		•	•
EXETER CENTRAL	4' only – all green	Devon		FF		•	•
EXMOUTH		Devon		FF		•	•
EXTON		Devon		FF		•	•
FALCONWOOD		London		HF/FF		•	•
FALMER		Sussex		FF		•	•
FARNBOROUGH NORTH		Hampshire	1L	FF		•	•
FARNHAM		Surrey		FF			•
FARNINGHAM ROAD		Kent		FF		•	•
FAVERSHAM		Kent		FF			•
FAYGATE		Sussex		HF			•
FISHBOURNE HALT		Sussex	LP	FF		•	•
FISHERSGATE HALT		Sussex	LP	FF		•	•
FOLKESTONE EAST		Kent	1L	FF	1965	•	•
FOLKESTONE HARBOUR		Kent	2L	FF	2001	•	•
FOLKESTONE HARBOUR		Kent	1L	BF	2001	•	•
FOLKESTONE Jct	Overpainted on Kenley	Kent	1L	BF		•	•
FOLKESTONE JUNCTION	renamed 1962	Kent	2L	FF		•	•
FOLKESTONE WEST		Kent	1L	FF			•
FORD		Sussex		FF		•	•
FRANT		Sussex		FF		•	•
FRATTON ""		Hampshire		FF		•	•
FRIMLEY		Surrey		FF		•	•
FULWELL		Middlesex		FF		•	•
GATWICK RACECOURSE	wood only	Sussex		wood		•	•
GILLINGHAM		Kent		BF/FF		•	•

"" = modified Gill Sans lettering used (termed Transport Medium)   1L = one line: 2L = two line: LP = lower panel

Station Name	County in 1956	Layout	Flange	Closed	Auction	Survived
GIPSY HILL	Surrey		FF		•	•
GODSTONE	Surrey		FF		•	•
GORING-BY-SEA no hyphens on FF	Sussex		HF/FF		•	•
GOUDHURST	Kent		FF	1961	•	•
GRANGE ROAD	Sussex		BF/FF	1967	•	•
GRAVESEND CENTRAL	Kent	LP	BF		•	•
GRAVESEND WEST	Kent	1L	HF	1953		
GREATSTONE-ON-SEA	Kent		FF	1967		•
GREENHITHE New discovery + new station 2008	Kent		BF		•	•
GREENWICH	London		HF		•	•
GROOMBRIDGE *heritage station 2011	Sussex		FF	1985*	•	•
GROVE FERRY AND UPSTREET	Kent	2L	FF	1966	•	•
GROVE PARK	London		HF/FF		•	•
GUILDFORD	Surrey		FF		•	•
GUNNERSBURY	Middlesex		HF/FF		•	•
HACKBRIDGE ""	Surrey		FF		•	•
HAILSHAM	Sussex		FF	1968		•
HALLING	Kent		FF			
HAM STREET AND ORLESTONE	Kent	1L	HF		•	•
HAMBLE HALT	Hampshire	1L	HF			
HAMPDEN PARK	Sussex		FF		•	•
HAMPTON ""	Middlesex		FF		•	•
HARRIETSHAM	Kent		FF		•	•
HARTFIELD	Sussex		FF	1967		•
HASSOCKS	Sussex		FF		•	•
HASTINGS	Sussex		FF		•	•
HAVANT	Hampshire		FF		•	•
HAYDONS ROAD	Surrey		FF		•	•
HAYES	Kent		BF		•	•
HAYWARDS HEATH	Sussex		FF		•	•
HEADCORN	Kent		HF/FF		•	•
HEATHFIELD	Sussex		FF	1965		•

"" = modified Gill Sans lettering used (termed Transport Medium)   1L = one line: 2L = two line: LP = lower panel

Station Name		County in 1956	Layout	Flange	Closed	Auction	Survived
HELLINGLY		Sussex		HF/FF	1965	•	•
HENFIELD		Sussex		FF	1966	•	•
HERNE BAY		Kent		FF		•	•
HERSHAM		Surrey		FF		•	•
HEVER		Kent		HF		•	•
HIGH BROOMS		Kent		HF			•
HIGHAM		Kent		HF/BF		•	•
HILDENBOROUGH		Kent		BF/FF		•	•
HINCHLEY WOOD		Surrey		FF		•	•
HINTON ADMIRAL		Hampshire		FF		•	•
HITHER GREEN		London		HF/FF		•	•
HOLBORN VIADUCT	o/p on Burgess Hill	London		wood	1990		•
HOLBORN VIADUCT		London		FF	1990		
HOLLINGBOURNE		Kent		FF		•	•
HOLMWOOD		Surrey		FF			•
HONITON		Devon		FF		•	•
HONOR OAK PARK		London		FF		•	•
HOOK		Hampshire		FF		•	•
HORAM		Sussex		HF/FF	1965		•
HORSEBRIDGE		Hampshire		FF	1964	•	•
HORSLEY	New discovery	Surrey		?			•
HORSMONDEN		Kent		FF	1961		•
HOVE		Sussex		FF		•	•
HURST GREEN		Surrey		FF		•	•
IDMISTON HALT		Wiltshire	LP	FF	1968	•	•
IFIELD	(some o/p on St. Helier FF totem)	Sussex		HF		•	•
ILFRACOMBE		Devon		FF	1970	•	•
ISFIELD station restored 1986		Sussex		HF	1969	•	•
ITCHEN ABBAS		Hampshire		HF	1973	•	•
KEARSNEY		Kent		FF		•	•
KEMSING		Kent		FF		•	•
KEMSLEY HALT		Kent	1L	FF		•	•

"" = modified Gill Sans lettering used (termed Transport Medium) 1L = one line: 2L = two line: LP = lower panel

Station Name	County in 1956	Layout	Flange	Closed	Auction	Survived
KENLEY	Surrey		BF/FF		•	•
KENT HOUSE	Kent		HF/FF		•	•
KIDBROOKE	London		HF		•	•
KINGSTON	Surrey		FF		•	•
KINGSWOOD	Surrey		BF/FF		•	•
KNOCKHOLT	Kent		BF/FF		•	•
LADYWELL	London		HF		•	•
LANCING	Sussex		HF		•	•
LEATHERHEAD ""	Surrey		FF		•	•
LEE FOR BURNT ASH	London	LP	HF		•	•
LEIGH HALT	Kent		FF		•	•
LENHAM	Kent		FF		•	•
LEWISHAM ""	London		HF/FF		•	•
LINGFIELD	Surrey		FF		•	•
LITTLEHAMPTON	Sussex		FF		•	•
LITTLEHAVEN HALT	Sussex	1L	HF		•	•
LONDON BRIDGE	London		wood		•	•
LONDON ROAD (Guildford) ""	Surrey	LP	FF		•	•
LONGFIELD FOR FAWKHAM & HARTLEY	Kent	2L	FF		•	•
LOUGHBOROUGH JUNCTION	London	2L	FF		•	•
LOUGHBOROUGH JUNCTION	London	LP	HF		•	•
LOWER SYDENHAM	London		BF/FF		•	•
MAIDEN NEWTON	Dorset		FF		•	•
MAIDSTONE BARRACKS	Kent		FF		•	•
MAIDSTONE EAST	Kent		FF		•	•
MARCHWOOD	Hampshire		FF	1966	•	•
MARDEN	Kent		HF/FF		•	•
MARGATE (some all green)	Kent		FF		•	•
MARSTON MAGNA	Somerset		FF	1966	•	•
MARTIN MILL	Kent		FF		•	•
MAYFIELD	Sussex		FF	1965		•

"" = modified Gill Sans lettering used (termed Transport Medium)   1L = one line: 2L = two line: LP = lower panel

Station Name		County in 1956	Layout	Flange	Closed	Auction	Survived
MAZE HILL ""	not all have modified letters	London		FF		•	•
MEOPHAM		Kent		FF		•	•
MERSTHAM		Surrey		HF/FF		•	•
MERSTONE		Hampshire (IOW)		HF	1956	•	•
MICHELDEVER		Hampshire		HF		•	•
MILBORNE PORT HALT		Somerset	LP	FF	1966	•	•
MILL HILL		Hampshire (IOW)		HF	1966	•	•
MILLBROOK		Hampshire		FF		•	•
MINSTER THANET		Kent	LP	FF		•	•
MITCHAM	*re-opened 2000	Surrey		FF	1997*	•	•
MITCHAM JUNCTION		Surrey	1L	FF		•	•
MORDEN ROAD HALT	*re-opened 2000	Surrey	1L	HF	1997*	•	•
MORDEN SOUTH		Surrey		FF		•	•
MORTIMER		Berkshire		FF		•	•
MORTLAKE ""		Surrey		FF		•	•
MOTTINGHAM		London		HF/FF		•	•
MOTTISFONT		Hampshire		FF	1964	•	•
MOUNTFIELD HALT		Sussex	LP	FF	1969	•	•
NEW BECKENHAM		Kent		BF		•	•
NEW CROSS		London		BF/FF		•	•
NEW ELTHAM		London		HF		•	•
NEW MALDEN	(also wooden totems)	Surrey		FF		•	•
NEW MILTON ""		Hampshire		FF		•	•
NEW ROMNEY & LITTLESTONE-ON-SEA		Kent	2L	FF	1967		•
NEW ROMNEY AND LITTLESTONE-ON-SEA		Kent	2L	HF	1967		•
NEWHAVEN HARBOUR		Sussex	1L	BF/FF		•	•
NEWHAVEN TOWN		Sussex	1L	BF		•	•
NEWINGTON		Kent		FF		•	•
NEWPORT		Hampshire (IOW)		HF	1966	•	•
NORMANS BAY HALT		Sussex	1L	FF		•	•
NORTH CAMP		Surrey		FF		•	•
NORTH DULWICH		London		BF		•	•

"" = modified Gill Sans lettering used (termed Transport Medium)   1L = one line: 2L = two line: LP = lower panel

Station Name		County in 1956	Layout	Flange	Closed	Auction	Survived
NORTH SHEEN	also HF	Surrey		BF/FF		•	•
NORTHAM		Hampshire		FF	1966	•	•
NORTHFLEET		Kent		BF		•	•
NORWOOD JUNCTION		Surrey	1L	FF		•	•
NUNHEAD		London		FF		•	•
NUTBOURNE HALT		Sussex	LP	FF		•	•
OAKLEY		Hampshire		FF	1963	•	•
OCKLEY & CAPEL		Surrey		HF		•	•
OKEHAMPTON	*Re-opened November 2021	Devon		FF	1972*	•	•
ORE		Sussex		FF		•	•
ORPINGTON		Kent		HF		•	•
OTTERY ST. MARY		Devon		FF	1967		•
OVERTON		Hampshire		HF		•	•
OXSHOTT ""		Surrey		FF		•	•
OXTED		Surrey		FF		•	•
PADDOCK WOOD		Kent		FF		•	•
PARTRIDGE GREEN		Sussex		FF	1966	•	•
PECKHAM RYE		London		FF		•	•
PETTS WOOD ""		Kent		FF		•	•
PEVENSEY AND WESTHAM		Sussex	2L	FF		•	•
PEVENSEY BAY HALT		Sussex	LP	FF		•	•
PINHOE	*re-opened 1983	Devon		FF	1966*	•	•
PLUCKLEY		Kent		BF/FF		•	•
PLUMSTEAD		London		HF		•	•
POKESDOWN		Hampshire		HF		•	•
POLEGATE		Sussex		FF		•	•
PORTON		Wiltshire		HF	1968	•	•
PORTSLADE & WEST HOVE		Sussex	2L	FF		•	•
PORTSMOUTH & SOUTHSEA		Hampshire		HF/FF		•	•
PORTSMOUTH HARBOUR		Hampshire	1L	HF/FF		•	•
PRESTON PARK		Sussex		FF		•	•

"" = modified Gill Sans lettering used (termed Transport Medium)   1L = one line: 2L = two line: LP = lower panel

Station Name	County in 1956	Layout	Flange	Closed	Auction	Survived
PULBOROUGH	Sussex		FF		•	•
PUTNEY	London		HF		•	•
QUEENBOROUGH ""	Kent		FF		•	•
QUEENS ROAD BATTERSEA	London	2L	FF		•	•
RAINHAM	Kent		FF		•	•
RAMSGATE	Kent		FF		•	•
RAVENSBOURNE	London		FF		•	•
READING (SOUTHERN) named from 1961	Berkshire	2L	FF	1965	•	•
READING SOUTH renamed in 1961	Berkshire	1L	HF	1965		
REEDHAM	Surrey		BF		•	•
RIDDLESDOWN	Surrey		FF		•	•
ROCHESTER	Kent		BF		•	•
ROPLEY *open as heritage station 1977	Hampshire		FF	1973*	•	•
ROTHERFIELD & MARK CROSS	Sussex	2L	FF	1965		
ROTHERFIELD & MARK CROSS	Sussex	1L	BF	1965	•	
ROWFANT	Sussex		BF/FF	1967	•	
RUDGWICK	Sussex		HF	1965		•
RYE	Sussex		FF		•	•
SALISBURY	Wiltshire		HF		•	•
SANDERSTEAD	Surrey		BF		•	•
SANDHURST HALT "" o/p on Wraysbury	Berkshire	LP	FF		•	•
SANDLING FOR HYTHE	Kent	LP	HF		•	•
SANDWICH	Kent		FF		•	•
SEAFORD ""	Sussex		FF		•	•
SEATON	Devon		FF	1966	•	•
SELHURST	Surrey		FF		•	•
SELLING	Kent		HF/FF		•	•
SELSDON	Surrey		BF	1983	•	•
SEMLEY	Wiltshire		FF	1966	•	•
SEVENOAKS	Kent		FF		•	•

"" = modified Gill Sans lettering used (termed Transport Medium)   1L = one line: 2L = two line: LP = lower panel

Station Name	County in 1956	Layout	Flange	Closed	Auction	Survived
SHEERNESS-ON-SEA	Kent		FF		•	•
SHEPHERDS WELL	Kent		FF		•	•
SHERBORNE	Dorset		FF		•	•
SHILLINGSTONE	Dorset		BF	1966		•
SHOLING	Hampshire		FF		•	•
SHOREHAM ""	Kent		FF		•	•
SHORTLANDS	Kent		FF		•	•
SIDCUP	Kent		HF		•	•
SIDMOUTH JUNCTION *re-opened 1971	Devon		FF	1967*	•	•
SITTINGBOURNE	Kent		FF		•	•
SITTINGBOURNE AND MILTON REGIS	Kent	3L	BF		•	•
SLADE GREEN	Kent		FF		•	•
SLINFOLD	Sussex		HF	1965	•	•
SMITHAM ""	Surrey		FF		•	•
SNODLAND	Kent		FF		•	•
SNOWDOWN & NONINGTON HALT	Kent	LP	HF/FF		•	•
SNOWDOWN & NONINGTON HALT	Kent	LP	BF		•	•
SOLE STREET	Kent		FF		•	•
SOUTH MERTON	Surrey		FF		•	•
SOUTHBOURNE HALT	Sussex	LP	FF		•	•
SOUTHEASE & RODMELL HALT	Sussex	LP	FF		•	•
SOUTHWATER	Sussex		FF	1966	•	•
SOUTHWICK	Sussex		FF		•	•
SPARKFORD	Somerset		FF	1966	•	•
ST. BUDEAUX VICTORIA ROAD	Devon	LP	HF		•	•
ST. DENYS ""	Hampshire		FF		•	•
ST. HELIER	Surrey		FF		•	•
ST. JOHNS	London		HF/FF		•	•
ST. JAMES PARK HALT	Devon	LP	FF		•	•
STAINES CENTRAL	Middlesex	1L	HF		•	•
STALBRIDGE	Dorset		HF	1966	•	•
STAPLEHURST "" also standard Gill Sans totems	Kent		HF/FF		•	•
STEYNING	Sussex		FF	1966		•

"" = modified Gill Sans lettering used (termed Transport Medium) | 1L = one line: 2L = two line: LP = lower panel

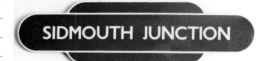

Station Name	County in 1956	Layout	Flange	Closed	Auction	Survived
STONE CROSSING HALT	Kent	1L/LP	BF		•	•
STONE CROSSING HALT	Kent	LP	FF		•	•
STONEGATE	Sussex		HF		•	•
STONELEIGH	Surrey		FF		•	•
STREATHAM ""	Surrey		FF		•	•
STREATHAM COMMON	Surrey		FF		•	•
STREATHAM HILL	Surrey		FF		•	•
STROOD	Kent		FF/BF		•	•
STURRY	Kent		HF		•	•
SUNBURY	Middlesex		HF		•	•
SUNDRIDGE PARK	Kent		FF		•	•
SUNNYMEADS	Buckinghamshire		FF		•	•
SURBITON	Surrey		FF		•	•
SUTTON	Surrey		FF		•	•
SUTTON COMMON	Surrey		FF		•	•
SWALE HALT	Kent		FF		•	•
SWANSCOMBE HALT	Kent	1L	FF		•	•
SWANSCOMBE HALT	Kent	LP	BF		•	•
SWAY	Hampshire		FF		•	•
SYDENHAM HILL	London		BF		•	•
SYON LANE	Middlesex		FF		•	•
TADWORTH ""	Surrey		FF		•	•
TAVISTOCK NORTH	Devon	1L	HF	1968	•	•
TEMPLECOMBE *re-opened 1983	Somerset		FF	1966*	•	•
TEYNHAM	Kent		FF		•	•
THORNTON HEATH	Surrey		FF		•	•
THREE BRIDGES	Sussex		HF/FF		•	•
THREE OAKS & GUESTLING HALT	Sussex	3L	FF		•	•
TONBRIDGE	Kent		FF		•	•
TOOTING	London		FF		•	•
TUNBRIDGE WELLS CENTRAL	Kent	LP	FF		•	•
TUNBRIDGE WELLS WEST *new heritage stn 1996	Kent	1L	FF	1985*	•	•
TWICKENHAM (light green only)	Middlesex		HF		•	•

"" = modified Gill Sans lettering used (termed Transport Medium)   1L = one line: 2L = two line: LP = lower panel

Station Name		County in 1956	Layout	Flange	Closed	Auction	Survived
UCKFIELD	*station re-sited 1991	Sussex		FF	1991*	•	•
UPPER HALLIFORD HALT		Middlesex	LP	BF		•	•
UPPER WARLINGHAM ""	(2L version is "")	Surrey	1L/2L	FF		•	•
VAUXHALL		London		FF		•	•
WADDON		Surrey		FF		•	•
WADDON MARSH HALT	*re-opened 2000	Surrey	1L	BF	1997*	•	•
WADEBRIDGE		Cornwall		FF	1967	•	•
WALDRON AND HORAM	renamed Horam 1953	Sussex		HF	1965		•
WALMER		Kent		FF		•	•
WALTON ON THAMES		Surrey		BF		•	•
WANBOROUGH		Surrey		HF		•	•
WANDSWORTH COMMON		London	2L	FF		•	•
WANDSWORTH ROAD		London	1L	FF		•	•
WANDSWORTH TOWN		London	1L	FF		•	•
WARBLINGTON HALT		Hampshire	LP	FF		•	•
WARMINSTER		Wiltshire		HF/FF		•	•
WARNHAM ""		Sussex		FF		•	•
WATERINGBURY		Kent		FF		•	•
WATERLOO	some wood: some all green	London		FF		•	•
WATERLOO	6 foot wooden all green variant	London		wood			•
WELLING		Kent		HF/FF		•	•
WEST BYFLEET		Surrey		HF		•	•
WEST CROYDON	some wooden non-standard letters	Surrey		HF/FF		•	•
WEST DULWICH		London		HF		•	•
WEST GRINSTEAD		Sussex		FF	1966	•	•
WEST MALLING		Kent		HF/FF		•	•
WEST MOORS		Dorset		FF	1964	•	•
WEST NORWOOD		London		HF		•	•
WEST ST. LEONARDS		Sussex		FF		•	•
WEST SUTTON		Surrey		FF		•	•
WEST WEYBRIDGE	Byfleet & New Haw from 1962	Surrey		HF		•	•
WEST WICKHAM	also BF	Kent		HF/FF		•	•
WESTCOMBE PARK		London		FF		•	•

"" = modified Gill Sans lettering used (termed Transport Medium) 1L = one line: 2L = two line: LP = lower panel

Station Name		County in 1956	Layout	Flange	Closed	Auction	Survived
WESTENHANGER	also BF	Kent		HF/FF		•	•
WESTGATE-ON-SEA		Kent		FF		•	•
WEYBRIDGE		Surrey		HF		•	•
WEYMOUTH	(also 4' totems FF)	Dorset		HF		•	•
WHIMPLE		Devon		FF		•	•
WHITCHURCH NORTH		Hampshire	1L	HF		•	•
WHITSTABLE & TANKERTON		Kent		BF/FF		•	•
WHITTON		Middlesex		FF		•	•
WHYTELEAFE		Surrey		FF		•	•
WHYTELEAFE SOUTH	named Warlingham to 1956	Surrey	1L	BF		•	•
WILTON SOUTH		Wiltshire	1L	HF	1966	•	•
WIMBLEDON		Surrey		wood			
WIMBLEDON CHASE		Surrey		FF		•	•
WINCHELSEA		Sussex		BF			•
WINCHESTER CITY		Hampshire		HF		•	•
WINCHFIELD		Hampshire		FF		•	•
WINDSOR & ETON RIVERSIDE		Berkshire	LP	HF		•	•
WINNERSH HALT ""		Berkshire	1L	FF		•	•
WITHYHAM		Sussex		BF	1967	•	•
WIVELSFIELD		Sussex		FF		•	•
WOLDINGHAM ""		Surrey		FF		•	•
WOODMANSTERNE		Surrey		FF		•	•
WOODSIDE	*re-opened 2000	Surrey		BF/FF	1997*	•	•
WOOLWICH ARSENAL		London		HF/FF		•	•
WOOLWICH DOCKYARD		London		HF/FF		•	•
WORPLESDON		Surrey		FF		•	•
WORTHING CENTRAL		Sussex	1L	FF		•	•
WRAYSBURY	+ all green totems BF	Buckinghamshire		FF		•	•
WYE		Kent	1L	FF		•	•
YALDING		Kent		FF		•	•
YEOFORD		Devon		FF		•	•
YEOVIL PEN MILL		Somerset	1L	HF		•	•
YEOVIL TOWN		Somerset		FF	1966	•	•
YETMINSTER		Dorset		FF?			

"" = modified Gill Sans lettering used (termed Transport Medium)   1L = one line: 2L = two line: LP = lower panel

Opening Comments

The map alongside shows the extent of the Western Region at inception on 1 January 1948. The boundaries were to a great extent based upon the former Great Western Railway (GWR) routes running from London to as far north as Caernarvonshire and down to the south-western extremity of England at **Penzance** in Cornwall. Before BR was formed, the GWR had thought of itself as the 'premier railway company'. It did not have the fastest engines (that was the LNER) or mighty Pacifics (the LMS) or a part-electrified network (the SR) but in all other respects they thought of themselves as superior: 'God's Wonderful Railway'. It had been built by, arguably, Britain greatest-ever engineer, Isambard Kingdom Brunel, who joined London to Bristol, Britain's premier port at that time, so creating the fastest route from the City of London to the New World. His ill-fated broad gauge vision created faster, smoother rides for the passengers, though his visionary thinking was out of step with everybody else. He engineered bridges, tunnels, stations, and even ships, the complete all-rounder you might say, and his legacy is still present all over this part of Britain.

The map shows how many stations and routes the WR operated. In all 406 stations in this region were fitted with totems, with concentrations in Glamorgan, 67 listed in the database such as **Swansea High Street**, and all around the 'Black Country' in the West Midlands, such as **West Bromwich**. In contrast, there were only two fitted stations in Brecknockshire, **Brecon** and **Llanwrtyd Wells**, three in Cardiganshire, **Aberystwyth**, **Borth** and **Lampeter**, and four each in London and Radnorshire.

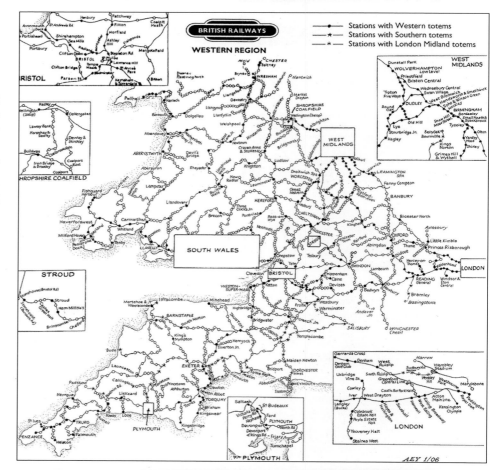

Brief Regional History

The Great Western Railway Company was founded in 1833, received its enabling Act of Parliament on 31 August 1835 and it ran its first trains in 1838. It steadily expanded during the mania of railway expansion in the 19th century from just 171 miles in 1841 to 2,504 miles by 1899. The drive for this expansion came from wealthy Bristol merchants who wanted to maintain their city's status as Britain's premier port. By collaborating with financiers in the City of London, the GWR began on a sound monetary footing. Brunel's vision was to out-perform the railways being built in the north-west that served Bristol's great rival, Liverpool. The WR main line out of London ran from **Paddington** through **Reading**, **Didcot**, **Swindon**, **Chippenham** and **Bath**.

Swindon was halfway between Brunel's two termini and it soon became the home of the GWR. The development of Swindon Works gave rise to the rapid growth of the town and hundreds of homes were built for the workforce. **Swindon** is the junction for the line to **Gloucester** and South Wales, whilst **Didcot** became the junction for the line through **Oxford** to **Birmingham**, **Shrewsbury**, **Chester** and into **Birkenhead**.

Junctions along these routes enabled other lines to be built, leading eventually to the network shown in the map opposite. The routes also contained ground-breaking engineering of the time, including beautiful stations at **Paddington**, **Bristol Temple Meads** and **Shrewsbury**, the unique brick-arch bridge at **Maidenhead** and tunnels at Box and beneath the River Severn.

By 1850 the GWR was carrying 2.5 million passengers a year and in 1923 they carried 140 million people. Freight became a major revenue source once the coal-rich valleys of South Wales and the West Midlands industrial heartlands had been reached. By 1900 over 37.5 million tonnes of freight were carried. A high percentage of this freight came from the West Midlands, but when the GWR reached here in 1852 they built a wooden structure (named Birmingham), as the rival LNWR did not agree to the use of their terminus at Curzon Street. It was renamed as **Birmingham Snow Hill** in 1858 and from there the route ran to **Wolverhampton Low Level** and on towards **Shrewsbury**.

Early in the 20th century the GWR began railway-owned bus services in Cornwall and in 1903 they introduced an early version of the auto-train service on the Stroud Valley line. They were innovative in transportation in the years before the WWI, but on its outbreak in 1914, they were nationalised for the war effort.

After the cessation of hostilities, the Government decreed that the many railway companies in Britain should be amalgamated. The GWR acquired six Welsh railway companies, the most important being the Cambrian, which extended their routes into Caernarvonshire; this was a valuable addition to their holiday excursion business.

The GWR was the only company to keep its identity through the Railways Act of 1921, which amalgamated it with the remaining independent railways within its territory. With these newly acquired assets, particularly in South Wales, they were able to directly control around 90% of the nation's coal movements, a cornerstone to their revenue stream and integral part of the British economy.

However, coal costs rose steadily so by 1934, they had recognised the need for other forms of traction. In February of that year, they ran their first diesel railcars and later twin sets ran between **Birmingham** and **Cardiff**. However, WWII loomed and the GWR was soon to be no more. It was finally merged at the end of 1947, when it was nationalised and became the Western Region of British Railways.

It was hoped that profitability might follow, but operating costs were still too high and closures became inevitable, even before Beeching's appointment. In 1955, there were 1,296 stations so only 30% were ever fitted with totems. By 1961 this had fallen to 1,045 and after the Beeching cuts only 422 remained. Rural and cross country routes fared badly, but even sizeable towns lost their stations, such as **Cirencester**.

Despite best efforts, this region's profitability was not forthcoming and, following the wholesale Beeching station closures, it was clear further cuts were needed. This came in the form of rationalisation of duplicate lines, so some historic routes were lost. These included **Birmingham Snow Hill–Wolverhampton Low Level**, which duplicated the London Midland Region's **Birmingham New Street–Wolverhampton High Level** line; this was the one subsequently chosen for electrification. Other later closures included **Cefn On, Gloucester Eastgate, Kingswear, Minehead** and **St. Annes Park.**

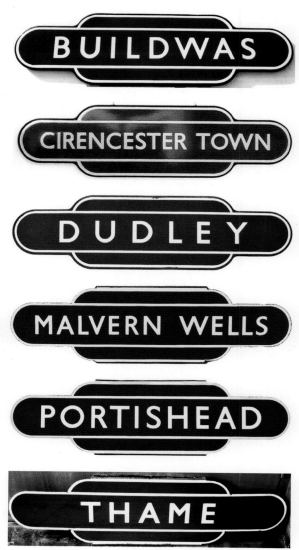

Western Region Totem Geography

Richard Furness & Alan Young

The WR had geographic diversity, which for the most part made track-laying fairly straightforward. The main London to Bristol line is often called 'Brunel's billiard table' as it has few gradients, allowing his trains to run fast. For many years the *Cheltenham Flye'* held many operational speed titles. In complete contrast, the South Devon banks between **Exeter** and Plymouth presented real challenges for steam locomotives. Leaving **Newton Abbot**, the line ascends Dainton Bank, and from **Totnes** it climbs Rattery Bank, peaking at Wrangaton summit, and then descending Hemerdon Bank to reach Plymouth. Dainton is the third-steepest main-line climb in Britain, with 2½ miles of between 1 in 36 and 1 in 57. Rattery is the seventh steepest: 4 miles at an average of 1 in 55, and a final half-mile of 1 in 65. Hemerdon is the fourth steepest: 3 miles of constant 1 in 42. Charles Collett's wonderful *King* class engines, introduced 1927, could handle medium loads unaided, but double heading was common, especially on the heavy summer expresses such as the *Cornish Riviera*.

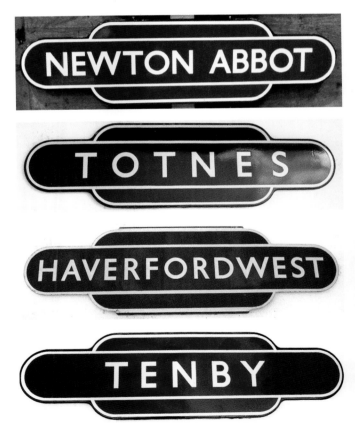

Further north, the western extremity is Pembrokeshire, home to some real collectors' pieces, such as the pair below left. Further north still lies the beautiful Cambrian Coast and one of Britain's great train journeys. Stations along this route, with the being, include: **Aberystwyth,** 17, to the south, and **Dovey Junction,** 9; **Aberdovey,** 3; **Barmouth,** 13; **Harlech,** 7; **Portmadoc,** 6; **Penychain,** 0; **Criccieth,** 1, and **Pwllheli,** 12, to the north. **Afon Wen,** 4, was closed in 1964. The number after the name is the number of auction appearances, as of December 2021.

The main line out of **Paddington**, through **High Wycombe**, **Bicester**, Banbury (sadly no totems), **Leamington Spa, Solihull** and into **Birmingham Snow Hill** marked the eastern boundary of the Western Region. Today, trains can still travel on the Chiltern route but now leave from Marylebone station instead of **Paddington**. The 1974 scene below shows overpainted B&W totems still in place at **Denham Golf Club**.

Alan Young's superb hand-drawn map at the start of the chapter shows the 406 stations that had totems fitted, but many more that did not. It is rumoured, but not yet proven, that Britain's first totems were installed at **West Ealing**. Totems, all half flanged (HF), were then installed at quite a slow rate, with by far the largest majority being installed before 1957. In the late-1950s, most of the new WR totems that were being installed were full-flange variants, even though the ER had already started taking down some of their station signage due to platform lighting upgrades.

Denham Golf Club station, on 6 July 1974. *Alan Young*

During the early and subsequent years, boundary changes happened quite often. The first changes occurred in April 1950, when the WR gained lines and stations in Oxfordshire, Shropshire and Warwickshire (from the LMR) and in Somerset and west of **Exeter** (from the SR), but lost lines in Shropshire (to the LMR) and in Berkshire, Dorset, Hampshire and Wiltshire (all to the SR). It was a pattern that seemed to repeat itself as tinkering often occurred. This eventually resulted in totems of one colour installed at stations overseen by a different regional management.

In these changes the WR surrendered the line jointly operated with the LMS from **Chester** to Birkenhead to the LMR but took control of other routes: **Shrewsbury** to **Wellington (Salop)**, to **Hereford**, and to Buttington, Bristol–**Avonmouth Dock**, and **Llandovery–Llandilo Bridge**. It is unlikely that WR totems were fitted prior to the 1950 regional changes, when it gained SR lines, and where several SR totems had already appeared (e.g. **Bodmin North**). Gains occurred on the Somerset & Dorset as far as Cole, but the WR lost the Chard and Yeovil byways to the SR. Chocolate-and-cream totems were only fitted on its newly acquired Devon lines at **Instow**, **Mortehoe & Woolacombe**, at **King's Nympton**, and at **Evercreech Junction** on the S&D.

In February 1958, the SR regained the lines west of Exeter but had fitted only ten stations with totems when the WR took over again in January 1963. In the north, major adjustments occurred as the southern boundary of the LMR bit deeply into traditional WR territory, so at the same time major adjustments at the northern edge of the WR meant the surrender of many lines and stations to the LMR: **Aberystwyth**, **Church Stretton**, Stourport-on-Severn, **Kidderminster**, **Stratford-upon-Avon** and King's Sutton formed the southern boundary of the enlarged LMR.

The 1963 boundary revision probably had no effect on totem installation – we think that no more were fitted in the areas concerned – and both the WR and LMR seemed blasé about stations displaying the wrong regional livery: SR signs still hung at WR stations (e.g. **Yeovil Pen Mill**) and WR signs at LMR stations (e.g. **Pwllheli**) well into the 1970s. The Western Region reached east into SR territory almost to **Salisbury**.

In these boundary changes, the WR had inherited numerous small 'halts' built by

its predecessor, the GWR. These were often close together and the opening map has tried to show a high percentage of these. On the SR there were more than thirty of these, many fitted with totems, but the WR was far less generous. In the **Stroud** valley only **Ham Mill Halt** was fitted with new FF totems following renaming in 1957, even though there were numerous other stations from **Stonehouse (Burdett Road)** to **Kemble**.

The WR opened some diminutive new halts, such as Cefntilla (opened 1954, closed 1955), Trouble House (opened 1959), Park Leaze (1960) and Boscarne Exchange Platform (1964), but all lacked totems: the last named would have been a real collectable item.

Kemble *in situ* early 1960s. *TSG library*

Totems were fitted at the only slightly larger **Poyle Estate Halt** (opened 1954) and **Colnbrook Estate Halt** (1961). The former carried fully-flanged totems, presumably fitted after 1957; these are rare, not having appeared yet in auction. They were preceded by two HF totems. But by the mid 1950s, most of the WR's rural lines were on borrowed time, being more of a social prop than a profitable transport facility.

The policy seemed to be that totems were installed only at major stations (e.g. **Brecon, Devizes, Dolgelley, Lampeter, Llandovery, Perranporth, Rhayader, Ross-on-Wye**), and branch termini (e.g. **Helston, Kingsbridge, Looe, Minehead, Newquay, Porthcawl** and **Portishead**), with none at intermediate stations. This approach denied some lines any totems at all (e.g. branches to Ashburton, Blaenau Ffestiniog Central, Bridport, Cardigan, Cinderford, Devil's Bridge, Fairford, Lambourn, and Moretonhampstead). Towns such as Bridgnorth, Bewdley, Bromyard, Monmouth, Stourport-on-Severn and neighbouring stations on lesser routes sadly never carried totems.

The WR had the opportunity, while it had ownership from 1950 until 1958 of the Marylebone–South Ruislip line, but it was first given to the ER and then acquired by the LMR. The LMR duly installed maroon totems at **Wembley Stadium** (overpainted on **Watford Junction**), **Wembley Hill, Sudbury & Harrow Road, Sudbury Hill (Harrow)** and **Northolt Park**: just imagine a chocolate-and-cream **Wembley Stadium**!

Turning to the main WR lines, totems were only installed at main stations. This is seen on the system map on the **Paddington–Penzance** route (via **Westbury (Wilts)** or **Swindon**), **Didcot–Oxford–Worcester–Hereford, Shrewsbury–Newport** and on the **Paddington** to **Birmingham Snow Hill** route. There were exceptions at some lesser stations (**Colwall, Dauntsey, Fladbury** and **Theale**), so these are real collectors' items.

On the WR lines in Cornwall, totems were quite numerous (the database lists 19 different stations) but the ex-SR route Salisbury-Exeter-Plymouth never received 'chocolate-and-creams', though around half carried green SR totems and several kept targets until closure, Seaton Junction for example. It was only in 1963 that the SR's Salisbury to Exeter came under WR control but Western brown totems were never fitted; this might well have confused many 1960s travelling passengers!

Pembrokeshire did rather well, with 13 totems for collectors to obtain. Even small places such as **Mathry Road** were fitted and the branch lines from **Clarbeston Road** to **Milford Haven** and **Neyland** all had totems. The database contains the only known survivor from **Milford Haven**, but in poor condition. Most of the small stations and halts (Welsh Hook or Sarnau for example) were deemed unworthy of such costs.

Similar perversity existed on the **Exeter** to **Paignton** route where full 'totemisation' occurred. This is one of our great British railway journeys, along the Devon seawall with a wonderful selection of totems, even **Exminster**; the three **Exmouth** line stations had SR green totems. However, it is the 'chocolate-and- creams' that collectors seem to clamour for: what a wonderful quartet right!

In the London area totems were abundant on the main lines to **Didcot** and **Princes Risborough**, with some omissions (Acton Main Line and South Ruislip). London itself had only a quartet of totem stations, including **Kensington Olympia**, later SR owned.

Area Focus:
The Valleys of South Wales

Totems from South Wales have always been popular as collector's items and it is where we find most of the tongue-twisting totem names. Many stations were closed here from early BR times, as a 30-year decline of the coal industry from 1950 onwards saw the social fabric of the area destroyed, but the true Welsh grit remained! The map below indicates totem fitting did not occur equally in all the eighteen valleys that make up the area: the central valley, the Rhondda from **Pontypridd**, however, was well provisioned.

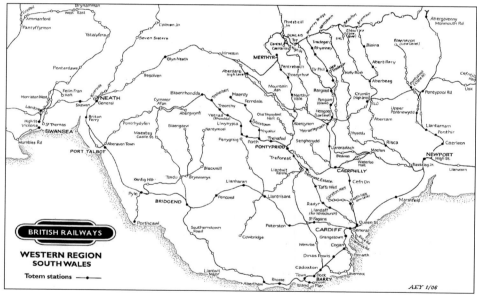

The Rhondda is at the centre of the valleys that stretch from the Swansea Tawe Valley in the west to the Welsh sections of the Wye Valley in the east. Totems from the Rhymney and Rhondda Valleys are depicted below, complemented by a classic pair at the top of the next page from the Merthyr Valley: these make a fine South Wales quartet.

Monmouthshire and Glamorgan contained copious amounts of rich coal and iron ore, all carried by railways to the nearby coastal ports. In 1910, over 10 million tonnes left the docks in Cardiff alone for export. The heart of the coal industry was the Rhondda Valley (actually two valleys shaped in a V). In 1860 it housed around 3,000 people: by 1910 it was 160,000 working in 66 pits that stretched up the valley(s). Travelling up the Rhondda Fawr (main), the sequence of totemed stations is **Porth**, **Dinas (Rhondda)**, **Tonypandy & Trealaw**, **Llwynypia**, **Ystrad Rhondda**, **Treorchy** and **Treherbert**. In the Rhondda Fach (little), the totemed stations were **Porth, Ynyshir, Tylorstown, Ferndale** and **Maerdy**: many are rare and others have not been seen since closure: all six Welsh totems depicted on this page are superb names.

Totem *in situ* in the Merthyr Valley.   Iconic sight in the Rhondda Valley.

When many of the stations were closed, everything was trashed pretty quickly, so those totems that have survived were fortunate indeed. There were neither roads nor railways here until 1850. Then in just a few years the Rhondda exploded industrially, transforming the once green valleys into a landscape dominated by coal mining.

If we move east, skipping over the Taff Valley with two lines through Mountain Ash to **Aberdare**, as they had few totems, we next encounter the Merthyr Valley where the giant Dowlais iron works was situated. This area saw very rapid development and possibly the greatest landscape transformation of all. Building of the single-track line was started in 1836, but it was not until 1856 that it was doubled tracked to cope with the huge growth in freight traffic. Brunel was the principal designer of the 24-mile route which astonishingly had twenty-three small feeder branches.

The journey runs from **Pontypridd** due north to **Merthyr.** In the past, **Pontypridd** had the longest platform of any station in the United Kingdom. The route from Cardiff had a fabulous array of totems at **Cardiff Queen Street**, **Radyr,** **Llandaff (for Whitchurch)**, **Taffs Well, Treforest, Pontypridd, Quakers Yard (Low Level), Merthyr Vale, Pentrebach** and **Merthyr** (made but not installed): a simply magical set of names.

The final valley route featured in this review is the Rhymney, whose railway was built for the sole purpose of connecting the iron workings and coal mines at the head of the valley to the port at Cardiff, 26 miles to the south. Incorporated in 1854, it was opened as a single track in sections over a six-year period. Other branches were added until around 1895, taking the total mileage to over 90 miles. Prior to inclusion into the enlarged GWR in 1923, the Rhymney Railway also ran the Taff Vale and Cardiff railways.

The Rhymney River forms the border between the counties of Glamorgan and Monmouthshire. Stations at the top of the valley lost their totems quickly and few have survived. Coming south down the valley, the totem sequence is **Rhymney, Pontlottyn, Tir Phil, Brithdir, Bargoed, Pengam (Glam), Hengoed, Ystrad Mynach, Llanbradach,** and **Caerphilly.** Sadly, some have not survived, so the collecting of the complete set is exceptionally challenging (see page 40 for a wonderful collection).

This is one of the few surviving valley lines today, the line to **Merthyr** and the one to **Treherbert** are the others: eight other valley lines in Central Glamorgan are gone. The extent of the cuts, detailed in the database pages, saw once-thriving places such as **Abertillery**, Tredegar, Mountain Ash, and **Aberdare** all lose their railways. Aberdare and Mountain Ash re-opened in 1988. **Cardiff–Barry** totems curiously continued out to **Aberthaw** (closed 1964). Other oddities include the abrupt end to totem stations west of **Blaenrhondda**, and isolated examples such as **Heath Halt Low Level**, **Glyn Neath, Blaina** and **Abertillery.** The Penarth loop never received totems.

Travels in the West Midlands

In 1845, a Bill was passed to build lines from Wolvercote Junction to **Worcester, Stourbridge, Dudley,** and **Wolverhampton,** with a branch to the Grand Junction Railway at Bushbury. The Bill also stated that the **Low Level** station should be built and run jointly with two other companies: the Shrewsbury & Birmingham Railway and the Birmingham, Wolverhampton & Dudley Railway (BW&DR). The GWR had reached **Birmingham** via the BW&DR and a logical extension of this would be to extend the line to **Wolverhampton.** These were the cornerstones to the routes subsequently operated by the enlarged GWR after 1923 and then by BR after 1947. Alan Young's map shows the ex-GWR route via **West Bromwich**, with the competing LMR lines to the south and north from **New Street** to **Wolverhampton High Level** shown in purple.

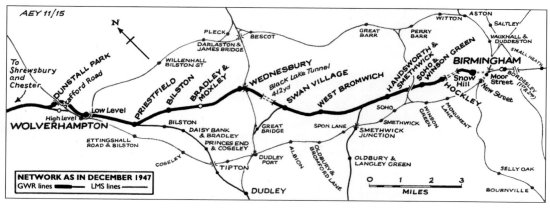

Over the decades, this route has, proven popular with travellers. In 1902, 43 trains ran daily, rising to 49 by 1939. In 1910, an agreement was signed with the South Eastern and Chatham Railway (SECR) so trains ran first to London Victoria and then *The Continental Express* ran through to Paris. Later, agreements with the London and South Western (LSWR) allowed trains through to Bournemouth, the forerunners of the legendary *Pines Express*. The famous Blue Pullman, which ran into **Paddington**, appeared in 1957 and initially this was popular, but ridership soon fell and by the time **Birmingham Snow Hill** eventually closed, the service had ceased.

The death knell for the ex-GWR line occurred in 1963 when the LMR took over. Electrification of the WCML soon afterwards meant the line through **Wednesbury** became redundant. There was a temporary increase in traffic while the upgrade work was in progress, but services were soon reduced on completion and the GWR line closed in stages. The last **Paddington** to Birkenhead express ran in March 1967 and the first section closed was **Priestfield** to **Dudle**y in September 1968. The whole line officially closed in March 1972, but sections remained open for freight usage.

Staffordshire had 21 WR totemed stations in its heyday, but only 8 after all the closures. Today, the line is reincarnated as the West Midlands Metro, with trams running past **Snow Hill** station, which has been rebuilt, and terminating at **New Street**. There are some lovely place names along the route (**Priestfield** and **Swan Village**) plus some 'totem filling' one- and two-line designs. A small selection is shown right.

In the West Midlands, the WR seemed to spend heavily on totems, with 100% provision on the lines around the Wolverhampton-Birmingham area. The totems here are almost all fully-flanged, fitted after the 1958 boundary changes to represent the WR's area tenure. The saturation

coverage included the quartet of superbly named 'Black Country' halts: **Old Hill (High Street) Halt, Darby End Halt, Windmill End Halt** and **Baptist End Halt**, all between **Old Hill** and **Blowers Green**.

The **Old Hill** to **Blowers Green** line opened on 1 March 1878 after some complex construction work in and around the widespread mining activities of the area. The cost of building bridges and undertaking earthworks was burdensome and without the financial might of the GWR, the line may never have been built. For BR to then put totems on all the halts where passenger traffic was limited was a little baffling. They also placed totems in the Dudley to Wolverhampton section, through **Tipton Five Ways, Princes End & Coseley** and **Daisy Bank & Bradley**; all superb names.

However, the ultimate future of all these lines was not to be in the WR, as they were transferred into LMR administration in 1963, and two-thirds of them were closed by 1972. Several of these Western totems, stranded in the LMR, survived *in situ* until the 1970s, well after BR's 1965 corporate identity policy had been adopted.

Summer Saturday at Snow Hill by Philip D. Hawkins FGRA. *Artist's copyright, used with written permission*

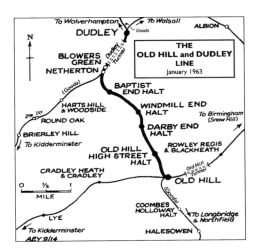

THE OLD HILL and DUDLEY LINE
January 1963

The map above shows the 3-mile long 'Bumble Hole' line, which towards the end carried only a handful of passengers daily. Alongside is a roundel from **Snow Hill** station; many of these once adorned the roof support columns in the central section of the station and conventional totems were found at the ends of the main platforms. Only **Snow Hill** and **Bristol Temple Meads** carried such 34-inch-diameter roundels.

Although much was swept away in a few short years, we have been fortunate to have some historic shots and paintings of much-loved lines, with **Snow Hill** and **Low Level** being magnets for trainspotting in the 1950s. **Snow Hill** station, nicknamed the 'Cathedral of Steam', was especially atmospheric on summer Saturdays, as named expresses headed to the seaside: going south, the *Cornishman*, and west, the *Cambrian Coast*.

The magnificent painting opposite by renowned artist Philip Hawkins FGRA captures the unique atmosphere on such a Saturday. The *Cornishman*, hauled by *Castle Class* No. 5070 *'Sir Daniel Gooch'*, arrives at Platform 7, thronged with passengers. For the journey to **Penzance**, the routing was via **Stratford-upon-Avon**, **Cheltenham Spa Malvern Road** and **Bristol.** Closure of the route from **Honeybourne** to **Cheltenham** meant BR using the ex-MR line from Birmingham to **Gloucester,** via the Lickey Incline, and once **Wolverhampton Low Level** closed, the service was extended, first to Sheffield and **Derby,** and later to **Bradford Forster Square**.

Rails Around Bristol

The next featured area is Bristol, home to Brunel's magnificent early trainshed, his mighty ship the SS *Great Britain*, the wonderful curve of **Temple Meads** and a host of collectable station totems. Bristol is both a city and county, steeped in British railway history: our database shows 14 totemed stations located in a relatively small area. **Temple Meads** is outstanding in railway history terms, which includes the broad gauge 'games', Brunel's own work and the wonderful architecture of Wyatt. The Tudor-style façade is a masterpiece and the massive, curved canopy makes this one of Britain's finest railway structures.

Electric overhead wires are not fitted here yet (at the time of writing, in 2021), as part of the **Paddington-Bristol** upgrade, so the station today is little different from that in totem times. In contrast, **York** has been rather spoilt by the overhead catenary wires and the track rationalisation. But structures such as **York**, Newcastle Central and **Temple Meads** were way ahead of their time and are testament to wonderful railway station design.

Temple Meads was also a great place for trainspotting in the mid-1950s, with 'Kings', 'Castles', 'Jubilees', 'Patriots' and other named engines all passing through every day. In 1954, the Bath Road depot (82A) on the eastern side of the lines at the southern end of the station complex had an allocation of 6 'Counties', 23 'Castles', 14 'Halls', plus numerous other engines. St. Philip's Marsh (82B), on the north side of the Gloucester line, had another 15 'Halls' plus 10 'Granges'. With trains coming in from **Paddington** to South Wales and the West Country, plus the cross-country expresses such as *The Cornishman*, *The Devon Scot* and *The Armada* to the north of England and Scotland, it is no wonder that so many artists have captured the heyday of steam here on canvas (such as on page 277) and so many trainspotters used to crowd the platforms. The classic pair of totems bearing the city name is seen below.

Bristol area railway map. *Alan Young*

Above: Bristol Temple Meads station viewed from the south.
Wikipedia Commons image

The map above shows that around 50% of the Bristol area stations were fitted with totems. The choice appears random, with a series of totems to **Avonmouth Dock** (but not beyond) and none on the **Portishead** branch, except for the terminus. There are also none on the ex-LMS line through Fishponds and Mangotsfield. **Filton Junction** was fitted, but not the next station, Patchway. **Henbury** also displayed totems, but not any of the stations on either side – a somewhat haphazard signage policy.

The quartet below shows stations close to **Temple Meads**, with the lower pair being the rarer (each 7 times in auction).

Many Bristol stations have been closed over the years, with the greatest cuts occurring south of the Avon on the line down to **Portishead**, and on the ex-Midland lines to the east through Mangotsfield. The picture above shows totems *in situ* on **Bristol Temple Meads'** long southern platform and left a roundel that used to hang inside the main central trainshed. The long south-facing platforms are shown to good effect in the panoramic photo of the station, above top, looking north towards the city. The demolition rubble in the right foreground is the remains of Bristol Bath Road (82A) engine shed: it closed on 28 September 1995 and was subsequently demolished.

The name Temple Meads derives from the Bristol's Temple Church and the original meadows that were alongside the River Avon, part of the Temple parish. Isambard Kingdom Brunel designed the first terminus on his broad-gauge line from **Paddington**. Built in the Tudor style, it opened in September 1840. The present station was expanded in the 1870s by Francis Fox and again in the 1930s by Percy Emerson Culverhouse: Brunel's Grade I-listed terminus is adjacent to the north.

King Edward II at Temple Meads by Bryan Evans 2013. *Author's collection*

Totems in Other Western Region Counties

In the 2002 book, the WR chapter concluded with an alphabetical review of desirable totems. The final section of this chapter presents a similar review, but arranged by county, hopefully to aid collectors in their local searches. Our database shows the WR had a presence in 17 English and 11 Welsh counties.

BERKSHIRE:

There were 16 stations fitted with WR totems in Berkshire. All have appeared in auction except **Abingdon** (now in Oxfordshire), where totems are not thought to have survived, but photo evidence shows them installed; it closed in 1963 and is believed to have been stripped of its signage soon afterwards. Rarities include **Hungerford,** 1 auction appearance; **Reading West,** 2; **Theale,** 2, and **Wargrave**, 3.

Pictures of rare totems from **Furze Platt Halt** and **Hungerford** are found on pages 294 and 295, but below is an equally uncommon photograph of a **Furze Platt Halt** totem *in situ*. All other station totems from Berkshire are fairly common, though the early flat variants from **Didcot** appear not to have survived, superseded by plentiful FF totems.

BRECKNOCKSHIRE

There are only two totemed stations found in this county and pictures of both feature in the database. **Llanwrtyd Wells** has been auctioned twice and **Brecon** only six times, the last appearance being recently in 2021; before that it was in auction a decade ago in 2011. The picture below shows the beauty around **Llanwrtyd Wells** with totems proudly displayed on both lamp standards and fence.

BRISTOL

This city and county were featured earlier, but we take the opportunity here of pointing out some other rarities. The first pair of totems from north of the city centre below have appeared in auction 5 and 6 times respectively.

The two totems above are on the line down to **Avonmouth** and both do come up in auction at regular intervals: 11 and 14 times respectively. **Ashley Hill** was closed in 1964, but **Sea Mills**, **Clifton Down** and **Shirehampton** are all still operational stations.

BUCKINGHAMSHIRE

This county has not featured prominently thus far. Quite a few of the traditionally coloured totems were overpainted in black-and-white (B&W)during the years of change. The database reveals 13 stations carried BR totems and none of them suffered closure during the Beeching and subsequent years. There are some rarities to collect, with both **Iver** and the LP version from **Langley (Bucks)** not appearing yet in auction. The one-line **Langley (Bucks)** appeared only as a B&W totem (9 times).

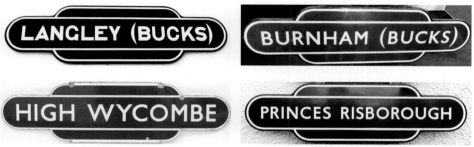

The line through the Chilterns saw much overpainting of the traditional chocolate totems into sterile B&W. Stations afforded this 'upgrade' included **Denham**, **Denham Golf Club**, **Gerrards Cross**, **Seer Green and Jordans** and **Beaconsfield**: traditional and BR 'upgrades' are shown below.

Finally the two most common Buckinghamshire station totems with 24 auction appearances each are **Bourne End** (6 traditional and 18 B&W) and **Taplow**.

CAERNARVONSHIRE

Five stations carried chocolate-and-cream totems, along the Cambrian Coast route. **Portmadoc** has appeared only 6 times in auction, with the unique **Penychain**, in Butlin's colours, yet to appear publicly.

Of the other three stations, **Criccieth** has 1 auction appearance, **Afon Wen**, 4, and **Pwllheli** is the most common having appeared 12 times.

CARDIGANSHIRE

Only three stations here, with **Lampeter** being closed in 1965. The rarest is **Borth**, with only 4 appearances: **Aberystwyth** has 17.

CARMARTHENSHIRE

Nine stations were fitted in this county, with two stations being closed during Beeching years (**Llandilo Bridge** and **St. Clears**). Most of the county's totems are rare with few auction appearances between them, in contrast to **Whitland** with 43 appearances in auction and Llanelly, 24. A rare quartet follows.

CHESHIRE

Just one station in Cheshire carried 'Chocolate and Cream'. This is **Saltney,** a 2007 TSG discovery and a minor station on the ex-GWR route a few miles west of Chester. Although the station was closed in 1960, the route is still open on the Shrewsbury to Chester line.

CORNWALL

This is a real collectors' area and whenever Cornish items appear in auction, a keen contest usually ensues, due to both rarity and because of the past holiday memories they invariably evoke. Rarities amongst the 19 totems available with 4 or fewer auction appearances include **Camborne, Carbis Bay, Falmouth, Helston, Looe, Newquay, Penzance, Perranporth, Saltash** and **St. Ives.** From recent photographic evidence it appears that only one totem was installed at **Carbis Bay**.

There were rather feeble attempts to overpaint lovely chocolate Cornish totems as BR had done in Buckinghamshire. The two photos below show BRs 'butchery'.

Four stations closed in the early 1960s, and **Falmouth** closed in 1970, only to re-open five years later. Fortunately, several Cornish branches survived Beeching's axe. Above is Alan Young's 1977 atmospheric photo of **Lostwithiel**, with totems still *in situ*.

Cornish totems seem desirable, whether rare or common. We think any from the sextet below would be welcome in any WR collection, especially **St. Austell** or **St. Erth**.

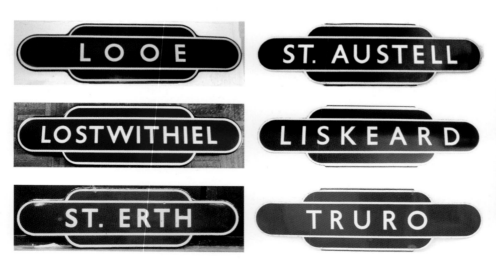

DENBIGHSHIRE

There are only six totems in this county, all of which have appeared in auction. The rarest is **Llangollen,** 3 times, followed by **Gwersyllt,** 6. Only **Llangollen** was closed (1965), but 20 years later it reopened as the area's heritage line terminus. It is a lovingly restored station situated next to the River Dee. The standard-gauge line is 10 miles long, running on part of the former Ruabon-Barmouth GWR route that closed in 1965. It was extended to **Corwen** in 2014.

Wrexham had two stations with totems, **Exchange** being less common than **General**.

DEVONSHIRE

This is another county favoured by collectors. There are 25 to complete the set, but **Teignmouth** totems rapidly disappeared, and none are thought to have survived. **Exminster**, **Keyham** and **South Molton** have yet to appear in auction and are great rarities. Uncommon Devon items are shown below and opposite top.

Paignton Summer 1972. *Rod Budd*

Kingswear Summer 1974. *Rod Budd*

Paignton totems are always sought after, and this picture taken in 1972 shows one proudly *in situ* on the first day of private operation of the line to Kingswear. Alongside is a lovely shot of nearby **Kingswear,** taken two years later. Notice the beautiful GWR crest on the carriage beneath the totem.

Both stations were on the former branch from **Newton Abbott**, and both now form part of the Dartmouth Steam Railway. The Devonshire network developed slowly and was not completed until after Queen Victoria's death. The county was, in a sense, split. The GWR developed the north east and south west and L&SWR developed the north west and south east; they crossed at **Exeter**. Sadly, the complete network operated for a mere 38 years, as Beeching closed many of the branch lines. During the 1960s, Devon lost some 40 stations from its total of nearly 120; a loss of one-third. Many were small country halts, but 8 were totemed WR stations, some of which have re-opened as part of heritage line development. One station not closed is the wonderfully named **St. Budeaux Ferry Road**. The name is pure Breton, coming from Saint Budoc, the Bishop of Dol (Brittany).

GLAMORGAN

This is the real heavyweight in the Western Region with 67 stations proudly carrying chocolate-and-creams. Many have not survived, so trying to collect a full set is a fruitless task. There are some simply wonderful names from a county with a rich cultural and industrial heritage. As well as its productive coal mining industry, the county was noted for copper, iron and tinplate, all requiring raw materials to be transported to various processing plants and then subsequent transfer of finished products to the major ports of **Cardiff** and **Swansea**. Totem appearances range from the very many, such as **Cardiff Queen Street**, 59 times in auction, or **Bridgend,** 40, to the ultra-rare, **Heath Halt Low Level**, 0; **Maerdy**, 0; or **Cefn On**, 2.

The photo below shows a **Ynyshir** totem we would have loved to have survived. During the writing of this book, we researched why the **Barry** area had four different totems: the result was unexpected. The two totems below were carried at the same station. Local people in the area always referred to the station as **Barrytown** and this name was carried until around 1959. When the HF totems were replaced by the more robust FF totems, BR decided to revert to the name of just **Barry**.

In addition, there is a terminus station at **Barry Island,** still open, and lines into the **Docks,** also still open, to facilitate exports. Now this is a wonderful rare quartet for Glamorgan collectors. Other desirables include the small group below.

GLOUCESTERSHIRE

A total of 20 different stations carrying totems are found in Gloucestershire, but over 50% were closed during the years of the cuts. We have no information regarding **Yate** and totems from here are not thought to have survived. The database pages contain photos of the three rarities: **Churchdown, Ham Mill Halt** and **Stonehouse (Burdett Road).** The county town is home to one of England's most beautiful cathedrals and both city stations carried totems. **Gloucester Eastgate** was a curiosity as an ex-LMS station that carried WR colours. It was, in many respects, a nicer station than **Gloucester Central.** Totems were made for **Cirencester Town** but never hung due to closure in 1964. **Chipping Campden,** not in auction, is also a rarity.

The quartet below used to hang proudly together in my (RF) former UK home. Three of these were closed, though **Ashchurch** was happily reopened in 1997. Only **Cheltenham Spa Lansdown,** opened in 1840 by B&GR, escaped Beeching's axe.

HEREFORDSHIRE

This beautiful county is represented by a small group of only six totems, with **Pontrilas** and **Ross-on-Wye** mustering just 1 and 2 public appearance respectively. Of the others, **Colwall** and **Ledbury** are often contested, but **Hereford** itself has a remarkable 27 auction appearances.

LONDON

There are just four stations here that carried the WR colours. Three of these feature in the database pages, and two variants are found on page 270.

MERIONETHSHIRE

This is a beautiful county at the heart of the Cambrian Coast with only seven stations that carried totems. Two stations were renamed, so the total number of totem variants available is ten, with two desirable names appearing below.

Middlesex extended from Enfield, Tottenham and Edmonton in the north-east to Staines, Feltham and Twickenham in the south-west. In addition to the main lines, the former county is criss-crossed by tube and overground lines, serving Finsbury Park, Highgate, Harrow and other places that were in the past well outside today's Greater London boundary. Some of the totems found here are common: **West Ealing** with 34 appearances, or **Hayes & Harlington** with 24, whilst others are rare, such as **Poyle Estate Halt,** 0; **Colnbrook Estate Halt,** 1; and **Staines West,** 2. A small selection is presented right.

MONMOUTHSHIRE

This ancient Welsh Marches county was formed in 1535 by the Laws of Wales Act but was abolished in 1972 when an expanded Monmouthshire was renamed as Gwent. Sixteen stations carried totems, but 1962 saw the effect of savage business economics, when most of them closed. There are some very desirable and attractively-named totems, but for three of them, **Aberbeeg**, **Ponthir** and **Upper Pontnewydd**, we have no information regarding any survivors. Six others have rarely been seen in public auctions, three of these once only.

The rugged coastline consists alternately of cliffs interspersed with stretches of sand and the area is generally the most mountainous in Wales; a large part of the Snowdonia National Park lies within Merionethshire. The famous castle at **Harlech** sits high on a rocky outcrop keeping guard over the whole bay. This is one of the strongest Welsh-speaking areas, epitomised by the two totems above.

MIDDLESEX

Fast WR lines cut through the heart of this county, west of London. It existed from Anglo-Saxon times until 1965, when most of the area became part of Greater London.

The former county is dotted with historic castles, all used to name GWR *'Castle'* Class locomotives. The names are well familiar to students of history: **Abergavenny**, Caldicot, **Chepstow**, Monmouth, Raglan and Usk. In addition, there are the beautiful ancient buildings of Llanthony Priory and Tintern Abbey. The pictures below, of two desirable lower-panel totems, complete this short county review.

MONTGOMERYSHIRE

This former Welsh county is named after one of William the Conqueror's Lieutenants, Roger de Montgomerie, who was the first Earl of Shrewsbury. Today it forms the northern section of the new Welsh county of Powys. The Cambrian Line from **Shrewsbury** to **Aberystwyth** and **Pwllheli** crosses Montgomeryshire from east to west. The county is represented by seven stations that carried totems, two of which closed in 1962. With the exceptions of **Machynlleth** and **Welshpool**, the remainder are fairly uncommon.

The county is almost completely mountainous, with a few fertile valleys amidst the hills. Two major rivers are found here, the River Severn flowing east into Shropshire and then down towards **Gloucester,** and the Dyfi, which flows west into the Irish Sea. The steep-sided valleys allowed the building of Lake Vyrnwy's reservoir and aqueduct system in the 1880s, to supply Liverpool with its drinking water.

OXFORDSHIRE

Oxfordshire was first recorded as an English county as far back as the 10th century. It is home to the University of Oxford, one of the world's most famous educational establishments, which was founded in 1096. The Cotswold Hills lie to the west, the Chilterns to the east, with a southern border formed by the River Thames. There are only seven stations that carried totems, the most common of which are **Henley-on-Thames,** 29 appearances, and **Oxford,** 25. All are known survivors and all have appeared in public auction. **Shipton for Burford** is the rarity (photo on page 299): it has appeared only once in auction and that in 1991.

These two pictures show uncommon **Kingham** totems displayed proudly in the Cotswold summer sunshine. The station opened in 1855 as Chipping Norton Junction.

The station which is on the Oxfordshire/Gloucestershire border, took its totem name in 1909. Alongside the **Kingham** totem below is an almost mint **Oxford**.

PEMBROKESHIRE

We move from the Cotswolds to wonderful West Wales and the county of Pembrokeshire. There are 13 totems to collect from this county, but we have no information about **Saundersfoot** and no survivors are currently known. Three of the 13 stations carrying totems were closed in 1964, but happily the remainder are still operational. The rarities here are **Milford Haven,** only just discovered; **Neyland,** no appearances, and **Pembroke,** 1, but the two stations in **Fishguard** and the one at **Tenby** also carried collectable totems.

Pembrokeshire's coastline is simply stunning. The whole of it forms the Pembrokeshire Coast National Park, which along with the Presili Hills, occupies a third of the county's area. The *Pembrokeshire Coast Express* ran from **Paddington** to **Pembroke Dock** from 1953 and FGW ran their HST 125s there on summer Saturdays until 2019. For those interested in castles, there are Carew, Cilgerran, Manorbier and **Pembroke** to visit. Like **Harlech** to the north, Cilgerran Castle commands a most dramatic location perched high above the Teifi Gorge. Pembrokeshire's county town is **Haverfordwest,** another collectors' treasure: a full totem for your money here!

RADNORSHIRE

This is a central Welsh county formed in the Laws of Wales Acts of 1535 onwards, but in 1974 its authority was abolished and it became part of Powys. There are only four stations carrying totems in the county, but two of them were closed in 1962. The combined number of auction appearances is only 12 so Radnorshire (or more correctly) Sir Faesyfed totems are rare, with **Llandrindod Wells** at just 7 appearances the most common: two of Radnorshire's totems follow.

SHROPSHIRE

This beautiful county stakes a claim to be the birthplace of Britain's industrial revolution in the 18th century. Historians have ample opportunity to study industrial archaeology in the Coalbrookdale/Ironbridge/Coalport area, classed as a UNESCO World Heritage site. Most of the south and west is an AONB (Area of Outstanding Natural Beauty) with outstanding scenery around **Church Stretton**. There are 16 WR stations that carried totems, some of which are rare: **Cosford,** 1 appearance and **Ellesmere,** 2, whilst the county town of **Shrewsbury** has 41. **Wellington,** my home town (RF), had two totem variants shown alongside. The earlier HF version, some with brown flanges is shown above and the less common FF version, is alongside. It would have been wonderful if Iron Bridge and Broseley (note the actual station name) or Coalbrookdale had been totem-fitted but, sadly. it was not to be.

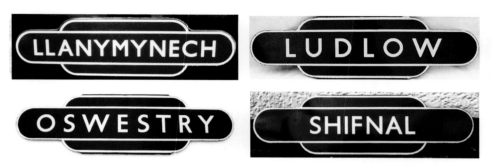

The most common Somerset totems are **Taunton,** 36; and **Keynsham & Somerdale,** 21; (2L version only 3 times). **Bath Spa** and **Wellington** both have 7.

There is one curiosity for the county, concerning the town of **Knighton** in Radnorshire. The town straddles the River Teme, the border between England and Wales. Our 2002 book contained an error as **Knighton** station is in Shropshire, but the town is in Wales!

SOMERSET

With 19 different station totems to collect, this county offers some very choice names. Somerset is a largely rural county of rolling hills, including the Blackdowns, the Mendips, the Quantocks and the superb Exmoor National Park, together with large flat expanses of land that includes the Somerset Levels. The city of **Bath** is famous for its Georgian architecture and is another UNESCO World Heritage Site. The seaside towns of **Weston-super-Mare,** Burnham-on-Sea and **Minehead** have attracted day-trippers for decades, initially arriving by train. Somerset rarities include **Bathampton,** 2 appearances; **Evercreech Junction,** 3; **Oldfield Park,** 3, and **Radstock West,** 0. **Bath Green Park,** the northern terminus of the S&D, is on many want lists and has surprisingly been in auction 9 times; **Weston Milton** has 9 appearances.

STAFFORDSHIRE

Industrial Staffordshire is criss-crossed by both WR and LMR railways. There are 21 chocolate-and-creams plus a further 64 LMR totems making this one of the higher overall county totals of stations that carried totems. Savage cuts in the 1960s and 1970s saw over 60% of WR stations closed, as the LMR lines were upgraded. Because of this most totems from WR stations have appeared in auctions fewer than 5 times each, including **Bilston West** and **Brierley Hill,** which have not yet appeared. This contrasts with **Swan Village,** 24, and **Wolverhampton Low Level,** 29. A rare quartet is shown left.

The first railway to be built across the county was the Grand Junction, between **Birmingham, Wolverhampton, Stafford** and Crewe. Amalgamations in and around the area led to the eventual formation of the London & North Western, with **Stafford** emerging as a major hub. However, the suspension of passenger services on the **Stafford** to **Uttoxeter** line in 1939 and Beeching's closure of the **Stafford** to **Wellington** line in 1964 eliminated the station's east-west traffic. The station is on the WCML and underwent major rebuilding between 1961 and 1962 using the Brutalist style.

Wolverhampton Low Level has also undergone a major transformation into the Grand Station banqueting hall and wedding venue, but it looked forlorn after closure.

WARWICKSHIRE

Totems were found at 33 stations in Warwickshire at the peak of totem signage. Of these, eight were closed, most of them in 1972, and two have subsequently re-opened (**Snow Hill** and an enlarged **Moor Street** incorporating the former terminus). When station signs were removed, collecting had gathered pace, so most totems, direction signs and other station enamels were saved. As a result, many Warwickshire totems are fairly common, having appeared 20 times or more in auction; two less common totems (4 appearances each) are shown right.

The shape of Warwickshire today is vastly different from the historic county and the boundaries that existed in the totem years. Areas historically part of Warwickshire included Coventry, Solihull, and most of Birmingham, all three becoming part of the West Midlands Metropolitan county in April 1974, following local government re-organisation. In 1931, Warwickshire was ceded the town of Shipston-on-Stour from Worcestershire and several villages, including **Long Marston** and Welford-on-Avon, from Gloucestershire. In addition, some stations became part of Warwickshire when Birmingham absorbed parts of Worcestershire in the 1930s. All this has meant we have corrected stations originally listed in the 2002 book. For those collectors wanting many letters on their totems, a 'wordy' sextet appears left!

The station at **Knowle & Dorridge** has been called Knowle, Dorridge and the actual totem name on different occasions during its lifetime. The official station name included 'and' instead of the ampersand that appears on the totem above. The ampersand was almost certainly used to make the wording fit without reducing letter size. This station was on the main ex-GWR line from Birmingham via **Warwick** to **Paddington** that opened in 1852. This passed through **Solihull, Widney Manor** and **Lapworth** before reaching **Hatton** where it splits to head south to **Stratford-upon-Avon**. All these lines were generously fitted with totems.

Over the years many railway books have included fine shots of *'Kings'* and *'Castles'* at speed through all these stations or working hard climbing Hatton Bank on the journey northwards. The bank was a 6-mile climb including a 3-mile section of 1 in 103, the steepest on the whole route from **Paddington** to **Birmingham Snow Hill**.

WILTSHIRE

This is traditionally thought of as a 'Southern' county, but WR lines crossed it heading for the West Country. West Country lines from **Paddington** run via **Swindon** to **Bristol**, then south to **Taunton** or via **Westbury** to **Taunton** direct. The WR presence is actually strong with sixteen stations carrying chocolate-and-creams. Closures between 1964 and 1966 halved this number, and most totems from Wiltshire are considered very collectable. With the exceptions of **Chippenham**, 35 appearances, and **Swindon,** 28, most of the remainder have not been publicly auctioned very often. We have no information about **Pewsey** totems.

Of this quartet, only **Castle Cary** was spared the axe. When **Devizes** closed in 1966, the track Rights of Way were quickly sold, so no possibility of either a reinstatement of the line or a recreational pathway along the former trackbed: a town of over 12,000 inhabitants is now denied a station. **Calne** totems were made but not used.

This trio of totems and their stations all survived the Beeching cuts and notice how much TLC is being given to the **Freshford** station gardens.

WORCESTERSHIRE

The final county, where chocolate-and-creams hung, is Worcestershire: here 26 stations carried them. Many are rare, with **Blakedown** and **Fladbury** not being in auction, **Baptist End Halt** and **Darby End Halt,** 1 each and **Grimes Hill & Wythall**, **Henwick**, **Malvern Wells** and **Stourbridge Town,** 2 each. **Stourbridge Junction** variants have appeared a total of 40 times. The quartet left shows totem faces filled to the brim.

The county is first recorded in 927 AD and in 1642 saw the first major battle in the English Civil War. Its county boundaries have been tinkered with for centuries. In 1965, **Smethwick** and **Rowley Regis** were added to the Borough of Warley, and **Dudley** was ceded to Staffordshire. Even bigger changes occurred in 1974 when Halesowen and **Stourbridge** were ceded to **Dudley,** which then joined with towns and cities in Staffordshire and Warwickshire to form the County of the West Midlands.

The rest of Worcestershire was amalgamated with Herefordshire. In 1998, these two counties were separated, and Worcestershire exists again.

It is a lovely rolling county, with the River Severn, Elgar's Malvern Hills, the historic city of Worcester, beautiful Broadway and **Droitwich Spa** all being places of note. The Gloucestershire and Warwickshire Railway is working miracles reinstating the former GWR main line from **Cheltenham** through beautiful Broadway and on towards **Honeybourne**, with the aim of one day re-connecting with **Stratford-Upon-Avon**.

A collectable Worcestershire totem still in *situ* in July 1979. *Alan Young*

Above: Seer Green & Jordans in 1976. *Alan Young*

Right: Ystrad Mynach in 1973. *Alan Young*

Closure

Initially, the Western Region divested itself of route miles quite slowly: 3,700 miles in 1951 down to 3,000 miles by 1965, but station closures over the same period saw 1,296 stopping points reduced to just 422. For me (RF) this timeframe has many happy early memories, with scenes such as these above immortalised by Alan Young.

Station Name	County in 1956	Layout	Flange	Closed	Auction	Survived
ABERBEEG	Monmouthshire		FF	1962		
ABERCYNON	Glamorgan		FF		•	•
ABERDARE HIGH LEVEL *re-opened 1988	Glamorgan	LP	HF	1964*	•	•
ABERDOVEY	Merionethshire		FF		•	•
ABERGAVENNY MONMOUTH ROAD	Monmouthshire	LP	HF/FF		•	•
ABERTHAW	Glamorgan		FF	1964		•
ABERTILLERY	Monmouthshire		FF	1962	•	•
ABERYSTWYTH	Cardiganshire		HF/FF		•	•
ABINGDON	Berkshire		HF	1963		
ACOCKS GREEN & SOUTH YARDLEY	Warwickshire	1L	FF		•	•
ACOCKS GREEN & SOUTH YARDLEY	Warwickshire	2L	FF		•	•
AFON WEN	Caernarvonshire		FF	1964	•	•
ALBRIGHTON some with brown flanges	Shropshire		HF		•	•
ASHCHURCH FOR TEWKESBURY *re-opened 1997	Gloucestershire	LP	FF	1971*	•	•
ASHLEY HILL	Bristol		FF	1964	•	•
AVONMOUTH DOCK	Bristol		FF		•	•
BADMINTON	Gloucestershire		HF	1968	•	•
BAPTIST END HALT	Worcestershire	LP	FF	1964	•	•
BARGOED	Glamorgan		FF		•	•
BARMOUTH	Merionethshire		HF		•	•
BARMOUTH JUNCTION Morfa Mawddach in 1960	Merionethshire	1L	HF			
BARMOUTH JUNCTION Morfa Mawddach in 1960	Merionethshire	LP	FF			•
BARRY name carried from 1959	Glamorgan		FF		•	•
BARRY DOCK	Glamorgan		FF		•	•
BARRY ISLAND	Glamorgan		FF		•	•
BARRYTOWN name carried up to 1959	Glamorgan		HF		•	•
BATHAMPTON	Somerset		FF	1966	•	•
BATH GREEN PARK	Somerset	LP	HF	1966	•	•
BATH SPA also early style flat totem	Somerset		HF		•	•
BEACONSFIELD (some o/p B&W)	Buckinghamshire		HF/FF		•	•
BEARLEY	Warwickshire		FF		•	•
BEDMINSTER	Bristol		FF		•	•
BEDWYN	Wiltshire		FF		•	•
BICESTER NORTH	Oxfordshire		HF		•	•
BILSTON (CENTRAL)	Staffordshire	LP	FF	1972	•	•

1L = one line: 2L = two line: LP = lower panel

Station Name	County in 1956	Layout	Flange	Closed	Auction	Survived
BILSTON WEST	Staffordshire		FF	1962		•
BIRMINGHAM MOOR ST.^^ *new station 2010	Warwickshire	LP	FF	1987*	•	•
BIRMINGHAM SNOW HILL *re-opened 1987	Warwickshire	LP	FF	1972*	•	•
BIRMINGHAM SNOW HILL *re-opened 1987	Warwickshire	LP	Roundel	1972*	•	•
BLACKWELL	Worcestershire		FF	1966	•	•
BLAENRHONDDA	Glamorgan		FF	1968	•	•
BLAINA	Monmouthshire		FF	1962		•
BLAKEDOWN	Worcestershire		FF			•
BLOWERS GREEN	Worcestershire		FF	1962	•	•
BORDESLEY	Warwickshire		FF		•	•
BORTH brown flanges	Cardiganshire		HF		•	•
BOURNE END * = black and white	Buckinghamshire		HF/FF*		•	•
BRADFORD-ON-AVON	Wiltshire		FF		•	•
BRECON	Brecknockshire		HF		•	•
BRENT	Devonshire		HF	1964	•	•
BRETTELL LANE	Staffordshire		FF		•	•
BRIDGEND	Glamorgan		FF		•	•
BRIDGWATER	Somerset		FF		•	•
BRIERLEY HILL	Staffordshire		FF		•	•
BRISTOL STAPLETON ROAD	Bristol	LP	FF		•	•
BRISTOL TEMPLE MEADS	Bristol	LP	HF		•	•
BRISTOL TEMPLE MEADS	Bristol	LP	Roundel		•	•
BRITHDIR	Glamorgan		FF		•	•
BRITON FERRY *re-opened 1994	Glamorgan		FF	1964*	•	•
BROMSGROVE	Worcestershire		FF		•	•
BUILDWAS	Shropshire		FF	1963	•	•
BUILTH ROAD HIGH LEVEL	Radnorshire	LP	HF		•	•
BUILTH WELLS	Radnorshire		FF	1962	•	•
BURNHAM (BUCKS)	Buckinghamshire		FF		•	•
CADOXTON	Glamorgan		FF		•	•
CAERLEON	Monmouthshire		FF	1962	•	•
CAERPHILLY	Glamorgan		FF		•	•
CALNE	Wiltshire		FF	1965	•	•
CAMBORNE	Cornwall		FF			•

^^ Birmingham Moor St. through platforms opened 2002: new enlarged station opened 2010 incorporating terminus platforms closed in 1987

1L = one line: 2L = two line: LP = lower panel

Station Name	County in 1956	Layout	Flange	Closed	Auction	Survived
CARBIS BAY	Cornwall		FF		•	•
CARDIFF GENERAL	Glamorgan	LP	FF		•	•
CARDIFF GENERAL	Glamorgan	1L	HF			
CARDIFF QUEEN STREET	Glamorgan	LP	HF		•	•
CARMARTHEN	Carmarthen		HF		•	•
CASTLE CARY	Somerset		FF		•	•
CEFN ON	Glamorgan		FF	1986	•	•
CHACEWATER	Cornwall		FF	1964	•	•
CHARLBURY	Oxfordshire		FF		•	•
CHELTENHAM SPA LANSDOWN	Gloucestershire	LP	HF		•	•
CHELTENHAM SPA MALVERN ROAD	Gloucestershire	LP	HF/FF	1966	•	•
CHEPSTOW	Monmouthshire		HF		•	•
CHIPPENHAM	Wiltshire		HF		•	•
CHIPPING CAMPDEN	Oxfordshire		FF	1966		•
CHIRK	Denbighshire		FF		•	
CHURCHDOWN	Gloucestershire		HF	1964	•	•
CHURCH STRETTON	Shropshire		FF		•	•
CIRENCESTER TOWN	Gloucestershire		FF	1964	•	•
CLARBESTON ROAD	Pembrokeshire		HF		•	•
CLIFTON DOWN	Bristol		FF		•	•
CLYNDERWEN *HF version not in auction*	Pembrokeshire		HF/FF			•
CODSALL *some brown flanges*	Shropshire		HF/FF		•	•
COGAN	Glamorgan		FF		•	•
COLNBROOK ESTATE HALT	Middlesex	LP	FF	1965	•	•
COLWALL	Herefordshire		FF		•	•
CORSHAM	Wiltshire		FF	1965		•
CORWEN	Merionethshire		FF	1964	•	•
COSFORD	Shropshire		HF		•	•
CRADLEY HEATH	Staffordshire		FF		•	•
CRADLEY HEATH & CRADLEY	Staffordshire		FF		•	•
CRAVEN ARMS & STOKESAY	Shropshire		FF		•	•
CRICCIETH	Caernarvonshire		HF		•	•
CRUMLIN HIGH LEVEL	Monmouthshire	LP	FF	1964	•	•
CULLOMPTON	Devonshire		FF	1964	•	•

1L = one line: 2L = two line: LP = lower panel

Station Name		County in 1956	Layout	Flange	Closed	Auction	Survived
DAISY BANK & BRADLEY		Staffordshire		FF	1962	•	•
DANZEY (FOR TANWORTH)		Warwickshire	LP	FF		•	•
DARBY END HALT		Worcestershire	LP	FF	1964		•
DAUNTSEY		Wiltshire		FF	1965		•
DAWLISH		Devonshire		HF/FF		•	•
DAWLISH WARREN		Devonshire		FF		•	•
DENHAM		Buckinghamshire		HF/FF		•	•
DENHAM	Overpainted B & W	Buckinghamshire		FF		•	•
DENHAM GOLF CLUB	(some o/p B&W)	Buckinghamshire		FF		•	•
DEVIZES		Wiltshire		FF	1966	•	•
DEVONPORT	black & white only	Devonshire		FF		•	•
DIDCOT		Berkshire		FF		•	•
DIDCOT	early flat totem	Berkshire		Flat			
DINAS POWIS		Glamorgan		FF		•	•
DINAS (RHONDDA)		Glamorgan	?	FF			
DOLGELLAU	name carried from 1960	Merionethshire		FF	1965	•	•
DOLGELLEY	name carried to 1960	Merionethshire		FF		•	•
DOVEY JUNCTION		Montgomeryshire		FF		•	•
DROITWICH SPA		Worcestershire		HF/FF		•	•
DUDLEY		Worcestershire		FF	1964	•	•
DUNSTALL PARK		Staffordshire		FF	1968	•	•
EALING BROADWAY		Middlesex		HF		•	•
EARLSWOOD LAKES		Warwickshire		FF			•
ELLESMERE		Shropshire		FF	1965		•
EVERCREECH JUNCTION		Somerset		FF	1966		•
EVESHAM		Worcestershire		HF			•
EXETER ST. DAVID'S		Devonshire	LP	HF		•	•
EXETER (ST. THOMAS)		Devonshire		HF		•	•
EXMINSTER	painted wood	Devonshire		wood	1964		
FALMOUTH	*re-opened 1975	Cornwall		HF	1970*	•	•
FERNDALE		Glamorgan		FF	1964	•	
FERRYSIDE		Carmarthenshire		FF		•	
FILTON JUNCTION		Gloucestershire		FF		•	•

1L = one line: 2L = two line: LP = lower panel

Station Name	County in 1956	Layout	Flange	Closed	Auction	Survived
FISHGUARD & GOODWICK *re-opened 2012*	Pembrokeshire		HF	1964*	•	•
FISHGUARD HARBOUR	Pembrokeshire		HF		•	•
FLADBURY	Worcestershire		FF	1966		•
FRESHFORD	Wiltshire		FF		•	•
FROME	Somerset		HF		•	•
FURZE PLATT HALT	Berkshire	LP	FF		•	•
GERRARDS CROSS *(some o/p B&W)*	Buckinghamshire		HF/FF		•	•
GLOUCESTER CENTRAL	Gloucestershire	LP	HF		•	•
GLOUCESTER EASTGATE *some HF brown flanges*	Gloucestershire	LP	HF/FF	1975	•	•
GLYN NEATH	Glamorgan		HF	1964	•	•
GOBOWEN	Shropshire		FF		•	•
GORING & STREATLY	Berkshire		HF		•	•
GORSEINON	Glamorgan		FF	1964	•	•
GOWERTON NORTH	Glamorgan		FF		•	•
GRANGETOWN	Glamorgan		FF		•	•
GREAT BRIDGE SOUTH	Staffordshire		FF	1964	•	•
GREAT MALVERN	Worcestershire		HF		•	•
GRIMES HILL & WYTHALL	Worcestershire		FF		•	•
GWERSYLLT	Denbighshire		FF		•	•
GWINEAR ROAD	Cornwall		HF	1964	•	•
HAGLEY	Worcestershire		FF		•	•
HALL GREEN	Warwickshire		FF		•	•
HAM MILL HALT	Gloucestershire		FF	1964	•	•
HANDSWORTH & SMETHWICK	Warwickshire	1L/2L	FF	1972	•	•
HANWELL	Middlesex		FF		•	•
HARLECH	Merionethshire		FF		•	•
HATTON	Warwickshire		FF		•	•
HAVERFORDWEST	Pembrokeshire		HF		•	•
HAYES & HARLINGTON *black & white only*	Middlesex		FF		•	•
HEATH HALT LOW LEVEL	Glamorgan	LP	Flat			•
HELSTON *early flat type sign*	Cornwall		special	1962	•	•
HENBURY	Gloucestershire		FF	1964	•	•
HENGOED (LOW LEVEL)	Glamorgan	LP	FF		•	•

1L = one line: 2L = two line: LP = lower panel

Station Name	County in 1956	Layout	Flange	Closed	Auction	Survived
HENLEY-IN-ARDEN	Warwickshire		FF		•	•
HENLEY-ON-THAMES	Oxfordshire		HF		•	•
HENWICK	Worcestershire		FF	1965	•	•
HEREFORD *some with brown flanges*	Herefordshire		HF/FF		•	•
HIGHBRIDGE & BURNHAM-ON-SEA *some brown*	Somerset	2L	HF*		•	•
HIGHBRIDGE for BURNHAM-ON-SEA	Somerset	2L	FF		•	•
HIGH WYCOMBE *(some o/p B&W)*	Buckinghamshire		HF		•	•
HOCKLEY	Warwickshire		FF	1972	•	•
HONEYBOURNE *re-opened 1981*	Worcestershire		HF	1969*	•	•
HORFIELD	Gloucestershire		FF	1964	•	•
HUNGERFORD	Berkshire		FF		•	•
INSTOW	Devonshire		HF	1965	•	•
IVER	Buckinghamshire		FF			•
JOHNSTON (PEM)	Pembrokeshire		HF		•	•
KEMBLE	Gloucestershire		HF		•	•
KENSINGTON OLYMPIA	London	LP	FF		•	•
KENSINGTON (OLYMPIA)	London	LP	FF		•	•
KENSINGTON (OLYMPIA) *cream o/p variant*	London	2L	FF*		•	•
KEYHAM	Devonshire		FF			•
KEYNSHAM & SOMERDALE	Somerset	1L/2L	FF		•	•
KIDDERMINSTER	Worcestershire		HF		•	•
KIDWELLY	Carmarthenshire		HF		•	•
KINGHAM	Oxfordshire		HF		•	•
KINGSBRIDGE	Devonshire		HF	1963	•	•
KINGSKERSWELL	Devonshire		FF		•	•
KINGS NYMPTON *early flat sign*	Devonshire		special		•	•
KINGSWEAR *Heritage station from 1972*	Devonshire		FF	1971*	•	•
KNIGHTON	Shropshire		FF		•	•
KNOWLE & DORRIDGE	Warwickshire		FF		•	•
LAMPETER	Cardiganshire		FF	1965	•	•
LANDORE	Glamorgan		FF	1964	•	•

1L = one line: 2L = two line: LP = lower panel

Station Name		County in 1956	Layout	Flange	Closed	Auction	Survived
LANGLEY (BUCKS)	black & white only	Buckinghamshire		FF		•	•
LANGLEY BUCKS		Buckinghamshire	LP	HF			•
LAPWORTH		Warwickshire		FF		•	•
LAWRENCE HILL		Bristol		FF		•	•
LEAMINGTON SPA GENERAL		Warwickshire	LP	HF		•	•
LEAMINGTON SPA MILVERTON		Warwickshire	LP	HF	1965	•	•
LEDBURY		Herefordshire		HF		•	•
LEOMINSTER		Herefordshire		FF		•	•
LIMPLEY STOKE		Wiltshire		HF	1966	•	•
LISKEARD	some were o/p B&W	Cornwall		HF		•	•
LITTLE KIMBLE	early non-standard design	Buckinghamshire		Flat		•	•
LLANBRADACH		Glamorgan		FF		•	•
LLANDAFF (FOR WHITCHURCH)		Glamorgan	LP	FF		•	•
LLANDILO BRIDGE		Carmarthenshire		FF	1963	•	•
LLANDOVERY		Carmarthenshire		FF		•	•
LLANDRINDOD WELLS		Radnorshire		HF		•	•
LLANELLY		Carmarthenshire		HF/FF		•	•
LLANGOLLEN	*new heritage station 1981	Denbighshire		FF	1965*	•	•
LLANHARAN	*re-opened 2007	Glamorgan		HF	1964*		•
LLANIDLOES		Montgomeryshire		FF	1962	•	•
LLANTARNAM		Monmouthshire		FF	1962		•
LLANTRISANT	*re-opened as Pontyclun 1992	Glamorgan		FF	1964*	•	•
LLANWRTYD WELLS		Brecknockshire		FF		•	•
LLANYMYNECH		Shropshire		FF	1967	•	•
LLWYNYPIA		Glamorgan		FF		•	•
LONG MARSTON		Warwickshire		HF	1966	•	•
LOOE		Cornwall		FF		•	•
LOSTWITHIEL		Cornwall		HF/FF		•	•
LUDLOW		Shropshire		HF		•	•
LYDNEY JUNCTION		Gloucestershire		FF		•	•
LYE		Worcestershire		FF		•	•
MACHYNLLETH		Montgomeryshire		HF/FF		•	•
MAERDY		Glamorgan		FF	1964		•
MAIDENHEAD		Berkshire		HF/FF		•	•
MALVERN LINK	some painted black on white	Worcestershire		HF		•	•

1L = one line: 2L = two line: LP = lower panel

Station Name	County in 1956	Layout	Flange	Closed	Auction	Survived
MALVERN WELLS	Worcestershire		HF	1965	•	•
MARSHFIELD	Monmouthshire		HF/FF	1959	•	•
MATHRY ROAD	Pembrokeshire		FF	1964	•	•
MELKSHAM *re-opened 1985	Wiltshire		FF	1966*	•	•
MERTHYR	Glamorgan		FF		•	•
METHYR VALE	Glamorgan		FF		•	
MILFORD HAVEN	Pembrokeshire		HF			•
MINEHEAD *Heritage station from 1976	Somerset		HF/FF	1971*	•	
MOAT LANE JUNCTION	Montgomeryshire	LP	FF	1962		
MONTGOMERY	Montgomeryshire		FF		•	•
MONTPELIER	Bristol		FF		•	•
MORFA MAWDDACH ^^ name carried from 1960	Merionethshire		FF		•	•
MORETON-IN-MARSH early design	Gloucestershire		Flat		•	•
MORTEHOE & WOOLACOMBE	Devon		HF	1970	•	•
NAILSEA & BACKWELL	Somerset		FF		•	•
NEATH GENERAL	Glamorgan		HF		•	•
NEATH GENERAL	Glamorgan	LP	FF		•	•
NEWBURY	Berkshire		HF/FF		•	•
NEWPORT HIGH STREET	Monmouthshire	LP	HF		•	•
NEWQUAY some were o/p black & white	Cornwall		HF		•	•
NEWTON ABBOT	Devonshire		FF		•	•
NEWTOWN	Montgomeryshire		HF		•	
NEYLAND	Pembrokeshire		HF	1964		•
OAKENGATES	Shropshire		HF		•	•
OLDBURY & LANGLEY GREEN	Worcestershire	1L/2L	FF		•	•
OLDFIELD PARK	Somerset		FF		•	•
OLD HILL	Staffordshire		FF		•	•
OLD HILL (HIGH STREET) HALT	Staffordshire	LP	FF	1964	•	•
OLTON	Warwickshire		FF		•	•
OSWESTRY	Shropshire		HF	1966	•	•
OXFORD	Oxfordshire		FF			•
PADDINGTON (some o/p B&W)	London		FF		•	•
PAIGNTON	Devonshire		FF		•	•
PANGBOURNE	Berkshire		FF			•

^^ Previous name up to 1960 was Barmouth Junction

1L = one line: 2L = two line: LP = lower panel

Station Name		County in 1956	Layout	Flange	Closed	Auction	Survived
PAR		Cornwall		HF/FF		•	•
PARSON STREET		Bristol		FF		•	•
PEMBREY & BURRY PORT		Carmarthenshire		HF		•	•
PEMBROKE		Pembrokeshire		HF		•	•
PEMBROKE DOCK		Pembrokeshire		FF		•	•
PENCOED	*re-opened 1992	Glamorgan		HF	1964*		
PENGAM (GLAM)		Glamorgan	LP	FF		•	•
PENTREBACH		Glamorgan		FF		•	•
PENYCHAIN	unique blue & yellow	Caernarvonshire		FF			•
PENZANCE		Cornwall		HF		•	•
PERRANPORTH		Cornwall		FF	1963	•	•
PERSHORE		Worcestershire		HF		•	•
PETERSTON	New discovery	Glamorgan		HF	1964		•
PEWSEY		Wiltshire		FF			
PILNING (HIGH LEVEL)		Gloucestershire	LP	FF		•	•
PONTHIR		Monmouthshire		FF	1962		
PONTLOTTYN		Glamorgan		FF		•	•
PONTRILAS		Herefordshire		FF	1958		•
PONTYPOOL (CRANE STREET)		Monmouthshire	LP	FF	1962		•
PONTYPOOL ROAD		Monmouthshire		FF		•	•
PONTYPRIDD		Glamorgan		HF		•	•
PORTH		Glamorgan		FF		•	•
PORTHCAWL		Glamorgan		FF	1963	•	•
PORTISHEAD		Somerset		HF	1964	•	•
PORTMADOC		Caernarvonshire		HF		•	•
PORT TALBOT		Glamorgan		HF/FF		•	•
POYLE ESTATE HALT		Middlesex	1L	HF/FF	1965		
PRIESTFIELD		Staffordshire		FF	1972	•	•
PRINCES END & COSELEY		Staffordshire		FF	1962	•	•
PRINCES RISBOROUGH	(some o/p B&W)	Buckinghamshire		FF		•	•
PURTON		Wiltshire		FF	1964	•	•
PWLLHELI		Caernarvonshire		HF		•	•
PYLE	*new station on site 1994	Glamorgan		FF	1964*	•	•
QUAKERS YARD (LOW LEVEL)		Glamorgan	LP	FF		•	•

1L = one line: 2L = two line: LP = lower panel

Station Name		County in 1956	Layout	Flange	Closed	Auction	Survived
RADSTOCK WEST	*early design	Somerset		Flat*	1959		•
RADYR		Glamorgan		FF		•	•
READING GENERAL	*some FF aluminium variants	Berkshire		HF/FF*		•	•
READING WEST		Berkshire		FF		•	•
REDLAND		Bristol		FF		•	•
REDRUTH	some o/p black & white	Cornwall		HF		•	•
RHAYADER		Radnorshire		FF	1962	•	•
RHOOSE	*re-opened 2005	Glamorgan		FF	1964*	•	•
RHYMNEY		Glamorgan		FF		•	•
RISCA	*re-opened 2008	Monmouthshire		FF	1962*	•	•
ROSS-ON-WYE		Herefordshire		FF	1964	•	•
ROUND OAK		Staffordshire		HF/FF		•	•
ROWLEY REGIS & BLACKHEATH		Worcestershire	1L	FF		•	•
ROYAL OAK	Underground platform only	London		HF/FF		•	•
RUABON		Denbighshire		FF		•	•
SALTASH		Cornwall		FF		•	•
SALTFORD		Somerset		HF	1970	•	•
SALTNEY	New discovery	Cheshire		FF	1960		
SAUNDERSFOOT		Pembrokeshire		FF			
SEA MILLS		Bristol		FF		•	•
SEER GREEN AND JORDANS	(some o/p B&W)	Buckinghamshire	1L	FF		•	•
SEER GREEN & JORDANS		Buckinghamshire	1L	FF		•	•
SEVERN TUNNEL JUNCTION		Monmouthshire	LP	FF		•	•
SHIFNAL	brown flanges	Shropshire		HF		•	•
SHIPTON FOR BURFORD		Oxfordshire	LP	FF		•	•
SHIREHAMPTON		Bristol		FF		•	•
SHIRLEY		Warwickshire		FF		•	•
SHREWSBURY		Shropshire		HF/FF		•	•
SKEWEN	*re-opened 1994	Glamorgan		HF	1964*		
SLOUGH		Berkshire		HF/FF			
SMALL HEATH & SPARKBROOK		Warwickshire	1L	FF			
SMETHWICK WEST		Staffordshire		FF		•	•
SOHO & WINSON GREEN		Warwickshire	1L	FF	1972	•	•
SOLIHULL		Warwickshire		HF			•

*some non-standard aluminium alloy FF totems were made and used by BR; see page 47. They have not appeared in auction

1L = one line: 2L = two line: LP = lower panel

Station Name		County in 1956	Layout	Flange	Closed	Auction	Survived
SOLIHULL		Warwickshire		FF		•	•
SOUTHALL	some o/p B&W	Middlesex		HF/FF		•	•
SOUTH MOLTON		Devonshire		FF	1966		•
SPRING ROAD		Warwickshire		FF		•	•
ST. ANNE'S PARK		Bristol		FF	1970	•	•
ST. AUSTELL		Cornwall		HF/FF		•	•
ST. BUDEAUX FERRY ROAD		Devonshire	LP	FF		•	•
ST. CLEARS		Carmarthenshire		FF	1964	•	•
ST. ERTH		Cornwall		FF		•	•
ST. FAGANS		Glamorgan		HF	1962	•	•
ST. IVES		Cornwall		FF		•	•
STAINES WEST		Middlesex		HF	1965	•	•
STARCROSS		Devonshire		FF		•	•
STONEHOUSE (BURDETT ROAD)		Gloucestershire	LP	FF		•	•
STOURBRIDGE JUNCTION		Worcestershire	1L/LP	HF/FF		•	•
STOURBRIDGE TOWN		Worcestershire		FF		•	•
STRATFORD-UPON-AVON		Warwickshire		HF		•	•
STROUD	*brown flanges	Gloucestershire		HF*		•	•
SWANSEA HIGH STREET		Glamorgan	LP	HF/FF		•	•
SWANSEA (VICTORIA)		Glamorgan	LP	FF	1964	•	•
SWAN VILLAGE		Staffordshire		FF	1972	•	•
SWINDON		Wiltshire		HF		•	•
TAFFS WELL		Glamorgan		FF		•	•
TAPLOW		Buckinghamshire		HF/FF		•	•
TAUNTON		Somerset		HF		•	
TEIGNMOUTH		Devonshire		HF			
TENBY		Pembrokeshire		FF		•	•
THAME		Oxfordshire		HF	1963	•	•
THEALE		Berkshire		FF			
THE LAKES HALT		Warwickshire		FF			•
TILEHURST		Berkshire		FF		•	
TIPTON FIVE WAYS		Staffordshire		FF		•	•
TIR PHIL		Glamorgan		FF			
TIVERTON JUNCTION		Devonshire		FF	1986	•	•

1L = one line: 2L = two line: LP = lower panel

Station Name	County in 1956	Layout	Flange	Closed	Auction	Survived
TONYPANDY & TREALAW	Glamorgan	1L	FF		•	•
TORQUAY two variants B&W and choc/cream	Devonshire		plastic		•	•
TORRE	Devonshire		FF			•
TOTNES	Devonshire		FF			•
TOWYN	Merionethshire		FF		•	•
TREFOREST	Glamorgan		FF		•	•
TREFOREST ESTATE	Glamorgan		FF		•	•
TREHAFOD	Glamorgan		FF		•	•
TREHERBERT	Glamorgan		FF		•	•
TREORCHY	Glamorgan		FF		•	•
TROEDYRHIW	Glamorgan		FF		•	•
TROWBRIDGE	Wiltshire		HF		•	•
TRURO	Cornwall		HF/FF		•	•
TWYFORD	Berkshire		FF		•	•
TYLORSTOWN	Glamorgan		FF			•
TYSELEY	Warwickshire		FF		•	•
UPPER PONTNEWYDD	Monmouthshire		FF	1962		
UXBRIDGE VINE STREET	Middlesex	LP	HF	1962	•	•
WARGARVE	Berkshire		FF			•
WARWICK	Warwickshire		FF		•	•
WEDNESBURY (CENTRAL)	Staffordshire	LP	FF	1972	•	•
WELLINGTON	Somerset		HF			•
WELLINGTON SALOP some brown flanges	Shropshire	LP	HF		•	•
WELLINGTON (SALOP)	Shropshire	LP	FF		•	•
WELSHPOOL	Montgomeryshire		HF		•	•
WESTBOURNE PARK	London		HF/FF		•	•
WEST BROMWICH	Staffordshire		FF	1972	•	•
WESTBURY WILTS	Wiltshire	LP	HF		•	•
WEST DRAYTON & YIEWSLEY	Middlesex	1L	HF		•	•
WEST EALING FF version not in auction	Middlesex		HF/FF		•	•
WESTON MILTON	Somerset		FF		•	•
WESTON-SUPER-MARE GENERAL	Somerset	LP	HF		•	•
WEST RUISLIP	Middlesex		HF/FF		•	•

1L = one line: 2L = two line: LP = lower panel

Station Name	County in 1956	Layout	Flange	Closed	Auction	Survived
WHITLAND	Carmarthenshire		HF/FF		•	•
WHITLOCK'S END HALT	Warwickshire	LP	FF		•	•
WIDNEY MANOR	Warwickshire		FF		•	•
WILMCOTE	Warwickshire		FF		•	•
WINDMILL END HALT	Staffordshire	LP	FF	1964	•	•
WINDSOR & ETON CENTRAL	Berkshire	LP	HF		•	•
WOLVERHAMPTON (LOW LEVEL)	Staffordshire	LP	FF	1972	•	•
WOOD END	Warwickshire		FF		•	•
WOOTTON BASSETT	Wiltshire		FF	1965	•	•
WOOTTON WAWEN PLATFORM	Warwickshire	2L	FF		•	•
WORCESTER FOREGATE STREET	Worcestershire	LP	HF		•	•
WORCESTER SHRUB HILL	Worcestershire	LP	HF		•	•
WREXHAM (EXCHANGE)	Denbighshire	LP	FF		•	•
WREXHAM GENERAL	Denbighshire		FF		•	•
YARDLEY WOOD	Warwickshire		FF		•	•
YATE *re-opened 1989	Gloucestershire		FF	1965*		
YATTON	Bristol		FF		•	•
YNYSHIR	Glamorgan		FF	1964		
YSTRAD MYNACH	Glamorgan		FF		•	•
YSTRAD (RHONDDA)	Glamorgan	LP	FF		•	•

1L = one line: 2L = two line: LP = lower panel

Other Western Region Collectables

Opening Comments

The designers, installers and travelling public during the decades that totems adorned our stations would not believe that these simple signs, over half a century later would become so hugely collectable. The term '*In situ* Files' was first used in our popular Totem Study Group (TSG) quarterly newsletters, which followed the publication of our 2002 totem book, to help document new discoveries. Many of these pictures are displayed for the first time outside the TSG group. The series ran for seven years, until March 2009, and we have delved into some of these as a source of 'new' material.

We have also included many evocative images from our personal libraries showing the humble totem sign hanging proudly in its rightful place.

Our contributors, Alan Young and Tim Clarke were prolific photographers of totems *in situ* during their final years and we are privileged to include so many of their views.

Some of the oddest totems ever installed on the BR network were not at stations. Lake Windermere boasts three former BR-operated piers for their pleasure boats and installed these oversized totems at the ends of the piers on two of them; **Bowness Pier** and **Ambleside Pier** (see page 128), which are not in the LMR database, as this is purely for station totems. We would speculate that they were between 4- and 5-feet in length. Neither of the two signs are known to survived at the time of writing, but it is intriguing to think that a Lake District collection somewhere has one of these gems in it. At **Lake Side** station, boats would berth alongside the station, (and still do). After closure in 1965, the station became derelict, but it was saved in 1973 by the Lakeside & Haverthwaite Railway, who operate the heritage line today. **Ashley Hill** (bottom right) lies just north of Bristol and closed in 1964. Today, the remains of one platform exist, but a new station known as Ashley Down is planned as part of the **Henbury** line project.

Top left: East London, 1975. *Alan Young*

Top Right: Somerset, 1975. *Alan Young*

Bottom right: G Churchward

All photos in this chapter are from our TSG library unless credited otherwise.

The Eastern Region

We look at the ER first then the other five regions, following the order of the preceding six regional chapters. The suburban system radiating from Liverpool Street into Hertfordshire, Middlesex and Essex was a very early candidate for the installation of fluorescent strip lighting on stations incorporating the station name on the Perspex cover. Such progress was inevitable, but the bad news for totem collectors was the wholesale removal of relatively new dark blue enamels. Some of this work started in earnest in the mid-1950s and **Cambridge** was an early victim by 1956. The totems would have been displayed for only three or four years. Similarly, **Alresford** totems were early victims of the major clearances that occurred somewhat prematurely.

The Essex branch lines to **Clacton on Sea** and **Walton on Naze** were similarly treated, but strangely, a few totems remained for several years at **Thorpe-le-Soken**, **Frinton-on-Sea** and **Kirby Cross**. There are no survivors known from **Alresford**, **Colchester**, **Great Bentley**, **Hythe**, **St. Botolphs**, **Weeley** or **Wivenhoe**.

Woodgrange Park is where one of the authors (DB) spent many happy hours in the signal box as a youngster, oblivious to the existence of totems outside, seen in 1975. **Barking** totems (below) were short-lived and disappeared during the modernisation of the station, which was officially reopened by HM The Queen on 15 February 1962.

The GE lines in Hertfordshire are very difficult to collect from and the **Hertford East** branch especially. Totems were short-lived at **Rye House**, seen here in 1959 just prior to electrification work. On the ex-LT&SR line from Fenchurch Street to **Shoeburyness**, there was another cull between 1957 and 1962 east of **Upminster**, with all the stations being re-signed except for **Grays** and **Tilbury Town** on the Tilbury loop. The right-hand image below shows totems at **Stepney East** (renamed Limehouse 1987) and top left, partly obscured by a tree, is a very rare **Westcliff on Sea** in 1955 just before removal.

The branch from **Seven Sisters** to **Palace Gates** (left) was opened by the GER in 1878; it was built to rival the GNR's **Wood Green** station and their branch to Alexandra Palace (closed 1954). The GER line never lived up to the company's expectations, due partly to a long uphill walk from the terminus and competition from the Piccadilly line to Arnos Grove opening in 1932. The **Palace Gates** branch closed in 1963 and few totems are known to exist from here and the intermediate stations of **West Green** and **Noel Park**. There are three totems in view at **Hoe Street**, which is on the Chingford line, becoming Walthamstow Central in 1968. We are unaware of any survivors.

Still in north-east London we have some more classic TSG views. **Hackney Downs**, on the Liverpool Street to Chingford and Enfield Town line had more than 30 totems spread over four platforms. One is rumoured to survive, but the bulk have strangely disappeared, along with all those at **Bethnal Green**, a favoured spotting haunt for East End enthusiasts. The EMU is on a recently electrified **Southend-on-Sea Victoria** to Liverpool Street service, which went straight from steam to overhead electric trains in 1956. The totems from both stations were removed between 1960 and 1961.

Palace Gates, just prior to closure in 1963. *Book Law Publications*

Above: Lea Bridge and Temple Mills yard beyond 1974. *Alan Young*

The North Woolwich branch 1975. *Alan Young*

This **West Ham (Manor Road)** was the very last totem still *in situ* during 1977. The view of **Lea Bridge** shows the station in very poor condition. It closed in 1985 but reopened in 2016 to much local fanfare. Nearby is **Clapton** on the Liverpool Street to Chingford line. These images show the former GER station just before the electrification of the line in the early 1960s, with some FF totems *in situ* and others about to be rather unceremoniously disposed of. None are known to have survived.

In the first-half of the 1970s, the North Woolwich branch line had a wonderful air of neglect. It had been forgotten and was not seen as a priority when it came to modernisation. The Port of London Authority stopped handling freight by rail in 1970, which exacerbated the decline. Trainloads of dock workers became a part of history and the only station on the line from **Stratford** Low Level with totems was **Silvertown** (above). The incline to the Connaught Road tunnel is in the distance. The station closed in 2006 and there is no trace of it today, being on the new Crossrail route.

Ponders End, Lea Valley line in 1967. *D. Fairhurst*

Above: Holbeach, Lincolnshire.
Tony Harden Collection

Finding pictures of **Newark Northgate** totems *in situ* has been very difficult and this view (above left) is the only one we have discovered. Fluorescent lighting caused the early demise of several other ECML dark blues; **New Barnet**, **Potters Bar** (by 1955 when the station was rebuilt), **Grantham** and **Retford** totems all came to a premature end. In Lincolnshire, only **Louth** (above) and **Skegness** had large lettered totems.

Woodbridge totems were still adorning the lovely East Suffolk line station in 1982 and this was probably the last station in East Anglia to carry its totems.

Woodbridge, Suffolk. *Alan Young*

In the 1970s, East Anglia was fertile ground for seeing totems in addition to growing crops! Some stations were overlooked for modernisation even into the early 1980s. The ex-GER buildings, ornate LNER lamps and peeling paintwork gave many East Anglian stations a certain charm. The branch lines to **Kings Lynn** and **Hunstanton** were well provided with totems. The classic BTF film of Sir John Betjeman's trip on a DMU to **Hunstanton** before closure is a real treat. The cameraman pans onto the totems at several stations *en route*. Gems such as **Dersingham**, **Snettisham** and **Heacham** *in situ* are pure nostalgia. **Holbeach** (M&GN) closed to passengers in 1959, but this building survives in residential use. **Shepreth** (below) is on the **Cambridge** to **Hitchin** line.

Shepreth, Cambridgeshire in 1973. *Alan Young*

A TSG member brought two new discoveries to our attention several years ago. A snow-covered **Drayton** is shown in 1958 just one year before closure. Situated on the M&GN branch from **Melton Constable** to Norwich City, this was the only station on the branch to be fitted with totems. The other revelation was the existence of totems at **Grimston Road** (a totem is above the bench and another to the left) further west on the M&GN. Both lines closed to passengers in 1959 and survivors are not known.

A delightful Cambridgeshire quartet is presented here, starting with **Kennett** near **Newmarket**. Alongside is a picture of **Ely,** an extremely rare totem and highly sought-after. **Linton** (below *in situ*) is also a very rare totem, with no known survivors; it was a former station (closed 1967) on the much lamented **Shelford** (below *in situ* 1970) to **Marks Tey** cross-country route via **Haverhill** and **Long Melford**, a sad loss on closure.

John Crook

This image of **Althorpe** in Lincolnshire is a wonderful record of a bygone era. The full title of the station was 'Althorpe for Keadby, Gunness and Burringham'; rather a lot for a totem to carry, but easily accommodated on the Running-n Board. Keadby (closed 1874) and Gunness & Burringham (closed 1916) once had separate stations.

Althorpe, Lincolnshire, 1973. *Alan Young*

The electrified Woodhead route had both MR and ER totems either side of the Pennine tunnel. At the junction station of **Penistone** (bottom left), a pair of EM1 1,500 volt DC locos are passing through with an eastbound coal train. During the research stage, we noticed that these totems have the larger letters; a feature unique to just 13 ER totems. **Whittlesea** is a most delightful name in the Cambridgeshire countryside; even today, the station retains a link with the past, as the level crossing is still worked manually. **Goxhill** station in Lincolnshire has the accolade of being the last station on the BR network to carry a full complement of totems, as late as 1988, by which time they had become very faded and almost white! The popularity of collecting totems in the intervening forty plus years is astonishing and none of us really know how many enthusiasts collect these artefacts today.

Top: Cambridgeshire, in 1974. *Alan Young*

Left: Lincolnshire, 1984. *Alan Young*

Alan Young has been a major contributor to our totem studies and publications; his hand-drawn maps are works of art. The **Northumberland Pk**. photo was sent in by Doug Fairhurst, while the remaining four were taken by Alan Young.

In Essex, **Cressing** and **Emerson Park Halt** stations only had two or three totems each. Both of these station totems are extremely difficult to find, having a total of only three combined auction appearances between them.

The London Midland Region

Totem collections sometimes have themes, such as engine sheds, seaside resorts, scenic byways or a particular area where the collector spotted trains as a youngster; the LMR has them all in abundance. The grand London termini were omitted when it came to totem installation except for the lesser-known and latterly run-down North London Railway **Broad Street** next-door to Liverpool Street. The North London line serves a great swathe of London's suburbia, through **Canonbury**, **Caledonian Road & Barnsbury**, **Camden Road**, **Gospel Oak**, **Hampstead Heath** and **Willesden Junction**, then entering Southern territory down to Richmond. This would be a difficult line to collect as both **Kentish Town West** and **Hampstead Heath** are very rare. After many years of neglect, the North London line underwent a renaissance and is currently operated by Transport for London with new links opening up a wide variety of connections. The **Canonbury** view (right), with Edwin Horne's typical NLR architecture from 1870, is a rustic delight. This building was demolished shortly after the photo was taken and flimsy bus shelters replaced solid brick-built waiting rooms.

Above: Canonbury, North London line, 1969. *Jim Connor*

Right: Pete Sargieson

London's Broad Street, in 1974, showing several large 4-foot totems. *Alan Young*

The short branch line to Stanmore was proposed by the Harrow & Stanmore Railway and opened by the LNWR in 1890. The terminus was renamed **Stanmore Village** in 1950 and totems were installed. However, just two years later the station closed, due to competition from the nearby Metropolitan Railway (Bakerloo) line station. There were only four or five totems installed there and no survivors are known. **Aylesbury High Street station** took its name in September 1950, to avoid confusion with nearby **Aylesbury Town** (GW/GC Joint). Sadly, **Aylesbury High Street** totems also had a short life, as the station closed to passengers in February 1953.

Belmont is worthy of mention here, as it was on the **Stanmore Village** branch. It outlived the terminus by twelve years, but it is believed that the few totems that were made were never installed at the station. Two were found in the station master's office at **Harrow & Wealdstone** station in the 1960s in mint condition and given away to a local enthusiast! **Kentish Town**, on the Midland line from St. Pancras, will always appeal to steam enthusiasts, being a major loco shed until its closure in 1963.

Above: A rationalised Bedford St. Johns, 11 May 1973.
Both images Alan Young

Fenny Stratford in early 1970s. *Alan Young*

In Bedfordshire a rather forlorn **Bedford St. Johns** retains just a few totems after the rationalisation and demolition of the station buildings had taken place in 1971. This station closed in 1984 and a new station opened to the west, slightly closer to **Bedford Midland**. Through the 1970s, the Bedford to **Bletchley** line was largely overlooked when it came to modernisation and totem removal. The line was once part of an important **Oxford–Bletchley–Cambridge** through-route until 1967. Only the section from Bletchley to Bedford was retained. Delightfully named **Woburn Sands** is a bit deceiving, as it is a long way from the sea. **Millbrook** was once home to a very large brick factory, which closed in 2008. Totems survive from all these stations.

Surely a candidate for 'The Best Kept Station Award' was **Fenny Stratford** (above); one of four stations on the line to be built in a Gothic Revival style at the behest of the 7th Duke of Bedford. The totem has been sadly vandalised and bent forward. The other stations with totems were **Lidlington** (below in 1973) and **Ridgmont**.

Above left: Years of grime and brake dust in North London.
Both photos by J. E. Connor

Upon leaving the original London Euston station with its magnificent Doric Arch, a steam-hauled journey north in the late 1950s would have been pure pleasure. Maroon enamels adorned nearly every station all the way to **Carlisle**. Today's Pendolino express services run at such high speeds that it is difficult to focus on station names, which become blurred. Some WCML stations lost their totems during the electrification work in the early 1960s; **Watford Junction**, **Tring**, **Rugby Midland** (above right *in situ*), **Coventry** (*in situ* below), **Birmingham New Street** (*in situ* above right), **Wolverhampton High Level** and **Stafford** were stripped of totems and most of these are rare today. The totem below right is known to be one of only two survivors from that station

The West Midlands area was richly supplied with maroon totems and had some classic names mixed with the more mundane. We cannot turn the clock back, but collectors can relive those far-off halcyon days by owning totems; they are enamel time capsules recapturing the heritage of British Railways.

In the last forty years, just six **Birmingham New Street** totems have appeared at auction, proving that there are few survivors from the large number installed. **Rugby Midland** also had a very large number of totems and we are aware of just one survivor, with no auction appearances to date. Aside from the main line early totem removals, the majority of West Midlands totems had a long lifespan, lasting well into the 1970s and upon removal they were mainly sold off through Collectors Corner and other local outlets. Some **Lichfield Trent Valley** totems carried the full title using the lower panel and a two-line version. An interesting fact emerges when we examine the whole LMR database; just seven stations had totems with an appendage in the lower panel.

Tim Clarke Collection

John Mann Collection

TSG Collection

Tim Clarke

Sudbury Hill Harrow is an example from the small group of maroon lower panels. This was an ex-GCR station that opened as South Harrow in 1906; it took its totem name in 1926. **Blake Street** is on the Birmingham to **Lichfield** line and the photo shows the maroon totem surmounted by a lamp from a previous era; it is a common totem, having been seen ten times at auction. **Melton Mowbray** lies on the Leicester to Peterborough cross-country route. The station retains most of its original buildings and canopies, which were refurbished in 2011. **Doe Hill** in Derbyshire (closed 1960) is one of the most amazing recent totem discoveries, with no survivors currently known, whilst **Appleby West** is now a Grade-II listed station on the scenic **Settle** & **Carlisle** route in Cumbria.

Maryport (middle right) is a very rare totem, having no auction appearances thus far. A former Maryport and Carlisle Railway station, it is still open today. **Ardwick** *in situ* (right) is awash with infrastructure from the 1,500 volt DC Manchester, Sheffield and **Wath** route via Woodhead tunnel. The station, just east of Manchester Piccadilly, is now one of the least used in the UK and narrowly escaped closure in 2007.

G C Lewthwaite

New Basford in Nottinghamshire was an ex-GCR station that stood on a high embankment. Closure came in 1964; rows of terraced houses billowing smoke from coal fires provide an evocative backdrop. **Quorn & Woodhouse** is eagerly sought by some Leicestershire collectors and another Leicestershire rarity is **Wigston Glen Parva** with just four auction appearances. Wigston once had three stations (**Wigston South** and **Wigston Magna** are the other two). All had closed by 1968 but a new South Wigston opened in 1986 situated 300 metres east of the former Glen Parva station.

These four classic images are from our TSG files. **Tebay** station and the engine shed both closed in 1968; the final year of steam-hauled trains on British Railways. Banking engines were supplied from **Tebay** for the long climb to **Shap** station (also closed in 1968) and the WCML summit at 914 feet. Both these totems have eight auction appearances apiece. The **Coleshill** totem overlooks decades of poorly renovated pre-grouping architecture and alongside is **Kenilworth** with very similar surroundings. It closed in 1965 and reopened in 2018: totems from here have been auctioned 14 times.

Two views from either side of the Dee estuary.
Above: Flint, in 1969. *A.F. Grimmett Collection*
Below: Bidston in 1977. *Alan Young*

Images from Tim Clarke and Alan Young

There is a mainly Lancashire theme here. **Kirkham and Wesham** is the junction for the branches to Blackpool, whilst **Kirkdale** is situated just north of Liverpool. On the Wirral, totems were still at **Bidston** (left) in 1977; the lines to West Kirby and Wrexham diverge here. In the photo, a Liverpool Central-bound Merseyrail EMU passes **Bidston** Dee Junction signal box. **Culcheth** was on the former Wigan Central to **Glazebrook** line, which closed to passengers in 1964 and to freight in 1968.

North of Liverpool, almost every station on the line to **Preston,** except Rufford, had totems. **Ormskirk** (left) hangs proudly in this mid-1960s view. Since 1970, **Ormskirk** station has been divided by an odd arrangement whereby third-rail trains from the south and the DMUs from the north both meet head on and are separated by buffer stops. There have been many calls to have through Liverpool to Preston trains again. **Stalybridge** lies to the west of the Pennines and the station has retained much of the original architecture, along with a buffet and real ale bar which is well worth a visit. The Lake District CK&PR line was a tragic loss in 1972; **Keswick**, **Troutbeck** and **Penruddock** are seen in their final days (above).

At the eastern end of the Woodhead tunnel were the short platforms at Dunford Bridge (no totems), shown in this late 1950s photo, a rare example of two different regional signs being displayed. This resulted from the transfer of Dunford Bridge from the LMR to the ER in February 1958. The rather grimy EM1 Bo-Bo electric loco, sporting green livery with orange and black lining, is seen on a westbound freight.

The North Eastern Region

This small collage shows some of the rarest imaginable NER totems. Both **Seaburn** and **Darlington Bank Top** are widely considered to be the 'Holy Grail' for NER aficionados. There are currently no known survivors from **Seaburn** and very few from **Darlington Bank Top**, as these were superseded by FF **Darlington** signs. **Howdon-on-Tyne** was still proudly hanging when Alan Young captured this immaculate specimen in July 1979. We are very lucky that Alan was a native of Tyneside and recorded a treasure trove of material for future generations to enjoy.

David Dippie

Right: Darlington Bank Top station interior. *Alf Miles Collection*

Below: A rare sight in 1979: an extremely good condition tangerine totem *in situ*.

North Wylam. *TSG library*

Scarborough totem in situ – on a diesel shunter! *TSG library*

This image of a Class 03 diesel shunting loco at **Scarborough Central** *circa* 1974 is the most unusual NER *in situ* photo we have. Totems had been superseded by fluorescent lighting but two were retained for use on the 03s with 'No. 1 and No. 2 station pilot' painted in the top panel. Adjacent is a HF **Barnard Castle** *in situ*: a former station on the branch line from **Darlington** to Middleton-in-Teesdale (what a great totem that would have been). Until 1952 it was possible to travel on the Stainmore route from **Barnard Castle** to **Tebay** on the WCML via **Kirkby Stephen East**. Magnificent **York** station had a very large number of HF totems and the unusual wrap-round pillar signs (below), but few are known to survive. Below, the FF York is rare and in mint condition. An **Ikley** totem is shown *in situ* in 1975 and recorded by one of our major contributors. The battered and weathered **Dinsdale** (alongside right) is extremely rare.

Considered by many to be 'the jewel in the crown' of Yorkshire's coastal towns is beautiful Whitby. The stunning colourful image right shows **Whitby Town** in 1974. The Church of St. Mary overlooks the town, and the ruin of Whitby Abbey can just be glimpsed on the right. This Benedictine monastery has stood for over 800 years and although ransacked by Henry VIII in 1540 during the Dissolution of the Monasteries, the surviving structure is both beautiful and eerie. Bottom right is **Whitby West Cliff** during the last year of operation in 1961. Note the totem on the right; one of just a handful to adorn the station and none of which are currently thought to have survived.

The closure and the loss of the picturesque lines, north to Loftus (closed in 1958) and south to **Scarborough Central** via Robin Hood's Bay (closed 1965) were tragic. They may have been uneconomic, but they were a lifeline to many hundreds of villagers and holidaymakers. If the lines had been retained, they might well have become one of Britain's best tourist attractions. The North Yorkshire Moors Railway now runs into Whitby again. From 2007, regular steam and diesel-hauled trains operated over the Esk Valley Line from Whitby to Grosmont, then down to Pickering, thus providing a service over the entire length of the original Whitby and Pickering Railway. Services were further improved in 2014 by the re-opening of a second platform at Whitby to enable services to increase out-and-back trips from three to five. It has proved hugely popular.

Below is **Saltburn** in 1967. The seaside town and its success were due to the vision of Henry Pease (one of the directors of the **Stockton** & **Darlington** Railway) and the opening of the railway line from Redcar to Saltburn in 1861. A trio of Metropolitan Cammell DMUs in their earliest livery with half-yellow ends add a bit of welcome colour to the seemingly lonely totem. These trusty DMU workhorses were a common sight in the Darlington and Newcastle areas between 1956 and the 1980s. Even today, a large original BR (NE) tangerine enamel adorns the station frontage. The three photos on this page all come from the Neil Cholmondley Collection, courtesy of Alan Young.

Tim Clarke

The late John Mann Collection

East Boldon, County Durham, in 1973. *Alan Young*

The two photos above show totems from **Whitby Town** and **Saltburn** hanging proudly and both totems always cause a stir at auction, even though they each have eight appearances to date. Below, the rather dour blackened buildings at **Percy Main** were brightened by the addition of several orange enamels, seen here in April 1973.

There is something nostalgic about Tyneside totems, as this 1973 image of a grimy **East Boldon** testifies, yet survivors are generally in remarkably good condition; seemingly escaping the attention of those who might have harmed them. This **Northallerton** image differs from the one in the NER chapter on page 168 and shows two totems prior to mid-1950s fluorescent lighting installation.

Percy Main station, in the early 1970s. *Alan Young*

The late John Mann Collection

We have devoted this page to the memory of the late John Mann of Sheffield, who travelled the length and breadth of the UK photographing stations and collecting images. His portfolio of over 60,000 prints is now administered by the **Disused Stations** website owner Nick Catford, who has kindly given us permission to use just a small NER selection. Nick's website is exceptional, in our opinion.

The **Redcar East** direction sign right is the most unusual we have seen, showing a transitional mixture of lettering and colours. Although the image is B&W, the top appears to be orange Gill Sans on white, whilst the bottom is lower case Gill Sans.

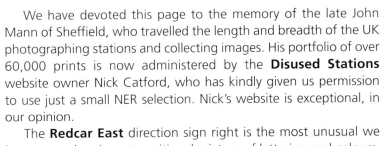

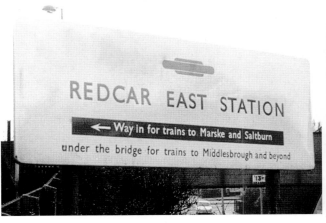

The Scottish Region

We start the Scottish section with rhododendron-rich **Achnashellach** station, on the **Dingwall** to **Kyle of Lochalsh** line, as it appeared in the early 1970s, with a Class 26 diesel approaching. Totems also once hung on the closed platform. **Kyle of Lochalsh** is shown bottom left with a Class 24 departing on a fish train. Totems were fitted only on either side of the approach road, with none under the canopies.

    Corrour is the highest and most remote station in the UK at 1,340 feet. We believe there were only four totems here. Scenic delight at **Newtonmore** is shown middle (right) on the Highland main line from **Perth** to Inverness. The postman carrying bags of mail is a reminder of bygone traffic, lost to the roads. There have been calls for this section of line to be doubled throughout, rather than the current mix of single and double line.

Middle left: Highland splendour, Corrour, 1974. *The late Paul Carter*

Middle right: Newtonmore, 1974. *Alan Young*

Left: Kyle of Lochalsh, 1974. *The late Paul Carter*

Tim Clarke   *Alan Young*

Glasgow's River Clyde gave rise to one of the world's greatest shipbuilding empires and other industries provided employment for hundreds of thousands of Glaswegians. Totems flanked the Clyde and some wonderful names emerged from the dark polluted surroundings. **Upper Greenock**, on the branch to **Wemyss Bay**, closed in 1967 and we would surmise that the railwayman posing by the lamp worked at the station. North of the river once stood **Clydebank Riverside**, which closed to passengers in 1964, and the totems are not known to survive. Six platforms served the shipyards and this fine CR building survives in residential use.

Canonbie (far left), on the former **Riddings Junction** to **Langholm** branch closed in 1964. Beautiful **Loch Awe** is a truly stunning location, nestling below Ben Cruachan, with the towering Gothic hotel and views across the loch to Kilchurn Castle. The year 1964 was a bad year for Scottish station closures and **Portobello**, east of Edinburgh, also succumbed; it was a busy junction in its heyday with several branch lines feeding into the station. **Dalmally** is one of only a handful of stations fitted with totems on the picturesque **Crianlarich Upper** to Oban line. The damage is unusual, with the stone chips normally associated with an inner city station. The **Ardlui** totem is a West Highland line treat, also in beautiful surroundings.

TSG library

Above and middle: Alan Young

Right: Elgin.
Courtesy Alan Young/Carl Marsden

Despite our widespread research, there are still snippets of information coming to light all the time. These two were discovered during the writing stages. We knew that wooden totems hung at **Balmossie Halt** and **Golf Street Halt** in the County of Angus, but we did not know that prior to being painted white with non-standard black lettering, they carried ScR light blue with standard white lettering, seen in July 1972.

This timeless image of **Elgin** in 1962 (right) proves what effect 170 years has had on monetary values. The three totems in this view would cost more today than the whole station cost to build in the 1850s! **Achnasheen** is a passing loop on the **Kyle of Lochalsh** line and once had a hotel on the platform; it was destroyed by fire in 1996. Only one **Achnasheen** totem has appeared at auction, in 2004. The trio to the right need little explanation, suffice to say that they are all pure Highland totem nostalgia.

Alan Young

Above: Jim Connor

Right: The late John Mann Collection

In this instantly recognisable view of Edinburgh's Princes Street above, including the Scott Monument and the castle overlooking Waverley station, a desirable BR (ScR) direction sign is surreptitiously attached to the railings. Waverley did not have totems, so such a direction sign would be hugely collectable. Totems from **Ladybank**, Fife, are not common; below, Alan Young's August 1978 photograph shows them still in situ.

The loss of the Waverley route, between Edinburgh and **Carlisle,** in the dark days of 1969 was a terrible blow to thousands of local people. Local and national opposition was vigorous, but fell on deaf ears in the corridors of power. Thankfully, some 35 miles reopened to Tweedbank in 2015, but the remainder to **Carlisle** will be hugely expensive to reinstate. Some 18 months after closure, our photographer visited

Gorebridge in 1970 and found grubby totems still *in situ*. Note the recycled lamppost from **Melrose** station! Further south, **Fountainhall** (former junction for the Lauder branch, closed in 1932) was captured in January 1969, just prior to closure of the line. **Balloch Pier** is an unusually positioned right-angled totem facing passengers arriving on the platform from the pier on the edge of Loch Lomond. Tyndrum Lower did not have totems but at least it did have this fine direction sign nearby.

Left: The late John Boyes, courtesy R. Barber/ARPT

Below: Kilmaurs, 24 August 1963. *G.C. Lewthwaite*

This 15-foot monster totem outside **Ayr** station in the late 1960s could well be the biggest in Britain. Closer inspection shows that all the letters and the borders are illuminated with fluorescent tubes; so perhaps it was visible from space? **Newton-on-Ayr** (below) is a rare totem with just one auction appearance in 2020. Alongside, the former G&SWR terminus at **Dalmellington** is shown shortly before closure in 1964.

Above left is a very rare image of a **Patna** totem *in situ*. This station was also on the Dalmellington branch; it closed to passengers in 1964.

There are only two ScR stations which carried these unusual plastic totems with raised letters. Standard totems were also fitted at **Girvan** and **Prestonpans**. Below is a rare picture of East Ayrshire **Kilmaurs** totems *in situ;* no survivors are currently known. The station was opened by the Glasgow, Barrhead & Kilmarnock Joint Railway in 1873; closure came in 1966, but a new station was opened by BR in 1984.

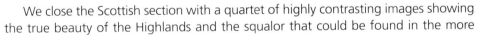

foreboding inner city areas. Idyllic **Corpach** is on the West Highland Extension line, whereas the **Dalmarnock** image, taken a few years after closure in 1964, has an almost sinister appearance. Above, one of the few totems at iconic **Glenfinnan** can be seen at seat level! The refreshment rooms at **Crianlarich Upper**, seen here in the mid-1970s, still supply weary West Highland Line travellers with sustenance to this day.

We close the Scottish section with a quartet of highly contrasting images showing the true beauty of the Highlands and the squalor that could be found in the more

The Southern Region

Venturing onto Southern metals, we are transported back to June 1975 as a Hastings-line 6L 'Thumper' DEMU No. 1017 passes **New Cross**. The lamp shades and barley sugar-twist lamp standards are delightful. A new find shown below is **Yetminster**, just south of Yeovil in Dorset; a survivor has yet to been seen. Unusually, for such a small station, **New Romney & Littlestone-on-Sea** had both HF and FF totems.

A totem that many seasoned collectors will have undoubtedly owned is the common **Elmstead Woods**, seen here in 1974, as a Class 33 coasts through with a parcels train. Although one of the most common SR totems at auction, the station did not possess anywhere near the number of totems that were installed at **Clapham Junction**; an approximation might be 200 spread over seventeen platforms and more than any other station.

Above: New Cross, London, 1975.
Alan Young

Above: Alan Young

Passengers would be in no doubt that they had arrived at **Uckfield** with the multitude of signage in this image from the 1970s by Tim Clarke, who also took the **East Dulwich**, **Martin Mill**, **Cheam**, **Eastbourne** and **Fishersgate Halt** views. Tim was instrumental in the research for the original 1991 book and three decades on, he has again provided us with valuable knowledge and photos. The dark-green totems with black flanges at **Dunbridge** are shown with all the paraphernalia of a bygone era adorning the station. Only one totem from here has ever appeared at auction in 2002.

An enamel **Holborn Viaduct** is not known to survive, but our image clearly shows two *in situ* back-to-back. **Axminster** totems were only wooden, to our knowledge. Lastly, we have a very rare Cornish green in the shape of **Callington,** which succumbed to closure in 1966; part of the branch survives today as far as Gunnislake.

This whole page is from Tim Clarke's collection. The **Sunnymeads** totem and barley sugar-twist lamp post are most attractive; further images follow of **Sevenoaks**, **Rye**, **Chertsey** and **Cowden**. The Southern Region had just four stations with three-letter signs; **Ash**, **Ore**, **Rye** and **Wye**; few letters but what wonderful memories they evoke.

The **Isfield, Slinfold** and **Cowden** images are pure nostalgia, epitomising a pastime from which we gain so much pleasure. The combination of signage and lamps from different eras all share the commonality of Southern green. **Appledore,** on the Ashford to **Hastings** line, was an afterthought when it came to totem installation and possessed only these second-rate painted wooden signs: note the absence of white lines.

Above: TSG library

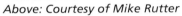

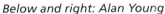

Above: Courtesy of Mike Rutter

Below and right: Alan Young

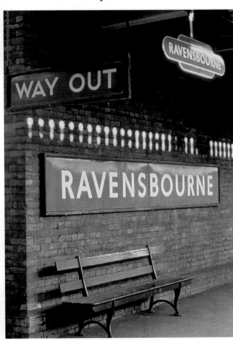

Unsurprisingly, being one of only two SR three-line Halt totems, **Three Oaks & Guestling Halt** totems are desirable and rare, with just six fitted and one 2018 Internet auction appearance. With just 6 fitted, 1 auction appearance in 2018 on the internet and the bonus of being the only three-line Halt totem, they are desirable. Whilst looking at rarities, **Ham Street and Orlestone** has made only one auction appearance, in 2012, at Derby. This sign illustrates why BR moved away from the half-flanged totem to the full-flanged totem. Sadly, vandalism like this ruined thousands of signs all over the BR network. Crease repairs, no matter how well executed, can affect the value of a totem.

This Somerset & Dorset *in situ* shot shows one of the rarest totems imaginable. Although **Shillingstone** totems are known to survive, none have ever appeared in a public auction. The much-loved line from **Bath Green Park** to **Bournemouth West** closed in 1966 as part of the Beeching cuts. Above top right are painted wooden totems at **Wimbledon**. We have noted that a few stations in several regions had totems displayed at right angles, such as these at **Sunnymeads** in 1977.

Above left: A nostalgic view in 1980. *Alan Young*

The Western Region

We start our WR journey with Cambrian scenery and a visit to **Dovey Junction** in 1980. Still with GWR lower quadrant signals and good old BR blue DMUs, it forms an important interchange between the branches to **Aberystwyth** and **Pwllheli** on the beautiful coastal lines. One of the intermediate stations heading north is **Harlech**; the condition of this example proudly hanging in 1974 is near-mint. **Avonmouth Dock** is staring at its awful corporate image replacement. The totem design is the clear winner.

In the West Midlands, this excellent view at **Old Hill** shows a totem and a pre-British Railways (ex-GWR) RIB with multiple destinations, one of which is the **Windmill End (Halt)** branch, locally known as the 'Bumble Hole' line. At just 3miles long, the branch to **Blowers Green** was poorly patronised in the 1960s and suffered closure by 1964, but what wonderful names were bestowed upon its tiny halts; **Old Hill (High Street) Halt**, **Darby End Halt** and **Baptist End Halt** are all very rare. We give our apologies for the top of the image below being absent but its rarity warrants inclusion.

Alan Young

Tony Hoskins

Cornwall has arguably some of the best totem names and scenery. Thankfully, most of the wonderful Cornish branch lines escaped the savagery of Beeching's cuts. These 1960s views show **Looe** and **St. Ives** *in situ*. **Looe** has only appeared twice at auction; last time in 2002 in Exeter, whilst the first auction for **St. Ives** was July 2021. Sadly, the branch to **Helston** was less fortunate and closed in 1962. Two of the early, flat squashed totems appear in this view, bottom left. Please see the WR database for a close-up. **Perranporth** was the only station with totems on the former **Newquay** to **Chacewater** direct branch line that closed in 1963, leading to a lengthy detour today via **Par**!

For reasons best known to the WR hierarchy, once the BR corporate identity policy was launched in 1965, there was an attempt to hide the former BR(WR) colour scheme with black-and-white overpainting, which was not an improvement. The idea was not widely adopted, but some Cornish stations were targeted, such as **Newquay**, **Redruth** and **Liskeard** (above right), where

even the ancillary signs have all been overpainted; what a waste of manpower and paint. Not one station in the whole of South Wales had B&W overpainting. The WR used the appendage 'Halt' almost as much as the SR. **Furze Platt Halt** is on the **Maidenhead** to Marlow branch, although the 'Halt' has been dropped today. Also, on the same line is **Bourne End**; these enamelled black-and-white totems superseded the HF chocolate-and-cream signs. The newest version is more common with three times as many auction outings than the older HF version.

Tim Clarke

Tim Clarke

A classic totem in its rightful surroundings.

Rare Llandilo Bridge totem *in situ*.

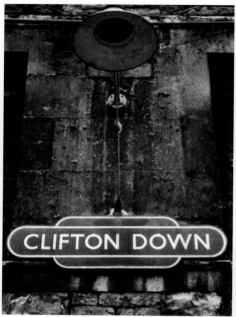

Tony Hoskins

Above: TSG library

Above: TSG library

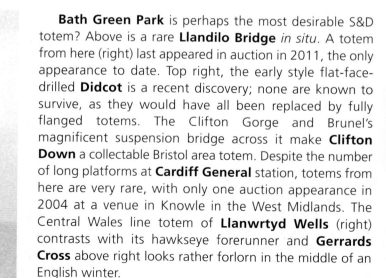

Bath Green Park is perhaps the most desirable S&D totem? Above is a rare **Llandilo Bridge** *in situ*. A totem from here (right) last appeared in auction in 2011, the only appearance to date. Top right, the early style flat-face-drilled **Didcot** is a recent discovery; none are known to survive, as they would have all been replaced by fully flanged totems. The Clifton Gorge and Brunel's magnificent suspension bridge across it make **Clifton Down** a collectable Bristol area totem. Despite the number of long platforms at **Cardiff General** station, totems from here are very rare, with only one auction appearance in 2004 at a venue in Knowle in the West Midlands. The Central Wales line totem of **Llanwrtyd Wells** (right) contrasts with its hawkseye forerunner and **Gerrards Cross** above right looks rather forlorn in the middle of an English winter.

Why totems were installed at obscure halts will always be a mystery and **Poyle Estate Halt** on the **West Drayton & Yiewsley** to **Staines West** branch, which closed in 1965, is the perfect example. During our research, we discovered that this halt had two HF totems (the second one is under the canopy), as seen alongside left in the mid-50s. These were replaced at some point with a single FF totem as per the image alongside right. The HF version, bearing slightly larger letters, is not known to survive. This is a very rare occurrence for such a minor halt. A picture of the FF survivor is shown in the database.

Kingswear terminus on the picturesque River Dart is shown in 1968. The station is well preserved since being closed in 1971 and taken over by the Dart Valley Railway in 1972. Note the unusual offset mounting bracket. **Kensington (Olympia)** is painted over a maroon **Willesden Junction,** made redundant after the main line platforms closed in 1962. **Shipton for Burford** is a pure Cotswold delight and very rare.

GW Main Line, in 1974. *Alan Young*   Birmingham Moor Street. *Alan Young*

Dartmouth, Devon, delight at Kingswear. *Jim Connor*

Totems in Retrospect

A Lincolnshire classic hangs in its rightful place in 1979. *TSG library*

Highly elusive Rickmansworth Church Street *in situ* just prior to closure in 1952. *TSG library*

Background to This Volume

Compiling this greatly expanded book on totems has been a real challenge. The authors lived over 1,750 miles apart for 95% of the time spent drafting, so the internet has been an equal partner in our endeavours. Thousands of e-mails have been exchanged since the autumn of 2019, when we began, and in the intervening months countless photographs, Word documents and Excel spreadsheets have been swapped. A great deal of new data has appeared since our 2002 book, making this volume necessary. There are 43 stations where totem signage has been discovered and more than 1,200 database amendments; we both felt this book should not be a rehash of our 2002 volume due to the past 20 years yielding so much new information. Our databases have been in continuous development since 2002.

We have lost count of the numbers of hours we have spent on this labour of love, but this is nothing compared to the pleasure we have gained from decades of totem collecting and the thrill of recording new survivors, checking auction appearances, and finding changes in flange styles and wording layouts. Only recently did photo evidence confirm the exact layout of **Bury-St-Edmunds**. Many hours have also been spent cross-checking our work with other experienced and knowledgeable collectors, who have received our very grateful thanks in the Acknowledgements.

As collectors ourselves, we appreciate that anyone starting their totem collections may be overwhelmed by the variety on offer and the numbers currently available. Approaching 1,000 totems seem to appear at auction every year but this is just a small percentage of those that have survived. We would estimate that tens of thousands are in the hands of collectors worldwide! We are still learning and there will be fresh data in the future, which we hope that readers will add to their copies – unless you want to keep it in mint condition, then you will need two copies! One of your authors has kept a 'master copy' of the 2002 book for 20 years to record all the database changes. These often change when railwayana auctions occur and we have left the book's cut-off date until December 2021, so they are as current as possible.

Letter Spacing Variations on Totems

During the drafting of this book, thousands of photographs have been examined in detail to ensure the most complete information is available to the reader. It has been noted that some totems from the same station show variations, depending on the date of manufacture and, indeed, the manufacturer. In 1948, BR issued standard instructions for signage but there are many instances where the standards were either ignored or slightly tampered with. The 1948 guide does not seem to give clear instructions about the spacing of the letters, even though the letters themselves were a standard size. A good example is **Kingussie** in the Scottish Highlands. Photos in our library show two quite distinct types, both perfectly genuine. The left-hand layout shows the nine letters spaced, so that the first and second 'I's coincide with the upper and lower curved lines. In the right-hand picture the letters 'K' and 'E' coincide with these same curved lines. The right-hand design seems more pleasing somehow, even though there are larger areas of blue at both ends.

A third example is shown right for the two stations in **Wath**, Yorkshire. In the upper totem, the four letters forming '**Wath**' are slightly more widely spaced than in the lower totem, but the lower panel '**Central**' is more compact than in the '**North**' totem again there is also a noticeable colour difference between the two stations.

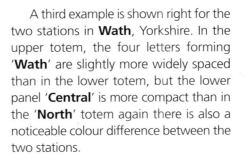

The final example comes from the LMR where the totems for **Stone** in Staffordshire show even more marked layout differences than **Kingussie**. However, in this instance the spaced-out variant seems more pleasing to our eyes than the left-hand layout.

Such examples clearly show the manufacturing variations that exist. In the space available it is simply not possible to list all of them. For the Southern Region we can mention **Adisham**, **Hellingl**y or **Oxted**, in the ER we list **Althorpe**, **Becontree**

There are other examples that are more difficult to spot but, again, both variants are *bona fide* BR totems. A good example is the SR's **Littlehampton** totems, where the letter spacing variation is not as pronounced as the **Kingussie** but is still discernible. The left-hand totem has the curved sections pointing to the right-hand side of the first 'T' and the top of the letter 'O'; on the right-hand design the curves point to the space between 'I' and the first 'T' on the left, and the space between the 'O' and the 'N' on the right. This example also shows significant colour variation, so the pair of totems almost certainly come from different suppliers.

and **Sandy**, the LMR list includes **Edge Hill** and **Lichfield City**, the ScR has **Ardlui** and **Carntyne**, whilst the WR includes **Newbury**, **Ruabon** and **Slough**. For all these regions there are other examples. We recently discovered **Pelaw** in the NER has both wide and compact designs, similar to **Stone**.

From the foregoing list, we show right the compact-lettered **Oxted** (SR) and **Sandy** (ER) totems alongside, with their respective more expanded counterparts beneath. All of these are *bona fide* BR totems, and we again might comment that where there are few letters, a more spread-out design seems visually appealing.

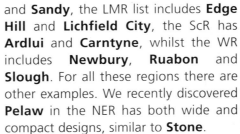

Thoughts on BR's Provision of Totems and Station Lighting

Tim Clarke

Totem provision around the BR network appears to have been haphazard, to say the least! There were many and various reasons why some stations were fitted with totems and others not, but the wide variation between the six individual regions is perhaps harder to understand.

The *Code of Instructions for Station Name and Direction Signs* document issued by the Railway Executive Committee (REC) in April 1948, clearly specifies the proportions, dimensions and lettering standards for the new totem nameplates, together with their positioning and quantities. However, it does not give any indication of any concentrated programme to replace existing signage with the new versions, quite understandable perhaps given the conditions of post-war austerity prevalent at the time of BR's formation. It is generally the case that totems did not start to be installed until around two years into BR's tenure.

So, what were the triggers for the installation of the new signage? Certainly, a desire to present a fresh image for the newly nationalised railway would have been seen to be important, and where better to start this than the major city terminals?

Curiously however, many of these large stations were often not favoured with totems, presumably because of cost. There were exceptions of course (**Bradford Exchange**, **Charing Cross**, **Manchester Central** or **Waterloo** for example) but most totems, where they existed in major termini, tended to be on suburban, through or underground platforms, or positioned outside the main trainshed area, as at **Brighton**, **Kings Cross** and **Paddington**. Collecting a complete set of main terminus station totems is therefore impossible, simply due to availability.

Perhaps then the impetus for fitting stations with totems in those earlier years was mainly to replace signage regarded as inadequate, or to provide it where none previously existed. In earlier times, the main form of station nameboard was the ubiquitous 'Running-In Board', backed up by station names displayed within lanterns lit by oil or gas. These were often etched or painted onto the glass itself, or sometimes were just paper, which were easily replaced.

As lighting improved the lanterns were largely replaced by suspended gas lamps with glass globes, or shaded electric bulbs. This new form of lighting did not offer an obvious opportunity to display the station name, so the 'lamp tablet' was born. Initially, most of these were simple small rectangular plates, framed glass on the Southern and enamel for the other companies, but some were also horseshoe shaped to match the curve of the gas lamp globes, such as the LNER **Palace Gates** shown above left.

The image-conscious Southern Railway later replaced most of their glass tablets with enamel 'target' nameplates, widely regarded as the predecessor to the totem, but some glass tablets lasted well into the 1960s without replacement. This was largely the situation at the formation of BR, plus the LMS 'hawkseye' nameboards, and a brand-new concept by the LNER, the fluorescent strip light with translucent shades bearing the station's name that became common in the Eastern Region soon after totems had been installed. So, if the new British Railways organisation originally had ambitions for a consistent application of their new signage policy throughout the network, in practice the individual regions implemented it very differently from each other, something that remained the case right through the BR period.

There were some obvious situations where new signage would be required quickly. Where stations were duplicated within a town, for example, they now needed to be differentiated from each other by renaming. Windsor, where the ex-GWR station became **Windsor & Eton Central** and the ex-SR station became **Windsor & Eton Riverside**, soon had regional totems provided at both stations.

It also seemed that some of the regions were quite keen to provide totems at some of the smaller stations where oil or gas lanterns were still extant, particularly the Scottish Region where many tiny stations were fitted. On the Southern, very few of these stations were ever provided with target signs, so a surprising number acquired totems instead. This was particularly noticeable on the minor lines of Sussex, where a significant number of the small stations retaining oil lighting right into the '60s, had totems fitted. As far as can be ascertained, none of these ever displayed targets.

In general, the initial installation of totems did seem not to have followed any logical pattern. Suburban systems around the major conurbations were where totems generally became most common, but not in every case. The West Yorkshire suburbs, for example, had relatively few stations fitted, seemingly reflecting the North Eastern Region's apparent reluctance to fit many totems at all. Predictably, London's suburbs were very generously supplied, but initially the Southern Region was slower to adopt them, as the existing SR targets were already doing much the same job. This would change later as BR appeared to become more focused on imposing their 'image'

over that of the Southern Railway. Thus, the like-for-like replacement of targets with totems carried on right until the new corporate identity brought any changes to a halt. The two photos below show Warlingham in Surrey in the early 1950s displaying Southern targets. In 1956, it was renamed as **Whyteleafe South** and was completely re-signed to carry totems and other new signage.

Warlingham to Whyteleafe South: targets (L) to totems (R) from 1956. *Alan Young*

The SR had an additional factor that possibly affected their thinking about the provision of multiple types of signage. This was the South-Eastern area's '10-car scheme' introduced in the 1950s to address capacity issues resulting from the growing numbers of peak-hour commuters. BR decided to build a fleet of 2EPB EMUs and attach them to the existing 8-car formations on South Eastern suburban services. This of course meant that nearly all the platforms affected needed to be extended by two coach lengths to accommodate the longer trains. This was generally done using precast concrete units, including concrete lamp posts with the new totems attached. However, in most (but not all) cases it appears these were provided at that time *only* on the extensions, the rest of the station retaining whatever was already there, usually SR targets, but sometimes half-flanged totems where they previously existed.

As a general rule (there are of course exceptions) those on the 'three lines' to **Dartford**, the main line to **Orpington** and the **Bromley North** branch appeared to be half-flanged, whilst those installed later on the line beyond **Dartford** to **Gillingham**, the line beyond **Orpington** to **Sevenoaks**, and the Mid-Kent line to **Hayes** (including the **Addiscombe** and **Sanderstead** branches) were of the black-edged FF variety. After all this was done, in later years, the other parts of most of the stations were re-signed, usually with the later white-flanged totems, but some retained SR targets to the end. This may explain why so many South Eastern suburban stations had more than one type of totem, and why some variants are so much rarer than the others, simply because there were just a few of them and only on the platform extensions.

Alan Young

However, the different policies (or lack of a national policy) by the individual regions concerning signage changes seem to be most prevalent when station rebuilds, renovations or new-builds are considered, especially when changes or additions to a station's lighting system were implemented. An example there is **Chesterfield Midland**, which was rebuilt in 1963. There is no evidence, so far, of the totems being put back after 'modernisation'.

Taking the Eastern Region first, the 'strip light' signs appeared to be the favoured option from a very early date, probably reflecting the success of the LNER installations. Their 1950s policy seemed to be to install fluorescent lights and remove the totems from a station fitted with these. It appeared to sound the death-knell for any totems already fitted, applying to an individual station, or sometimes to those on an entire route. An example here was electrification in Essex where wholesale removal took place. In some cases, this happened only a few years after totem installation and this led to many highly desirable totem names being lost to collectors, such as **Cambridge**. Naturally, there were exceptions such as at **Grimsby Docks** (top left), where totems and strip lights co-existed. It was also possible that individual totems were 'missed' when the others were removed. As noted in the chapter on the North Eastern Region, this also happened at some NER locations, but not always. **Benton** lost its totems when named strip lights were fitted and the same appeared to be the case at **York**.

However, at other stations, new totems were still being installed, as Alan Young described on page 161. In contrast though, named strip lights happily co-existed with totems at **Darlington** for many years and it is possible that these were both fitted at the same time, perhaps replacing the earlier **Darlington Bank Top** totems? Another example of NER totems and named strip lights being displayed together was at **Beverley** (bottom left) in 1974.

It appeared that both the ScR and LMR were perfectly happy for named strip lights and totems to co-exist with each other on the same platforms. This was the case at some major LMR stations, two significant examples being **Preston** and **Carlisle**. However, the early phases of the West Coast Main Line electrification and modernisation in the Manchester area mixed these two types of station name displays on smaller stations as well, with totems being fitted to new lamp posts with 'street lamp' style heads in addition to the named strip lights. Examples of this treatment were found at **Macclesfield** and **Wilmslow**.

Similarly, in the early phases of the creation of the Scottish Region Glasgow 'Blue Train' network stations were fitted with named strip lights but displayed totems simultaneously. **Hillfoot** and **Alexandria** are examples, whilst some major stations elsewhere (**Ayr** and **Kilmarnock)**, also displayed both together.

Tim Clarke

The Western Region was different. There seemed a marked reluctance to provide totems at small stations, but not so much at larger and suburban stations. Again, lighting changes had an impact, where lighting was improved by providing increased numbers of new lamp posts carrying conventional electric lights. Both half-flanged totems, relocated from the earlier posts and new full-flanged totems provided for the extra numbers that could be seen together. Sometimes these were even of different layout, e.g. **Neath General**!

Provision of named strip lights was also random. There were examples where they were provided in addition to totems and others where the ER approach of complete replacement was followed. **Teignmouth** and **Bristol Temple Meads** both lost all their totems when the named strip lights were installed, although the latter did retain its 'roundel' totems under the trainshed roof. In contrast, when **Whitland** was rebuilt, named strip lights were found in the open platform areas and totems under the canopies. **Tenby** was the same, although only the 'up' platform was rebuilt.

The SR did not appear to be a great supporter of the named strip light, with remarkably few locations having them, more so considering the total number of stations they operated. Where they were fitted though, they mostly replaced SR targets (and a few totems) in the same 'scorched earth' style as the ER. Even in the late 1950s, the new station at Gatwick Airport and the rebuilt station at Chichester were both fitted with named strip lights and no totems, yet the new **Hurst Green** station in '61 had totems and no strip lights!

There were a very few stations that carried both; **Weymouth** had named strip lights and large 4ft totems together on the new island platform built by the Southern Region in 1957. They retained the conventional half-flanged totems with gas lighting on the station's old GWR side. Both **Twickenham** and **Portsmouth & Southsea** also carried both, though in each case it is believed that they were each on different parts of the station. In conclusion then, whatever good intentions the new management of British Railways might have had in 1948 for a consistent new image across the whole network, regional differences soon became apparent and corporate intentions were never properly fulfilled. This inconsistency can only be explained by regional managers implementing their own interpretation of the image and probably their own preferences.

Even when the new 1965 British Rail corporate identity policy came along, this still didn't succeed in eliminating regional differences. The new signage might have shown a common black-on-white Rail Alphabet typeface, but the Southern Region began installing large plastic nameboards at the same time as small enamel lamp tablets appeared at some stations on the London Midland Region and larger printed metal nameboards elsewhere. Some things don't change!

343

Saved by the Scrap Man, But Not Always!

The scrap men were not the collectors' favourite people, as they consigned thousands of rare totems to landfill sites and many were recycled in furnaces! Just occasionally, there were some more entrepeneurial scrap men who would see the potential value in redundant totems and sell them to collectors. One of the saddest aspects of this hobby is the number of times that we have said 'Not known to survive', and this is largely due to the careless nature of those that were tasked with removing not only totems, but all the paraphernalia that made railway stations so charming in their heyday. The old gas lamps, canopies and brick-built waiting rooms with real fires were anathema to the modernisers! Electrification and new forms of station lighting consigned our beloved totems to become little more than worthless junk.

Kentish Town West in 1966, prior to being burnt down in 1971. *Jim Connor*

Lower Edmonton (Low Level) circa 1963. *Doug Fairhurst*

The image above shows **Kentish Town West** prior to a devastating fire which completely gutted the old wooden railway station on 18 April 1971. The two-line arrangement of wording can be seen and there are six totems in this view alone. We are aware of only one survivor and the rest would have likely perished in the fire.

An odd fate befell some **Lower Edmonton** totems during re-signing in the early 1960s. The line from **Hackney Downs** to Enfield Town is impossible to collect as a complete set of totems, because many stations have no survivors. Lower Edmonton was the junction of a former branch line to **Angel Road** on the Lea Valley line, and during the electrification work many trains were diverted over this single line branch. At the separate Lower Edmonton (Low Level), some former totems from the main station were re-used and one can be seen here precariously hanging from a platform lamp. The DMU has arrived from **Angel Road** as we look towards Edmonton Junction.

John Mann Collection   Rochford (Essex) 1955. *H.C. Casserley*   *Author's Collection*

Out of the ten stations on the Enfield Town line with totems, just a few examples survive from **Seven Sisters**, **White Hart Lane**, **Lower Edmonton** and **Bush Hill Park**. All were removed by the time electrification of the line was completed in June 1962.

There were few totems at the Essex resort of **Walton on Naze** and these have evaded collectors since removal. In contrast to the demise of totems at **Kentish Town West**, the next station heading west is **Gospel Oak**. During its costly rebuild in the mid-1950s, it received a good complement of FF totems which have been in auction 10 times. While drafting this volume, we discovered that **Pelaw** also had HF totems. This 1969 view above right shows one *in situ* with slightly wider spaced lettering than the FF version. The devastating wholesale removal of totems on the Shenfield to **Southend-on-Sea Victoria** line has been well documented, but these two views alongside do not appear elsewhere. **Rochford** totems were very short-lived and had disappeared by the time that new electric trains started running in 1956. The closure of the M&GN system in 1959 included **Moulton** (right); totems from here have been in auction three times.

Who were these mysterious individuals that were responsible for the loss and burial of so many historical artefacts? We have certainly never spoken to or heard tales from the hundreds of men that were employed to strip stations of their signage. Perhaps they are keeping a low profile for good reason.

Moulton (Lincs) 30 January 1959. *G. C. Lewthwaite*

The pure nostalgia of railway stations in the BR period and the memories that come with the ownership of totems from these places is summed up below. **Old Hill** was once a busy West Midlands junction, with services to both Halesowen and **Dudley**. The station survives but the junctions have long gone. The delightful station at **White Notley** is on the **Witham** to Braintree line. Just three totems adorned the station. Once part of a through route to **Bishops Stortford** which was closed to passengers in 1952, the line remained in use for occasional freight traffic until the final section from Bishops Stortford to Easton Lodge succumbed in 1971. The random selection of stations to receive totems omitted Braintree & Bocking, but a dark blue enamel with the full title was fitted to the signal box.

Therein lies the conundrum regarding the saving of some signs and the scrapping of others in the same decade. Peculiarities abound in this strange hobby. The totems at **Runcorn** are very rare, with no survivors currently known, but the next station, **Frodsham** heading south on the **Chester General** line, has appeared at auction on 15 occasions. This delightful image was taken in 1963 with a coal yard full of the detritus and vehicles of a bygone age.

Some East Anglian M&GN stations were equipped with these large RIBs incorporating the totem logo around the name. We became aware of this rare survivor from North Walsham (Town) only during the final preparation of this last chapter!

Our research and databases will evolve as new information appears and long-forgotten treasures are found. We have tried to cover every aspect of this subject, but the full story will always elude us, owing to the seemingly random policies that covered both totem installation and removal. We wish all collectors good luck in their quest for the 'dream like' totems they desire and perhaps we will meet again at live auctions, which have been suspended for two years due to the global pandemic. One thing we have taken comfort from is the fact that we are so very fortunate to have hobbies at a time when millions of people have been forced to stay at home.

Whilst in the north Midlands area, we highlight some unusual signage at **Trent** station that did escape the scrapman. This former Midland Railway station was east of **Sawley Junction,** between Derby and Nottingham; it opened in 1862 and was closed in January 1968. The station itself was unusual in that it did not serve any community, being simply an interchange, with a complex series of tracks to the north, south and west. Following closure, some of the north loop trackwork was removed, despite much local opposition and the station itself was very quickly demolished. Almost nothing else survived. The sign below measures 20in x 25in and is the only one to have appeared in auction. It is unusual because of its size and having a grey background, rather than sporting the reversed colours of a maroon totem on white.

The former branch line from **Paddock Wood** in Kent to Hawkhurst (no totems) closed to passengers in 1961 and the complete set of totems above would not have hung for very long. The **Burton-on-Trent** totem included below passed through the Sheffield Railwayana Auction in March 2000, its only known appearance so far. This 'lucky' totem was apparently rescued from two skips, so cheating the clearance gang on both occasions. We are therefore happy that at least one example has survived. It was rescued in rather 'battered and bruised' condition but after some restoration, it lives on, proudly carrying the LMR colours.

Some totems escaped the scrapman, only to perish or be very badly damaged after preservation. The two examples below highlight the damage an intense domestic fire can wreak. The extreme heat has caused the surface of the enamel to melt or disintegrate, indicating a fire temperature above those used when the totem was made (see page 27). Both **Burnham (Bucks)** and **Pinhoe** are not particularly common, so the damage sustained is a real shame. Clever and painstaking restoration however can remove most of the destruction caused by the fire, saving them again from scrap!

Normans Bay Halt, Sussex. *Tim Clarke Collection*

Evidence, as if it were needed, is provided here of the quirky nature of SR station signage, particularly the provision of totems at minor halts. Even in the final weeks of completing this mammoth project, we were shown this view of **Normans Bay Halt** in Sussex. We had no layout details and they are clearly a one-line arrangement, whereas the next station travelling west is **Pevensey Bay Halt** and that had the Lower Panel arrangement. To date, **Normans Bay Halt** totems are not known to survive.

The scrapman wrought devastation at very many stations on the BR network, as the photo below shows. This is the former GSWR station at **Cumberland Street** in the southern Glasgow suburbs. The damaged and discarded totem had been left on the demolished station platform, as worthless rubbish. The station opened in 1900 but was recommended for closure by Beeching, eventually succumbing in 1966. It opened as **Eglinton Street**, but was renamed in 1924 to avoid confusion with the ex-Caledonian station of the same name nearby that also carried BR totems.

Remains of Cumberland Street station in late 1960s. *John Wells*

Closing Remarks

We have often considered the reasons behind the popularity of collecting totem signage and one frequently overlooked aspect is their compact size. How many of us have gone to Collectors' Corner and taken one home on the train? Both authors have done just that! If totems had all been made 4ft long, they would have been far more unwieldly to carry and display. In that respect, the designers produced a perfectly proportioned sign which has stood the test of time. They will carry the legacy of British Railways on for many more years than the designers could possibly have envisaged; totem collecting today is as popular as it has ever been.

STOP PRESS!

In the final few hours before our 2002 totem book went to press, we were notified that a **Bradford Forster Square** totem had turned up for the first KRA auction of 2002 at Kidlington. Could lightening strike twice? Well as it happens, yes it could, as on 18 July 2021, just 2 days before this complete manuscript left us, it was discovered from photographic evidence, that **Stewarton** in Ayrshire carried totems. This made 42 new stations discovered since our last book was published and one more was yet to come, (see page 351). Below is the photo that confirms the discovery. We are most grateful to the Stewarton Historical Society for this new information. Naturally, no totem from there has been seen thus far.

Stewarton is on the Glasgow South West main line, around 19 miles south of the old terminus at Glasgow St. Enoch. The stations at **Dunlop** and **Lugton** lie to the north and to the south is **Kilmaurs**. All these stations, together with **Stewarton**, closed in 1966, and only **Lugton** has not been re-opened. Today's upgraded line is well used, with passenger numbers exceeding 325,000 annually since 2017.

Stewarton station northbound in 1962. *Courtesy Stewarton Historical Society, Ayrshire*

Buildings on the southbound platform are quite different, as seen below in 1962, with a solitary totem installed in the centre under the main canopy. The station was opened in 1871 by the Glasgow, Barrhead and Kilmarnock Joint Railway, but in November 1966, wholesale closures in the area saw it become redundant. This lasted barely seven months and in June 1967, it re-opened. The line was singled and Platform 2 taken out of service in 1975, but this was also reversed, when in 2009, the route was upgraded and double-tracked, with Platform 2 being re-instated.

Courtesy Stewarton Historical Society, Ayrshire

Even though we thought we had concluded the unearthing of new data on British Railways' totems, discoveries such as this clearly show we are all still learning. Fortunately, visionary people have taken many photographs at a time when major change was occurring and it is those photographs that keep us all on our toes!

The original plan for the publishing of the book was October 2021 in time for the 2021 Christmas market, but unforseen delays due to global logistical issues pushed this back to the Spring of 2022. This had the bonus effect of allowing even more recent research to be included, one of the most curious being the discovery of a fourth variant of totems from **Snowdown & (and) Nonington Halt**. Our databases had already listed three different designs, but in October 2021 a three-line version appeared on an Internet auction. All four variants are shown together here for the first time. The three-line version, which comes fully white flanged, carries conventional Gill Sans lettering: all the remaining trio have GS Condensed letters in one main line, but all the designs carry '**Halt**' in the lower panel. It is most curious that such a small Kent station that only opened in 1914 received so much attention.

HF variant condensed letters.

FF white flange variant condensed letters.

FF black flange variant condensed letters.

3-line FF variant standard sized letters.

During October 2021, more research was undertaken on Hawkeseye station signs (see page 12). This came about because our library acquired a book listing the design company as G C Hawkes of Birmingham. Further 'digging' showed this was not quite correct as the company was O C Hawkes, a manufacturer of glass-based products from Victorian times. The LMS had been experimenting with station sign design and colours from around 1930 and by 1931, gave more serious credence about changing station liveries. In reality, they did not immediately start to stamp their image on stations, signal boxes and other assets until around 1936, so for well over a decade after formation, pre-grouping liveries were seen throughout their region. As a result, many stations in the early 1930s had a shabby, run-down appearance.

When stations needed repainting, most of them were decked in LNWR colours, light and dark brown with cream as the contrast colour. Poster boards and other signage were black and white and like the Furness Railway, enamel signage was white letters on a dark blue background. However in 1931 they began to experiment with more readable signage and the end result was most surprising. Their 4-year development work led them to the use of yellow with black lettering, a colour combination that had no former history either in the LMS itself or in their pre-grouping constituents.

The actual length of the Hawkseye changed depending on the number of letters in each stations name. Some of them were curious in appearance, sometimes being cast in two sections.

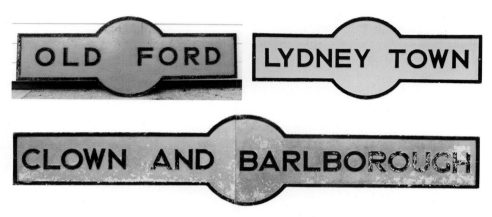

The two direction signs above are examples of the final development colours but note the weighting of the font was not consistent. Such signs were slowly introduced from late 1934 and the impact of the design is very clear, readable even in the most inclement of conditions.

The new signage had another unique characteristic. The yellow background was impregnated with millions of small glass particles to further improve readability. They used a development partner, Hawkes Ltd of Birmingham. Reference to Grace's Guide of British Industrial History shows this company has had a long and proud history in glass product manufacture. It had been founded in 1859 by John Hawkes but in 1870, it was taken over by his brother Obed Charles Hawkes and completely re-branded.

By 1914 they were manufacturers of the widest range of glass-based products available and were noted suppliers to HM Government for road signage from 1913 onwards. Being the leading supplier of glass-based products it would have been natural for the LMS to use them in their signage development programme. It is no coincidence that the new LMS station running-in boards were termed 'Hawkseyes', or maybe this should read Hawkes' eyes!

Alongside are examples of the signs *in situ*. The right-hand picture shows a prototype sign at Radlett in Hertfordshire. Notice the curved sections above and below the lettering is elliptical, whereas in the final design shown nearside at Elm Park, this had changed to a circle of 18in diameter. It is not clear at this time which font was utilised, but further work may reveal this detail. Two of these now very-collectable artefacts are shown in their final 1934 form (above right) in yellow and black livery.

When the LMS was merged with the GWR, LNER and SR at the end of 1947 to form British Railways, the six BR regions were given regional liveries. The BR Midland Region colour scheme reflected the most widely used LMS colours, maroon and cream. The cream was the standard BR shade used on all regions (except the North Eastern), and the red was a dark shade similar to the ex-MR LMS colour. Cream was used on planking and canopy valencing, with the red on ironwork, framing, doors etc. as usual. The official BR specification from 1960 gives the colours as BS 381C 'Gulf Red' and 'Light Biscuit' in which case the red is brighter than the LMS shade. The paints dried very matt, though, which lessened the impact of this attractive livery. From early 1949 onwards, poster boards & station signs were red with white lettering, including enamelled station signs on which the red was a darker shade. This meant the very readable black lettering on the bright yellow background was lost in favour of BR corporate colours and the million or so glass beads embedded in the hawkseye were covered. The LMR was slow to install totems compared to the other regions, so many Hawkseyes were painted in maroon and cream as a 'stop gap'.

The grand London termini, together with their associated engine sheds, were magnets for trainspotters over the decades that totems adorned some of the stations. We all have our favourites and it is frustrating to find that due to random installation, some termini had either few or no totems whatsoever. Even those that were fitted, such as **Kings Cross** or **Paddington**, the number of platforms that displayed totems was minimal. We have only seen evidence of totems at **Kings Cross** on the former Moorgate widened lines platform where the line came back into daylight from Hotel Curve. The only other platform which had totems was **Kings Cross York Road** and these are very rare.

Paddington totems were installed at a few locations along Platform 1 and strangely on the other side of the station where the Underground's Metropolitan Line emerged. This type of London Underground installation was repeated at **Royal Oak** and **Westbourne Park**. Totems from **Broad Street** (closed 1986) are the easiest of the London termini to find, coming in the form of both standard and four-foot variants. South of the River Thames, there was also random provision, with totems installed at just **Waterloo**, **Cannon Street**, **Charing Cross**, **Holborn Viaduct** plus wooden signs at **London Bridge**.

The major London omissions were Euston, Marylebone, St. Pancras and Victoria, but as we polished the manuscript ready for the Publisher, a listing on an internet auction site in late 2021 showed this was not quite the case. It is well documented that conventional totems were not fitted at **St. Pancras,** but the LMR enamel Poster Board Header below, which incorporates the famous name within a totem in reversed colours, is believed to be a unique design.

Other stations, such as **Blackburn**, **Leicester London Road**, **Longton** and **Preston** had enamel Poster Board Headers with the totem in standard colours in addition to regular totems. Further investigation found a couple of old **St Pancras** pictures showing these enamels in situ above posters tucked away on the side walls under the magnificence of Barlow's trainshed roof. They measure 52in long and this survivor is in very good condition, as the photo shows. This qualified to be our 43rd and final discovery (see page 23), proving that this wonderful hobby still springs surprises on all of us.

And finally! In early November 2021 we were sent a rather interesting photograph of **Bamber Bridge** station in Lancashire. It was sent to show the standard totem in situ, but the station also possessed an unusual RIB with British Railways in a reverse coloured totem placed above the station name. We are not aware of many signs of this type on the BR network.

References

Anderson, V.R. and Twells, H.N. (2007) **LMS Lineside Part 1; stations, lamps and nameboards**; Wild Swan Publications Ltd, Didcot OX11 8DP; ISBN 978-1-905184-31-6

Awdry, Christopher (1990) **Encyclopaedia of British Railway Companies**; Guild Publishing London. Book reference CN8983

Baker, S.K. (2019) **Rail Atlas of Great Britain and Ireland** (15th Edition); Crécy Publishing Ltd, Manchester, M22 5LH. ISBN 978-0 8609368-1-7

Brennand, D. (1991) **British Railways Totem Station Signs**; Connor and Butler Publishing Ltd, Colchester, Essex, CO1 9DL. ISBN 947699-18X

Brennand D. and Furness, R.A. (2002) **The Book of British Railways Station Totems**; Sutton Publishing Ltd, Stroud, GL5 2BU. ISBN 0 7509 2997 9

Bryan, Tim (2017) **Railway Stations (Britain's Heritage)**; Amberley Publishing, Stroud, Gloucestershire, GL5 4EP. ISBN 978-1-445669-00-7

Buck, G. (1992) **A Pictorial Survey of Railway Stations**; Oxford Publishing Company. ISBN 978-0-86093-459-2e

Carter, E.F. (1959) **An Historical Geography of Railways of the British Isles**; Cassell & Company, Red Lion Square, London, WC1. (Now Octopus Publishing, London, EC4.)

Edwards, C. (2001) **Railway Records: A Guide to Sources**; Public Records Office, Richmond. Cromwell Press, Trowbridge. ISBN 1-903365-10-4

Freeman, M. & Aldcroft, D. (1985) **The Atlas of British Railway History**; Routledge, Hall & Chapman, 29W 35th Street, New York, 10001. ISBN 0-7099-0542-4

Furness, R.A. (2009) **Poster to Poster Volume 1: Scotland**; J D F & Associates Ltd, Gloucestershire, GL2 4AL. ISBN 978-0-9562092-0-7

Furness, R.A. (2011) **Poster to Poster Volume 4: The Eastern Counties**; J D F & Associates Ltd, Gloucestershire, GL2 4AL. ISBN 978-0-9562092-3-8

Furness, R.A. (2014) **Poster to Poster Volume 7: The Glorious South-West**; J D F & Associates Ltd, Gloucestershire, GL2 4AL. ISBN 978-0-9562092-6-9

Grace's Guide (1914) **The Company Guide to British Industrial History**; Registered UK Charity 1154342{Editor@gracesguide.co.uk}

Jowett, Alan (1985) **Jowett's Railway Atlas**; Guild Publishing London; Book reference CN2155

Lawrence, David (2018) **British Rail Architecture 1948–97**; Crécy Publishing Ltd, Manchester, M22 5LH. ISBN 978-0-8509368-5-5

Maggs, Colin (1987) **GWR Principal Stations**; Ian Allan Publishing Ltd, Shepperton, Middlesex. ISBN 978-0-7110171-3-9

Quick, Michael (2020) **Railway Passenger Stations in Great Britain: A Chronology**; Electronic version 5.02 available from Railway and Canal Historical Society website

Railway Clearing House (1956) **Official Hand-Book of Stations**; British Transport Commission, 203 Eversholt Street, London, NW1 1BU.

Simmons, J. and Biddle, G. (1997) **The Oxford Companion to British Railways History**; Oxford University Press. ISBN 0-19-211697-5

Waller, Peter (2020) **Atlas of Railway Station Closures** (2nd Edition); Crécy Publishing Ltd, Manchester, M22 5LH. ISBN 978-0-8609369-7-8